# The New French Law of Contract

# The New French Law of Contract

SOLÈNE ROWAN

OXFORD
UNIVERSITY PRESS

OXFORD
UNIVERSITY PRESS

Great Clarendon Street, Oxford, OX2 6DP,
United Kingdom

Oxford University Press is a department of the University of Oxford.
It furthers the University's objective of excellence in research, scholarship,
and education by publishing worldwide. Oxford is a registered trade mark of
Oxford University Press in the UK and in certain other countries



First Edition published in 2022

Impression: 1



Published in the United States of America by Oxford University Press
198 Madison Avenue, New York, NY 10016, United States of America

British Library Cataloguing in Publication Data

Data available

Library of Congress Control Number: 2022932382

ISBN 978–0–19–881088–9 (pbk.)
ISBN 978–0–19–881087–2 (hbk.)

DOI: 10.1093/oso/9780198810872.001.0001

Printed and bound by
CPI Group (UK) Ltd, Croydon, CR0 4YY

*For Gregg, Louis, Théodore, and Madeleine*

# Preface

In the *New French Law of Contract*, I have sought to describe, explain, and analyse the new general principles of contract law in the reformed Civil Code, including those on contract formation, the validity of the contract, the interpretation and supplementation of terms, the regulation of unfair terms, privity of contract, change of circumstances, breach of contract, and remedies. In doing so, I have relied extensively upon, and cited from, the translation of the new articles of the Civil Code by Professors John Cartwright, Bénédicte Fauvarque-Cosson, and Simon Whittaker, which is published on the French Ministry of Justice's website (<http://www.textes.justice.gouv.fr/art_pix/THE-LAW-OF-CONTRACT-2-5-16.pdf> (2016 version) and <http://www.textes.justice.gouv.fr/art_pix/Translationrevised2018final.pdf> (2018 version)). I am very grateful to them for giving me permission to use their translation.

I have benefited from the help of a number of colleagues to whom I would like to express my sincere gratitude. I am particularly indebted to my doctoral supervisor and mentor, Professor John Bell, who encouraged me to write on the reform of French contract law and has given me a great deal of support and feedback along the way. Throughout my career he has always been generous with his time and advice, and I cannot thank him enough. My gratitude is also due to Professor Hugh Beale for his attentive reading of the draft manuscript of the book. Despite being very busy, he gave me incredibly detailed feedback and his insightful comments have been invaluable and spared me from some embarrassments.

I also wish to record my appreciation for the support of Professor Sally Wheeler, Dean of the College of Law at the Australian National University where I spent two-and-a-half years as a Futures Fellow. The flexibility and generous funding that accompanied that position were essential in enabling me to complete the book. Although now back in the UK, I am delighted to have kept my ties with the ANU as an Honorary Professor. I look forward to visiting Sally and my former colleagues in Canberra in the future.

I have benefited from the considerable help, attention to detail, and hard work of my dedicated and efficient research assistant, Steven Daly.

This book is dedicated to the people who matter most to me: my husband, Gregg, and my three children, Louis, Théodore, and Madeleine. My husband is a constant source of support and love. I am incredibly fortunate to have him by my side. He has unfailingly supported my ambition to juggle a demanding career with raising our children. In the many moments when I am downhearted for falling short of the high standards that I set for myself as a mother and an academic, he reminds me that I can only do my best and that my best is good enough. I have also benefited from his comments on the book. My final thanks are to my wonderful children, who have been endlessly patient and supportive, not least during the long lockdowns in Melbourne when I wrote much of this book. They make life feel like a constant roller coaster and there is not a moment to breathe when they are around, but I would not have it any other way.

Solène Rowan, London<br>15 November 2021

# Contents

# Table of Cases

## COMMONWEALTH AND UNITED KINGDOM

## FRANCE

French civil and criminal cases are not generally known by the names of the parties. They are listed below in chronological order.

# Table of Legislation and Other Materials

## LEGISLATIVE PROJECTS, LAW COMMISSION REPORTS, AND OTHER REPORTS

### FRANCE

# 1
# The Genesis of the New French Law of Contract

'My real glory is not to have won forty battles: Waterloo will erase the memory of all these victories. What nothing will erase, what will live eternally, is my Civil Code.'[1] So said Napoleon Bonaparte in a prophecy that on any view has been vindicated. Although enacted more than 200 years ago and one of the oldest codified laws still in force in the world, the French Civil Code remains the principal private law legislative instrument in France today.

Some parts of the Code have, however, been revised to keep pace with changing times. This book is concerned with the modernization of the section on the law of contract, which was comprehensively amended and restructured in 2016. The revised section came into force on 1 October 2016,[2] marking the end of the articles of the 1804 Code familiar to many generations of practitioners and scholars, and inaugurating a new era of 150 articles[3] that are a more extensive and contemporary statement of French contract law. These articles contain a host of rules that over the previous two centuries had been developed and applied in cases and also a range of significant innovations.

The reforms were a major event in France. Such an extensive overhaul of an important part of the Civil Code is a rare thing. Indeed, since its enactment in 1804, almost all of the articles on contract law had remained completely untouched, making this the first re-examination of the subject in over 200 years. It was also the culmination of several attempts at reform in this area that had begun more than 100 years previously and intensified over the preceding fifteen years.

The reforms are also relevant beyond France's borders, particularly in the many jurisdictions that over time have drawn upon the Code as a model to forge their

[1] C-F de Montholon, *Récits de la captivité de l'Empereur Napoléon à Sainte-Hélène* (Paulin: Paris, 1847) 401.

[2] 'Ordonnance no 2016-131 du 10 février 2016 portant réforme du droit des contrats, du régime général et de la preuve des obligations', JORF no 0035 of 11 February 2016. The Ordonnance was translated into English by J Cartwright, B Fauvarque-Cosson, and S Whittaker: <http://www.textes.justice.gouv.fr/art_pix/THE-LAW-OF-CONTRACT-2-5-16.pdf> (2016 version) and <http://www.textes.justice.gouv.fr/art_pix/Translationrevised2018final.pdf> (2018 version) accessed 1 September 2021. The translations of the new articles contained in this book are theirs.

[3] Articles 1101 to 1231-7 regulate contracts but there have also been reforms in other areas (the 'general legal regime of obligations' and the 'proof of obligations') and in total 353 new articles were introduced. The focus of this book is solely on the new contract law regime.

*The New French Law of Contract.* Solène Rowan, Oxford University Press. © Solène Rowan 2022.
DOI: 10.1093/oso/9780198810872.003.0001

own laws. During the nineteenth and twentieth centuries, the 1804 Code had unparalleled reach, serving as a source of inspiration and even a template in many European countries and parts of Africa, Asia, Central and South America, and North America.[4] France became 'one of the few legal systems that exerted such a dominant influence on other jurisdictions that the country is generally regarded as the "lead jurisdiction" of an entire legal family that stretches from Chile to Vietnam'.[5] In many of these jurisdictions, law reformers and other members of the legal community followed the reforms closely.[6]

## A The Reasons for the Reforms

Whilst the longevity of the Civil Code is generally seen as a strength, it had become apparent to many that the contract law section was overdue for modernization. The reforms were born from a realization that the Code had ceased to be an accurate statement of the law of contract applied by French courts, and had fallen in influence abroad and attractiveness to international business.

### 1 An outdated and incomplete statement of contract law

Until the reforms, most of the section of the Code on contract law had remained unaltered, even as society and technology changed almost beyond recognition. Instead, the courts progressively re-interpreted the articles, which as generally high-level propositions or statements of principle lent themselves to adaptation.

In itself, this was unremarkable. The original draftsmen had foreseen that the judiciary would have a prominent role in adjusting and developing the law. As Portalis noted:

[4] On the 'extraordinary influence' of the Civil Code in the world, see K Zweigert and H Kötz, *An Introduction to Comparative Law*, trans T Weir (3rd edn, OUP: Oxford, 2009) 98.

[5] S Vogenauer, 'The Avant-projet de réforme: An Overview' in J Cartwright, S Vogenauer, and S Whittaker (eds), *Reforming the French Law of Obligations, Comparative Reflections on the Avant-Projet de Réforme du Droit des Obligations et de la Prescription* (Hart Publishing: Oxford, 2009) 7; The Civil Code was a global 'ambassador' for French law: B Fauvarque-Cosson and S Patris-Godechot, *Le code civil face à son destin* (La Documentation Française: Paris, 2006) 8–9.

[6] One such jurisdiction, Peru, announced soon after the French reforms that it would overhaul its own Civil Code: Ministerial Resolution no 0300-2016-JUS of 17 October 2016. Workshops on the new French law of contract were also organized in jurisdictions that have not used the Civil Code as a model. For example, there was a workshop at the University of Oxford in September 2017. Publications on the reforms in English include J Cartwright and S Whittaker (eds), *The Code Napoléon Rewritten: French Contract Law after the 2016 Reforms* (Hart Publishing: Oxford, 2017); S Rowan, 'The New French Law of Contract' (2017) 66 ICLQ 805; S Rowan 'The Reform of French Contract Law: The Struggle for Coherency' in TT Arvind and J Steele (eds) *Contract Law and the Legislature: Autonomy, Expectations, and the Making of Legal Doctrine* (Hart Publishing: Oxford, 2020). A number of their findings and observations are reproduced or referenced herein.

> ... the task of the legislator is to determine those principles most conducive to the common good.... The skill of the judge is to put these principles into action, to develop and extend them to particular circumstances by wise and reasoned application.[7]

However, over the course of two centuries, it had become excessive. Most articles had been substantially developed, extended, or limited. Many were interpreted by analogy, *a contrario*[8] or even *contra legem*.[9] On their own and without explanation of how they had been interpreted by the courts, a significant number were all but meaningless. Indeed in several areas the courts had shaped rules that were almost entirely new.

To read the Civil Code therefore did not give a clear or precise picture of French contract law. Instead, this was largely to be found in decided cases. In a jurisdiction with a tradition of codified law in which previous judicial decisions are not formally a binding source of law, this was regarded as ironic and unsatisfactory.

The growing body of cases interpreting the Civil Code also meant that knowledge and understanding of contract law became the preserve of lawyers, contrary to the original aim that the Code would be clear and intelligible to lawyers and non-lawyers alike. This was compounded by the separate development outside of the Code of supplementary rules applicable to particular types of contracts. For example, regulations on consumer law and insurance law were enacted through specific legislation, without being integrated into the Code.[10] In short, the Code had ceased to be a comprehensive, coherent, and self-contained legislative instrument; modernization had become essential.

## 2 Loss of international influence

There was also a realization that the international influence of the Civil Code had declined. This was felt acutely at the turn of the twenty-first century amidst the preparations for the Code's 200th anniversary. One sign of the times was that, when reforming their own civil codes, states that had once drawn upon the Code, such as the Netherlands and Quebec, actually chose to depart from it.

In parallel, there were moves within the European Union towards harmonizing contract law in Europe beyond simply the well-trodden terrain of consumer

[7] JEM Portalis, 'Discours préliminaire du premier projet de Code civil', in PA Fenet, *Receuil complet de travaux preparatoires du Code civil* (Vidocq: Paris, 1836).

[8] 'From the contrary', that is an interpretation that adopts the opposite solution to a rule contained in the Code where the conditions of that rule are not fulfilled.

[9] 'Against the law', that is an interpretation that contradicts the clear wording of a provision of the Code.

[10] For a detailed account of the process of 'codification, decodification and recodification' of French private law, see Vogenauer (n 5) 4–7.

protection. The European Parliament had advocated work being undertaken on a European civil code or contract code[11] and in 2001 the European Commission began a debate on the future of European contract law.[12] In France, these projects were met with anxiety and even hostility. This was partly because the input of French lawyers had at that stage been minimal and the projects were also feared to portend the creation of a rival to the Civil Code.[13] Some were concerned that the disconnect between the Code and the law as applied in practice would diminish its sway in these European level projects. If the Code was ever again to be a model or exert real influence over, or even serve as, a counter-weight to future harmonization proposals, it simply had to be modernized.

## 3 Lack of appeal to international business

A final important factor behind the reforms was a recognition that French contract law was materially less attractive as a choice of law for cross-border contracts than the equivalent regimes of some common law countries. When selecting their governing law, international businesses often preferred the laws of England or New York. There was a widely held view that these were more commercial and in tune with whether particular outcomes made economic sense. French law compared unfavourably on measures such as pragmatism and the promotion of transactional certainty, which have less prominence in France and were often counterbalanced by considerations of substantive fairness (*justice contractuelle*). Nowhere was this more apparent than in the extensive powers of the courts to interfere with the terms of the contract. This had become a source of real uncertainty, to which business is generally averse.

These perceptions were compounded by several reports on 'Doing Business' that were published by the World Bank between 2004 and 2006.[14] France was ranked in a very unhappy 44th place for ease of doing business, behind less developed countries such as Botswana and Jamaica amongst others. The reports were particularly critical of the 'French civil law tradition' and its restraining effect on commerce. It was portrayed as being economically inefficient, complex, and unpredictable, and as generally inferior to the main common law systems.

Although tendentious and based on a methodology that was contentious,[15] these reports were nevertheless 'electroshocks'[16] in France, adding to a growing

[11] See European Parliament Resolution A2-157/89 and Resolution A3-0329/94.

[12] 'Communication from the Commission to the Council and the European Parliament on European Contract Law' (COM (2001) 398 final) <https://eur-lex.europa.eu/LexUriServ/LexUriServ.do?uri=COM:2001:0398:FIN:EN:PDF> accessed 1 September 2021.

[13] Fauvarque-Cosson and Patris-Godechot (n 5) 8–9.

[14] 'Doing Business in 2004: Understanding Regulation' (World Bank and OUP: Washington DC, 2003); 'Doing Business in 2005: Removing Obstacles to Growth' (World Bank and OUP: Washington DC, 2004); 'Doing Business in 2006: Creating Jobs' (World Bank and OUP: Washington DC, 2005).

[15] See Fauvarque-Cosson and Patris-Godechot (n 5) 152–7.

[16] Ibid.

awareness that French contract law would need to be modernized in order to be a serious and credible option for international business. As the then French Minister of Justice, Christiane Taubira, said in the Senate in 2014:

> ... our law [of contract] dates from over two centuries ... Times have changed ... Our law does not inspire anyone in the world ...There is a battle of influence in Europe between our continental law ... and the common law ... This battle is ... permanent ... It is necessary to modernise our law of contract and obligations.[17]

## B The Objectives of the Reform

This was the context in which the French government began to grapple with the need for reform. It promulgated three objectives which were identified by the drafters of the reforms in their 'Report to the President of the Republic'[18] in which they explained the new articles and their rationale. These were that the contract law section of the Civil Code should be more up to date, accessible, and predictable; be more attractive to international business and competitive with the major common law regimes; and promote fairness.[19]

The drafters sought to achieve the first objective in a combination of ways. The first was to use more simple and modern language than used in the 1804 Code. According to the Report to the President, the aim was that laymen unfamiliar with legal jargon should be able to understand the rules and see how justice is done.[20]

Second, the drafters sought to codify principles that had been established in decided cases. The need to do so was significant and pressing. In France, judicial decisions, even those of the highest court, the *Cour de cassation*, do not have nearly

[17] Official report of the session of 23 January 2014 in the 'Sénat': <www.senat.fr/seances/s201401/s20140123/s20140123014.html> accessed 1 September 2021; interview in 'Les Echos' magazine: <www.youtube.com/watch?v=K9V-DqNw2kQ> accessed 1 September 2021.

[18] 'Report to the President of the Republic relating to Ordonnance no 2016–131 of 10 February 2016 on the reform of contract law, the general regime and proof of obligations', JORF no 0035 of 11 February 2016.

[19] Ibid., 1–2. These goals were reaffirmed in the reports published by the National Assembly and the Senate when ratifying the decree: S Houlié, 'Rapport fait au nom de la commission des lois constitutionnelles, de la législation et de l'administration générale de la République sur le projet de loi, modifié par le Sénat en deuxième lecture, ratifiant l'ordonnance no 2016-131 du 10 février 2016 portant réforme du droit des contrats, du régime général et de la preuve des obligations' (Assemblée Nationale: no 429, 29 Nov 2017) <https://www.assemblee-nationale.fr/dyn/15/rapports/cion_lois/l15b0429_rapport-fond> accessed 1 September 2021; F Pillet, 'Rapport fait au nom des lois constitutionnelles, de législation, du suffrage universel, du Règlement d'administration générale (1) sur le projet de loi ratifiant l'ordonnance no 2016-131 du 10 février 2016 portant réforme du droit des contrats, du régime général et de la preuve des obligations' (Sénat: no 33, 11 Oct 2017) <https://www.senat.fr/rap/l17-022/l17-0221.pdf> accessed 1 September 2021.

[20] Ibid., 2.

the same importance as in common law systems.[21] There is no formal system of precedent, as will be explained in Chapter 2 on the consideration of the sources of contract law. Appellate cases are innumerable in comparison with England. The *Cour de cassation*, for instance, comprises six chambers and more than 100 judges who deal with over 25,000 disputes each year.[22] As of 2020, there were thirty-six regional courts of appeal, comprising over 1,000 judges.[23] It is therefore much more difficult than in England to identify decisions to which importance should be attached and to distil binding principles. There is also a greater risk of inconsistency between decisions. These difficulties are compounded by the brevity and terse style of judgments in France which reveal little of the reasoning of the court. The aim was to reduce the uncertainties inherent in relying on past cases.

Third, the drafters revised the structure of the 1804 Code to give each section more defined scope and clarity.[24] A clear distinction is now drawn between the sources of obligations,[25] the legal regime governing obligations,[26] and the proof of obligations (*preuve des obligations*).[27] The articles relating to contract law are ordered in a sequence that corresponds to the life cycle of the contract, dealing first with contract formation, followed by validity, interpretation, unfair terms, privity, and finally remedies for breach.[28]

These clarifications were also perceived to go some way towards fulfilling another goal of the reforms, which was to restore the international status of French contract law, both as a model for other countries and amongst European law reformers, in case a European civil code should ever be drafted. A codified set of laws presented clearly that is easier to read and more accessible was thought to be essential. At the very least, French contract law principles should be readily understood.

Codifying the case law and adopting this new structure have resulted in the contract law provisions of the Code becoming more comprehensive. It has also led to the articles being extensively re-numbered. Some of the iconic articles of the 1804 Code have disappeared. For instance, the enunciation of the fundamental principles of the binding force of contract and good faith in performance, which for many generations was found in old article 1134, is now split between new articles 1103 and 1104.

[21] On the role of the courts and the status of decided cases as a source of law in the civil law, see J Bell, *French Legal Culture* (Butterworths Lexis: London, 2001) 66–72; J Cartwright, 'Un regard anglais sur les forces et les faiblesses du droit français' RTD 2015.691, 693.

[22] According to the 2019 report of the *Cour de cassation*: <https://www.vie-publique.fr/sites/default/files/rapport/pdf/276165.pdf> accessed 1 September 2021.

[23] Statistics of the Ministère de la Justice, 'Les chiffres-clés de la Justice 2020' <http://www.justice.gouv.fr/art_pix/Chiffres_Cl%E9s_nov2020.pdf> accessed 1 September 2021. England has only forty-two Justices of Appeal.

[24] 'Report to the President' (n 18) 2.

[25] Articles 1100 to 1303-4 of the Civil Code.

[26] Articles 1304 to 1352-9 of the Civil Code.

[27] Articles 1353 to 1386-1 of the Civil Code.

[28] 'Report to the President' (n 18) 2.

The second objective as described in the Report to the President[29] was to make French contract law more commercially orientated, attractive to potential foreign investors, and competitive with major common law regimes. It was hoped that this would encourage the choice of French law as the governing law in international contracts.[30] The Report explains as follows:

> In a globalised economy where the laws of different countries are themselves in competition, the absence of evolution of contract law... penalises France on the international scene... [a more modern and predictable contract law] would attract foreign investors and businesses wanting to choose French law as the governing law of their contract.[31]

This was even cast as an opportunity for French law to capitalize on Brexit. For example, one French parliamentarian said that 'Brexit gives us the opportunity to make continental law prevail over the law of common law countries'.[32]

Neither the Report to the President nor the French parliamentary debates shed light on precisely how the drafters intended to fulfil this objective. Such brief references as were made to enhanced commerciality related to remedies for breach of contract, where the drafters sought to reduce the need for recourse to the court and introduce greater optionality and flexibility. The injured party can now act unilaterally to suspend performance (*exceptio non adimpleti contractus*), reduce the contract price, and terminate.

The third objective—substantive fairness (*justice contractuelle*)[33]—involved achieving a fair balance between the substantive interests of the parties. In France, the courts have long been seen as the guardians of this balance.[34] Over the years there have been many well-known cases in which courts have interfered with the contract in order to redress a bad bargain or unfair terms.[35] The drafters sought to enhance these powers and amplify considerations of fairness. For example, greater prominence is now given to the principle of good faith and there are wider powers

[29] Ibid., 1–2.

[30] The Senate criticized this objective, arguing that the attractiveness of the law does not depend only on legal factors but also on the economic power of the State and the reputation of its legal system and law firms: see Pillet, 'Report to the Senate' (n 19) 12.

[31] 'Report to the President' (n 18) 1–2.

[32] Pillet, 'Report to the Senate' (n 19).

[33] S Smorto, 'La Justice Contractuelle' Revue Internationale de Droit Comparé 2008.60.

[34] S Whittaker, 'Contracts, Contract Law and Contractual Principle' in J Cartwright and S Whittaker (eds), *The Code Napoléon Rewritten, French Contract Law After the 2016 Reforms* (Hart Publishing: Oxford, 2017) 29; Smorto (n 33).

[35] Using the notion of *cause*: see Chapter 7 on unfair terms and notably the *Video cassette* decision: Civ (1) 3 July 1996, D 1997.500, note P Reigné; see also the well-known *Chronopost* decision: Com 22 Oct 1996, D 1997.121, note A Sériaux; Com 30 May 2006, D 2006.1599, note X Delpech and D Mazeaud.

for the court to strike down unfair terms and adjust the agreed risk allocation where unforeseen circumstances arise.

To some extent this objective was in conflict with the second objective of making French contract law more commercially attractive. This was addressed in the Report to the President in the following terms:

> It appeared necessary ... not to recast the law of contract in its entirety but to modernise it... while still preserving the spirit of the Civil Code which is favourable to both consensualism to encourage economic exchanges and protective of the weakest... Enhancing the attractiveness of our law does not require us to relinquish balanced legal solutions that are not only protective of the parties but also effective and responsive to changes in the market economy... The reforms propose solutions that seek to achieve a balance between the rights and duties of the parties.[36]

There will be consideration in the chapters that follow as to whether the competing objectives have been successfully reconciled in the reforms, and of the coherency of the balance that is struck between the classical tensions of freedom of contract, transactional certainty, and the protection of the weak.

## C The Long Road to Reform

The road to reform was a long one, requiring sustained persistence for the revision of the section of the Civil Code on contract law to come to fruition. Momentum first really began to build in 2004 at around the time of the celebration of the bicentenary of the enactment of the Code, which marked the beginning of what became a serious push towards reform. In the years that followed, several proposals were published, only to fall away, before the 2016 reforms were finally enacted.

The first reform project in this period, commonly referred as the 'Catala proposals',[37] was published in 2005. Drafted mainly by academic lawyers, it contained proposals for the reform not only of French contract law but of all the core areas of French private law. Despite generating considerable interest and enthusiasm, the draft reforms never reached the statute book, due largely to an insufficiency of political will at that time.[38] This was followed in 2008 and 2009 by two further reform projects, which contained many of the same ideas. Both were under the

[36] 'Report to the President' (n 18) 2 and 5.

[37] *Avant-Projet de Réforme du Droit des Obligations (Art 1101 à 1386 du Code civil) et du Droit de la Prescription (Art 2234 à 2281 du Code Civil) under the direction of P Catala, 22 Sept 2005* (Documentation Française: Paris 2006) translated into English by J Cartwright and S Whittaker: <http://www.justice.gouv.fr/art_pix/rapportcatatla0905-anglais.pdf> accessed 1 September 2021.

[38] Vogenauer (n 5) 17.

auspices of the Ministry of Justice[39] and neither was ultimately adopted. This is not to say, however, that any of the three projects were in vain. The proposals that were made and the commentary and discussion that ensued served as the foundations on which the 2016 reforms were later built. With the clarity of hindsight, these proposals deserve great credit and arguably were essential stepping stones without which the reforms might never ultimately have been adopted.

Another essential ingredient was political will. Having previously been lacking, this came to the fore between 2010 and 2016, despite a change in the prevailing political colour following the French presidential election in 2012, which saw François Hollande succeed Nicolas Sarkozy. The two Ministers of Justice who held office during this period each established working groups comprising lawyers, business representatives, and ministers to draft what would become the final reform proposals.

There was also a degree of political dexterity in the enactment of the reforms. The French government was concerned that full debates of the proposals in the French Parliament would lead to delay and possibly even their failure. It therefore invited Parliament to grant legislative authority for the enactment of the reforms by government decree (*ordonnance*). This meant that the normal parliamentary process could be bypassed and the proposals passed without full scrutiny. To justify this course, the Ministry of Justice argued that French contract law was in urgent need of reform, the objectives of the proposed reforms were uncontroversial, and the fundamental principles on which contract law was based would remain unchanged. It also pointed to the proposed text being the culmination of the various reform proposals published over the preceding ten years, all of which had been the subject of intense scrutiny.[40]

This met with considerable opposition on the basis that reform by decree was inappropriate for such an important area of private law.[41] The Senate was particularly vocal in disputing the propriety of the proposed procedure. Ultimately, however, the French Parliament authorized the government to proceed. The draft proposals were published in February 2015,[42] and a short period of consultation

[39] Ministère de la Justice, *Projet de réforme du droit des contrats*, July 2008. A new version was drafted in 2009. See also F Terré, *Pour une reforme du droit des contrats: Réflexions et propositions d'un groupe de travail sous la direction de François Terré* (Paris: Dalloz, 2008).

[40] See Christiane Taubira's intervention in Parliament on 16 April 2014: <https://www.youtube.com/watch?v=OFrpvFh-I4s> accessed 1 September 2021.

[41] The *Conseil Constitutionnel* was petitioned by members of the Senate to review the constitutionality of the Government being granted authority to legislate on such an important topic without parliamentary debate. The *Conseil Constitutionnel* held that the process adopted by the Government complied with article 38 of the Constitution, which allows the Government to legislate by decree in certain circumstances; it was limited and had clear and precise goals. See its decision Cons Const 12 Feb 2015, no 2015-510 DC. See also F Ancel, 'Le procès en illégitimité: retour sur le processus d'élaboration de l'ordonnance du 10 février 2016' RDA 2017, no 15.83.

[42] 'Projet d'Ordonnance portant réforme du droit des contrats, du régime général et de la preuve des obligations' published 25 February 2015 <http://www.justice.gouv.fr/publication/j21_projet_ord_reforme_contrats_2015.pdf> accessed 1 September 2021.

followed. At the end of this period, the text was revised by the Ministry of Justice before being published in final form in February 2016.[43] It came into effect on 1 October 2016.

The final remaining hurdle was for the government decree to be ratified by the French Parliament. This had to occur within the prescribed period of eighteen months, failing which the decree would be void. A ratification bill was presented to Parliament in June 2017. There was some hope that it would pass without modification. However, Parliament and in particular the Senate sought to reopen the debate and reformulate some of the most controversial innovations.[44] It did so with some success,[45] several articles being modified quite substantially.[46]

Ratification finally occurred on 20 April 2018, with the amended articles formally taking effect on 1 October 2018.[47] The amendments that had been made in the interim had the somewhat peculiar and unsatisfactory effect that there are no fewer than three different contract law regimes in operation in France. Contracts that were entered before 1 October 2016 are governed by the law prior to the reforms; those entered between 1 October 2016 and 30 September 2018 are subject to the principles in the 2016 decree; and those entered from 1 October 2018 are governed by the principles of the 2016 decree as amended by the 2018 ratification law.

This was not, however, the end of the journey. Although extensive, the 2016 reforms did not amend in any significant respect the articles of the Civil Code relating to contractual liability and compensatory and agreed damages. These were held over by the drafters to be addressed separately along with extra-contractual liability as part of a later and broader project to reform civil liability in France.[48] As the Report to the President stated:

> Contractual liability cannot be reformed in isolation from extra-contractual liability: it is generally accepted that, fundamentally, these two forms of liability are mechanisms of the same nature, resting on the existence of an action giving rise

[43] 'Ordonnance no 2016-131 du 10 février 2016' (n 2).

[44] M Mekki 'La loi de ratification de l'ordonnance du 10 février 2016—une réforme de la réforme?' D 2018.900.

[45] On these changes, see the various articles by prominent French commentators in 'Le nouveau droit des contrats après la loi de ratification du 20 avril 2018' RDC Hors-série June 2018.

[46] Others were clarified but not substantially amended.

[47] 'Loi no 2018-287 du 20 avril 2018 ratifiant l'ordonnance n° 2016-131 du 10 février 2016 portant réforme du droit des contrats, du régime général et de la preuve des obligations', JORF no 0093 du 21 avril 2018.

[48] Ministère de la Justice, *Projet de réforme de la responsabilité civile* (March 2017), <http://www.justice.gouv.fr/publication/Projet_de_reforme_de_la_responsabilite_civile_13032017.pdf>; translated from French into English by S Whittaker in consultation with J-S Borghetti: *Reform Bill on Civil Liability* (March 2017) <http://www.textes.justice.gouv.fr/art_pix/reform_bill_on_civil_liability_march_2017.pdf> accessed 1 September 2021.

> to liability, harm, and a causal relationship between the two. Only differences of regime distinguish between them, based essentially on the special character of the action giving rise to liability in the contractual context.[49]

The first proposals made as part of this project were published in April 2016 and a period of consultation was initiated, which closed at the end of July 2016. New proposals taking account of comments that had been submitted were published in March 2017.[50] The Reform Bill on Civil Liability contains eighty-three new articles in which there are a number of significant innovations.[51] At the time of writing (June 2021), the proposals of the 2017 Reform Bill are yet to be implemented. It is presently unclear whether this will happen and, if so, when and in what form.[52]

As a result, the analysis of contractual liability and compensatory and agreed damages in this book is confined to the original articles in the 1804 Civil Code, which were renumbered but otherwise substantially replicated in the 2016 reforms and continue to apply. Occasional reference is made to some of the main proposed changes and innovations, which could potentially be introduced in the future,[53] but this is not intended to be comprehensive.

[49] 'Report to the President' (n 18) 17; translation of S Whittaker in his chapter entitled 'A Common Framework for Civil Liability?' in J-S Borghetti and S Whittaker (eds), *French Civil Liability in Comparative Perspective* (Hart Publishing: Oxford, 2019) 21.

[50] *Projet de réforme de la responsabilité civile* (n 48).

[51] For example, the introduction of a form of mitigation (proposed articles 1237 and 1263) and civil fines (*amende civile*) which are punitive in nature (proposed article 1266-1).

[52] In July 2020, several senators who were impatient to see reforms enacted put forward proposals amending the 2017 reforms: '23 propositions pour simplifier la vie des Français en facilitant la réparation des dommages' (Sénat: 22 July 2020) <20200722_23_propositions_Responsabilite_civile.pdf (senat.fr)> accessed 1 September 2021. This was followed by a 'proposition de loi': <https://www.senat.fr/leg/ppl19-678.html> accessed 1 September 2021.

[53] On the draft project, see J-S Borghetti and S Whittaker (eds), *French Civil Liability in Comparative Perspective* (Hart Publishing: Oxford, 2019).

# PART I

# INTRODUCTION TO THE KEY PRINCIPLES OF CONTRACT LAW

# 2
# The Place of Contract Law in the Law of Obligations and the Sources of Contract Law

Before embarking upon the study of French contract law, it is helpful to understand its place within the wider law of obligations and the main sources from which the principles that are set out in the following chapters have been shaped.

## A The Place of Contract Law within the Law of Obligations

Civil Code[1]
Art. 1100.—Obligations arise from juridical acts, juridically significant facts or from the sole authority of legislation.

They can arise from the voluntary performance or from the promise of performance of a moral duty towards another person.

Art. 1100-1.—Juridical acts are manifestations of will intended to produce legal effects. They may be based on agreement or unilateral.

As far as is appropriate, they are subject, both as to their validity and as to their effects, to the rules governing contracts.

Art. 1100-2.—Juridically significant facts consist of behaviour or events to which legislation attaches legal consequences.

Obligations which arise from a juridically significant fact are governed, according to the circumstances, by the sub-title relating to extra-contractual liability or the sub-title relating to other sources of obligations.

In France, contract law forms part of the law of obligations, sitting alongside extra-contractual liability (*la responsabilité extra-contractuelle*) and

[1] 'Ordonnance no 2016-131 du 10 février 2016 portant réforme du droit des contrats, du régime général et de la preuve des obligations', JORF no 0035 of 11 February 2016. The Ordonnance was translated into English by J Cartwright, B Fauvarque-Cosson, and S Whittaker: <http://www.textes.justice.gouv.fr/art_pix/THE-LAW-OF-CONTRACT-2-5-16.pdf> (2016 version) and <http://www.textes.justice.gouv.fr/art_pix/Translationrevised2018final.pdf> (2018 version) accessed 1 September 2021. The translations of the new articles contained in this book are theirs.

*The New French Law of Contract*. Solène Rowan, Oxford University Press. © Solène Rowan 2022.
DOI: 10.1093/oso/9780198810872.003.0002

quasi-contracts. This is reflected in the structure of the reformed Civil Code, in which Title III—'The Sources of Obligations' (*Des Sources d'Obligations*)—is divided into three sub-titles. These are: 'Contract' (Sub-Title I);[2] 'Extra-Contractual Liability' (Sub-Title II);[3] and 'Other Sources of Obligations' (Sub-Title III).[4] It can be seen that contract law is dealt within the first sub-title and extra-contractual liability, which was referred to prior to the reforms as 'delictual liability' (*la responsabilité délictuelle*), in the second. The cryptically-named third sub-title—Other Sources of Obligations—deals with quasi-contracts,[5] which is explained at new article 1300.

The place of contract law in the law of obligations is illustrated in how the main French student and practitioner textbooks typically tackle the subject, alongside extra-contractual liability and quasi-contract as part of a broader examination of the law of obligations.[6] Rarely do textbooks deal solely with contract law.

It is also discernible in new article 1100 of the Code, which provides that all obligations arise from 'juridical acts' (*actes juridiques*), 'juridical facts' (*faits juridiques*) or from 'the sole authority of legislation' (*l'autorité seule de la loi*). In simple terms, juridical acts give rise to contractual obligations whereas juridical facts are the source of extra-contractual obligations and quasi-contracts.

Juridical acts are defined in new article 1100-1 as voluntary acts that are intended to produce (and do produce) legal effects. They may be either bilateral, of which the paradigm is a contract, or unilateral, for example a will or a promise of a reward that is made to the public at large. Paragraph 2 of article 1101-1 provides that both bilateral and unilateral juridical acts, so far as appropriate, are subject to the rules of the Code on contract law.

Juridical facts are defined in new article 1100-2 and consist of conduct or events which give rise to legal effects by operation of law. This may be an event that is external to the will or choice of the person that is the subject of the legal effects, such as a death, or a voluntary act of that person which gives rise to legal effects, whether or not that was the party's intention. An example is the publication of a defamatory statement which results in a liability to pay damages. As the basis for extra-contractual obligations and quasi-contracts, juridical facts are governed by

[2] Sub-Title I of Title III of the Civil Code (articles 1102 to 1231-7).

[3] Sub-Title II of Title III of the Civil Code (articles 1240 to 1245-17).

[4] Sub-Title III of Title III of the Civil Code (article 1300 to 1303-4).

[5] Principally what in other laws would be treated as unjust enrichment and benevolent intervention.

[6] J Bell, S Boyron, and S Whittaker, *Principles of French Law* (2nd edn, OUP: Oxford, 2008) 294. See, for example, the main student textbooks: F Terré, P Simler, Y Lequette, and F Chénedé, *Droit civil: les obligations* (12th edn, Dalloz: Paris, 2018); 'Book 1: Les Sources des obligations' with four titles on 'Le contrat', 'La responsabilité extracontractuelle', 'Les régimes spéciaux de responsabilité', and 'Les quasi-contrats'; P Malaurie, L Aynès, and P Stoffel-Munck, *Droit des obligations* (10th edn, LGDJ: Paris, 2018) is divided into three parts: 'Responsabilités extracontractuelles', 'Contrats et quasi-contrats', and 'Régime général'; A Bénabent, *Droit des obligations* (18th edn, LGDJ: Paris, 2019) is also divided into three parts: 'Les obligations d'origine volontaire: le contrat', 'Les obligations d'origine légale', and 'Le régime général des obligations.'

the rules of the Code on extra-contractual liability and other sources of obligations respectively.

This categorization and the distinction between juridical acts and facts is long-standing in the French law of obligations,[7] although it was not mentioned in the 1804 Code and was only formally introduced as part of the reform process. In truth, however, the distinction is more theoretical than practical. It has been described as 'an expression of a dogmatic taxonomy, rather than being used for significant normative purposes'.[8] It is no more than the idea that there are 'two fundamental sources of obligation ...: a promise and a wrong'.[9]

Despite these attempts at categorization, neither the relationship nor the boundary between the principles governing contractual and extra-contractual obligations has ever been strictly delineated in French law. Indeed, they have been described as 'among one of the most complex and finely-balanced questions of the law of obligations',[10] and are a source of much contention.[11]

In some circumstances, French law imposes a strict barrier between the rules that regulate the two sources of obligations. This is most evident in the 'no-option' rule on contractual and extra-contractual liability (*principe de non-cumul des responsabilités*).[12] Its effect is to prevent the party injured by a breach of contract from bringing a claim based on extra-contractual liability, even where the requirements for both contractual and extra-contractual liability are met. Instead, the claim can only be in contract.[13] As the *Cour de cassation* has held, the injured party 'cannot rely on the rules of delictual liability against the party in breach even where he would have an interest in doing so'.[14] There can therefore be no concurrent liability and the injured party cannot choose their preferred basis of claim. The rules relating to contractual liability take precedence, and extra-contractual liability is confined to cases in which there is no breach of contract.

The no-option rule has been attributed to 'a juristic preference for keeping legal categories distinct'.[15] It avoids extra-contractual liability undermining the

[7] For a detailed explanation, see Terré, Simler, Lequette, and Chénedé (n 6) [5].

[8] Ibid.

[9] Ibid.

[10] P Wéry, *Droit des obligations* (2nd edn, Larcier: Bruxelles, 2011) [619] cited in O Deshayes, T Genicon, and Y-M Laithier, *Réforme du droit des contrats, du régime général et de la preuve des obligations* (2nd edn, LexisNexis: Paris, 2018) 62.

[11] For a description and analysis of the debates, see S Whittaker, 'A Common Framework for Civil Liability' and Y-M Laithier 'The Relationship between Contractual and Extra-Contractual Liability as between Parties to a Contract' in J-S Borghetti and S Whittaker (eds), *French Civil Liability in Comparative Perspective* (Hart Publishing: Oxford, 2019).

[12] Ibid.

[13] There are a small number of exceptions to the rule of non-cumul, see Dehayes, Genicon, and Laithier (n 10) 72. A new one would also be created in draft paragraph 1 of article 1233-1 of the 2017 Reform Bill on Civil Liability.

[14] Com 26 Sept 2018 no 17-15306; Com 10 March 2015 no 13-10003.

[15] Bell, Boyron, and Whittaker (n 6) 328; Dehayes, Genicon, and Laithier (n 10) 72–4. See also P Ancel, 'Le concours de la responsabilité délictuelle et de la responsabilité contractuelle' RCA 2012.2, dossier no 8, [11]; P le Tourneau (ed), *Droit de la responsabilité et des contrats, Régimes d'indemnisation*

allocation of risks in the contract.[16] As Deshayes, Genicon, and Laithier have explained, 'in this way the refusal of an option to the creditor protects the function and effectiveness of contracts as *un acte de prévision*, that is to say, a juridical act by which the parties can plan and make provision for their future relationship'.[17] This protection is regarded as necessary in view of the breadth of extra-contractual liability in French law.[18] In particular, the availability of compensation for pure economic loss gives rise to a risk of the defaulting party being liable to third parties in ways and amounts that are unforeseeable.[19] This creates 'a far from theoretical risk that the contractual regime may be circumvented to the advantage of the extra-contractual regime'.[20]

However, despite the apparent cleanness of the no-option rule, the line between the rules governing contractual and extra-contractual liability is often blurred. For example, there are general principles that apply indistinctly in both contexts, such as the principle of full compensation (*réparation intégrale du préjudice*) and the principle that there must be a causal link between the breach of duty and the loss suffered by the victim. Similarly, both forms of liability are said to be based on 'fault'.[21] As regards extra-contractual liability, this is stated in article 1240 of the Code, which provides that 'any human action whatsoever which causes harm to another creates an obligation in the person by whose fault it occurred to make reparation for it'. In a contractual context, the courts and commentators often refer to breach of contract as a 'fault' (*la faute contractuelle* or *l'inexécution fautive*), even where liability is strict and despite the contract law section of the Civil Code not using this term and referring only to breach of contract (*l'inexécution du contrat*).

A number of the commonalities and differences between contractual and extra-contractual liability would be given formal recognition in the event that the 2017 Reform Bill on Civil Liability is enacted.[22] These include certain conditions

(11th edn, Dalloz: Paris, 2017) [3213.321]–[3213.322]; P Rémy, 'La responsabilité contractuelle: histoire d'un faux concept' RTD civ 1997, 354.

[16] Civ 11 Jan 1922, S 1924.1.105, note R Demogue GAJC no 182; see also Whittaker, 'A Common Framework for Civil Liability' (n 11), and Laithier, 'The Relationship between Contractual and Extra-Contractual Liability as between Parties to a Contract' (n 11).

[17] Dehayes, Genicon, and Laithier (n 10) 63.

[18] Ibid., 72–4.

[19] J-S Borghetti, 'The Effects of Contracts and Third Parties' in J Cartwright and S Whittaker (eds), *The Code Napoléon Rewritten: French Contract Law after the 2016 Reforms* (Hart Publishing: Oxford, 2017) 227, 249–53.

[20] Dehayes, Genicon, and Laithier (n 10) 63.

[21] This would be the case even if the draft reforms in relation to civil liability are enacted, see ibid., 75: 'The *Projet de réforme* proclaims its loyalty to the ... model ... [that] civil liability is above all based on breach of a duty which is imposed by the law and, accordingly, it is the defendant's fault or unlawful act which occupies a central place.'

[22] See Chapter I, p10–1: Ministère de la Justice, *Projet de réforme de la responsabilité civile* (13 March 2017), <http://www.justice.gouv.fr/publication/Projet_de_reforme_de_la_responsabilite_civile_13032017.pdf>; translated from French into English by S Whittaker in consultation with J-S Borghetti: *Reform Bill on Civil Liability* (March 2017) *Reform Bill on Civil Liability* (March 2017),

of liability and grounds of exoneration or exclusion of liability. Both forms of liability would also be newly situated in a broader category of 'civil liability' (*la responsabilité civile*)[23] and there would be a more defined framework for their relationship.[24] The reform project seeks to provide 'a common framework for the two categories of liability, but distinguishes between them where it considers this normatively appropriate'.[25]

## B The Main Sources of French Contract Law

The binding sources of law in France are varied and include the Constitution, European Union law,[26] international treaties,[27] legislation, and customs.[28] Some sources, although not formally binding, are nevertheless influential. These include decided cases and the work of academic lawyers.[29]

The focus of this section is on the primary and most influential sources in the development of French contract law.[30] These are codified legislation, decided cases, and legal writings (*la doctrine*).

### 1 Legislation

Most principles of French contract law are found in the section of the Civil Code on contract. However, this is by no means a comprehensive and self-contained statement of the codified law that applies to contracts. There are for example regulations on consumer law that were introduced through separate legislation and have not been integrated into the Civil Code and are instead found in the Consumer Code.[31]

<http://www.textes.justice.gouv.fr/art_pix/reform_bill_on_civil_liability_march_2017.pdf> accessed 1 September 2021.

23 Whittaker, 'A Common Framework for Civil Liability' (n 11) 27.

24 On the project, see generally J-S Borghetti and S Whittaker (eds), *French Civil Liability in Comparative Perspective* (Hart Publishing, Oxford, 2019).

25 Whittaker, 'A Common Framework for Civil Liability' (n 11) 20.

26 Especially in the area of consumer law.

27 In the context of contract law, see The United Nations Convention on Contracts for the International Sale of Goods, Vienna, 11 April 1980 <https://treaties.un.org/doc/Treaties/1988/01/19880101%2003-03%20AM/Ch_X_10p.pdf> accessed 1 September 2021.

28 In the context of contract law, see article 1194 of the Civil Code: 'Contracts create obligations not merely in relation to what they expressly provide, but also to all the consequences which are given to them by equity, usage or legislation'. It recognizes the importance of customs. Customs have been especially important in the context of commercial contracts: see Terré, Simler, Lequette, and Chénedé (n 6) [11].

29 Bell, Boyron, and Whittaker make the useful distinction between 'formal' and 'influential' sources, see (n 6) 14.

30 Terré, Simler, Lequette, and Chénedé (n 6) [10]–[11].

31 For a detailed account of the process of 'codification, decodification and recodification' of French private law, see S Vogenauer, 'The *Avant-projet de réforme*: An Overview' in J Cartwright, S Vogenauer,

The same is true of the law regulating certain types of commercial transactions, which resides in the Commercial Code.

### (a) The Civil Code

The Civil Code provides the overall framework of the law of contract and contains the general principles applicable to all types of contract (*droit commun des contrats*).[32] It seeks to regulate the important stages in the life of the contract, including formation and validity, interpretation, and the legal effects as between the contracting parties and on third parties. There are also many special rules for specific categories of contract (*droit des contrats spéciaux*) such as contracts of sale (*vente*)[33] and agency (*mandats*).[34]

The contractual principles contained in the Civil Code are the product of a confluence of influences.[35] Their historical roots are in Roman law, canon law, customary law, the rationalizing and systematizing works of eminent jurists, such as Robert Joseph Pothier[36] and Jean Domat,[37] and the Enlightenment and the post-revolutionary ideas of the eighteenth century. One of the achievements of the 1804 Civil Code was to create a generalized law of contract that drew from the law of individual contracts in Roman law and its subsequent reinterpretation by scholars in later centuries, and the spirit of individualism and liberalism of the revolutionary age.

New and external influences have supplemented and built upon these historical sources. For example, as will be shown at various points, comparative law and international contract law projects such as the Principles of European Contract Law (PECL) and the UNIDROIT Principles were a source of inspiration for several new provisions and innovations in the 2016 reforms. This has resulted in a Code that is more in tune with a number of other European legal systems,[38] whilst at

and S Whittaker (eds), *Reforming the French Law of Obligations, Comparative Reflections on the Avant-Projet de Réforme du Droit des Obligations et de la Prescription* (Hart Publishing: Oxford, 2009) 4–7.

[32] Administrative contracts are subject to different rules. French law makes a formal distinction between public and private law, with contracts that are characterized as public being governed by special rules and subject to the jurisdiction of the administrative courts. Such contracts are outside of the scope of this book. For a discussion of administrative contracts, see J Bell and F Lichère, *Contemporary French Administrative Law* (CUP: Cambridge, 2022) ch. 9.

[33] Articles 1582 to 1701 of the Civil Code.

[34] Articles 1984 to 2010 of the Civil Code.

[35] Terré, Simler, Lequette, and Chénedé (n 6) [7]–[9].

[36] See, for example, R J Pothier, *Traité des obligations* (1761; reprint Dalloz: Paris, 2017).

[37] See, for example, J Domat, *Les lois civiles dans leur ordre naturel* (1689-1694; reprint Hachette Livre: Paris, 2018).

[38] Y-M Laithier, 'Exécution Forcée en Nature' in J-S Borghetti and S Whittaker (eds), *French Civil Liability in Comparative Perspective* (Hart Publishing: Oxford, 2019) 257, 260–1 said this in the context of the new provisions on enforced performance in kind but it is equally true in relation to many other aspects of the reforms. See also, Borghetti (n 19).

the same time retaining important values and doctrines that were enshrined in the 1804 Code.

One such doctrine that is referred to extensively in the following chapters is the theory of the autonomy of the will (*théorie de l'autonomie de la volonté*). This epitomized the central themes of individualism and liberalism in the 1804 Code and still plays a significant role in the reformed Code.[39] The theory holds that contracts are above all regulated by the will of the parties, who are free to bind themselves to whomever and on whatever terms they decide. Voluntarily created obligations, as an expression of the will of the parties, have the force of law and require adherence. They must be given effect by the courts, which cannot substitute their own will for that of the parties. Any restrictions on their freedom, whether based on public policy or otherwise, should be kept to a minimum.

Underlying this theory is a philosophy that prevailed at the time of codification: a natural law belief that contracting parties are driven by reason and are the best judges of their own interests.[40] It is founded on an assumption that something that a party has agreed to is fair and just or, as Alfred Fouillée famously said, 'whatever is contractual is just' (*Qui dit contractuel dit juste*).[41]

The reformed Code still firmly upholds the liberal tradition of giving effect to the will of the parties,[42] on which many principles in the Code are founded. It will be shown however that the reforms have adapted the theory to modern times, with a discernible shift in emphasis towards promoting fairness and counterbalancing some of the vices of freedom of contract. This reflects an unease that first developed in the nineteenth century in regard to *laissez-faire* economic philosophy and a growing appreciation of the limits of the idea that individuals are the best judges of their interests. What is voluntarily agreed is not always fair. In many situations, the contracting parties are not of equal bargaining power and the freedom of contract that individuals supposedly enjoy is in fact illusory.[43] The 'Report to the President of the Republic' in respect of the 2016 reforms explained that 'one of the essential aims pursued by the [reform is] ... to find a balance between contractual fairness and the autonomy of the will.'[44]

[39] The *Conseil Constitutionnel* elevated *autonomie de la volonté* to the level of a fundamental principle of constitutional importance: Cons Const 27 Nov 1959, D 1960.555, note L Hamon; Cons Const 8 Sept 1961, D 1963.381, note L Hamon; Cons Const 28 Nov 1973, D 1974.269.

[40] Terré, Simler, Lequette, and Chénedé (n 6) [22–23].

[41] A Fouillée, *La science sociale contemporaine* (2nd edn, Librairie Hachette: Paris, 1885) 410.

[42] G Chantepie and M Latina, *La réforme du droit des obligations, Commentaire théorique et pratique dans l'ordre du Code civil* (2nd edn, Dalloz: Paris, 2018) [85].

[43] P le Tourneau and M de Poumarède, *Répertoire de droit civil: bonne foi* (Dalloz: Paris, 2017) [66]: 'Since around the decade 1980-1990, good faith has been magnified and placed on a pedestal.' The decline of autonomy of the will led some commentators to argue that French contract law should be based on a model of contractual solidarity: R Demogue, *Traité des obligations en général, t 6* (Rousseau: Paris, 1931) no 3. Cited in Terré, Simler, Lequette, and Chénedé (n 6) [42].

[44] 'Report to the President of the Republic relating to Ordonnance no 2016–131 of 10 February 2016 on the reform of contract law, the general regime and proof of obligations', JORF no 0035 of 11 February 2016, 4.

### (b) Specific legislation: The examples of the Commercial Code and Consumer Code

The student or practitioner of French contract law must look beyond the Civil Code in a number of circumstances. For certain types of contract, it is supplemented by other codes. The most important are the Commercial Code (*Code de commerce*) and the Consumer Code (*Code de la consommation*), which contain rules that apply to specific types of commercial contracts and business-to-consumer contracts respectively.[45]

#### *(i) The Commercial Code*

French law gives special status to commercial contracts (*contrats commerciaux*). They are governed by the general principles of the Civil Code, but are also subject to specific rules that are set out in the Commercial Code, which was originally enacted in 1807 and reformed in 2000.

'Commercial contract' has a technical significance in French law and is not to be understood merely as a descriptor or catch-all for agreements that are commercial in nature. There are defined activities or transactions that qualify a contract as commercial. These are essentially *actes de commerce* and contracts entered into by the traders (*commerçants*) that engage in them.[46] They include for example the *actes de commerce* listed at article L110-1 and L110-2 of the Commercial Code, such as 'buying and selling goods with a view to making a profit', 'manufacturing', 'buying and selling land', and a range of contracts for the provision of services such as carriage contracts, banking and insurance contracts, and bills of exchange (*lettres de change*). Other examples are contracts entered into by the types of legal entities listed at article L210-1, such as partnerships and companies.

As a further sign of their distinctiveness, commercial contracts are subject to the jurisdiction of special commercial courts (*tribunaux de commerce*). The judges that sit in these courts are not career judges but peer-elected business people. Whilst they may have some background in the law, this is not a requirement. As a result, there is generally greater emphasis on practicality in the application of the law in the resolution of disputes.

#### *(ii) The Consumer Code*

Contracts between 'professionals' (*professionnels*) and 'non-professionals or consumers' are also classified separately in French law. In addition to the general principles of the Civil Code, they are subject to specific rules in the Consumer Code. This code resulted from a pan-European legislative drive in the 1980s to enhance

[45] There are other categories of contract that have become regulated by specific codes, for instance insurance contracts and employment contracts, which are separated from the general law of contract of the Civil Code.

[46] For more details on French commercial law in English, see Bell, Boyron, and Whittaker (n 6) 453–80.

and protect consumer rights. Whilst the idea that the law should protect contracting parties in weaker bargaining positions dates from long before then, consumer contracts were formally categorized separately from other types of contract from between 1993 and 1995, following the 1992 EU Directive on Unfair Terms in Consumer Contracts. The Consumer Code has subsequently been amended on multiple occasions in response to European and domestic legislative changes, most recently in 2017.[47]

As with the Commercial Code, identifying whether a contract falls within this classification is important because of the distinct rules that apply to consumer contracts. Some of these rules have significant consequences, including criminal and punitive civil law sanctions. As Whittaker has summarized, '[French] consumer law goes beyond "contract law" as traditionally understood ... it often enlists the criminal or administrative powers to contribute to the protection of consumers: indeed, most consumer law started with criminal law or in administrative rule-making rather than with "contract law" in the traditional sense.'[48] It is therefore essential for the criteria for consumer contract status to be clearly defined and, with that aim in view, definitions of 'consumer', 'non-professional', and 'professional' were recently added to the Consumer Code.[49]

### (c) The relationship between general contract law and specific contract law

The relationship between the general contract law principles and the special rules that apply to specific types of contracts, such as commercial contracts and consumer contracts, has historically been a source of controversy[50]—under which new article 1105 of the Civil Code seeks to draw a line. It does so by providing that, where both general and special rules apply, the former gives way to the latter.[51] In other words, the general principles are subject to the special rules. The article states that:

[47] By Ordonnance no 2016-301 of 14 March 2016 and ratified, with amendments, by law no 2017-203 of 21 February 2017 (loi no 2017-203 du 21 février 2017 ratifiant les ordonnances no 2016-301 du 14 mars 2016 relative à la partie législative du code de la consommation et no 2016-351 du 25 mars 2016 sur les contrats de crédit aux consommateurs relatifs aux biens immobiliers à usage d'habitation et simplifiant le dispositif de mise en œuvre des obligations en matière de conformité et de sécurité des produits et services).

[48] S Whittaker, 'Contracts, Contract Law and Contractual Principle' in J Cartwright and S Whittaker (eds), *The Code Napoléon Rewritten: French Contract Law after the 2016 Reforms* (Hart Publishing: Oxford, 2017) 29, 36.

[49] Consumer Code, article liminaire (modified by loi no 2017-203 of 21 February 2017 which ratifies the Ordonnance).

[50] For a detailed explanation of the evolution of article 1105 and the controversy it provoked, see F Ancel, B Fauvarque-Cosson, and J Gest, *Aux sources de la réforme du droit des contrats* (Paris: Dalloz, 2017) [33.22].

[51] Ibid. See also 'Report to the President' (n 44) 4: 'The general rules laid down by the Ordonnance will in particular be set aside when it is impossible to apply them simultaneously with certain rules provided for by the Civil Code to govern special contracts, or those in other codes such as the Commercial Code or the Consumer Code.'

> Whether or not they have their own denomination, contracts are subject to general rules, which are the subject of this sub-title.
>
> Rules particular to certain contracts are laid down in the provisions special to each of these contracts.
>
> The general rules are applied subject to these particular rules.

The effect in commercial and consumer contracts is that the special rules in the Commercial Code and the Consumer Code qualify those in the Civil Code.[52]

## 2 Decided cases

Decided cases are not formally a binding source of law in France. The role of the court, at least in theory, is merely to apply and give effect to the law. To rely upon decided cases is impermissible; the basis for a ruling must always be in statute. This means that, even where the facts are similar, lower courts cannot follow a previous decision of a superior court. The *Cour de cassation* is also not bound by its own past decisions.

The non-binding nature of court decisions is a product of history. At the time of the French Revolution, the legislature distrusted and was hostile to the judiciary, which was perceived to aspire to a law-making role and threaten its authority.[53] The legacy of these early jealousies is a strict doctrine of separation of powers in which the judiciary is prevented from interfering with the legislative function. This has been inscribed in the law since 1790.[54] Article 5 of the Civil Code imposes clear limits on the role of the court, providing that 'judges are not permitted to adjudicate by means of general and statutory rulings in the cases brought before them'.

Despite the passive function that is traditionally ascribed to the judiciary, the importance and influence of decided cases in the development of French contract law has been substantial. In practice, the judiciary has played a significant role in shaping the law, creating entire bodies of 'judge-made' law. For this reason, decided case are widely acknowledged as a ' "de facto source of law" and lower courts generally follow the decisions of higher courts'.[55]

[52] Ancel, Fauvarque-Cosson, and Gest (n 50) [33.23]: 'The fact remains that cumulation (*cumul*), even if it was not intended, is not expressly ruled out by the text: the meaning of the formulation "subject to" may leave the door open to a combined application when the rules of the general law are not incompatible with those of the special law.'

[53] B Nicholas, *The French Law of Contract* (Clarendon Press: Oxford, 1992) 12.

[54] See article 10 of law 16–24 August 1790 on judicial organization (loi des 16-24 août 1790 sur l'organisation judiciaire) <https://www.legifrance.gouv.fr/loda/id/JORFTEXT000000704777/> accessed 1 September 2021.

[55] H Beale, B Fauvarque-Cosson, J Rutgers, and S Vogenauer, *Cases, Materials and Text on Contract Law, Ius Commune Casebooks for the Common Law of Europe* (3rd edn, Hart Publishing: Oxford, 2019) 80.

Persuasive precedents are usually established in cases where the *Cour de cassation* articulates new general principles (*arrêts de principe*) or sets consistent lines of reasoning (*jurisprudence constante*). Decisions of special 'formations' of the *Cour de cassation* have enhanced status. This can be a full bench,[56] known as the *Assemblée Plénière*, that includes its most senior members, which is typically convened to adjudicate on important issues of law and questions of principle, or where there is persistent conflict between decisions of lower courts or lower courts and the *Cour of cassation* itself.[57] It can also be a *Chambre Mixte* comprising senior members of its different chambers,[58] which is typically convened to resolve conflicts in decisions of those chambers or to settle matters of jurisdiction if it is unclear within which chamber the case falls.[59] Decisions of these special formations have particular weight and authority and therefore promote legal certainty.

The importance of judicial decision-making in French law is closely tied to the inherent limitation of its codified system in that the original Civil Code enshrined only broad principles derived from political and social conditions and beliefs that prevailed at the time of codification in 1804. These principles were generally so broadly worded as to leave considerable room for interpretation. Indeed, in order for the Code to evolve with the times, they have had to be interpreted to take account of developments in the intervening period. In the words of Portalis, one of the drafters of the 1804 Code, the role of the judge is to put the laws enacted by Parliament 'into action, to develop and extend them to particular circumstances by wise and reasoned application'.[60] This approach is still followed today. It has been articulated by the *Cour de cassation* in the following terms:

> Whilst remaining within its role, our Court contributes to the gradual creation of the new state of law which will shape the society of tomorrow . . . [61] Even though it is careful to avoid hasty reversals of case law, which would not be compatible with the need for legal certainty, the *Cour de cassation* does not hesitate to correct its most settled doctrines when these no longer seem to it to correspond to social or economic reality or no longer accord with the development of ideas and morals.[62]

[56] 'About the Court' <L'organisation de la Cour de cassation | Cour de cassation> accessed 1 September 2021.

[57] Article L 431-6 of the Code of Judicial Organization.

[58] About the Court' <L'organisation de la Cour de cassation | Cour de cassation> accessed 1 September 2021.

[59] Article L 431-5 of the Code of Judicial Organization.

[60] JEM Portalis, 'Discours préliminaire du premier projet de Code civil', in PA Fenet, *Recueil complet de travaux préparatoires du Code civil* (Vidocq: Paris, 1836).

[61] Cour de cassation, *Rapport annuel 1975* (Paris, 1976) 101. Cited in Bell, Boyron, and Whittaker (n 6) 26.

[62] *Rapport de la Cour de cassation: Années judiciaires 1976 et 1977* (Paris, 1978), 119. Cited in Bell, Boyron, and Whittaker (n 6) 27.

In the area of contract law, the creativity of the courts has been substantial. As will be shown at various points in the following chapters, over the period of more than 200 years between the enactment of the 1804 Civil Code and the 2016 reforms, French judges gradually developed the principles laid down by the first drafters in ways that sought to address a range of lacunae and deficiencies in the original Code, progressively re-interpreting articles which, as high-level propositions or statements of principle, generally lent themselves to adaption. Well-known examples include the extension of the principle in old article 1134 that contracts should be performed in good faith to the pre-contractual negotiation, formation, and termination stages; the extensive use of *cause* in old articles 1108 and 1131 to interfere with contracts and promote substantive fairness; giving primacy to specific performance and restrictively interpreting old article 1142, which emphasized damages to the exclusion of other remedies.

Whilst the reformed Code is a more accurate and up-to-date statement of the law of contract in France, now taking account of a considerable number of significant decided cases, this will not diminish the important role of judicial decision-making. The new provisions of the Code remain very general and still leave lacunae, uncertainties, and significant power of decision and interpretation in the hands of the courts. It will continue to be for the judges, and in particular those of the *Cour de cassation*, to tackle these issues. As Whittaker and Cartwright have rightly said, the reforms are:

> very unlikely to lead to the abandonment of the freedom which ... the courts have long enjoyed in relation to the development of the law of contract and the law of obligations more generally. First and foremost, this is because many of the new provisions themselves invite creative development either because of the breadth of the legal propositions which they set out ... or the breath of the adjudicative discretion which the provisions give to the courts.[63]

## 3 The important role of academic writings

It can often come as a surprise to lawyers from a common law background to find that academic legal writings are also a source of law in France. However, *la doctrine*, defined by Nicholas as 'the whole body of writing about the law by those learned in it' has in practice achieved this status.[64] Influential forms of writing include academic treatises, articles, and case notes (*notes d'arrêt*).

[63] J Cartwright and S Whittaker 'Introduction' in J Cartwright and S Whittaker (eds), *The Code Napoléon Rewritten: French Contract Law after the 2016 Reforms* (Hart Publishing: Oxford, 2017) 1, 10–11.

[64] Nicholas (n 53) 19.

The significance of academic writing is long-standing. It has been traced back to the eleventh and twelfth centuries and, specifically, to the authority enjoyed by universities in the study and elaboration of the 'ius commune' and the guidance that they gave to courts on its interpretation.[65] Its growth was assisted by the constraints on the law-making powers of the courts that were first established in revolutionary France. The judiciary have often turned for inspiration to the ideas and theoretical framework provided by academics to justify developing the law.[66]

The importance of legal writings has continued to the present day. A significant reason is the brevity and sparseness of French judgments, especially those of the *Cour de cassation*. Whilst the *Cour de cassation* issued new guidelines on 1 October 2019 requiring its chambers to issue more detailed judgments,[67] the reality is that judgments of the court continue to be laconic, terse, and formalistic in style. They rely on highly technical language and jargon, and as such are opaque and reveal little of the reasoning of the court. This is compounded by the absence in most cases of any detailed explanation of the facts of the case. The rationale is that the role of the highest court is limited to reviewing questions of law, with findings of facts being left for lower courts to determine (*pouvoir souverain des juges du fond*). However, this prevents the reader from situating the decision on the legal question in a factual context which, as common lawyers know, can be very helpful in interpreting and understanding decisions.

Until 1 October 2019, judgments, including most of those discussed in this book, were set out in one single, very long sentence. This began with the name of the court and concluded with the verb 'quashes' or 'dismisses' to presage the decision.[68] The main body of the decision—entirely contained in the single sentence—was made up of subordinate clauses[69] which contained the reasons[70] for the ruling.[71] This format was regarded as complying with article 455 of the Civil Procedure Code, which requires that the judgment 'must set out succinctly the respective claims of the parties and their grounds'; that it 'must be motivated'; and that it 'pronounces the decision in the form of an operative part'.[72] It also reflected the syllogistic form (*syllogisme judiciaire*) that continues to be foundational in legal reasoning in France: the legal rule is stated, following by a brief description of the facts and concluding with the decision. The format is the same for courts of all

[65] Ibid., 19–20.

[66] Bell, Boyron, and Whittaker (n 6) 34.

[67] 'The new mode of drafting court decisions and their reasoning in expanded form | Cour de cassation' <Le nouveau mode de rédaction des décisions de la Cour et la motivation en forme développée | Cour de cassation> accessed 1 September 2021.

[68] Known as the *dispositif*. On this, see K Zweigert and H Kötz, *An Introduction to Comparative Law* (3rd edn, Clarendon Press: Oxford, 1998) 122; Nicholas (n 53) 13.

[69] Beginning with 'attendu ... que' ('whereas').

[70] They are called '*motifs*'.

[71] Zweigert and Kötz (n 68) 122.

[72] Article 455 of the Civil Procedure Code <https://www.legifrance.gouv.fr/codes/article_lc/LEGIARTI000006410706/> accessed 1 September 2021.

levels although, since findings of fact are made by lower courts, their judgments tend to be longer and more descriptive of the facts.[73]

Faced with the relative obscurity of French judgments, academic case notes (*notes d'arrêt*) have come to serve the vital function of explaining the facts of cases and the reasons for a particular decision. They typically explain and opine on what has been decided and situate the judgment in the broader context of other decided cases and relevant principles. For some cases, fuller academic articles cover the same topics more expansively. Through these cases notes and articles, legal commentators provide the discursive analysis that the judgments are lacking. This can also serve as an important source of feedback for the courts,[74] which is facilitated by the relatively collaborative relationship enjoyed by the judiciary and academic lawyers in France; judges often teach in universities and participate in academic conferences, while academic lawyers sometimes move to the bench.[75]

The influence of legal writings over French contract law has been immense. A striking example is the way in which the courts adopted and developed René Demogue's ground-breaking division of contractual obligations as being either *de moyens* (to exercise reasonable care in the performance of the obligation) and *de résultat* (to bring about a contemplated result) in the 1920s. This remains good law today and will be considered in Chapter 10 in the section on loss compensation.[76]

The importance of the contribution of French academic lawyers can also be seen very clearly in their major influence in bringing about the 2016 reforms. It is widely recognized that two academic projects, known as the 'Catala proposals'[77] and the 'Terré project'[78], together with the voluminous academic commentary that followed their publication, served as foundations on which the new articles of the Civil Code were later developed. This contribution was hailed by Beale, writing when he was a Law Commissioner in England,[79] in the following terms:

> It is remarkable—and admirable—that such reform of the law has been undertaken for the most part by academics. In England, professionals would not allow this. Not only would it need to go through the Law Commission or another governmental institution but practitioners would impose that they play a large—and

[73] Nicholas (n 53) 13.

[74] Bell, Boyron, and Whittaker (n 6) 34.

[75] Ibid., 35.

[76] See Chapter 10, pp 225–8.

[77] *Avant-Projet de Réforme du Droit des Obligations (Art 1101 à 1386 du Code civil) et du Droit de la Prescription (Art 2234 à 2281 du Code Civil) under the direction of P Catala, 22 Sept 2005* (Documentation française: Paris, 2006) translated in English by J Cartwright and S Whittaker: <http://www.justice.gouv.fr/art_pix/rapportcatatla0905-anglais.pdf>.

[78] F Terré (ed), *Pour une réforme du droit des contrats: Réflexions et propositions d'un groupe de travail sous la direction de François Terré* (Dalloz: Paris, 2009).

[79] Professor Hugh Beale was a Law Commissioner for England and Wales, with responsibility for the Commercial and Common Law Team from 2000 to 2007.

conservative—role in the process. Without a doubt, the French process reflects the significance of *la doctrine*, little considered today in English law.[80]

As with decided cases, the role of academic writings is likely to remain vital after the 2016 reforms in helping judges interpret the new provisions of the Code, which like their predecessors are drafted in broad terms and are often incomplete.[81]

[80] H Beale, 'La réforme du droit Français des contrats et le "droit européen des contrats": perspective de la Law Commission anglaise' RDC 2006.146. Beale did recognize, however, that more significance is today given to legal writings in England than in the past.
[81] Cartwright and Whittaker (n 63) 10–11.

# 3

# Introductory Provisions

## The Definition of Contract, the Fundamental Principles of Contract Law, and the Classification of Contract

The reformed Civil Code has an initial section entitled 'Introductory Provisions', which contains a definition of the term 'contract', sets out the fundamental principles of French contract law, and identifies and describes a number of different categories of contract. In the main, the reforms made in these provisions do not break new ground. Instead, the primary focus was on codifying established principles previously developed in decided cases, with the aim of enhancing clarity, certainty, and predictability.

## A Definition of Contract

> **Civil Code**[1]
> Art. 1101.—A contract is a concordance of wills of two or more persons intended to create, modify, transfer or extinguish obligations.

'Contract' is defined at article 1101 as 'a concordance of wills of two or more persons intended to create, modify, transfer or extinguish obligations'. It is founded on the mutual assent of the parties (*l'accord des volontés*). Their wills or, to use the terminology of English law, their intentions[2] are paramount in importance.[3]

This is a conventional definition of contract. It is rooted in the theory of the autonomy of the will (*théorie de l'autonomie de la volonté*), which is at the heart of French contract law.[4] This holds that contractual obligations are the product of

[1] 'Ordonnance no 2016-131 du 10 février 2016 portant réforme du droit des contrats, du régime général et de la preuve des obligations', JORF no 0035 of 11 February 2016. The Ordonnance was translated into English by J Cartwright, B Fauvarque-Cosson, and S Whittaker: <http://www.textes.justice.gouv.fr/art_pix/THE-LAW-OF-CONTRACT-2-5-16.pdf> (2016 version) and <http://www.textes.justice.gouv.fr/art_pix/Translationrevised2018final.pdf> (2018 version) accessed 1 September 2021. The translations of the new articles contained in this book are theirs.

[2] G Chantepie and M Latina, *La réforme du droit des obligations, Commentaire théorique et pratique dans l'ordre du Code civil* (2nd edn, Dalloz: Paris, 2018) [77]–[78].

[3] Although in England assent alone is not sufficient for the creation of a contract and, in addition, the doctrine of consideration requires reciprocal undertakings or performance.

[4] See p 21 in Chapter 2 for the sources of this theory; F Terré, P Simler, Y Lequette, and F Chénédé, *Droit civil, Les obligations* (12th edn, Dalloz: Paris, 2018) [606].

*The New French Law of Contract.* Solène Rowan, Oxford University Press. © Solène Rowan 2022.
DOI: 10.1093/oso/9780198810872.003.0003

the consent of the parties, who should only be bound if, and to what, they truly intend.[5] Intention is mainly a subjective concept in French law, as will be shown later, particularly in relation to the rules on mistake and interpretation.[6] For a contract to be formed, the parties must subjectively intend the same thing. Where there is a conflict between the actual and the declared intention of the parties, their actual intention prevails.

This definition is markedly different from the one in the 1804 Civil Code. Old article 1101 did not even mention the consensual character of contractual obligations. Instead, it referred to 'an agreement by which one or several persons bind themselves to one or several others to transfer, to do, or not to do something'. This tripartite distinction between 'obligations to give, to do, and not to do' has now disappeared entirely from the Code, reflecting the more complex reality that contracts not only create obligations but can also modify, transfer, and extinguish them.[7]

The central role of mutual assent in the formation of a contract[8] is readily discernible in a number of other provisions of the Code, of which articles 1113, 1118, 1128, and 1172 are examples. Article 1113 provides that 'a contract is formed by the meeting of an offer and an acceptance by which the parties demonstrate their will to be bound'. In the same vein, article 1118 states that 'an acceptance is the manifestation of the will of the offeree to be bound on the terms of the offer'. The consent of the parties is the first entry in a list of conditions that according to article 1128 must be fulfilled in order for a contract to be valid. Article 1172, in laying down a rule that no particular form is required in contracting, states in paragraph 1 that 'on principle contracts require only the consent of the parties'.

## B The Fundamental Principles of Contract Law

**Civil Code**

Art. 1102.—Everyone is free to contract or not to contract, to choose the person with whom to contract, and to determine the content and form of the contract, within the limits imposed by legislation.

Contractual freedom does not allow derogation from rules which are an expression of public policy.

Art. 1103.—Contracts which are lawfully formed have the binding force of legislation for those who have made them.

[5] A Bénabent, *Droit des obligations* (18th edn, LGDJ: Paris, 2019) [281].

[6] Ass Plén 12 May 1989, JCP 1989.II.21322, note G Lyon-Caen; Civ (1) 2 March 1982, GP 1982.2.Pan 245; see the section on mistake in Chapter 5 and Chapter 6 on interpretation.

[7] O Deshayes, T Genicon, and Y-M Laithier, *Réforme du droit des contrats, du régime général et de la preuve des obligations* (2nd edn, LexisNexis: Paris, 2018) 57–8; Chantepie and Latina (n 2) [81].

[8] Terré, Simler, Lequette, and Chénédé (n 4) [21]–[30].

Art. 1104.—Contracts must be negotiated, formed and performed in good faith.

This provision is a matter of public policy.

Immediately after defining the term 'contract', the Introductory Provisions section sets out three principles that are of prime importance in French contract law: freedom of contract, the binding force of contract, and good faith. These principles are intended to give 'general guidance ... and are aimed at facilitating the interpretation of principles of contract law and to fill gaps when necessary'.[9] The drafters of the new Civil Code emphasized that they should not be read as 'superior to [the principles] that follow' or relied upon 'to justify increased interventionism' from the judiciary.[10] However, it is nonetheless highly symbolic that they are grouped together and the very first provisions, putting them at the apex of all contractual rules.[11]

## 1 Freedom of contract

New article 1102 enunciates the principle of freedom of contract in three concisely stated but fundamental propositions: 'everyone is free to contract or not to contract, to choose the person with whom to contract and to determine the content and form of the contract, within the limits imposed by the law'. The principle of freedom of contract is long-standing and uncontentious in French contract law, despite not appearing in the 1804 Civil Code. Indeed, in 2013 it was elevated by the *Conseil Constitutionnel* to the status of a constitutional norm on the basis that it derives from article 4 of the Declaration of the Rights of Man and the Citizen of 1789, according to which 'freedom consists in being able to do everything that does not harm another' within limits which 'can only be determined by legislation'.[12] In view of its importance, it is perhaps surprising that the principle has only been formally recognized for the first time in the reformed Code.

[9] 'Report to the President of the Republic relating to Ordonnance no 2016–131 of 10 February 2016 on the reform of contract law, the general regime and proof of obligations', JORF no 0035 of 11 February 2016, 4.

[10] Ibid.

[11] On the controversy generated by these three principles being grouped together in the new Civil Code and whether they should be seen as guiding or merely introductory in nature, see A Ghozi and Y Lequette, 'La réforme du droit des contrats: brèves observations sur le projet de la chancellerie' RDC 2008.2609; R Cabrillac, 'Le projet de réforme du droit des contrats: Premières impressions' JCP 2008.190; L Leveneur, 'Projet de la Chancellerie de réforme du droit des contrats: à améliorer' Contrats, Conc, Consomm 2008.10. See generally Chantepie and Latina (n 2) [105]; Deshayes, Genicon, and Laithier (n 7) 59; M Mekki, 'The General Principles of Contract Law in the "Ordonnance" on the Reform of Contract Law' (2016) 76, Louisiana LR 1193, 1198. <https://digitalcommons.law.lsu.edu/lalrev/vol76/iss4/15> accessed 1 September 2021.

[12] Cons Const 13 June 2013, no 2013-672 DC. Decision of law no 2013-504 of 14 June 2013 relating to job security (*loi no 2013-504 du 14 juin 2013 relative à la sécurisation de l'emploi*).

The principle is far from being absolute. It is limited by legislation in a relatively large number of circumstances. As examples, the freedom as to whether or not to enter into a contract is fettered for motorists who must purchase and cannot drive without insurance cover;[13] the freedom of an employer to choose with whom they enter into a contract of employment is subject to rules against discrimination on the basis of sex, race, or religious belief;[14] and the freedom to determine the content of a contract[15] is curtailed by 'rules of public policy'[16] that impose mandatory obligations from which the parties cannot derogate. Two important limitations on the principle that are based on public policy can be found in article 1128, which provides that the content of a contract must be lawful and cannot involve conduct that is prohibited by law, and the principle of good faith in article 1104 which, as will be explained below,[17] imposes obligations of loyalty, cooperation, and coherence.[18]

## 2 The binding force of contract

Article 1103 declares, in almost identical terms[19] to paragraph 1 of old article 1134, the principle that legally formed agreements have the force of law between the parties.[20] It provides that 'contracts which are lawfully formed have the binding force of legislation for those who have made them'. This near-sacrosanct text is understood as meaning that contracts must be given effect by the courts and adhered to by the parties. It is often referred to by the Latin formulation *pacta sunt servanda*, which means that one must perform that which one has promised. Not only is this regarded as promoting legal certainty but it is also cited as a key justification for the central role of specific enforcement as a remedy for breach of contract.[21]

The principle of binding force is well-established and subject to fewer limitations than freedom of contract, but it is not absolute either. A number of the rules that limit the principle share the common purposes of achieving greater contractual

[13] Article L211-1 of the Insurance Code.

[14] Article L122-45 of the Labour Code.

[15] The freedom to determine the form of a contract is limited, for example, by new article 1216-3 of the Civil Code, which imposes requirements of form in the context of the assignment of contracts. The assignment must be in writing in order to be valid.

[16] Paragraph 2 of article 1102 of the Civil Code. This wording largely resembles article 6 of the Civil Code, which provides that 'one may not, by private agreement, derogate from legislation which concerns public policy or good morals'.

[17] See pp 35–41 on Good faith (article 1104) in this chapter.

[18] On the relationship between freedom of contract and mandatory rules, see C Pérès, 'Mandatory and Non-Mandatory Rules in the New Law of Contract' in J Cartwright and S Whittaker (eds), *The Code Napoléon Rewritten: French Contract Law after the 2016 Reforms* (Hart Publishing: Oxford, 2017) 167.

[19] 'Convention' has been replaced by 'contrat'.

[20] J-P Chazal, 'De la signification du mot loi dans l'article 1134, alinéa 1er du code civil' RTD civ 2001.265.

[21] S Rowan, *Remedies for Breach of Contract: A Comparative Analysis of the Protection of Performance* (OUP: Oxford, 2012) 49–50.

equilibrium between the parties or avoiding unfair outcomes. Examples include new article 1231-5 of the new Civil Code, which allows the court to reduce or even increase the agreed liability under a penalty clause 'if it is manifestly excessive or derisory'; new article 1171, which confers on the court a power to invalidate non-negotiable terms in standard form contracts that are unfair; and new article 1195, which confers a power on the court to revise or terminate a contract which has become unduly onerous due to unforeseen circumstances. Some of these powers were newly introduced by the reforms and create novel ways in which the court can interfere with the contract in the interest of fairness. They are considered in detail in the following chapters.[22]

## 3 Good faith

### (a) The important role of good faith

The principle of good faith is similarly well-established in French contract law. It was originally enshrined in paragraph 3 of article 1134 of the 1804 Civil Code. This provided that legally formed agreements 'must be performed in good faith'.[23] It was however only from the 1980s that the principle attracted significant attention, when the courts began what proved to be a swift expansion of its scope to pre-contractual negotiations and contract formation.[24] Its enlarged scope is reflected in new article 1104, which states that contracts must be 'negotiated, formed and performed in good faith'. This is stipulated to be 'a matter of public policy', meaning that it cannot be disapplied by agreement between the parties.

Giving greater prominence to good faith was amongst the more important changes brought about by the reforms. Its new location amongst the key contractual principles, and characterization as 'a matter of public policy', cement its status as a fundamental principle of French contract law.[25]

The new Civil Code does not contain any definition of good faith. Some commentators have expressed concern that, as a result, the principle is mistrusted by commercial parties for conferring too much discretion on the court and being

[22] See the section on protection against unfair terms in Chapter 7, and the sections on force majeure and *imprévision* in Chapter 9.

[23] For further reading, see D Houtcieff, *Le principe de cohérence en matière contractuelle* (Puam: Aix-en-Provence, 2001); R Jabbour, *La bonne foi dans l'exécution du contrat* (LGDJ: Paris, 2016); S Tisseyre, *Le rôle de la bonne foi en droit des contrats: essai d'analyse à la lumière du droit anglais et droit européen* (PUAM: Aix-en-Provence, 2012); B Fages, *Le comportement du contractant* (PUAM: Aix-en-Provence, 1997).

[24] For this timeline, see P Le Tourneau and M Poumarède, *Répertoire de droit civil: bonne foi* (Dalloz: 2017) [65]; see also [22].

[25] Terré, Simler, Lequette, and Chénédé (n 4) [128]; Le Tourneau and Poumarède (n 24) [3]. In earlier reform projects, good faith was classified as a 'principe directeur'. For a discussion of the previous location and categorization of good faith in the Code, see Le Tourneau and Poumarède (n 24) [16].

vague and inimical to contractual certainty.[26] This was, however, most likely intended by the drafters at least to some extent, with a view to ensuring that the principle can continue to be applied and developed with the same flexibility that has characterized its evolution to date. Indeed, for several commentators, its utility is inextricably linked to the absence of any more specific rules or guidance. This allows 'the judge to control the loyalty of contracting parties in the different contractual and pre-contractual stages'.[27]

In the absence of a definition, the case law from prior to the reforms can be expected to remain a source of guidance as to when and how good faith will apply.[28] This should however be approached with a degree of caution. In view of its fluid nature, the duties that arise from the principle are not fixed and cannot be categorized too rigidly.

### (b) Good faith in the case law

The role of good faith in French law is primarily in regulating and promoting standards of conduct for contracting parties.[29] It is a source of obligations that apply to each stage in the life of the contract, that is, to pre-contractual negotiations, contractual performance, and termination.[30] What is actually required in practice will vary depending on the stage and the particular circumstances of the case.

#### *(i) Pre-contractual negotiations*

At the pre-contractual stage, which is described at greater length in the examination of contract formation in the next chapter,[31] the principle of good faith limits party freedom of negotiation and to call off negotiations.[32] The process of

[26] P Malaurie, L Aynès, and P Stoffel-Munck, *Droit des obligations* (10th edn, LGDJ: Paris, 2018) [458]. On the other hand, a push by some commentators for good faith to have a wider role in regulating contractual relations has not been adopted in the case law either: see especially D Mazeaud, 'Loyauté, solidarité, fraternité: la nouvelle devise contractuelle?' in *Mélanges François Terré* (PUF Dalloz, Juris-Classeur: Paris, 1999) 603; D Mazeaud 'Le nouvel ordre contractuel' RDC 2003.295; Y Lequette, 'Bilan des solidarismes contractuels' in *Mélanges Paul Didier* (Economica: Paris, 2008) 247.

[27] Deshayes, Genicon, and Laithier (n 7) 63.

[28] Malaurie, Aynès, and Stoffel-Munck (n 26) [458–9]; S Whittaker and R Zimmermann, 'Good Faith in European Contract Law: Surveying the Legal Landscape' in S Whittaker and R Zimmermann (eds), *Good Faith in European Contract law* (CUP: Cambridge, 2000) 7, 32–9 who point out that legal systems that recognize good faith as a standard tend to offer illustrations of groups of situations in which it applies rather than give a definition.

[29] Le Tourneau and Poumarède (n 24) [19]–[20], [77], and [83]; Deshayes, Genicon, and Laithier (n 7) 63; Chantepie and Latina (n 2) [110]; P Stoffel-Munck, *L'abus dans le contrat: Essai d'une théorie* (LGDJ: Paris 2000) [731]; in agreement: Malaurie, Aynès, and Stoffel-Munck (n 26) [459]; M Fabre-Magnan, *Droit des obligations, Contrat et engagements unilateral* (2nd edn, PUF: Paris, 2010) 80–3; L Cadiet and P Le Tourneau, *Répertoire du droit civil: Abus de droit* (Dalloz: Paris, 2015) [83]; Com 10 July 2007, Bull civ 2007.IV.188, note P Stoffel-Munck and note P-Y Gautier, RDC 2007. 1107, obs L Aynès, and 1110, obs D Mazeaud, RTD Civ 2007.773, obs B Fages, RTD Com 2007.786, obs P Le Cannu and B Dondero.

[30] Deshayes, Genicon, and Laithier (n 7) 98–9.

[31] See the section on pre-contractual negotiations at pp59–66 in Chapter 4 (n XX).

[32] Article 1112 of the Civil Code.

negotiating a contract is regarded as collaborative and the parties are expected to conduct themselves 'ethically' and 'loyally'.[33]

In practical terms, this has translated into a number of different duties that apply to negotiating parties. One is to refrain from any conduct that could mislead the other as to the true purpose of the negotiations. There will be a breach of this duty where, for example, a party engages in negotiations with the sole intention of obtaining confidential information[34] or dissuading the other party from negotiating with third parties.[35]

It also precludes breaking off negotiations in a way which is 'abusive'[36] or 'intolerable'.[37] This will occur where the negotiations are terminated abruptly or vexatiously,[38] for example if they are nearing the fruition of an agreement or the sole motivation is to harm the other party.[39] There will also be a breach where a party behaves as if an agreement is within reach despite having no intention of concluding it.[40]

Another notable example is a general[41] duty on negotiating parties to share decisively important information with one another (*devoir d'information*).[42] This serves to ensure that they each enter into the contract in full knowledge of key relevant facts[43] and, in consequence, that their consent is real. The degree and scope of the duty depend heavily on the nature of the parties and the type of contract. It has particular prominence and value in protecting weaker parties, who cannot always inform themselves as may be desirable.[44] The paradigm is consumer contracts, where the duty is regarded as essential and is correspondingly more onerous.[45] This explains the requirement on business suppliers of goods and services (*professionnels*) to provide consumers with information 'in a readable and understandable form' on the essential characteristics of the performance, the price, the date of performance, and any rights to complain, as well as the *professionnel*'s own details.[46] In contrast, an experienced businessperson cannot expect the other

[33] Deshayes, Genicon, and Laithier (n 7) 98–9.
[34] Le Tourneau and Poumarède (n 24) [37]: Com 3 Oct 1978, Bull civ IV no 208.
[35] Paris, 19 Jan 2001, D 2001 IR.677.
[36] Com 13 Nov 2013, no 12-25.043.
[37] Deshayes, Genicon, and Laithier (n 7) 98–9.
[38] Com 22 April 1997 no 94-18.952 D 1998.45, note P Chauvel; Le Tourneau and Poumarède (n 24) [41].
[39] Civ (1) 1 April 1976, Bull civ I no 122, RTD civ 1977.127, obs G Durry.
[40] Com 31 March 1992, no 90-14.867, Bull civ IV no 145; Com 18 Jan 2011, no 09-14.617; Riom 10 June 1992, RJDA 1992.732, RTD civ 1993. 343, obs J Mestre; Reims, 13 Dec 1989, Juris-Data, no 049 587; Com 18 June 2002, no 99-16.488. See also UNIDROIT Principles article 2.1.15 [3].
[41] There are multiple duties to inform in specific contexts, for example, consumer law: articles L111-1 and L112-1 of the Consumer Code.
[42] Article 1112-1 of the Civil Code.
[43] On the different 'purpose' (*finalité*) of good faith see Malaurie, Aynès, and Stoffel-Munck (n 26) [458].
[44] Terré, Simler, Lequette, and Chénedé (n 4) [332].
[45] Paris, 18 June 1999 JCP 2000.II.10322, note Psaume; Civ (1) 28 Oct 2010, D 2010.2580.
[46] Article L111-1 of the Consumer Code; see also article L411-1 of the Consumer Code relating to the conformity of products and services.

party to share information which is publicly available.[47] The onus of undertaking appropriate research and obtaining any necessary advice is on them.

*(ii) Performance*

During the performance of the contract, the principle of good faith requires that the contracting parties conduct themselves ethically. This involves behaving loyally (*devoir de loyauté*), cooperating (*devoir de coopération*) and being logical and coherent (*devoir de cohérence*).

(a) A duty of loyalty

Pursuant to the duty of loyalty, the parties must perform their obligations faithfully, conscientiously, and diligently.[48] A supplier of temporary labour must therefore ensure that their recruitment processes are sound and diligent.[49] Where a party has a choice as to how to perform, they must choose the most efficient way. For example, in a delivery contract where the price is calculated by reference to distance and the precise route has not been agreed, the carrier must take the shortest route available to avoid the other party incurring expense unnecessarily.[50]

Loyalty also requires that contracting parties persevere in the performance of their obligations, which must be rendered for the entire duration of the contract term and proactively.[51] This has been held to mean that a lawyer must actively manage the case of their client until conclusion;[52] doctors and dentists should supervise and tend to their patients until they have recovered, including by providing postoperative care;[53] and construction workers must work diligently until satisfactory completion of the project.[54]

A related aspect of loyalty is that the parties must facilitate the performance of the contract by being engaged and vigilant. For instance, a banker who failed to report irregular and abnormal activity in the account of a client was held to have breached the duty.[55] This was also true of a landlord who omitted to seek payment

47 Com 17 July 2001, D 2002 Somm 1004, note G Pignarre; Civ (3) 6 March 2002, RTD civ 2003.82, note J Mestre and B Fages; Civ (3) 9 Oct 2012, D 2013.Pan 396, note S and M Mekki; Com 24 Sept 2003, no 00-21.863, RDC 2004.260, note D Mazeaud, RTD civ 2004.86, note J Mestre and B Fages.

48 Terré, Simler, Lequette, and Chénedé (n 4) [128]; Malaurie, Aynès, and Stoffel-Munck (n 26) [459]; Y Picod, *Le devoir de loyauté dans l'exécution du contrat* (LGDJ: Paris, 1989) 11.

49 Civ (1) 26 Feb 1991, Bull civ I no 77 D 1991.605, note C Lapouyade-Descamps. In another context, see Civ (1) 31 March 1992, Bull civ I no 93.

50 Civ 28 Nov 1905, D 1909.1.193 (*Chemins de fer Paris-Lyon-Méditerranée c Floccard*).

51 Le Tourneau and Poumarède (n 24) [89].

52 Ibid. Aix-en-Provence, 9 July 1961, D 1961.593.

53 Civ (1) 9 Oct 1985, no 84-10.245 Bull civ I no 251, D 1986.417, note J Penneau, Gaz Pal 1986.1.150, note P Bertin; Civ (1) 21 March 1995, no 93-12.768, RCA 1995, no 214.

54 Civ (3) 28 Oct 2003, no 02-17.484, RDC 2004.231, note A Bénabent.

55 Com 30 Oct 1984, no 83-12.997 Bull civ IV no 285; Com 27 Feb 1996, no 94-15.176 RJDA 1996, no 651; Paris, 5 March 2002, D 2002.1897, note V Avena-Robardet.

of rent from the tenants over a period of years, only then to demand the full outstanding amount from their guarantor.[56]

As with the duty of information, what is required by the duty of loyalty will vary depending on the nature of the parties and the type of contract. It is particularly exacting where there is a relationship of trust between them or one party is responsible for looking after the interests of the other. Contracts of agency, for example, 'are governed by a duty of loyalty and a reciprocal duty to share information' pursuant to paragraph 2 of article L134-4 of the Commercial Code. Financial advisers are required to 'act with loyalty and act in equity in the best interests of their clients' under article L541-8-1 of the Monetary and Financial Code.

The duty of loyalty takes on particular significance in an employment context, requiring employers to inform employees of important workplace changes and make appropriate adjustments to their contracts of employment in the light of new circumstances.[57] It was held, for example, that an employer had failed to act in good faith by informing employees of plans to relocate their workplace at the last minute, despite having taken the decision several months previously.[58] The same was true of an employer who attempted to force an employee to retire before she could benefit from a seniority clause which would have increased her retirement entitlements.[59] It is a duty that also works both ways and is capable of being breached by the employee, as occurred, for example, where a rogue employee regularly insulted his co-workers and publicly disparaged the services of his employer.[60]

### (b) A duty of cooperation

There is general acceptance that the principle of good faith does not require a party to prioritize the interests of the other party to the detriment of their own.[61] The parties are, however, obliged in some circumstances to cooperate and take account of the interests of the other.[62] This is particularly pertinent where there is a relationship of trust or inequality of bargaining power between the parties. The duty has been found to exist in consumer contracts, agency contracts, employment contracts,[63] and tenancy agreements. As an example, a professional landlord

[56] Civ (1) 16 July 1998, no 96-17.476, JCP E 1999.128, note B Fages; Civ (1) 23 Jan 1996, Bull civ III no 22, RTD civ 2009.317, note B Fages.

[57] Article L6321-1 of the Labour Code; Soc 25 Feb 1992, D 1992.390, note M Defossez; G Couturier, 'Vers un droit du reclassement?' Dr soc 1999.497: 'employers, who are under a requirement to perform in good faith, have a duty to ensure that employees can adapt as their jobs evolve'. In addition to the employment context, see article L212-6 of the Consumer Code: in contracts between professionals and consumers, clauses which create a significant imbalance between the rights and obligations of the parties are abusive.

[58] Soc 4 April 2006, no 04-43.506.

[59] Soc 4 June 2002 no 00-42.280, D 2002 IR 2027; JCP 2003.I.152, no 9, note G Viney.

[60] Soc 25 June 2002 no 00-44.001.

[61] Com 2 July 2002, no 00-13.459; Com 3 Oct 2006, no 04-13.214, D 2007.765, note D Mazeaud.

[62] Le Tourneau and Poumarède (n 24) [95]–[109].

[63] See article L6321-1 of the Labour Code.

who did not draw his tenant's attention to the fact that he had failed to give notice in the prescribed way (registered letter) was found to be in breach of the duty of good faith.[64]

In common with the duties of information and loyalty, what is required by the duty to cooperate is dependent on the nature of the parties and the type of contract. There are certain situations, for example, in which a party must share information which they know could have a negative impact on the willingness of the other party to enter into the contract. Bankers are under a duty to warn customers of the risks involved in speculative transactions[65] or excessive borrowing.[66]

The duty of cooperation has also translated into obligations to facilitate and refrain from obstructing contractual performance.[67] In one case, the *Cour de cassation* found that it was bad faith for an employer suddenly to discontinue a shuttle bus service that had been provided to the claimant employee for a decade. This had the effect that the claimant, whose role and hours meant that she was unable to use public transport, was no longer able to work at her contracted times.[68] Another employer was held to have acted in bad faith by requiring an employee to improve her performance at a time when activity was so quiet that it was unfeasible for her to do so.[69] In a landlord and tenant context, it has been held that a tenant cannot insist on significant building works being undertaken in an unrealistically short period of time.[70]

There is a duty to cooperate in commercial contracts where the parties share a common goal and common interests, for example in commercial distributorship agreements.[71] In one case, during the term of a distributorship agreement between BP and a service station for the sale of petrol, BP decided to sell petrol through its own agents, who were offered more favourable rates. Unable to compete, the service station brought a claim for breach of contract. The Paris Court of Appeal found that, despite not being expressly set out in the contract, there was a duty on BP to provide the service station, as a distributor, with the means to compete. In not doing so, BP failed to act in good faith. This was upheld by the *Cour de cassation*.[72]

[64] Civ (3) 5 Nov 2003, no 01-17.530.

[65] Com 5 Nov 1991, no 89-18.005 Bull civ IV no 327; Com 10 Dec 1996, no 94-16.082 Bull civ II no 307 Juris-Data no 1996-00-4769; Com 22 May 2001, no 98-14.087 Bull civ IV no 94 Juris-Data no 2001-00-9673.

[66] Com 13 Feb 2019, no 17-14.785 D actu 3 April 2019, obs X Delpech.

[67] Article L134-4 of the Commercial Code for agency contracts.

[68] Soc 10 May 2006, no 05-42.210, D 2006 IR.1482, D 2007 Pan 179, Dr soc 2006.803, obs R Savatier, JCP S 2006.1727, note B Bossu; Paris, 28 Feb 2014, no 11.23308.

[69] Com 18 May 1978, D 1979 JuIR 140; see also Paris, 27 April 1998, Juris-Data no 1998-02-0939.

[70] Civ (3) 5 June 1991, no 89-21.166, Bull civ III no 163.

[71] Chantepie and Latina (n 2) [105]; Terré, Simler, Lequette, Chénedé (n 4) [128]; Bénabent (n 5) [298].

[72] Com 3 Nov 1992, no 90-18.547 Bull civ IV no 338, RTD civ 1993.124, note J Mestre; see also Com 24 Nov 1998, Bull civ IV no 277, JCP G 1999.II.10210.

### (c) A duty to act consistently or coherently

The last key manifestation of the principle of good faith is the requirement that contracting parties behave consistently (*venire contra factum proprium*) in performing their obligations under the contract.[73] Conduct that is inconsistent or contradictory is regarded as dishonest and incompatible with their relationship. In one case, concerning a professional who had taken out documentary credit with a bank, the *Cour de cassation* held that the professional, 'could not, in good faith, claim to be ignorant of the legal scope of the modification [of the contract] that he himself had requested'.[74] The duty was also breached by the supplier of motor vehicles which, in the context of a crisis in the automobile market, required its distributors to make significant financial sacrifices that endangered their viability. Since the supplier did not impose the same sacrifices on its own business and notably continued to pay dividends to its shareholders, it was held to have acted abusively.[75]

## (c) Omissions from new article 1104

### *(i) Termination*

The reforms did not codify the principle that the termination of a contract must be in good faith. It is, however, uncontentious that the court can refuse to order termination when sought in bad faith[76] or in a manner that 'can be characterised as disloyal speculation'.[77] The case law from prior to the reforms is therefore likely to hold good. In one such case, the injured party was found to have acted in bad faith by seeking to terminate despite not having complained about the breach for nineteen years.[78] The same conclusion was reached in another case where the attempt to terminate was made shortly after the terminating party had induced the other party to make significant capital investments and borrow high amounts of money.[79]

Good faith is also relevant to the exercise of a contractual right to terminate. In principle the court can do no more than ascertain whether the conditions stipulated in the termination clause have been satisfied. However, in practice, termination clauses are interpreted restrictively by reference to the principle of good faith. If exercised in bad faith, they will not be enforced.[80] This is neatly illustrated by a

[73] See Malaurie, Aynès, and Stoffel-Munck (n 26) [459].

[74] Com 4 July 2006, no 05-10.529; Civ (3) 28 Jan 2009, no 07-20.891; Com 8 March 2005, Bull civ IV no 44.

[75] Com 15 Jan 2002, no 99-21.172, JCP 2002.II.10157, note C Jamin RTD civ 2002.294, note J Mestre and B Fages.

[76] CA Poitiers 1st Civ Chamber, 4 July 2006, Juris-Data no 2006-313835.

[77] Civ (3) 29 April 1987, RTD civ 1987.536, note J Mestre; Civ (3) 3 June 1992, GP 1992.II.656, note J-P Barbier.

[78] CA Poitiers 1st Civ Chamber, 4 July 2006, Juris-Data no 2006-313835.

[79] Com 20 Jan 1998, no 96-18.353, D 1998.413, note C Jamin.

[80] Com 31 March 1978, Bull civ IV no 102; Civ (3) 6 June 1984, Bull civ II no 111; Civ 14 March 1956, Bull civ I no 133; Civ (1) 31 Jan 1995, D 1995.389, note C Jamin; Y Picod, 'La clause résolutoire et la règle morale' JCP 1990.I.3447.

case from 1994[81] in which the Limoges Court of Appeal refused to enforce a termination clause where the injured party had sought to rely on the defaulting party's breaches in exercising the right as a pretext to enter into more profitable transactions with third parties. This decision was upheld by the *Cour de cassation*.

*(ii) Sanctions for failure to act in good faith*

Whilst article 1104 is silent on the remedies for the breach of a duty of good faith during the performance of the contract, it is apparent from decided cases that there can be either civil liability and/or a temporary neutralization of a right. Good faith cannot, however, affect the substance of the rights and obligations in the contract. In a well-known case, the *Cour de cassation* held that 'whilst good faith enables the court to sanction the disloyal use of a contractual prerogative, it does not allow the court to compromise the substance of the rights and obligations that have been legally agreed by the parties'.[82] This has been interpreted by commentators as clarification from the highest level that good faith is a tool to moderate the behaviour of the contracting parties and promote minimum standards of conduct,[83] but 'not a way for the judge to rewrite the contract'[84] or interfere with its substantive terms.[85]

### (d) Good faith and abuse of rights

Closely related to good faith is the general doctrine of abuse of rights, which is well established in French law. 'A right ends where abuse begins', as Planiol famously remarked.[86] The doctrine prevents and indeed sanctions the abusive exercise of a right that has been legally conferred. 'Abuse' refers to the misuse, that is, the improper and objectionable use, of the right.[87] The practical effect is to set limits on how the right can be exercised, which cannot be in ways that are inadmissible, despite there being no such restriction on the face of the right.[88] At its core is the idea that certain rights, even though broad and largely unfettered, cannot be misused.

[81] Civ (3) 12 Jan 1994, no 91-17023.

[82] Com 10 July 2007 no 06-14.768 Bull civ 2007.IV.188.

[83] Deshayes, Genicon, and Laithier (n 7) 63.

[84] Ibid.

[85] See also Chantepie and Latina (n 2) [110].

[86] M Planiol, *Traité élémentaire de droit civil* (9th edn, LGDJ: 1923).

[87] HC Gutteridge, 'Abuse of Rights' (1933) 5 CLJ 22; J Gordley, 'The Abuse of Rights in the Civil Law Tradition' in R De La Feria and S Vogenauer (eds), *The Prohibition of Abuse of Law: An Emerging Principle of EU Law?* (Hart Publishing: Oxford, 2011) 33; K Zweigert and U Drobnig, *International Encyclopaedia of Comparative Law* (Brill, Nijhoff: Online Edition, 2018) Volume XI: Torts, Chapter 2.

[88] P Catala and J-A Weir, 'Delict and Torts: A Study in Parallel—Part II' (1963–1964) 38 Tul L Rev 221; S Whittaker, 'Comments on "Abuse of Law" in European Private Law' in R De La Feria and S Vogenauer (eds), *The Prohibition of Abuse of Law: An Emerging Principle of EU Law?* (Hart Publishing: Oxford, 2011) 253; Zweigert and Drobnig (n 87); S Saintier, 'The Elusive Notion of Good Faith in the Performance of a Contract, Why Still a "Bête Noire" for the Civil and the Common Law?' [2017] JBL 441; J-H Crabb, 'The French Concept of Abuse of Rights' (1964) 6 Inter-Am L Rev 1; J Voyame, B Cottier, and B Rocha, 'Abuse of Rights in Comparative Law' in *Council of Europe, Abuse of Rights and Equivalent Concepts: The Principle and Its Present Day Application* (Council of Europe: Strasbourg, 1990) 23; F Ranieri, 'Bonne foi et exercice du droit dans la tradition du droit civil' (1998) RIDC 1055.

Notwithstanding the importance of the doctrine, there has never been any provision in the Civil Code preventing the abuse of rights. Rather, it is almost exclusively a creation of the courts, having been devised and expanded towards the end of the nineteenth century in the context of neighbour disputes.[89] From these beginnings, it now applies in a wide range of areas—from family law to competition law—and has become particularly significant in contract law.[90]

In a contractual context, the doctrine serves mainly to limit the exercise of discretionary powers that are conferred by the contract.[91] The focus is on whether the discretion has been perverted,[92] and there are commonalities with the French administrative law doctrine of abuse of power (*détournement de pouvoir*).[93] Considerations that are relevant to this question include whether the discretion has been exercised within its proper limits, for its intended purpose, in pursuance of a legitimate interest (*intérêt légitime*), and on proper grounds (*juste motif*).[94]

As an example, the Civil Code requires that a unilateral right to fix the contract price is not exercised abusively.[95] If called upon to do so, the right-holder must show that the right has been exercised rationally[96] and be able to justify the price. Similarly, in a contract of agency, it has been held that the principal must have a legitimate basis for exercising a power to terminate the contract, even though the power was expressed to be unilateral and exercisable 'whenever [the principal] likes'.[97] Nor can a landlord exercise a unilateral discretion to approve or reject a proposed assignee of the lease for a collateral purpose.[98] This is also true of the

[89] Cadiet and Le Tourneau (n 29) [5]. See L Josserand, *De l'abus des droits* (1st edn, Rousseau: Paris, 1905).

[90] Cadiet and Le Tourneau (n 29) [79].

[91] Stoffel-Munck (n 29) [731]; Fabre-Magnan (n 29) 80–2.

[92] Stoffel-Munck (n 29) [731].

[93] G Texier, 'L'abus de droit en matière de droit public' in J Mestre, *L'abus dans le droit des affaires*, Droit & Patrimoine 2000.83, 57 ff; M Hauriou commenting on CE 27 Feb 1903, S 1905.3.17; O de David Beauregard-Berthier, 'La notion de détournement de procédure en droit administratif' 2006 Droit administratif: Lexis Nexis Jurisclasseur [9]; Stoffel-Munck (n 29) [731]; Cadiet and le Tourneau (n 29) [26].

[94] Stoffel-Munck (n 29) [634]–[802], in particular [783]–[789]; F Chénedé, 'Les conditions d'exercice des prérogatives contractuelles' RDC 2010.709 [14]; G Courtieu, *Arts 1382 à 1386—Fasc 131-20: Droit à la réparation—Abus de droits et abus de pouvoirs* (Lexis Nexis Jurisclasseur, 2005) [26]–[47]; Cadiet and Le Tourneau (n 29) [27]–[29], [85]–[99], and [197].

[95] In 'framework contracts' (*contrat-cadre*), see new article 1164 of the Civil Code. See also new article 1165 of the Civil Code.

[96] Terré, Simler, Lequette, and Chénedé (n 4) [387]; Deshayes, Genicon, and Laithier (n 7) 313–16.

[97] Com 3 July 2001, no 98-16.691, D 2001 AJ.2826; Civ (1) 28 Jan 2003, Bull civ 2003.I.27; Com 14 Oct 1997 no 95-16.937; Com 10 March 1976, D 1976 Somm 49, note P Stoffel-Munck.

[98] Req 16 Nov 1927 DP 1928.I.61 Rapport Bricourt; Com, 19 Feb 1963, JCP 1963.II.13299; CA Lyon 17 May 2001 RJDA 2001, no 1204; Com 3 Nov 2004, no 02-17.919, RDC 2005.288 note P Stoffel-Munck; Com 5 Oct 2004, no 02-17338; Com 19 Feb 1963, JCP 1963.II.13299; Com 2 July 2002, no 01-12.685, D 2003.93, note D Mazeaud, RDC 2003.50, note P Stoffel-Munck; Com 4 Oct 2004, no 2-17338; Civ (3) 14 April 1982, JCP 1982.IV.217; CA Paris 7 April 1995, Rev societies 1995.771; see also in the context of leases: Com 5 Dec 1995, no 93-18.936, RJDA 1996, no 456; Civ (3) 22 Feb 1968, D 1968.607, RTD civ 1968.735, obs G Cornu.

unilateral discretion of an employer to terminate an employment contract at the end of the probation period.[99]

The relationship between abuse of rights and good faith has attracted academic interest in France, being described as 'close, even intimate',[100] and the courts frequently refer to the principles interchangeably.[101] However, at least in the context of contractual discretion, French commentators have increasingly drawn a distinction between the two principles, which they have shown to have different objectives.[102] In assessing good faith, the court focuses on the conduct of the decision-maker, making a moral and value judgement and seeking to promote minimum standards of conduct. This differs from the doctrine of abuse of rights, where the focus is on whether the right has been perverted, intentionally or otherwise.[103] In the words of Stoffel-Munck, 'the question is not to determine whether a right has been perverted hypocritically, selfishly, with an intention to harm but rather to assess if it has been perverted at all'.[104]

## C Classification of Contract

**Civil Code**

Art. 1105.—Whether or not they have their own denomination, contracts are subject to general rules, which are the subject of this sub-title.

Rules particular to certain contracts are laid down in the provisions special to each of these contracts.

The general rules are applied subject to these particular rules.

Art. 1106.—A contract is synallagmatic where the parties undertake reciprocal obligations in favour of each other.

It is unilateral where one or more persons undertake obligations in favour of one or more others without there being any reciprocal obligation on the part of the latter.

[99] Civ (3) 11 May 1976, D 1978.269, note J-J Taisne; for a finding that the exercise of a mobility clause in an employment contract is abusive, see Civ (3) 2 Feb 2005, Bull civ III no 24; Paris 24 March 1999, D 1999.IR 141. See also in the context of employment: Soc 9 May 1990, no 87-40.261, Bull civ V no 210, JCP E 1991.II.126; Soc 5 May 2004, no 02-41.224, Bull civ V no 123, D 2004.IR.1641; Soc 5 May 2004, no 02-41.224, Bull civ V no 123, D 2004 IR.1641.

[100] Stoffel-Munck (n 29) [62].

[101] G Courtieu, *Arts 1382 à 1386—Fasc 131-20: Droit à la réparation—Abus de droits et abus de pouvoirs* (Lexis Nexis Jurisclasseur, 2005) [26]–[47]; Cadiet and Le Tourneau (n 29) [81]; Fabre-Magnan (n 29) 80–3.

[102] Stoffel-Munck (n 29) [668]ff and [731]ff; Cadiet and Le Tourneau (n 29) [81]; Fabre-Magnan (n 29) 80–2 for whom 'the doctrine of abuse of rights is better suited to deal with [the misuse of] unilateral contractual discretions' than good faith; Malaurie, Aynès, and Stoffel-Munck (n 26) [459].

[103] Fabre-Magnan (n 29) 80–2; Malaurie, Aynès, and Stoffel-Munck (n 26) [459].

[104] Stoffel-Munck (n 29) [731]; in agreement: Malaurie, Aynès, and Stoffel-Munck (n 26) [459]; Fabre-Magnan (n 29) 80–3; Cadiet and Le Tourneau (n 29) [83].

Art. 1107.—A contract is onerous where each of the parties receives a benefit from the other in return for what he provides. It is gratuitous where one of the parties provides a benefit to the other without expecting or receiving anything in return.

Art. 1108.—A contract is commutative where each of the parties undertakes to provide a benefit to the other which is regarded as the equivalent of what he receives.

It is aleatory where the parties agree that the effects of the contract—both as regards its resulting benefits and losses—shall depend on an uncertain event.

Art. 1109.—A contract is consensual where it is formed by the mere exchange of consents, in whatever way they may be expressed.

A contract is solemn where its validity is subject to form prescribed by legislation.

A contract is real where its formation is subject to the delivery of a thing.

**(2016 version)**
*Art. 1110.—A bespoke contract is one whose stipulations are freely negotiated by the parties.*

*A standard form contract is one whose general conditions are determined in advance by one of the parties without negotiation.*

**(2018 version)**
Art. 1110.—A bespoke contract is one whose stipulations are negotiable by the parties.

A standard form contract is one which comprises a collection of non-negotiable terms which are determined in advance by one of the parties without negotiation.

Art. 1111.—A framework contract is an agreement by which the parties agree the general characteristics of their future contractual relations. Implementation contracts determine the modalities of performance under a framework contract.

Art. 1111-1.—A contract of instantaneous performance is one whose obligations can be performed as a single act of performance.

A contract of successive performance is one of which the obligations of at least one of the parties are performed in a number of acts of performance over a period of time.

After enunciating the three fundamental principles of French contract law—freedom of contract, the binding force of contract, and good faith—the

Introductory Provisions of the new Civil Code turn to the classification of contracts in articles 1105 to 1111-1. Several distinct classes of contract are identified and briefly defined. In each article there are up to three classes, which in most cases are grouped together on the basis that they either relate to, or are in opposition to, one another. How a contract is classified is important because, to varying degrees, it can affect the rules that apply to it.[105]

Some of these classes and groupings also appeared in the 1804 Civil Code. These include the following: 'nominate' and 'innominate' contracts; 'synallagmatic' and 'unilateral' contracts; 'onerous' and 'gratuitous' contracts; and 'commutative' and 'aleatory' contracts.[106] Others are new: for example, 'instantaneous' contracts and contracts of 'successive performance';[107] and 'standard form' and 'bespoke' contracts.[108] The classes are not mutually exclusive but can and often do overlap. Indeed, it is entirely normal for a contract to belong to multiple different classes.

This system of classifying contracts according to their type has roots in Roman law, which similarly identified and provided rules for contracts by class. This was, however, to the exclusion of principles of contract that applied on a general and systematic basis. The 1804 Civil Code retained—at least to an extent—the Roman preference for classification but embraced a general theory of contract. As Nicholas noted, 'the unitary principle of contract is superimposed on the individual contracts'.[109]

## 1 Traditional classifications of contract

### (a) Nominate and innominate contracts

There is a long-standing distinction in French law between nominate and innominate contracts, both of which are defined in the new Civil Code at new article 1105. Nominate contracts (*contrats nommés*)—also known as 'special contracts', 'typical contracts', and 'named contracts'—are contracts that are of recognized types, in contradistinction to those that are of no particular type. Nominate contracts are governed not only by the general principles of contract law in the Civil Code but also by special legislation, some of which is found in other codes, as well as principles developed in decided cases. Contracts are innominate (*contrats innomés*) where they do not fall within one of the recognized categories of nominate contracts.

[105] B Nicholas, *The French Law of Contract* (Clarendon Press: Oxford, 1992) 47: 'The first step in interpreting a contract is therefore to "qualify" or characterize it, i.e. to determine whether it falls within the limits of one or other of the special contracts. This is a question of law subject to the control of the *Cour de cassation* and there is much jurisprudence on the distinctions between various contracts.'

[106] Old articles 1102 to 1107 of the Civil Code; Deshayes, Genicon, and Laithier (n 7) 56.

[107] Article 1111-1 of the Civil Code.

[108] Article 1110 of the Civil Code.

[109] B Nicholas, 'Rules and Terms—Civil Law and Common Law' (1973-1974) 48 Tul L Rev 946, 951.

A number of the types of nominate contracts in the original Civil Code were inherited from Roman law, with new ones emerging over time.[110] Examples include contracts of sale (*vente*), lease agreements (*bail*), contracts of donation (*donation*), and agency agreements (*mandat*). Perhaps the most common is the contract of sale, which is regulated by the general provisions on contract, and the specific provisions on sale in the Civil Code, and various provisions in other codes such as the Commercial Code[111] and the Consumer Code.[112] In total there are more than 100 articles on contracts of sale in the Civil Code, dealing with a range of issues such as the obligations of the seller and the buyer and nullity for *lésion*.[113] As explained in the discussion on the relationship between the general contract law principles and the special rules that apply to specific types of contract in Chapter 2,[114] where there is a conflict between articles, article 1105 provides that the specific take precedence over the general.[115]

### (b) Synallagmatic and unilateral contracts

The mutually opposing classes of synallagmatic and unilateral contracts that originally appeared in the 1804 Civil Code were retained in the new Code.[116] A synallagmatic contract creates reciprocal obligations,[117] whereas a unilateral contract involves performance by only one party for the benefit of the other party. By way of illustration, a contract for the sale of goods is synallagmatic because the seller supplies the goods in return for payment by the buyer. In contrast, a donation is unilateral because the duty to perform resides only in one party, the donor, and all rights under the contract belong to the other, the donee.

### (c) Gratuitous and onerous contracts

Gratuitous and onerous contracts are also recognized in the new Civil Code. According to new article 1107, there is a gratuitous contract 'where one of the parties provides a benefit to the other without expecting or receiving anything in return'. The paradigm is a contract of donation, which as noted in the preceding paragraph is also unilateral. Unlike in England, gratuitous contracts are binding and enforceable, becoming so upon acceptance by the donee,[118] who can thereafter

[110] P Malaurie, L Aynès, and P-Y Gautier, *Droit des contrats spéciaux* (11th edn, LGDJ: Paris, 2020) [56].
[111] See, for example, articles L441-1 to L441-2 for the general terms and conditions of sales under the Commercial Code.
[112] See, for example, articles L112-1 to L112-9 for the information concerning the price and conditions of sale that must be provided to consumers.
[113] Articles 1582 to 1701 of the Civil Code.
[114] See pp22–4 in Chapter 2.
[115] Paragraph 3 of article 1105, but see the criticism of Deshayes, Genicon, and Laithier (n 7) 67.
[116] Article 1106.
[117] Deshayes, Genicon, and Laithier (n 7) 68.
[118] E Steiner, *French Law: A Comparative Approach* (OUP: Oxford, 2010) 223: 'By accepting the gift, the beneficiary makes the agreement a binding contract.'

sue the donor for any failure to make the donation.[119] There are also no formality requirements.

In opposition to gratuitous contracts in article 1107 are onerous contracts. These are characterized by each party receiving some benefit for the performance of their obligations. There must be an element of exchange or bargain, a concept familiar to English lawyers as the crux of the doctrine of consideration. A contract for the sale of goods is onerous as well as synallagmatic because there is a burden on both parties, with the seller transferring goods in return for payment by the buyer.[120]

### (d) Commutative and aleatory contracts

New article 1108 provides for commutative and aleatory contracts. Any contract that falls within either of these classes is necessarily also synallagmatic and onerous, illustrating the scope for contracts to belong to multiple classes. A contract is commutative 'where each of the parties undertakes to provide a benefit to the other which is regarded as the equivalent of what he receives'. There must be an agreement as to what each party will provide and receive, which they are deemed to regard as having equal value. This is exemplified by a sale of goods contract.

In contrast, a contract is aleatory where 'the effects of the contract—both as regards its resulting benefits and losses—shall depend on an uncertain event'. The deemed equivalence of the commutative contract is absent since the subject-matter of the contract relates to an event that was uncertain when the contract was entered. It is therefore incapable of being valued, still less deemed to be regarded by the parties as having the same value as the reciprocal performance. As an example, an insurance policy is aleatory in that whether a claim will be made is inherently uncertain.

## 2 Classifications of contract newly introduced by the reforms

The reforms gave formal recognition to several classes of contract that did not appear in the 1804 Civil Code but over time came to be recognized by the courts or commentators.

### (a) Contracts of instantaneous performance and successive performance

These include contracts of instantaneous performance and contracts of successive performance,[121] which are found in new article 1111-1. Instantaneous performance refers to the obligations of both parties being performed in a single act, however long that might last. Successive performance is fragmented, with at least one of the parties performing their obligations in a manner that is not unitary. It makes

[119] This is subject to some formalities in the case of donations.
[120] Deshayes, Genicon, and Laithier (n 7) 70.
[121] For example, Soc 28 Oct 1992, no 89-45.500, Bull civ V no 521.

no difference whether the duration of the performance is fixed or indeterminate. A contract for the construction of a house is of instantaneous performance, regardless of the time that it takes to perform. Lease agreements and contracts of employment are of successive performance, whatever their duration.[122]

### (b) Consensual, solemn, and real contracts

The tripartite classification of consensual, solemn, and real contracts in article 1109 is also novel. All three classes relate to the manner of the formation of the contract and, in particular, the way in which the parties express the meeting of their wills. A consensual contract is made by the combination of an offer and an acceptance. This is consistent with the fundamental principle of French law known as *consensualisme*, which holds that only an exchange of consent is required to conclude a binding contract. It makes no difference how this is done and it is trite that a contract can be made in various different ways, for example verbally or by the rendering of performance. This is reflected in paragraph 1 of article 1172 of the new Civil Code, which states unequivocally that 'on principle, contracts require only the consent of the parties'.[123]

As an exception to *consensualisme*, solemn contracts are formed only by the completion of formalities that are prescribed in law. By way of example, paragraph 3 of new article 1216 requires that the assignment of a contract be in writing,[124] failing which it will be void. In real contracts, the formation of the contract is dependent on the delivery of a thing (*chose*). Common examples—all with roots in Roman law—are the loan, the deposit, and the pledge.[125]

### (c) Framework and implementation contracts

Framework contracts and implementation contracts were also introduced as part of the reforms. According to new article 1111, framework contracts enable 'parties [to] agree the general characteristics of their future contractual relations'. No actual obligations are created,[126] only a contractual apparatus through which the parties can organize their future commercial affairs and, at some later time, enter into implementation contracts containing particulars of the performance to be rendered. Such contracts are a feature of some distribution relationships, for instance between oil companies and fuel retailers. A number of commentators have criticized the designation of framework contracts as fully fledged contracts on the basis that they do not create obligations, which is a requirement of the definition of 'contract' in new article 1100, but instead are organizational in nature.[127]

122 Examples given by Bénabent (n 5) [23].
123 Paragraph 1 of article 1172.
124 Paragraph 3 of article 1216: an assignment must be established in writing, on pain of nullity.
125 For example, see article 1919 of the Civil Code.
126 Chantepie and Latina (n 2) [152].
127 Terré, Simler, Lequette, and Chénedé (n 4) [79], [119].

### (d) Bespoke and standard form contracts

Perhaps the most significant but also the most controversial new classes introduced by the reforms are bespoke contracts and standard form contracts, which are paired in opposition to each other in new article 1110.[128] Whilst neither class was referred to in the 1804 Code, their formal recognition was considered by the drafters to have become necessary in view of the prevalence and importance of standard form contracts in modern practice.[129]

The controversy arose from the definitions of the classes that were adopted in 2016, which drew strong criticism and ultimately were revised when the Ratification Bill was approved by Parliament in 2018. Originally the article stated that 'a bespoke contract is one whose stipulations *are freely negotiated* by the parties. A standard form contract is one whose general conditions are determined in advance by one of the parties without negotiation.'

Some commentators perceived the definition of standard form contract to be too broad since it caught not only non-negotiable contracts in standard form but also those that had not been negotiated despite being negotiable.[130] Although at first glance somewhat nuanced, this distinction is important in view of the significant consequences that attach to a contract being classified as in standard form. Several provisions in the Civil Code confer significant protection on the party who agrees to accept a standard form contract.[131] One example is new article 1171, under which the court now has the power to deem not written any term 'of a standard form contract which creates a significant imbalance in the rights and obligations of the parties to the contract'. There are also specific rules in new article 1190 for the interpretation of standard form contracts: 'in case of ambiguity, a bespoke contract is interpreted against the creditor and in favour of the debtor, and a standard form contract is interpreted against the person who put it forward'.

The effect of the original definition was that these provisions would be applicable even where the party agreeing to accept the standard form contract had the opportunity to negotiate its terms but chose not to do so. This was argued to be overzealous and undesirable.[132] On this basis, the article was revised to state that 'a bespoke contract is one whose stipulations *are negotiable* by the parties. A standard form contract is one which comprises *a set of non-negotiable clauses* which are determined in advance by one of the parties' (emphasis added). As a result, 'standard form contracts' are those that contain clauses that are 'non-negotiable' instead of not negotiated. Equally, bespoke contracts need only contain stipulations that are

[128] T Revet, 'L'incohérent cantonnement, par l'Assemblée nationale, du domaine du contrat d'adhésion aux contrats de masse' D 2018 Chron 124. Cited in Deshayes, Genicon, and Laithier (n 7) 78.

[129] F Ancel, B Fauvarque-Cosson, and J Gest, *Aux sources de la réforme du droit des contrats* (Dalloz: Paris, 2017) [22.13].

[130] Deshayes, Genicon, and Laithier (n 7) 83.

[131] Ibid., 78–90; Chantepie and Latina (n 2) [145]–[150].

[132] Chantepie and Latina (n 2) [145]; Deshayes, Genicon, and Laithier (n 7) 81.

'negotiable', with the requirement that they are 'freely negotiated' by the parties having been dropped. A contract will therefore be bespoke as long as the terms are capable of being negotiated. It is no longer necessary that they are actually negotiated.

## D Concluding Observations

The new 'Introductory Provisions' section of the reformed Civil Code is not ground-breaking and mainly gives formal recognition to existing principles. What does, however, stand out is the codification of the three long-established and fundamental principles of freedom of contract, the binding force of contract, and good faith. This was regarded by the drafters as having symbolic importance, since the principles reflect a number of policy choices that are encapsulated in the reforms. As the 'Report to the President of the Republic', in which the drafters explained the new articles and their rationale, states, 'this choice to highlight three fundamental principles expresses one of the essential aims pursued by the Ordonnance: to find a balance between contractual fairness and the autonomy of the will'.[133]

The codification of these principles aligns French law more closely with a number of international contract law instruments. Both the Principles of European Contract Law (PECL)[134] and the UNIDROIT Principles[135] similarly recognize their fundamental importance whilst articulating them in different ways. In the PECL, the duties to act in good faith and of fair dealing[136] are stated separately from the duty of cooperation.[137] There are also separate provisions in the UNIDROIT Principles for good faith and inconsistent behaviour.[138] This should not, however, be understood as meaning that the duties to cooperate and not to act inconsistently are distinct from the general principle of good faith, rather than specific applications of it. Separate enumeration of the principles was simply intended 'to meet the concern [of] business people, but also lawyers from the common law tradition who are not necessarily familiar with sweeping good faith provisions'[139] and might

[133] 'Report to the President' (n 9) 4. Translation of S Whittaker 'Contracts, Contract Law and Contractual Principle' in J Cartwright and S Whittaker (eds), *The Code Napoléon Rewritten: French Contract Law after the 2016 Reforms* (Hart Publishing: Oxford, 2017) 29, 45.

[134] Articles 1:102, 1:103, 1:1201, and 1:203.

[135] Article 1.1 (freedom of contract), article 1.3 (binding force of contract), and article 1.7 (good faith) of the UNIDROIT Principles. See also article 2.1.4(2) (irrevocability of offer) and articles 2.1.15 to 2.1.16 (obligations of loyalty and confidentiality in the course of contractual negotiations as further manifestations of good faith).

[136] Article 1:201.

[137] Article 1:202.

[138] Articles 1.7 (Good faith and fair dealing) and 1.8 (Inconsistent behaviour).

[139] S Vogenauer in S Vogenauer (ed), *Commentary on the UNIDROIT Principles of International Commercial Contracts (PICC)* (2nd edn, OUP: Oxford, 2015) 227.

not read good faith as containing a duty to cooperate or one to avoid inconsistent behaviour.[140] It was considered to be 'safer to spell out [these rules] explicitly'.[141]

The differences between the positions in France and England are more substantial. Whilst English law has long embraced freedom of contract and the binding force of contract, it has largely resisted notions of good faith and contractual fairness.[142] This reflects a traditional judicial imperviousness to expansive and abstract doctrines.[143] Attempts to generalize from discrete rules that sanction bad faith in specific situations have usually failed[144] and there has been a tendency for developments to occur incrementally, not in broad sweeps.[145] In the famous words of Bingham LJ, the courts have developed 'piecemeal solutions in response to demonstrated problems of unfairness'.[146] The implication of terms and the rules on promissory estoppel, misrepresentation, economic duress, and undue influence have been variously cited as performing a similar role to good faith.[147]

The differences are not simply of technique but also substantive. This is exemplified by the approach in English law to pre-contractual negotiations and termination clauses. There is no equivalent to the general duty in France to negotiate and perform a contract in good faith and the pre-contractual negotiation phase is not regarded as giving rise to a legally-protected relationship.[148] The parties are free to

[140] Ibid.

[141] Ibid.

[142] For a summary of English law on this point, see H Beale (ed), *Chitty on Contracts* (33rd edn, Sweet & Maxwell: London, 2020) [39] ff.

[143] In the context of pre-contractual negotiations, see: Lord Ackner in *Walford v Miles* [1992] 2 AC 128 (HL) 138; Lord Denning in *Courtney & Fairbairn Ltd v Tolaini Brothers (Hotels) Ltd* (1975) 1 WLR 297 (CA) 30. In the context of contract performance: *Mid Essex Hospital Services NHS Trust v Compass Group UK and Ireland Ltd* [2013] EWCA Civ 200 (CA) [105] per Jackson LJ; *MSC Mediterranean Shipping Company SA v Cottonex Anstalt* [2016] EWCA Civ 789 (CA); Lord R Goff, '"Opening Address", Second Annual JCL Conference in London on 11 September 1991' (1992) 5 Journal of Contract Law 1, 4.

[144] See Lord Denning's attempt to recognize a general doctrine of 'inequality of bargaining power' in *Lloyds Bank Ltd v Bundy* [1975] QB 326 (CA) (see in particular Lord Denning at 339) which was rejected by the House of Lords in *National Westminster Bank Ltd v Morgan* [1985] AC 686 (HL); Lord Scarman at 707–8. See also, *MSC Mediterranean Shipping Company SA v Cottonex Anstalt* [2016] EWCA Civ 789 (CA) where Moore-Bick LJ observed that: '... the better course is for the law to develop along established lines rather than to encourage judges to look for what the judge in this case called some "general organising principle" drawn from cases of disparate kinds'.

[145] S Whittaker, 'Contracts, Contract Law and Contractual Principle' in J Cartwright and S Whittaker (eds), *The Code Napoléon Rewritten: French Contract Law after the 2016 Reforms* (Hart Publishing: Oxford, 2017) 29, 46.

[146] *Interfoto Picture Library Ltd v Stiletto Visual Programmes Ltd* [1989] QB 433 (CA) 439 (per Bingham LJ).

[147] See the exhaustive list of 'good faith in current legal doctrines' in Chapter 15 dedicated to good faith in M Chen-Wishart, *Contract Law* (6th edn, OUP: Oxford, 2018). The courts also thrive to give effect to express terms imposing a duty of good faith: *Mid Essex Hospital Services NHS Trust v Compass Group UK and Ireland Ltd* [2013] EWCA Civ 200 (CA); *Berkeley Community Villages Ltd v Pullen* [2007] EWHC 1330 (Ch) (Morgan J), although the term to act in good faith is unlikely to be construed broadly, see *Mid Essex* at [154] per Beatson LJ.

[148] For a summary of the English position, see J Cartwright, *Contract Law: An Introduction to the English Law of Contract for the Civil Lawyer* (3rd edn, Hart Publishing: Oxford, 2016) 74 ff. See also M Bridge, 'Good Faith, the Common Law and the CISG' (2017) 22 Unif L Rev 1, 18; M Bridge, 'Doubting Good Faith' (2005) 11 NZBLQ 449; J Steyn 'The Role of Good Faith and Fair Dealing in Contract

act in their own best interests and withdraw until the contract has been concluded and they are not subject to any general duties such as that of sharing information.

A further difference is that English courts generally do not interfere with the exercise of a right to terminate the contract under a termination clause. There is unwillingness to disturb the manner in which the parties have chosen to allocate risk in the event of breach. Instead, termination clauses will generally be upheld, even where the impact upon the defaulting party is severe.[149] It does not matter that the loss resulting from the breach is trivial or that the breach could easily be cured without inconveniencing the injured party. Nor is the extremity of the consequences for the defaulting party a relevant consideration and there is no requirement that the parties behave proportionally.[150]

There is similar circumspection towards the doctrine of abuse of rights, which English law has traditionally regarded with suspicion[151] and been thought to reject.[152] The reasons are manifold: it is difficult to prove abuse;[153] for the court to find abuse would involve making a moral judgement, which is thought to be more appropriate to criminal law than tort and contract;[154] there are fears of uncertainty;[155] and restraining contracting parties where they are acting within the formal limits of their rights arouses unease.[156]

However, there have been signs in recent times of a degree of *rapprochement* between the two jurisdictions, at least in the context of good faith in performance. In *Yam Seng Pte Ltd v International Trade Corporation Ltd*,[157] a case which concerned a distributorship agreement, Leggatt J (as he then was) sought to demonstrate that the traditional hostility in England to good faith is misplaced. Whilst acknowledging that English law was not ready to recognize a requirement of good

Law: A Hair-Shirt Philosophy?' [1991] Denning Law Journal 131–34; E McKendrick 'Good Faith in the Performance of a Contract in English Law' in L DiMatteo and M Hogg (eds), *Comparative Contract Law: British and American Perspectives* (Oxford: OUP, 2015), 196.

149 See, for example, *Union Eagle Ltd v Golden Achievement Ltd* [1997] AC 514 (PC).

150 D Harris, 'Incentives to Perform, or Break Contracts' (1992) 45 CL 29, 41–2; E Peel, *Treitel on the Law of Contract* (12th edn, Sweet & Maxwell: London, 2007) [18–061]. The courts have sometimes taken a strict approach to the interpretation of widely drafted termination clauses. By way of example, see *Rice v Great Yarmouth BC* [2003] TCLR 1 (CA). For a criticism of this practice, see S Whittaker, 'Termination Clauses' in A Burrows and E Peel (eds), *Contract Terms* (OUP: Oxford, 2007) 253.

151 *Bradford Corp v Pickles* [1895] AC 587 (HL); *Allen v Flood* [1898] AC 1 (HL). On why such authorities should not be taken to reject abuse of rights, see S Rowan, 'Abuse of Rights in English Contract Law: Hidden in Plain Sight?' (2021) 84 (5) MLR 1066.

152 Gutteridge (n 87); Rowan, 'Abuse of Rights in English Contract Law: Hidden in Plain Sight?' (n 151).

153 FH Lawson, 'Notes on the History of Tort in the Civil Law' (1940) 22 Journal of Comparative Legislation and International Law 136, 162; D-J Devine, 'Some Comparative Aspects of the Doctrine of Abuse of Rights' (1964) 1964 Acta Juridica 148, 149; J Murphy, 'Malice as an Ingredient of Tort Liability' [2019] CLJ 355, 371–3 disagreeing with this argument.

154 Gutteridge (n 87) 43; Lawson (n 153) 162; Murphy (n 153) 372.

155 Lord Hoffmann in *OBG Ltd* v *Allan* [2008] 1 AC 1 [14]; Gutteridge (n 87) 42.

156 Gutteridge (n 87) 35 and 45.

157 *Yam Seng Pte Ltd v International Trade Corporation Ltd* [2013] EWHC 111 (QB).

faith as a duty implied by law in all commercial contracts, he argued in favour of the recognition of an implied duty of good faith in performance 'based on the presumed intention of the parties'.[158] This duty is objective in nature, to be judged by the standard of 'reasonable and honest people',[159] and its content includes, as a minimum, the core value of honesty; it can also require adherence to reasonable commercial standards of fair dealing.[160] Being based on the presumed intention of the parties, it arises by implication, giving effect to their expectations and the agreed common purpose of the contract.[161]

This attempt to recognize an implied duty of good faith in English law has been controversial[162] and reaction in later cases has been mixed.[163] It has, however, revived the debate on the relevance of good faith in England,[164] as well as bringing to the fore its role in 'relational contracts'[165] such as distributorship and employment

[158] Ibid., [131]–[132], [135]–[136].

[159] Ibid., [144] and [150].

[160] Ibid., [137]–[152]; for a more recent decision of Leggatt LJ (sitting in the High Court) on good faith, see *Al Nehayan v Kent* [2018] EWHC 333 (Comm) [167]–[176]; see also Leggatt J, 'Contractual Duties of Good Faith' Lecture to the Commercial Bar Association, 18 October 2016 <https://www.judiciary.uk/wp-content/ uploads/2016/10/mr-justice-leggatt-lecture-contractual-duties-of-faith.pdf> accessed 1 September 2021 [30]. There has been controversy over the meaning of good faith, in particular whether it is mainly concerned with issues of honesty or wider in scope. This is illustrated by the recent criticism of *Chitty on Contracts* (33rd edn, London: Thomson Reuters, 2019) by Fraser J in *Bates v Post Office Ltd* [2019] EWHC 606 (QB) [708]–[711] for confining good faith to honesty. He said 'there is more to a duty of good faith than a requirement to act honestly . . . the parties must refrain from conduct which in the relevant context would be regarded as commercially unacceptable by reasonable and honest people'.

[161] *Yam Seng* (n 157) [148]–[149]; Leggatt J (n 160) [41] and [61].

[162] The inherent difficulties with the principle of good faith proposed by Leggatt J are well-documented in burgeoning academic literature: S Whittaker, 'Good Faith, Implied Terms and Commercial Contracts' (2013) 129 LQR 463; E Granger, 'Sweating over an Implied Duty of Good Faith' [2013] LMCLQ 418; H Collins, 'Implied Terms: The Foundation in Good Faith and Fair Dealing' (2014) 67 CLP 297; M Bridge, 'Limits on Contractual Freedom' (2019) 7 The Chinese Journal of Comparative Law 387; M Bridge, 'Does Anglo-Canadian Contract Law Need a Doctrine of Good Faith?' (1984) 9 Canadian Bus LJ 385. Good faith as a general organizing principle has also been rejected by the courts, see *Mid Essex Hospital Services NHS Trust v Compass Group UK and Ireland Ltd* [2013] EWCA Civ 200 (CA) (2013) BLR 265 [105]; *Greenclose Ltd v National Westminster Bank Plc* [2014] EWHC 1156 (Ch) [150].

[163] *Mid Essex Hospital Services NHS Trust v Compass Group UK and Ireland* [2013] EWCA Civ 200 [105] (per Jackson LJ): 'there is no general doctrine of "good faith" in English law'; *MSC Mediterranean Shipping Company SA v Cottonex Anstalt* [2016] EWCA Civ 789 (CA) [45]: Moore-Bick LJ has observed that there is 'a real danger that if a general principle of good faith were established it would be invoked as often to undermine as to support the terms in which the parties have reached agreement'; *Greenclose*: Andrews J [150]: 'there is no general doctrine of good faith in English contract law and such a term is unlikely to arise by way of necessary implication in a contract between two sophisticated commercial parties negotiating at arms' length'. But see also *Bates v Post Office Ltd (No 3)* [2019] EWHC 606 (QB) [702]ff.

[164] The topic is now considered more fully in textbooks. See, for example, the new chapters fully dedicated to the subject in Chen-Wishart (n 147) and P Davies, *JC Smith's The Law of Contract* (OUP: Oxford, 2018).

[165] The nature of 'relational contracts' and whether they are an established category of contract has been the subject of debate in the literature: see, for example, H Collins, 'Is a Relational Contract a Legal Concept?' in S Degeling, J Edelman, and J Goudkamp (eds), *Contract in Commercial Law* (Thomson Reuters: London, 2016); ZX Tan, 'Disruptive Doctrine? Revisiting the Doctrinal Impact of Relational Contract Theory' (2019) Legal Studies 39, 98. In *Bates v Post Office Ltd* (n 164), Fraser J held that it is an established concept in the case law, [702].

contracts. These relationships do not fit the classical model of commercial contracting parties engaged in one-off transactions, seeking only to further their own self-interest in an individualistic and if necessary antagonistic manner. They are long-term and involve expectations of trust, communication, and cooperation, as well as significant investment by the parties.[166]

As for the doctrine of abuse of rights, although it has generated little discussion in the English cases and literature on contract law, recent developments in the context of contractual discretion[167] and damages clauses[168] suggest that the courts are increasingly imposing outer limits on how contractual rights and freedoms are exercised in order to prevent their misuse.[169] In the context of contractual discretionary powers, there is recognition of an implied term regulating how the power is exercised that is founded on concepts of honesty, good faith, propriety of purpose, reasonableness, rationality, arbitrariness, capriciousness, and perversity. Where the parties exercise the right[170] to agree to a damages clause fixing the sum payable in the event of a breach, it will be assessed by reference to notions of legitimate interest, unconscionability, exorbitance, and extravagance. If it does not serve a legitimate interest in performance and is extravagant, exorbitant, or unconscionable in amount, it will be unenforceable. In both of these contexts, as in good faith, a degree of *rapprochement* between French law and English law can therefore be discerned.

166 *Yam Seng* (n 157); *Bristol Groundschool Ltd v Intelligent Data Capture Ltd & Ors* [2014] EWHC 2145 (Ch); *D&G Cars Ltd v Essex Police Authority* [2015] EWHC 226 (QB); and more recently see *Bates v Post Office Ltd* (n 164) in which Fraser J set out criteria to identify relational contracts [725].

167 *Braganza v BP Shipping Ltd* [2015] UKSC 17 (SC).

168 See *Cavendish Square Holding BV v Talal El Makdessi* [2015] UKSC 67 (SC) with its conjoined appeal *ParkingEye Ltd v Beavis* [2016] AC 172 (SC).

169 Rowan, 'Abuse of Rights in English Contract Law: Hidden in Plain Sight? (n 151).

170 See, for example, Lord Diplock using the term 'right' in this context in *Robophone Facilities Ltd v Blank* [1966] 1 WLR 1428, 1446.

# PART II
# FORMATION OF THE CONTRACT

# 4
# The Agreement

One of the more significant innovations in the reforms was the introduction in the new Civil Code of an entirely new section on contractual negotiation and formation. This was not addressed at all in the 1804 Code. As a result, the rules governing the formation of contracts developed in the cases over time. The absence of a body of codified rules was regarded by commentators as a 'major lacuna' in French contract law.[1] To general approbation, this has now been filled by fifteen new articles[2] that regulate pre-contractual negotiations (articles 1112 to 1112-2), offer and acceptance (articles 1113 to 1122), and pre-contractual agreements (articles 1123 to 1124).

## A Pre-Contractual Negotiations

**Civil Code[3]**
**(2016 version)**
*Art. 1112.—The commencement, continuation and breaking-off of precontractual negotiations are free from control. They must mandatorily satisfy the requirements of good faith.*

*In case of fault committed during the negotiations, the reparation of the resulting loss is not calculated so as to compensate the loss of benefits which were expected from the contract that was not concluded.*

[1] O Deshayes, 'La formation des contrats', RDC 2016/HS, 21; G Chantepie and M Latina, *La réforme du droit des obligations, Commentaire théorique et pratique dans l'ordre du Code civil* (2nd edn, Dalloz: Paris, 2018) [139].

[2] The section entitled 'Conclusion of Contracts' contains twenty-two articles in total: fifteen regulate all contracts; the other seven (articles 1125 to 1127-6) relate specifically to contracts made by electronic means and implement Directive 2000/31/EC of the European Parliament and of the Council of 8 June 2000 on certain legal aspects of information society services, in particular electronic commerce, in the Internal Market ('Directive on electronic commerce'), arts 9–11. The focus of this chapter is on the articles that apply to all contracts.

[3] 'Ordonnance no 2016-131 du 10 février 2016 portant réforme du droit des contrats, du régime général et de la preuve des obligations', JORF no 0035 of 11 February 2016. The Ordonnance was translated into English by J Cartwright, B Fauvarque-Cosson, and S Whittaker: <http://www.textes.justice.gouv.fr/art_pix/THE-LAW-OF-CONTRACT-2-5-16.pdf> (2016 version) and <http://www.textes.justice.gouv.fr/art_pix/Translationrevised2018final.pdf> (2018 version) accessed 1 September 2021. The translations of the new articles contained in this book are theirs.

*The New French Law of Contract.* Solène Rowan, Oxford University Press. © Solène Rowan 2022.
DOI: 10.1093/oso/9780198810872.003.0004

> **(2018 version)**
> Art. 1112.—The commencement, continuation and breaking-off of precontractual negotiations are free from control. They must mandatorily satisfy the requirements of good faith.
>
> In case of fault committed during the negotiations, the reparation of the resulting loss is calculated so as to compensate neither the loss of benefits which were expected from the contract that was not concluded nor the loss of the chance of obtaining these benefits.
>
> Art. 1112-1.—The party who knows information which is of decisive importance for the consent of the other, must inform him of it where the latter legitimately does not know the information or relies on the contracting party.
>
> However, this duty to inform does not apply to an assessment of the value of the act of performance.
>
> Information is of decisive importance if it has a direct and necessary relationship with the content of the contract or the status of the parties.
>
> A person who claims that information was due to him has the burden of proving that the other party had the duty to provide it, and that other party has the burden of proving that he has provided it.
>
> The parties may neither limit nor exclude this duty.
>
> In addition to imposing liability on the party who had the duty to inform, his failure to fulfil the duty may lead to annulment of the contract under the conditions provided by articles 1130 and following.

The formation of a contract is often preceded by negotiations. Particularly for substantial commercial contracts, these can be lengthy and intensive. French law affords extensive protection to the parties during this process, whatever the duration. The rationale is that negotiation should be a collaborative process in which they each act in good faith. In some circumstances there is even a requirement to share information.

## 1 Freedom to contract limited by a principle of good faith

The starting principle is that everyone is free to negotiate and enter, or indeed opt not to enter, into a contract. As new article 1112 states in the first sentence, 'the commencement, continuation and breaking-off of pre-contractual negotiations are free from control'. It is therefore *prima facie* not wrongful to put an end to contractual negotiations. In the absence of contrary agreement, either party can withdraw until the contract is formed without incurring liability.[4] This is illustrated by a case in which a trader sued a potential buyer for having broken off talks relating to the supply and installation of glazing and mirrors. It was held that the buyer was at liberty not to buy from the trader, even though the trader had incurred significant expense in providing quotes and showcasing the mirrors.[5]

However, this freedom is by no means absolute. It is qualified in article 1112 by the statement that '[pre-contractual negotiations] must mandatorily satisfy the requirements of good faith'. This is intended to protect negotiating parties and is in line with the fundamental principles of freedom of contract in article 1102 and good faith in article 1104 that are explored in Chapter 3.[6]

The requirement of good faith in pre-contractual negotiations is long-standing in French law. It was developed in decided cases over time and its codification was therefore uncontentious. This is not to say, however, that the article is unremarkable. There is now—for the first time—a textual basis for the requirement, which the 1804 Civil Code lacked. Paragraph 3 of old article 1134 imposed a duty to act in good faith only in the performance of the contract, which the courts extended to the pre-contractual stage and new article 1112 formalizes.[7]

Pre-contractual good faith sets standards for how the parties conduct themselves during negotiations.[8] It is their behaviour when negotiating that can fall beneath these standards and thereby be wrongful, not simply a decision by one party to bring the negotiations to an end.[9] As explained by the Pau Court of Appeal:

> Whereas it must be recognised, in actual fact, that in the preliminary phase of negotiations, during which the conditions of the contemplated contract are studied and discussed, certain obligations of rectitude and loyalty rest on the parties, these obligations clearly relate not to the conclusion of the eventual contract [ . . . ] but rather to the conduct of the negotiations themselves.[10]

Good faith requires that the negotiations are not broken off in a manner that is 'abusive'[11] or 'intolerable'.[12] The parties must conduct themselves 'ethically' and 'loyally'.[13] Decided cases assist in identifying where this line is drawn. It has been held, for example, that conducting parallel negotiations with several potential

[4] Civ (1) 20 Dec 2012, no 11-27340 cited in H Beale, B Fauvarque-Cosson, J Rutgers, and S Vogenauer (eds) *Cases, Materials and Text on Contract Law, Ius Commune Casebooks for the Common Law of Europe* (3rd edn, Hart Publishing: Oxford, 2019) 432.

[5] CA Pau, 14 Jan 1969, *Société Miroiterie Fraisse* D 1969.716; CA Paris 21 June 1965, Soc Airwell c SARL Publicite 28, D 1965.815.

[6] See Chapter 3, pp32–44.

[7] O Deshayes, T Genicon, and Y-M Laithier, *Réforme du droit des contrats, du régime général et de la preuve des obligations* (2nd edn, LexisNexis: Paris, 2018) 97.

[8] Ibid., 98–9.

[9] Ibid., 98–9.

[10] CA Pau, 14 Jan 1969, Societe Miroiterie Fraisse D 1969.716; Civ (1) 20 Dec 2012, no 11-27340.

[11] Com 13 Nov 2013, no 12-25.043.

[12] Deshayes, Genicon, and Laithier (n 7) 98.

[13] Ibid., 99; Chantepie and Latina (n 1) [174].

counterparties is not wrongful in the absence of an exclusivity agreement,[14] unless motivated by an intention to harm,[15] accompanied by fraud, or one or more negotiating parties are induced to believe that the negotiations are exclusive.[16]

There will however be a breach where a party embarks on negotiations without any intention of concluding a contract, or continues to negotiate having taken the decision not to do so.[17] This is also true where the negotiations are terminated without any legitimate justification,[18] abruptly or vexatiously,[19] especially where significant expense has been incurred. In one case, a French company that had engaged in prolonged negotiations for a dealership arrangement with a US manufacturer, which included an expensive trip to the US, was successful in establishing bad faith when the negotiations were terminated 'abruptly' in a brief telephone call with no explanation or justification, despite having reached an advanced stage. The *Cour de cassation* upheld the Colmar Court of Appeal's decision that there had been 'an improper breaking off of negotiations'.[20]

A breach of the duty to negotiate in good faith is a 'fault' that can give rise to extra-contractual liability under new article 1240 of the Civil Code. The victim can claim damages for the resulting loss but not a declaration that the contract came into being. Loss can include wasted expenditure[21] or injury to feelings (*dommage moral*) for the vexatious manner in which the negotiations were ended.[22] It can also include being deprived of the chance of concluding a contract with a third party where the wrongdoer has prolonged the negotiations with the victim, thus preventing them from doing so.[23]

However, compensation does not extend to the loss of benefits expected from the contract or the lost chance of obtaining them.[24] This is now stated expressly in

[14] CA Versailles, 5 March 1992, RTD civ 1992.753, note J Mestre, translated by Beale, Fauvarque-Cosson, Rutgers, and Vogenauer (n 4) 429.

[15] Although an intention to harm is not necessary for a breach of pre-contractual good faith to be established: Civ (3) 3 Oct 1972 no 71-12993, Bull civ III no 491, translated by Beale, Fauvarque-Cosson, Rutgers, and Vogenauer (n 4) 439.

[16] Com 26 Nov 2003, no 00-10.949 and 00-10.243 Bull civ IV no 186 D 2004.869, note AS Dupré Dallemagne, JCP 2004.I.163, note G Viney, RDC 2004.257, note D Mazeaud (the *Manoukian* decision), translated by Beale, Fauvarque-Cosson, Rutgers, and Vogenauer (n 4) 430.

[17] Com 18 June 2002, no 99-16.488; Com 26 Nov 2003, no 00-10.243, Bull civ 2003.IV.186.

[18] Civ (1) 20 Dec 2012, no 11-27.340; Civ (3) 18 Dec 2012, no 10-30.764, RDC 2013.545, note O Deshayes.

[19] Deshayes, Genicon, and Laithier (n 7) 99.

[20] Com 20 March 1972, JCP 1973.II.17543 (*Société des Etablissements Gerteis and Société Vilber-Lourmat*) translated by Beale, Fauvarque-Cosson, Rutgers, and Vogenauer (n 4) 437–9.

[21] Com 18 Jan 2011, no 09-14.617; Chantepie and Latina (n 1) [178].

[22] Paris 12 March 2008, Juris-Data no 2008-357913.

[23] Civ (3) 28 June 2006, no 04-20.040 Bull civ III no 164; Civ (3) 7 Jan 2009, no 07-20.783, Bull civ III no 5; Com 18 Sept 2012, no 11-19.269 Bull civ IV no 163; Chantepie and Latina (n 1) [178]; Deshayes, Genicon, and Laithier (n 7), citing the 'Report to the Senate', see F Pillet, 'Rapport fait au nom des lois constitutionnelles, de législation, du suffrage universel, du Règlement d'administration générale (1) sur le projet de loi ratifiant l'ordonnance no 2016-131 du 10 février 2016 portant réforme du droit des contrats, du régime général et de la preuve des obligations' (Sénat: no 33, 11 Oct 2017) <https://www.senat.fr/rap/l17-022/l17-0221.pdf> accessed 1 September 2021.

[24] The solution is long-standing: see the famous *Manoukian* decision (n 16).

article 1112. It has been justified on various grounds. The first is that the fault is in the abusive manner in which the right to break off negotiations is exercised, not in the act itself;[25] second, the general freedom to withdraw from negotiations 'would be illusory if the courts awarded damages which included the recovery of the expectation interest .... The victim of the legal wrong would be in the same position as if the contract had been concluded.'[26]

## 2 A general duty to provide information

In addition to the obligation to negotiate in good faith in article 1112, the Civil Code imposes a general duty to provide information (*devoir d'information*) on negotiating parties. Under article 1112-1, a party must share information within their knowledge that is decisively important to the consent of the other where that other party is legitimately ignorant or reliant on them for the information. This is a matter of public policy, meaning that it is not possible for the parties to limit or exclude their liability for breach.[27]

The duty is intended to ensure that the parties are only bound if their consent is real. In the 'Report to the President of the Republic', where the drafters of the reform discussed the new articles, it was characterized as 'an essential principle for ensuring balance in contractual relations', protecting weaker parties who are not always able to inform themselves.[28] It has been described by commentators as a 'preventive measure' that averts 'upstream' any defect in consent.[29] The defects in consent of mistake, fraud, and violence are considered in Chapter 5 on the validity of the contract.

The proposal to introduce the duty generated divergent views when the draft reforms were published. No duty to inform of general application had previously been recognized in France. Whilst in a number of judgments prior to the reforms a form of duty to provide information had been found to exist, these were decided case-by-case rather than by reference to established principles or criteria.[30] A general duty, independent and separate from good faith, would therefore alter the pre-contractual landscape. Some welcomed the proposal, arguing that establishing a clear framework for the duty rather than relying on the vagaries of incremental

[25] 'Report to the President of the Republic relating to Ordonnance no 2016–131 of 10 February 2016 on the reform of contract law, the general regime and proof of obligations', JORF no 0035 of 11 February 2016, 5.

[26] Beale, Fauvarque-Cosson, Rutgers, and Vogenauer (n 4) 458; 'Report to the President' (n 25) 5.

[27] Paragraph 5 of article 1112-1 of the Civil Code.

[28] 'Report to the President' (n 25) 5; F Terré, P Simler, Y Lequette, and F Chénedé, *Droit civil: les obligations* (12th edn, Dalloz: Paris, 2018 [332].

[29] Terré, Simler, Lequette, and Chénedé (n 28) [329].

[30] C Aubert de Vincelles 'Validity of Contract: Dol, Erreur and Obligation d'Information' in J Cartwright and S Whittaker (eds), *The Code Napoléon Rewritten: French Contract Law after the 2016 Reforms* (Hart Publishing: Oxford, 2017) 82.

development by the courts would enhance legal certainty.[31] However, business representatives raised several concerns. These included that the duty was too broadly cast, would cause uncertainty as to what should be disclosed and when, and would prevent the negotiation of the best possible deal.[32] Some doubted the need to go beyond special legislation that already required the provision of information in certain circumstances and the existing case law.

Acknowledging these concerns in the Report to the President,[33] the drafters characterized the duty as a compromise between various competing interests, with those of the information-holder protected in several different ways. These are a requirement that strict conditions be satisfied for the duty to arise, the exclusion of the value of the subject-matter of the contract from the scope of the duty,[34] and the burden of proof being imposed on the ignorant party. They bear the onus of showing that there was a duty to inform, that it was breached, and that they would not have entered into the contract on substantially the same terms had the information been available to them.[35]

### (a) In what circumstances does a negotiating party have a duty to inform the other?

Three conditions must be satisfied for the duty to arise. These are that the information is decisively important for the ignorant party and this is known to the information-holder; the information-holder has actual knowledge of the information; and the ignorance of the ignorant party is legitimate.

#### *(i) The information must be of decisive importance for the ignorant party*

The first condition is that the information is of decisive importance to the ignorant party to the knowledge of the information-holder.[36] 'Information of decisive importance' is defined in paragraph 3 of article 1112-1 as having 'a direct and necessary connection with the content of the contract or the character of the parties'. It has to be capable of influencing the consent of the victim and causing them either not to enter into the contract at all or to do so on substantially different terms.[37]

An estimate or assessment of the value of the promised performance does not qualify as information that must be shared.[38] This preserves the liberty of

[31] F Ancel, B Fauvarque-Cosson, and J Gest, *Aux sources de la réforme du droit des contrats* (Dalloz: Paris, 2017) [25.11]–[25.61] some parts of which are translated in Beale, Fauvarque-Cosson, Rutgers, and Vogenauer (n 4) 575–6; Deshayes, Genicon, and Laithier (n 7) 103.

[32] Ibid.

[33] And also in the book they wrote, see Ancel, Fauvarque-Cosson, and Gest (n 31) [25.12].

[34] 'Report to the President' (n 25) 5; Deshayes, Genicon, and Laithier (n 7) 102–3.

[35] Paragraph 4 of article 1112-1 of the Civil Code.

[36] Deshayes, Genicon, and Laithier (n 7) 105; article 1135 of the Civil Code.

[37] Terré, Simler, Lequette, and Chénedé (n 28) [333].

[38] Paragraph 2 of article 1112-1 of the Civil Code.

negotiating parties to speculate and strike good (and bad) bargains.[39] A well-known example is the 'Baldus' case[40] in which an unwitting seller of photographs, not realizing the photographer was famous, sold the negatives at a considerable undervalue to a buyer who knew of the seller's ignorance but said nothing. Dismissing a claim by the seller for nullity for fraudulent concealment of their true value, the *Cour de cassation* found that no duty to inform had arisen.

*(ii) Actual knowledge of the information by the information-holder*

The second condition is that the information-holder has actual knowledge of the information. Constructive knowledge, that is, knowledge that in the circumstances a party can be presumed to hold, will not do.[41] This diverges from several decisions prior to the reforms in which professionals were presumed, based on their professional status, to have certain knowledge.[42] Drawing a line under this presumption has been welcomed on the basis that liability would otherwise be too extensive and burdensome.[43]

*(iii) Legitimacy of ignorance or reliance*

The third condition is that the ignorance of, or the reliance on, the information-holder to provide the information is legitimate.[44] In negotiations, parties are expected to take responsibility for informing themselves appropriately through research, obtaining advice, and other means. As Deshayes, Genicon, and Laithier summarized, 'the duty to inform begins only where the duty to find the information for oneself ends'.[45] It is therefore only in relatively limited circumstances that reliance on the other party to share information can be warranted.[46]

Legitimacy is assessed having regard to the conduct of the ignorant party and the relationship between the parties. Where the information is easily ascertainable and would have been ascertained by the exercise of normal vigilance or minimal effort, their ignorance is considered to be of their own making and not legitimate. In other words, they only have themselves to blame.[47] It was held, for instance, that an experienced businessman who purchased a convenience store could not

[39] Deshayes, Genicon, and Laithier (n 7) 106.

[40] Civ (1) 3 May 2000 Bull civ I no 131, JCP 2001.II.10510, note Jamin, Défrenois no 19, 1106, note Mazeaud and note Delebecque (*affaire des photographies de Baldus*).

[41] R Sefton-Green, 'Formation of Contract: Negotiation and the Process of Agreement' in J Cartwright and S Whittaker (eds), *The Code Napoléon Rewritten: French Contract Law after the 2016 Reforms* (Hart Publishing: Oxford, 2017) 63; Civ (1) 28 May 2008, no 07-13.487, Bull civ I no 154.

[42] See, for example, Civ (1) 1 March 2005 no 04-10.063, Bull civ I no 109, RDC 2005.1051, obs D Fenouillet.

[43] Ancel, Fauvarque-Cosson, and Gest (n 31) [25.31]; Chantepie and Latina (n 1) [186]; Terré, Simler, Lequette, and Chénedé (n 28) [334].

[44] Article 1112-1 of the Civil Code.

[45] Deshayes, Genicon, and Laithier (n 7) 105.

[46] Chantepie and Latina (n 1) [187].

[47] Ibid.

complain that the seller had omitted to mention the opening of a new supermarket in the area where this was known publicly and had been well-documented in the press.[48]

However, information that is difficult for the ignorant party to ascertain[49] should be shared. This was held, for example, in respect of certain information relating to the characteristics of a basement that was only accessible by the seller.[50]

Where one party is a professional (*professionel*) and therefore more knowledgeable than the other, or the relationship is one of trust, disclosure can be required even of information that is readily accessible.[51] This often arises from the nature of the contract that is under negotiation. Examples are contracts that are collaborative in nature (*contrat de collaboration*) or involve a convergence of the interests of the parties, and those that create a relationship of confidence, for example, agency agreements.[52] Similarly, it is well-established that a professional will usually be under a duty to share information with a lay person.[53]

### (b) Remedies

Breach of the duty to inform gives rise to extra-contractual liability under new article 1240 in the form of compensatory damages for loss suffered as a result of the decisive information not being disclosed.[54] There are also various grounds on which the contract can be annulled. These arise where the breach of the duty to inform vitiates consent and the conditions in the new articles on defects in consent are satisfied.[55] This will be the case where the information is withheld with an intention to deceive and the conditions in new article 1137 on fraud are satisfied;[56] and where the information is withheld negligently causing a mistake that satisfies the conditions in new articles 1132 to 1136. Vitiating factors are considered in Chapter 5 on the validity of the contract.[57]

[48] Com 17 July 2001, D 2002.Somm 1004, note G Pignarre; Civ (3) 6 March 2002, RTD civ 2003.82, note J Mestre and B Fages; Civ (3) 9 Oct 2012, D 2013 Pan 396, note S and M Mekki; Com 24 Sept 2003, no 00-21.863 RDC 2004.260, note D Mazeaud, RTD civ 2004.86, note J Mestre et B Fages.

[49] Civ (3) 28 April 1971, JCP 1971.II.16841, RTD civ 1971.868.

[50] Civ (3) 15 Nov 2000, no 99-11.203, Bull civ III no 171; Civ (3) 27 March 1991, no 89-16.975, Bull civ III no 108.

[51] Deshayes, Genicon, and Laithier (n 7) 105–6.

[52] Civ (1) 22 Dec 1954, D 1955.254.

[53] Civ (1) 19 June 1985, Bull civ I no 201.181. Such a duty does not, however, automatically arise: Civ (1) 3 June 1998, Bull civ I no 198; 19 Feb 202, RTD civ 2003.82, note J Mestre and B Fages; Civ (1) 24 Nov 1976, Bull civ I.370.291.

[54] But not the loss of the chance to obtain the profits expected from the contract: Com 31 Jan 2012, no 11-10.834; Com 10 July 2012, no 11-21.954.

[55] Paragraph 6 of article 1112-1 of the Civil Code.

[56] See article 1137 of the Civil Code (*réticence dolosive*).

[57] See Chapter 5, pp 86–102.

## B Offer and Acceptance

**Civil Code**

Art. 1113.—A contract is formed by the meeting of an offer and an acceptance by which the parties demonstrate their will to be bound.

This may stem from a person's declaration or unequivocal conduct.

A contract is formed by an offer made by one party being accepted by the other. In this way the parties express their agreement to be bound.[58] New articles 1113 to 1122 define 'offer' and 'acceptance' and deal with issues that commonly arise in the formation of a contract.[59] These include the distinction between offers and invitations to treat, offers to the public at large, the withdrawal of offers, the time at which the contract is formed, acceptance by silence, and the withdrawal of an acceptance.

### 1 Offer

**Civil Code**

Art. 1114.—An offer, whether made to a particular person or to persons generally, contains the essential elements of the envisaged contract, and expresses the will of the offeror to be bound in case of acceptance. Failing this, there is only an invitation to enter into negotiations.

Art. 1115.—An offer may be withdrawn freely as long as it has not reached the person to whom it was addressed.

Art. 1116.—An offer may not be withdrawn before the expiry of any period fixed by the offeror or, if no such period has been fixed, the end of a reasonable period.

The withdrawal of an offer in contravention of this prohibition prevents the contract being concluded.

The person who thus withdraws an offer incurs extra-contractual liability under the conditions set out by the general law, and has no obligation to compensate the loss of profits which were expected from the contract.

Art. 1117.—An offer lapses on the expiry of the period fixed by the offeror or, if no period is fixed, at the end of a reasonable period.

It also lapses in the case of the incapacity or death of the offeror or death of the offeree.

[58] Paragraph 1 of article 1113 of the Civil Code. The Civil Code adopts the offer and acceptance model developed by Robert Joseph Pothier. This was transplanted into English law but is applied differently because intent is judged objectively in England.

[59] 'Report to the President' (n 25) 6.

New article 1114 defines an 'offer' as a statement that contains all the essential elements of the proposed contract and conveys the willingness of the maker to be bound upon acceptance by the other party. It must be precise and comprehensive.[60] No particular form is required and the offer can be expressed or made by conduct that is unequivocal (*offre tacite*).[61]

### (a) Offer and invitations to treat

According to article 1114, where these fundamental characteristics are not present, a pre-contractual proposal is merely an invitation to treat (*invitation à entrer en négociation*). The effect is to categorize as an invitation to treat anything that is not an offer. Unhelpfully, the article is silent on precisely what is necessary for a proposal to constitute an offer[62] and the 'essential elements of the envisaged contract' that are required. Despite various attempts by academic commentators to articulate these essential elements,[63] they have generally fallen to the courts to work out on a case-by-case basis having regard to the type and subject-matter of the contract.[64] It has been held, for example, than an offer to enter into a lease agreement must identify the property and the rent but not the date of commencement of the term.[65] An offer of sale must state the subject-matter and the price to be paid.[66] It was therefore held that an advertisement that stated 'price to be debated' was no more than an invitation to treat.[67]

Article 1114 is also silent on what is a manifest intention to be bound. Helpful guidance can again be found in cases decided prior to the reforms. For instance, the *Cour de cassation* has held that the requisite intention to be bound is not established where the proposal can be withdrawn capriciously,[68] or by a request for

[60] B Haftel, 'La conclusion du contrat dans le projet d'ordonnance portant réforme du droit des obligations' Gaz Pal 2015.120, 6.

[61] Paragraph 2 of article 1113 of the Civil Code. As an example, where a tenant remains in a rented property after the term of the lease has expired, it is considered that he tacitly offers to renew it. If the landlord makes no objection, the lease will be renewed: article 1738 Civil Code.

[62] In consumer contracts, additional essential elements are required by legislation: see, for example, article L111-1 of the Consumer Code which states that before being bound by the contract the consumer must be provided, in a legible and comprehensible manner, with the following information: (1) the essential characteristics of the goods or service; (2) the price; (3) in the absence of immediate performance of the contract, the date or deadline of delivery or performance; (4) contact and personal information relating to the professional; (5) if applicable, information relating to legal guarantees and the functionalities of digital content; and (6) the possibility of recourse to a consumer mediator.

[63] See, for example, J-L Aubert, *Notions et rôle de l'offre et de l'acceptation dans la formation du contrat* (LGDJ: Paris, 1970) [52], where the essential elements were suggested to be those without which it would be impossible to identify the contract has been concluded.

[64] Terré, Simler, Lequette, and Chénedé (n 28) [109]; see, for example, Civ (3) 28 Oct 2009, D 2009.2752, JCP 2009.574, no 7, note G Loiseau.

[65] Civ (3) 28 Oct 2009 D 2009.2752, JCP 2009.574 no 7, note G Loiseau.

[66] Article 1583 of the Civil Code.

[67] Paris 29 Jan 1996, D Affaires 1996.389, Defrenois 1996.1360, note D Mazeaud.

[68] Terré, Simler, Lequette, and Chénedé (n 28) [167]; Com 4 June 1996, Bull civ IV no 240.

information about the possible renewal of an existing contract,[69] or a proposal that is 'subject to confirmation' or 'without obligation'.[70]

### (b) Offers to the public at large and displays in shops

Offers to the public at large are treated no differently than offers to individuals,[71] as now reflected in article 1114, which states that offers can be made 'to a particular person or to persons generally'. There are therefore no specific principles governing public offers.[72] The *Cour de cassation* has made clear that 'an offer made to the public binds the offeror to the first person accepting in the same conditions that if the offer had been made to a specified person'.[73]

Displaying goods for sale in a shop has been held to constitute an offer.[74] A contract is formed when the customer places the goods in their basket, unlike in England where this occurs only when the goods are paid for. The Paris Court of Appeal, in a judgment which the *Cour de cassation* upheld, has held that 'the sale takes place as soon as the customer, choosing from the shelf an item offered for sale at a price that he is prepared to accept, places it in the basket or bag provided and which he is required to use until the goods are checked out at the till'.[75]

### (c) Withdrawal of the offer

An offer can be withdrawn at any time before being received by the offeree[76] and only becomes effective upon receipt.[77] It must then be held open for acceptance either for whatever period of time is specified in the offer or otherwise for a reasonable period of time.

These simple rules belie that, prior to the 2016 reforms, this was an area of real confusion, which the drafters sought to address in new articles 1115 and 1116.[78] There was particular uncertainty as to the extent of the offeror's ability to withdraw their offer. The basic principle was that an offer could be withdrawn at any time until accepted by the offeree. Until then, the parties were free to choose whether or not to enter into the contract. In a case in 1919, the *Cour de cassation* explained that 'an offer being insufficient to bind by itself the offeror, it can, in general, be withdrawn as long as it has not been validly accepted'.[79]

[69] Civ (1) 24 Nov 1998, D 1999 Somm 110, note P Delebecque.

[70] Com 6 March 1990, JCP 1990.II.21583, note B Gross, D 1991, translated by Beale, Fauvarque-Cosson, Rutgers, and Vogenauer (n 4) 210–11.

[71] A Vialard, 'L'offre publique du contrat' RTD civ 1971.750.

[72] A Bénabent, *Droit des obligations* (18th edn, LGDJ: Paris, 2019) [70]; J Bell, S Boyron, and S Whittaker, *Principles of French Law* (2nd edn, OUP: Oxford, 2008) 303; B Nicholas, *The French Law of Contract* (Clarendon Press: Oxford, 1992) 63–5.

[73] Civ (3) 28 Nov 1968, Bull civ III no 507 JCP 1969.II.15797, RTD civ 1969.348, note G Cornu and Y Loussouarn; A Vialard (n 71).

[74] Terré, Simler, Lequette, and Chénedé (n 28) [170].

[75] CA Paris 14 Dec 1961, JCP 1962.II.12547, Gaz Pal 1962.I.135; Civ 20 Oct 1964, D 1965.62. Cited and translated in Beale, Fauvarque-Cosson, Rutgers, and Vogenauer (n 4) 221–2.

[76] Articles 1115 and 1116 of the Civil Code.

[77] Regardless of whether the offeree knows of the offer, see Deshayes, Genicon, and Laithier (n 7) 121.

[78] Chantepie and Latina (n 1) [204]–[206].

[79] Civ (3) 3 Feb 1919, DP 1923.1.126.

Whilst the basic principle seems straightforward enough, the courts progressively imposed a duty on the offeror to keep the offer open for any period of time specified in the offer or, where no period of time was prescribed, for a reasonable period of time where the terms of the offer were burdensome and demanding.[80] Subsequently, the requirement that the terms be burdensome and demanding was dropped. The result was that any offer in which no period of time for acceptance was specified had to be kept open for a reasonable period of time. This duty was, however, clearly contrary to the basic principle and became the source of considerable contention.[81]

The reforms formalize this duty, effectively reversing the basic principle that the offeror could freely retract their offer prior to acceptance.[82] Now an offer must be kept open for the period of time specified in the offer or otherwise a reasonable period of time, unless it has not yet reached the offeree. What is reasonable will depend on the circumstances of each case and is a matter for the lower court hearing the case to decide on the facts, without scope for review by the *Cour de cassation* (*pouvoir souverain d'appréciation des juges du fond*). It is apparent from past judgments that the period will generally be calculated as the 'time necessary for the offeree to examine the offer and reply to it'.[83] In making this calculation, the courts have taken account of factors such as the nature of the contract,[84] the characteristics of the offeree, commercial usage, and the geographical distance between the parties.[85] In one case, a purported acceptance that was sent three months after the date of the offer, which stated that it had to be accepted 'quickly', was held to be too late as the offer had already lapsed.[86] However, an acceptance that was communicated five weeks after the making of an offer that required an 'immediate response' was not out of time. Relevant factors were that the offer was for the sale of real property and made to a company that required director approval in order to accept.[87]

Articles 1115 and 1116 do not state whether the withdrawal of an offer is effective when communicated by the offeror or only when received by, or brought to the attention of, the offeree. This is relevant where the withdrawal is sent by the offeror before the offer is accepted by the offeree but only received by the offeree after their acceptance of the offer. The absence of any provision on this point is in contrast with the equivalent rules on acceptance in new article 1118, which expressly states that the withdrawal of an acceptance by the offeree only takes effect

[80] Civ (3) 8 Feb 1968, no 65-10.600; Civ (3) 25 May 2005, no 03-19.411, Bull civ III no 117.

[81] Civ (3) 20 May 2009, no 08-13.230, Bull civ III no 118 RDC 2009.1325, note Y-M Laithier RTD civ 2009.524, note B Fages; Chantepie and Latina (n 1) [204].

[82] Chantepie and Latina (n 1) [205]; Deshayes, Genicon, and Laithier (n 7) 124; Terré, Simler, Lequette, and Chénedé (n 28) [178].

[83] CA Paris 12 June 1869, D 1870.2.6.

[84] Com 6 Feb 1973, Bull civ IV no 65; Civ (3) 21 Oct 1975, Bull civ III no 302 (the purported acceptance of an offer for the sale of a building nine years after the offer was made was held to be too late).

[85] Terré, Simler, Lequette, and Chénedé (n 28) [172].

[86] Civ (3) 8 Feb 1968, Bull civ III no 52.

[87] Civ 3, 25 May 2005 JCP 2005.I.172, note P Grosser, RDC 2006.311, note D Mazeaud.

when received by the offeror. This asymmetry has been inferred by commentators to mean that, in contrast with the position on acceptance, the withdrawal of an offer is effective upon being sent by the offeror. It does not need to reach the offeree in order to be effective.[88] The explanation proffered is that French law seeks to uphold the common intention of the parties and that, where an offer is withdrawn before being received, there is no meeting of the minds that could form a contract.[89]

### (d) Wrongful withdrawal of the offer

Withdrawal of an offer before the expiry of the period of time stipulated in the offer, or a reasonable period of time, will give rise to extra-contractual liability (*rétractation fautive*). According to paragraph 3 of article 1116, the remedy is damages to compensate the loss occasioned to the offeree. Prior to the reforms, there was inconsistency and uncertainty in the decided cases on the available remedy. In some cases, it was held that a wrongful withdrawal was ineffective, such that a contract was formed where the offeree had accepted the offer.[90] In others, the offeree was confined to an award of damages.[91] This came to be 'one of the most uncertain and discussed topics of French contract law'.[92] The clarity brought by new article 1116 is therefore welcome.[93]

Unhelpfully, however, the article provides very little guidance on the type of loss that can be compensated or how damages are to be assessed. Instead, it is expressed in the negative, stating only that compensation cannot include damages for loss of the profits that are expected from the contract.

Commentators have suggested that the main recovery for the wrongful withdrawal of an offer should be for the lost opportunity of entering into, and obtaining, the advantages expected from the contract.[94] This is faithful to the aim of compensation for extra-contractual liability of putting the innocent party in the position in which they would have been but for the wrong. It also censures the aspect of the conduct of the offeror that is objectionable, which is to have 'made the offeree believe that he could conclude a contract within a certain time',[95] only then to frustrate that expectation and the attendant aspiration of making a profit. In practical terms, the recoverable loss might include expenses incurred by the offeree in assessing the offer and possibly also the cost of foregone opportunities, for instance alternative contracts that were renounced or other offers that were declined.

[88] Chantepie and Latina (n 1) [206] and [227]; Deshayes, Genicon, and Laithier (n 7) 122–3; Terré, Simler, Lequette, and Chénedé (n 28) [177].

[89] Deshayes, Genicon, and Laithier (n 7) 122–3; Chantepie and Latina (n 1) [206].

[90] Civ (1) 17 Dec 1958, D 1959.33, translated by Beale, Fauvarque-Cosson, Rutgers, and Vogenauer (n 4) 229; Civ (3) 10 May 1968, Bull civ III no 209; Civ (3) 7 May 2008, no 07-11.690, Bull civ III no 79, RDC 2008.1109, note T Genicon, and 1239, note F Collart Dutilleul; RTD civ 2008.474, note B Fages.

[91] Terré, Simler, Lequette, and Chénedé (n 28) [179].

[92] Deshayes, Genicon, and Laithier (n 7) 128.

[93] D Mazeaud RDC 2006.2.311; T Genicon, RDC 2008.1109.

[94] Deshayes, Genicon, and Laithier (n 7) 129–30; Terré, Simler, Lequette, and Chénedé (n 28) [180].

[95] Deshayes, Genicon, and Laithier (n 7) 130; Terré, Simler, Lequette, and Chénedé (n 28) [180].

Some have criticized article 1116, arguing that damages are relatively toothless where the offeree remains willing to accept the offer. Only by compelling the formation of the contract can their expectations be properly satisfied. Others counter that such fulsome protection would ordinarily be excessive and, if genuinely desired by the offeree, can in any case be achieved through a pre-contractual agreement such as a unilateral promise to contract (*promesse unilatérale de contrat*).[96] This is 'a contract by which one party, the promisor, grants another, the beneficiary, a right to have the option to conclude a contract whose essential elements are determined, and for the formation of which only the consent of the beneficiary is missing'.[97] It would confer on the offeree a right to elect to enter into a contract on the agreed terms, if they wish to do so. If the offeror withdraws the promise to contract, according to paragraph 2 of article 1124, the contract would nevertheless be formed.[98]

### (e) Lapse of offer

An offer will lapse at the end of any period of time specified in the offer or otherwise upon the expiry of a reasonable period of time.[99] This mirrors the position prior to the 2016 reforms. Again, the new Civil Code is silent on what constitutes a reasonable period, which is for the court to determine on the facts in the given case.[100]

An offer will also lapse where the offeror dies or becomes subject to an incapacity before acceptance occurs.[101] This rule was introduced in the 2016 reforms, bringing an end to a somewhat anomalous line of decisions[102] that an offer which specifies a period of time for acceptance survives the death of the offeror and is binding on their successors.[103] Such an offer will now lapse on the death of the offeror. An analogous principle also applies where it is the offeree who dies. The offer lapses and no rights pass to the offeree's successors.[104]

In contrast with the international instruments that inspired the 2016 reforms, such as the Principles of European Contract Law (PECL) and the UNIDROIT

[96] Deshayes, Genicon, and Laithier (n 7) 131–2.

[97] Paragraph 1 of article 1124 of the Civil Code.

[98] Paragraph 2 of article 1121 of the Civil Code states that 'revocation of the promise during the period allowed to the beneficiary to exercise the option does not prevent the formation of the contract which was promised'.

[99] Paragraph 1 of article 1117 of the Civil Code.

[100] See, for example, Civ (3) 24 Jan 2012 no 10-27.965; Com 27 April 2011 no 10-17.177.

[101] Paragraph 2 of article 1117 of the Civil Code.

[102] N Dissaux and C Jamin, *Projet de réforme du droit des contrats, du régime général et de la preuve des obligations: rendu public le 25 février 2015: commentaire article par article* (Dalloz: Paris, 2015) 16. Citing Civ (3) 10 May 1989, no 87-18.130 Bull civ III no 109; Civ (1) 25 June 2014, no 13-16.529, D 2014.1574, note A Tadros.

[103] Civ (3) 10 Dec 1997, no 95-16461 Bull civ III no 223.

[104] Dissaux and Jamin (n 102) 16. Citing Civ (1) 5 Nov 2008, no 07-16.505 D 2010 226, obs S Amrani-Mekki.

Principles,[105] the new Civil Code does not deal with the effect of an offer being refused. It was, however, well-established in cases decided prior to the reforms that, where the offeree rejects the offer or makes a counter-offer, the offer would lapse. This rule should continue to apply.

## 2 Acceptance

**Civil Code**
Art. 1118.—An acceptance is the manifestation of the will of the offeree to be bound on the terms of the offer.

As long as the acceptance has not reached the offeror, it may be withdrawn freely provided that the withdrawal reaches the offeror before the acceptance.

An acceptance which does not conform to the offer has no effect, apart from constituting a new offer.

Art. 1119.—General conditions put forward by one party have no effect on the other party unless they have been brought to the latter's attention and that party has accepted them.

In case of inconsistency between general conditions relied on by each of the parties, incompatible clauses have no effect.

In case of inconsistency between general conditions and special conditions, the latter prevail over the former.

Art. 1120.—Silence does not count as acceptance except where so provided by legislation, usage, business dealings or other particular circumstances.

Art. 1121.—A contract is concluded as soon as the acceptance reaches the offeror. It is deemed to be concluded at the place where the acceptance has arrived.

Art. 1122.—Legislation or the contract may provide for a period for reflection, which is a period within which the offeree cannot give his acceptance, or a period for withdrawal, which is a period within which a party may withdraw his consent.

A contract is concluded where an offer is accepted by the offeree. Acceptance requires a statement or other unequivocal conduct (*acceptation tacite*) that indicates assent to the terms of the offer.[106] According to new article 1118, this manifests the 'will of the offeree' to enter into the contract (*manifestation de volonté*). The wording of the article echoes that in article 1101, which defines a contract as 'a

[105] UNIDROIT Principles (article 2.1.5), the Principles of European Contract Law (PECL) (article 2:203), the Vienna Convention on Contracts for the International Sale of Goods (CISG) (article 17).
[106] Civ (1) 21 June 1983, Bull civ I no 176; Civ (1) 28 Feb 1989, Bull civ I no 93.

concordance of wills of two or more persons intended to create, modify, transfer or extinguish obligations'.[107]

### (a) Acceptance by silence

New article 1120 sets out the long-established principle that silence does not amount to acceptance. It has repeatedly been held by the *Cour de cassation* that an acceptance must be externalized in some way. This is reflected in its classic statement that 'acceptance of a contract can be tacit but it can only result from acts which evidently demonstrate the intention to accept the proposed contract'.[108] The theoretical basis for the principle is freedom of contract, which holds that a party cannot be bound without evidence that they intend to commit themselves.[109] It also promotes certainty. Silence is too equivocal to manifest a willingness to be bound and it would be too burdensome to require that an offer be expressly rejected or else deemed to be accepted.[110]

The article recognizes that exceptions can arise by legislation, custom, or business dealings, or in other special circumstances. An example in legislation is paragraph 5 of article L112-2 of the Insurance Code, which provides for the automatic renewal of contracts of insurance unless the insured party gives a direction to the contrary. A particular profession or place[111] may have a custom or the parties may establish a practice in their business dealings that requires an offer to be expressly rejected in order not to be binding.[112] 'Particular circumstances' have been held to include a specific agreement between the parties that silence will constitute acceptance[113] and an offer that is made solely in the interest of the offeree.[114]

### (b) Counter-offer

Where the offeree's response to an offer proposes changes to the terms of the offer or different terms entirely, this amounts to a counter-offer and a rejection of the original offer.[115] A counter-offer can be accepted in the same way as any other offer. It appears to be suggested by article 1118 that acceptance requires unqualified assent to all of the terms of the offer, which if correct would mean that any qualification at all in a purported acceptance would be a counter-offer. However, there is consensus amongst commentators that this is not correct and that assent to the key

[107] See Chapter 3 on the definition of contract, pp 31–2.
[108] Civ (1) 16 April 1996, Bull civ I no 181.
[109] Deshayes, Genicon, and Laithier (n 7) 153.
[110] Chantepie and Latina (n 1) [239].
[111] Com 9 Jan 1956, Bull civ IV no 13; Com 13 May 2003, Bull civ IV no 82, *Contrats, Conc, Consomm*, 2003, comm 124, obs L Leveneur.
[112] Civ (1) 3 Dec 1985, Bull civ I no 330; Com 28 Feb 1989, Bull civ IV no 74 and 21 Nov 1989, Bull civ IV no 292; Civ (1) 4 June 2009, Bull civ I no 113, D 2009.2137, note F Labarthe.
[113] Civ (1) 12 Jan 1988, no 86-12.849.
[114] Req 28 March 1938, DP 1939.I.5, note P Voirin; Civ (1) 1 Dec 1969, JCP 1970.II.16445, note J-L Aubert.
[115] Paragraph 3 of article 1118 of the Civil Code.

elements of the proposed contract is sufficient.[116] Some have argued that this would have been clearer if the drafters of the reforms had adopted the distinction drawn in the PECL or the UNIDROIT Principles between 'material' and 'non-material alterations' to the terms of the offer.[117] In both instruments, an offer is accepted and a contract formed even where the response contains amendments to the terms of the offer, provided that they do not materially depart from those terms. The additional or different terms become part of the contract.

### (c) The acceptance of general conditions of business

The acceptance of general conditions of business is dealt with in new article 1119. An offeror who wishes to contract on their general conditions of business, which typically are a pre-prepared set of standard terms (that in most cases can reasonably be assumed to be favourable to the offeror) must overcome two additional hurdles.[118] The first is to bring the terms to the attention of the offeree in a manner that is accessible and reader-friendly. This has been held not to be satisfied where the terms were in very small print,[119] faint in colour,[120] and drowning in a mass of less significant terms.[121] There are a large number of cases in which limitation clauses in particular have fallen foul of this requirement. These include one such clause that was written in miniscule characters on a car park receipt[122] and another that was drowned and therefore difficult to discern amongst sixteen other clauses and also inconsistent with a promotional flyer that was given to the offeree.[123]

The second hurdle is to give notice of the terms to the offeree before the contract is formed. It is for the offeror to prove that the attention of the offeree was directed to the terms prior to their acceptance.[124] A statement in an order form that signing the form would amount to acceptance of terms on the reverse side of the form has been held to be sufficient in principle.[125] In contrast, terms displayed on notices or signs in a car park or a hotel which the customer can read only after entering into the contract have been held to be ineffective.[126]

### (d) Incompatible general terms of business

Particular complexities can arise where both parties have sought to impose their general conditions of business on the other and some of the terms are incompatible. The long-standing solution in French law, which is now codified in paragraph

[116] Deshayes, Genicon, and Laithier (n 7) 144–5 and 151.
[117] Ibid.; article 2:208 PECL and article 2.1.11 UNIDROIT Principles.
[118] In the context of consumer contracts, see article L112-1 of the Consumer Code.
[119] Com 27 Nov 2007, no 06-16.523; Com 19 Dec 2000, no 98-11.577.
[120] Com 17 Feb 1998, no 95-21.668.
[121] Civ (1) 27 Feb 1996, Defrenois 1996.742, note J-L Aubert; Chantepie, and Latina (n 1) [232].
[122] Civ (1) 31 May 1983, Bull civ I no 159.
[123] Civ (1) 27 Feb 1996 Defrenois 1996.742, note J-L Aubert.
[124] Bénabent (n 72) [77].
[125] Civ (1) 3 Dec 1991, no 89-20.856; Com 6 June 1995, no 93-21.786.
[126] Civ (1) 19 May 1992 Bull civ I no 146.

2 of new article 1119, is that the incompatible terms have no effect and are deemed not to be accepted. Only compatible terms will be incorporated into any contract that is nonetheless formed. Any resulting gaps in the contract are filled by the court through a process known as supplementation, which is described in Chapter 6.[127] The rationale for excising incompatible terms is that a contract is the product of consensual agreement. Terms on which there is no consensus should be taken not to have been agreed.

A conflict between the general terms of business of the parties therefore does not necessarily lead to the failure of the contract. It can, though, give rise to considerable uncertainty. The discretion in the court to supplement the contract is broad. Rarely can the parties be confident as to the terms that will end up governing their relationship.[128]

### (e) The time of acceptance

New article 1121 provides that an acceptance takes effect upon reaching the offeror. This achieves clarity on the timing of the formation of the contract and also brings French law more closely in line to various projects for the harmonization of European contract law.[129] It was, however, a surprisingly vexed issue prior to the reforms.[130] There was uncertainty as to whether an acceptance was effective when sent by the offeree to the offeror (*théorie de l'émission*) or only upon receipt by the offeror (*théorie de la réception*). The 1804 Code gave no guidance. In relation to special categories of contract, the Code pointed in different directions in different contexts. For instance, paragraph 2 of article 932 states that the acceptance of a donation is effective only when brought to the attention of the donor. In contrast, article 1985 provides that the acceptance of a contract of agency can take effect when the agent begins performing the contract.

In the absence of guidance, the issue fell to be determined on a case-by-case basis by the lower courts, without scope for review by the *Cour de cassation*, which refrained from interfering on the basis that the issue was one of fact rather than law. Exceptionally, however, it did give a ruling on the point in one case, which was that acceptance required receipt by the offeror, such that the mere sending of the

[127] See Chapter 5 and the section on supplementation, pp 130–4; Chantepie and Latina (n 1) [236].

[128] This contrasts with the 'all or nothing' approach in England, where the terms of one party alone will be found to apply to the exclusion of those of the other party. In what has come to be known as the 'battle of the forms', both parties are incentivized to try to have the 'last shot' by being the last to provide their terms to the other, such that those are the terms that are incorporated. This has drawn criticism for being too rigid and in some cases the approach has been rejected. See Lord Denning in *Butler Machine Tool Co Ltd v Ex-Cell-O Corp (England) Ltd* [1979] 1 WLR 401 (CA); Burton J in *GHSP Inc v AB Electronic Ltd* [2010] EWHC 1828 (Comm) [2011] 1 Lloyd's Rep 432 holding that the terms of the contract were to be found in the terms to be implied by the Sale of Goods Act 1979; Edwards-Stuart J in *Transformers & Rectifiers Ltd v Needs Ltd* [2015] EWHC 269 (TCC) [2015] BLR 336.

[129] Chantepie and Latina (n 1) [242]; see, however, PECL article 2:202(1).

[130] 'Report to the President' (n 25) 6.

acceptance was insufficient. The facts were that the offeror offered to sell her house to the offeree, which responded by sending an acceptance in the post on 2 April 2004. In the meantime, the offeror had second thoughts about selling and on 1 April 2004 sent a letter to the offeree withdrawing the offer. Affirming the decision of the Montpellier Court of Appeal that no contract had been formed, the *Cour de cassation* held that, as the withdrawal of the offer had been sent before the acceptance was received, there was no 'meeting of the minds'.[131] This position is now formalized in article 1121.

### (f) Withdrawal of acceptance and cooling off periods

An acceptance of an offer can be withdrawn as long as the communication of the withdrawal reaches the offeror before the communication of the acceptance.[132] The offeree can therefore withdraw an acceptance made by post by using a more expeditious means of communication such as email or telephone. This contrasts with the withdrawal of an offer, which is effective when sent.[133]

New article 1122 states that a cooling off period may be provided by legislation or the contract itself. This could be to allow time for consideration of the offer, with the offeree unable to accept the offer during the designated period, or withdrawal, conferring a right on the beneficiary to withdraw their offer or acceptance. Although almost entirely governed by consumer law,[134] cooling-off periods were considered by the drafters to be appropriate for inclusion in the new Civil Code as a general principle.[135]

## C Intention to Create Legal Relations

There is no article in the Civil Code requiring that the parties must intend to create legal relations in order to enter into a contract. The closest is new article 1113, which states that 'the formation of contract requires the meeting of an offer and an acceptance demonstrating the will of each of the parties to be bound'. This is, however, a well-established principle, and it is well understood that parties do not always intend to be bound even when in agreement, and not all agreements have legally binding consequences.

[131] Civ (3) 17 Sep 2014, no 13-21.824, Bull civ III no 108 D 2015, note S Amrani-Mekki and M Mekki. This is in line with the subjective approach to intention in French law.

[132] Article 1121 of the Civil Code. It is consistent with article 1118 of the Code.

[133] See preceding section on withdrawal of the offer.

[134] See articles L221-8 to L221-28 of the Consumer Code.

[135] 'Report to the President' (n 25) 6; criticized in N Molfessis, 'La formation du contrat' JCP 2015 supplement to no 21. Article 1122 has therefore no independent force and is merely a reinstatement of the already existing law governing cooling-off periods.

## 1 Social and domestic agreements, gentlemen's agreements, and agreements in principle

A distinction is often drawn in French academic literature between a number of different types of non-contractual agreements, namely, acts of courtesy (*actes de courtoisie*), agreements to perform services gratuitously (*actes de complaisance*), gentlemen's agreements (*engagements d'honneur*),[136] and agreements in principle (*accords de principe*).[137]

An act of courtesy is a social or domestic arrangement such as a dinner invitation that has been accepted or a parent's promise to their son of a gift for passing exams.[138] Since it is presumed that there is no intention to create legal relations, acts of courtesy are not legally binding.

An agreement to perform services gratuitously, for example to give a ride in a car or provide first-aid, is generally not binding either, being based on a willingness to act without receiving anything in return. It has therefore been held that an agreement to share the cost of a business trip by car did not give rise to a contract, which meant that the driver and owner of the car was not under a contractual duty to ensure the safety of the passenger. As a result, when the car was involved in an accident, no contractual liability arose.[139] In some circumstances the courts have found that a person who helps another in a dangerous situation, for example salvage at sea, can seek remuneration under a 'contract of assistance' (*convention d'assistance*), although the basis of the contractual relationship in these situations is unclear and controversial.[140]

Gentlemen's agreements (*engagements d'honneur*) have given rise to differing approaches in the cases. When made between family members or friends, they do not have legal force.[141] A promise to 'make a gesture' towards a friend was therefore held to create no more than a moral obligation.[142] However, in other situations, particularly in a commercial context, they have been found to be binding. There appear to be two main reasons. The first is that the parties should not be allowed to use the guise of a gentlemen's agreement to oust the jurisdiction of the court on matters that in substance are contractual in nature. The second is that, by engaging themselves in honour, the parties have actually emphasized their mutual commitment, which is all the more reason to hold them to their promises.[143] It has been

[136] B Oppetit, 'L'engagement d'honneur' D 1979, Chron 107; B Beignier, *L'honneur et le droit* (LGDJ: Paris, 1995).

[137] P Malaurie, L Aynès, and P Stoffel-Munck, *Droit des obligations* (10th edn, LGDJ: Paris, 2018) [437]–[442].

[138] Ibid.

[139] Civ (1) 6 April 1994, no 91-21047, Bull civ I no 136 RTD civ 1994.866, note O Jourdain. Cited and translated by Beale, Fauvarque-Cosson, Rutgers, and Vogenauer (n 4) 303–4.

[140] Malaurie, Aynès, and Stoffel-Munck (n 137) [438].

[141] Req 25 Feb 1835, Jurgen cited in Malaurie, Aynès, and Stoffel-Munck (n 137) [441].

[142] Malaurie, Aynès, and Stoffel-Munck (n 137) [440]. See also CA Colmar, 31 Dec 1850, De Loys c Dufay, DP 1853.2.164.

[143] Com 23 Dec 1968, Bull civ IV no 374, D 1969, SomRT 71 RTD com, 1969.555; Malaurie, Aynès, and Stoffel-Munck (n 137) [440].

held for instance that an obligation that was expressed as 'a purely moral undertaking of which no breach should be considered a breach of the remainder of the agreement' was sufficiently unequivocal as to be binding.[144]

Agreements in principle *(accords de principe)*, letters of intent (*lettres d'intention*), and agreements 'subject to contract' are generally not binding. As a relatively common feature of pre-contractual negotiations, where the parties remain free to withdraw,[145] they are usually intended to pave the way for further negotiations and ultimately the agreement of a binding contract. Only where, despite using these terms, the parties have in fact reached agreement on all essential matters such as the reciprocal performances and the duration and price of the contract have the courts found a binding contract to have been made.[146] Whether a party intends to be bound is a factual question for determination by a lower court.

## 2 Pre-contractual agreements

**Civil Code**

Art. 1123.—A pre-emption agreement is a contract by which a party undertakes that, in the event that he decides to enter into a contract, he will make the first proposal for that contract to the beneficiary of the pre-emption agreement.

Where a contract has been concluded with a third party in breach of a pre-emption agreement, the beneficiary of that agreement may obtain reparation of the loss that he has suffered. Where the third party knew of the existence of the pre-emption agreement and of the beneficiary's intention to take advantage of it, the beneficiary may also sue for nullity or may ask the court to substitute him for the third party in the contract that has been concluded.

The third party may give written notice to the beneficiary requiring him to confirm, within a period which the former fixes and which must be reasonable, the existence of a pre-emption agreement and whether he intends to take advantage of it.

Such a written notice must state that if he does not reply within that period, the beneficiary of the pre-emption agreement will no longer have the right to claim either to be substituted in any contract concluded with the third party, or nullity of the contract.

Art. 1124.—A unilateral promise is a contract by which one party, the promisor, grants another, the beneficiary, a right to have the option to conclude a contract

[144] Com 23 Jan 2007, no 05-13.189, Bull IV no 12, cited and translated in Beale, Fauvarque-Cosson, Rutgers, and Vogenauer (n 4) 319–20.

[145] Malaurie, Aynès, and Stoffel-Munck (n 137) [441].

[146] Com 4 Feb 1986, translated and noted in Beale, Fauvarque-Cosson, Rutgers, and Vogenauer (n 4) 330–1.

> whose essential elements are determined, and for the formation of which only the consent of the beneficiary is missing.
>
> Revocation of the promise during the period allowed to the beneficiary to exercise the option does not prevent the formation of the contract which was promised.
>
> A contract concluded in breach of a unilateral promise with a third party who knew of its existence, is a nullity.

In contrast with agreements in principle and letters of intent, which are generally not binding, pre-contractual agreements such as pre-emption agreements (*pactes de préférence*) and options to conclude a contract (*promesses unilatérales*) are enforceable. There was no provision in the 1804 Code for these forms of agreement. This was rectified in the reforms by the insertion of two new articles.[147]

### (a) Pre-emption agreements (*pactes de préférence*)

New article 1123 defines a pre-emption agreement as 'a contract by which a party undertakes that, in the event that he decides to enter into a contract, he will make the first proposal for that contract to the beneficiary of the pre-emption agreement'. The beneficiary has a right of first refusal to enter into the contract, in preference to, and priority over, others. Pre-emption agreements are often found in commercial leases, requiring the owner of the leased premises to offer the tenant the first right of refusal in the event that they decide to sell.

It is a breach of the pre-emption agreement for a contract to be concluded with a third party without the beneficiary being given an opportunity of first refusal. Any resulting losses are compensable in damages. The beneficiary can also claim the nullity of the contract or to be substituted for the third party in the contract[148] where the third party knew both of the existence of the pre-emption agreement and of their intention to exercise the pre-emption right. A distinction is therefore drawn between third parties depending on whether they are in good or bad faith, with nullity and substitution reserved for those who are in bad faith.[149] A beneficiary that chooses to be substituted for the third party must adopt the terms that have been agreed by the third party.[150]

[147] 'Report to the President' (n 25) 6.

[148] Paragraph 2 of article 1123 of the Civil Code.

[149] 'Report to the President' (n 25) 6; Ch Mixte 26 May 2006, no 03-19376, Bull mixt no 4, D 2006.1861, note P-Y Gautier, note D Mainguy, D 2006.2638, obs S Amrani-Mekki and B Fauvarque-Cosson, RTD civ 2006.550, obs J Mestre and B Fages, cited by Dissaux and Jamin (n 102) 28; Haftel (n 60).

[150] Deshayes, Genicon, and Laithier (n 7) 166–7 note that if the beneficiary does not wish to be bound by the terms negotiated by the third party and the promisor, they should seek nullity. The promisor will then have to give them priority on the terms agreed initially when they decide to enter into a contract.

There is some protection for third parties that suspect that a pre-emption agreement might exist and as a precaution wish to ascertain the true position. In paragraph 3 of article 1123 is a new mechanism[151] for giving written notice to the beneficiary requesting confirmation as to whether there is a pre-emption agreement and, if so, whether the beneficiary intends to avail themselves of it. The notice must specify a fixed period of time for a response, which has to be reasonable. It must also state that if a response is not received within that period then the beneficiary will lose the right to claim the nullity of the contract or substitution.[152] This should serve to reduce the uncertainty for the third party[153] and the risk of any pre-emption agreement being breached.

### (b) Unilateral promises to contract (*promesses unilatérales*)

The other form of pre-contractual agreement provided for in the Civil Code is the unilateral promise to contract. According to the definition in paragraph 1 of article 1124, this is a contract by which the beneficiary has an option to conclude a contract on terms that have already been agreed with the promisor. An example is a unilateral promise to purchase real property (*promesse unilatérale de vente*), by which the beneficiary has an exclusive right, exercisable for a defined period of time, to buy a property on agreed terms.

Where the unilateral promise is revoked during the period allowed for the beneficiary to exercise their right, thus breaching the agreement, this does not prevent the formation of the promised contract. It is open to the beneficiary to seek specific enforcement.[154] This ensures the effectiveness of the unilateral promise,[155] and draws a line under a controversial line of cases in which the *Cour de cassation* refused specific enforcement and awarded damages only where the beneficiary exercised their option after the withdrawal of the unilateral promise.[156] It had, however, attracted criticism, being described as 'a controversial decision which poisoned French contract law'.[157] This was on the basis that unilateral promises are fully constituted contracts[158] and, as such, should be specifically enforceable in the same way as any other contract that has been breached.[159]

[151] The *Cour de cassation* had previously refused to require a third party who had knowledge of a pre-emption agreement to investigate the intention of the beneficiary to exercise its pre-emptive right (Civ (3) 29 June 2010, no 09-68.110 RDC 2010, 30, obs E Savaux).

[152] Paragraph 4 of article 1123 of the Civil Code.

[153] 'Report to the President' (n 25) 6; Deshayes, Genicon, and Laithier (n 7) 170–1.

[154] 'Report to the President' (n 25) 6.

[155] Ibid. See also recently Civ (3) 23 June 2021, no 20-17.554 and Civ (3) 20 Oct 2021, no 20-18.514.

[156] Civ (3) 15 Dec 1993, no 91-10199 Bull civ I no 174 D 1994 Somm 230, obs O Tournafond D 1994.507, note F Bénac-Schmidt.

[157] Deshayes, Genicon, and Laithier (n 7) 179.

[158] See Chapter 10 and the section on specific enforcement, pp198–208.

[159] M Fabre-Magnan 'Le mythe de l'obligation de donner' RTD civ 1996.85, 101 ff; D Mazeaud JCP 1995.I.22366.

A contract that is concluded in breach of a unilateral promise with a third party who knows of the promise is null and void. There is no scope for the beneficiary to claim to be substituted to the position of the third party, in contrast with the knowing breach of a pre-emption agreement. The divergence has been attributed to substitution being unnecessary for unilateral promises since the beneficiary continues to be entitled to exercise the option.[160] This is in contrast with the beneficiary under a pre-emption agreement who has no right to contract but only a right of first refusal.[161]

## D Concluding Observations

The introduction of a new section of the Civil Code on contractual negotiation and formation helps to fulfil one of the main objectives of the reforms: that of making French contract law more up-to-date and intelligible. Long-standing principles that were developed in the cases over time have been codified, and the law is presented in a clear and accessible manner.[162] Aside, however, from these laudable achievements, the changes made in 2016 are relatively unremarkable.

From a comparative perspective, perhaps the most notable feature of the section is the formal recognition of pre-contractual good faith and a general duty to inform during negotiations. New articles 1112 and 1112-1 reflect a moral conception of the contract that is shared by many French lawyers. At its core is the idea that parties should refrain from behaving selfishly.[163] This has been openly acknowledged by the drafters of the reforms.[164] It has also been acknowledged by commentators. The new provisions serve 'contractual loyalty ... [but] correlatively restrict certainty of transactions' according to Aubert de Vincelles,[165] and reveal 'a specific conception of the contract ... [reflecting] the general strategic orientations of the reforms' in the words of Deshayes, Genicon, and Laithier.[166] This conception is 'solidarist, welfarist ... as opposed to market-individualistic'.[167]

The formal recognition of pre-contractual good faith and a duty to inform brings French law closer to a number of international contract law instruments. Article 1112 substantially reproduces article 2:301 of the PECL and article 2.1.15

160 Deshayes, Genicon, and Laithier (n 7) 191.

161 Ibid., 164 ff.

162 It has been argued by Aubert de Vincelles (n 30) 79 that mere codification has the disadvantage that many of the difficult questions that existed before the reforms remain and that this does not bring greater certainty.

163 Bénabent (n 72) [279]–[285]; Deshayes, Genicon, and Laithier (n 7) 79 and 102–3; see Sefton-Green (n 41) 68 for whom by recognizing this duty, French law is not purely moralistic but also implements market-efficiency considerations.

164 See 'Report to the President' (n 25).

165 Aubert de Vincelles (n 30) 79 ff.

166 Deshayes, Genicon, and Laithier (n 7) 102–3.

167 Sefton-Green (n 41) 60–1.

of the UNIDROIT Principles on good faith. A duty to inform can also be found at article 3.2.5 of the UNIDROIT principles and article 4:107 PECL, although in both cases it requires only that a party discloses information where non-disclosure would otherwise amount to fraud.

The new provisions are, however, in stark contrast with the position in England, where the relationship of parties in pre-contractual negotiations is not generally regarded as legally-protected.[168] They are free to withdraw, and to act in their own best interests, until a contract is formed. The risk of the negotiations being unsuccessful and a contract not being formed is shared, with the parties ordinarily unable to claim against one another if the risk materializes.

Unlike in France, the relationship of the negotiating parties is regarded as adversarial rather than cooperative.[169] Negotiating parties do not owe each other any general duties. There is therefore no general duty to negotiate in good faith, which is regarded with suspicion as vague and of uncertain content. Abusive behaviour is instead addressed through specific rules.[170]

There is similarly no general duty to disclose information, even where one party knows that the other is mistaken about the subject-matter of the contract. As Rix LJ explained in *ING Bank NV v Ros Roca SA*, 'silence is golden, for where there is no obligation to speak, silence gives no hostages to fortune'.[171] Generally no liability arises if a party does not disclose material information during negotiations. Only exceptionally in certain types of contract[172] or contractual relationships is disclosure required.[173] Beale, comparing English and French law, neatly summarizes the difference in the following way: 'English law can appear harsh and unfair [to French lawyers]... many English lawyers support this individualistic approach... what in France constitutes abusive behaviour is in England considered as necessary behaviour for business.'[174]

[168] For a summary of the English position, see J Cartwright, *Contract Law: An Introduction to the English Law of Contract for the Civil Lawyer* (3rd edn, Hart Publishing: Oxford, 2016) 74 ff.

[169] *Walford v Miles* [1992] 2 AC 128 (HL) 138 (Lord Ackner).

[170] *Interfoto Picture Library Ltd v Stiletto Visual Programmes Ltd* [1989] 1 QB 433 (CA) 439 (Bingham LJ). For example, misrepresentation, promissory estoppel, and fraud. For an analysis of the circumstances in which English law imposes liability for misconduct by a negotiating party, see J Cartwright and M Hesselink 'Introduction' in J Cartwright and M Hesselink (eds), *Precontractual Liability in European Private Law* (CUP: Cambridge, 2008) 1–18.

[171] *ING Bank NV v Ros Roca SA* [2012] 1 WLR 472 (CA) at [92].

[172] For example, in contracts of utmost good faith such as insurance contracts.

[173] For example, if the parties negotiating the contract are in a partnership.

[174] H Beale, 'La réforme du droit Français des contrats et le "droit européen des contrats": perspective de la Law Commission anglaise' RDC 2006.146.

# 5
# The Validity of the Contract

**Civil Code**[1]

Art. 1128.—The following are necessary for the validity of a contract:

1. the consent of the parties;
2. their capacity to contract;
3. content which is lawful and certain.

Art. 1178.—A contract which does not satisfy the conditions required for its validity is a nullity. Nullity must be declared by a court, unless the parties establish it by mutual agreement.

An annulled contract is deemed never to have existed.

Acts of performance which have been carried out give rise to restitution under the conditions provided by articles 1352 to 1352-9.

Irrespective of whether or not the contract is annulled, an injured party may claim reparation for any harm suffered under the conditions set out by the general law of extra-contractual liability.

Art. 1179.—Nullity is absolute where the rule that is violated has as its object the safeguard of the public interest.

It is relative where the rule that is violated has as its sole object the safeguard of a private interest.

Art. 1180.—Absolute nullity may be claimed by any person who can demonstrate an interest, as well as by the *ministère public*.

It may not be remedied by affirmation of the contract.

Art. 1181.—Relative nullity may be claimed only by the party that the legislation intends to protect.

It may be remedied by affirmation.

[1] 'Ordonnance no 2016-131 du 10 février 2016 portant réforme du droit des contrats, du régime général et de la preuve des obligations', JORF no 0035 of 11 February 2016. The Ordonnance was translated into English by J Cartwright, B Fauvarque-Cosson, and S Whittaker: <http://www.textes.justice.gouv.fr/art_pix/THE-LAW-OF-CONTRACT-2-5-16.pdf> (2016 version) and <http://www.textes.justice.gouv.fr/art_pix/Translationrevised2018final.pdf> (2018 version) accessed 1 September 2021. The translations of the new articles contained in this book are theirs.

*The New French Law of Contract*. Solène Rowan, Oxford University Press. 
DOI: 10.1093/oso/9780198810872.003.0005

Where more than one person has the right to bring an action for relative nullity, renunciation by one of them does not prevent the others from bringing proceedings.

Art. 1184.—Where a ground of nullity affects only one or more terms of the contract, it entails the nullity of the whole act only if this term or these terms constituted a decisive factor in the undertaking of the parties, or of one of them.

The contract is upheld where legislation deems a contract term not written, or where the purposes of the rule not followed requires it to be upheld.

New article 1128 of the Code sets three conditions for a contract to be valid. These are that: (1) the consent of the parties is genuine and free from defect; (2) the parties have the capacity to enter the contract; and (3) the content of the contract is lawful and certain. If one or more of these conditions is not met, the contract can be annulled.

The focus in this chapter is on the main grounds of non-fulfilment of these conditions in practice, which are defects in party consent, illegality, and uncertainty as to the content of the contract. In these areas as elsewhere in the Code, the 2016 reforms mainly codified established principles developed in past cases with the aim of enhancing clarity, certainty, and predictability.[2]

## A Defects Vitiating Consent

**Civil Code**

Art. 1130.—Mistake, fraud and duress vitiate consent where they are of such a nature that, without them, one of the parties would not have contracted or would have contracted on substantially different terms.

Their decisive character is assessed in the light of the person and of the circumstances in which consent was given.

Art. 1131.—Defects in consent are a ground of relative nullity of the contract.

Art. 1144.—In the case of mistake or fraud the period for bringing an action for nullity runs only from the day when they were discovered, and in the case of duress the period runs only from the day when it ceased.

A cardinal precept of French law is that the contract is founded on the mutual assent of the parties,[3] who can only be bound if their consent is real and free from defect. If it is not, the contract can be annulled. The reforms brought together the factors that

[2] F Ancel, B Fauvarque-Cosson, and J Gest, *Aux sources de la réforme du droit des contrats* (Dalloz: Paris, 2017) [24.21]–[24.40].

[3] Article 1101 of the Civil Code; see Chapter 3 and the section on definition of contract, pp 31–2.

can vitiate party consent—mistake (*erreur*), fraud (*dol*), and duress (*violence*)[4]—in a new section entitled 'Defects in Consent'. It begins with a common regime for all three vitiating factors in new articles 1130 and 1131. This is followed by a series of articles that deal with the defects sequentially: mistake is covered in articles 1132 to 1136, fraud in articles 1137 to 1139, and duress in articles 1140 to 1144.

## 1 Mistake (*erreur*)

> **Civil Code**
> Art. 1132.—Mistake of law or of fact, as long as it is not inexcusable, is a ground of nullity of the contract where it bears on the essential qualities of the act of performance owed or of the other contracting party.
>
> Art. 1133.—The essential qualities of the act of performance are those which have been expressly or impliedly agreed and which the parties took into consideration on contracting.
>
> Mistake is a ground of nullity whether it bears on the act of performance of one party or of the other. Acceptance of a risk about a quality of the act of performance rules out mistake in relation to this quality.
>
> Art. 1134.—Mistake about the essential qualities of the other contracting party is a ground of nullity only as regards contracts entered into on the basis of considerations personal to the party.
>
> Art. 1135.—Mistake about mere motive, extraneous to the essential qualities of the act of performance owed or of the other contracting party is not a ground of nullity unless the parties have expressly made it a decisive element of their consent.
>
> However, mistake about the motive for an act of generosity is a ground of nullity where, but for the mistake, the donor would not have made it.
>
> Art. 1136. A mistake as to value is not a ground of nullity where, in the absence of a mistake about the essential qualities of the act of performance, a contracting party makes only an inaccurate valuation of it.

Mistake (*erreur*) is not defined in the new Code but is commonly understood to mean an erroneous assumption of law[5] or fact. It has been described by one commentator as 'a false image of reality'.[6]

[4] Article 1130 of the Civil Code.
[5] See, for example, Civ (3) 24 May 2000, Bull civ III no 114, D 2001 Somm 1135, note D Mazeaud, JCP 2000.II.10494, note C Duvert, RTD civ 2000.824, note J Mestre and B Fages.
[6] C Aubert de Vincelles 'Validity of Contract: Dol, Erreur and Obligation d'Information' in J Cartwright and S Whittaker (eds), *The Code Napoléon Rewritten: French Contract Law after the 2016 Reforms* (Hart Publishing: Oxford, 2017) 79, 94.

Not all mistakes vitiate consent. In order to do so, a mistake must be sufficiently serious to justify the contract being set aside. This is intended to achieve a balance between substantive fairness (*justice contractuelle*), which prevents a party from being bound where their consent is not real, and the security and stability of transactions, which would be threatened if contracts could easily be undermined without regard to the interests of the other party.[7]

A mistake is considered to be sufficiently serious and therefore to justify the nullity of the contract where several cumulative requirements are met. These are that: the mistake bears on the 'essential qualities' of the subject-matter of the contract; it is decisive to the consent of the mistaken party so that, without it, they would not have contracted or would have contracted on substantially different terms; it is 'excusable'; and it does not relate to an assumed risk.

### (a) Mistake as to 'essential qualities'

#### *(i) The definition of 'essential qualities'*

The first requirement—set out in article 1132—is that one or both parties is under a misapprehension as to 'the essential qualities of the act of performance owed or of the other contracting party'.[8] To be essential, a quality must have been expressly or impliedly agreed and taken into consideration by the parties when entering the contract. It therefore has to be part of the subject-matter of the contract.[9] This will be so where the quality is 'linked to the very nature, substance and use'[10] of the contract's subject-matter or inherent in the contract. It also suffices that the quality is fundamentally important to the parties or they agree that it is so.

Examples of qualities that have been held to be essential include the authenticity of a work of art,[11] the suitability for development of a piece of land,[12] and the use[13] to which the goods or land can be put. In the well-known 'Poussin' cases,[14] for example, a painting was sold at auction for a relatively low price after the sellers had

[7] M Fabre-Magnan, *Droit des obligations, Contrat et engagement unilatéral* (4th edn, PUF: Paris, 2016) [337] cited and translated in H Beale, B Fauvarque-Cosson, J Rutgers, and S Vogenauer (eds), *Cases, Materials and Text on Contract Law, Ius Commune Casebooks for the Common Law of Europe* (3rd edn, Hart Publishing: Oxford, 2019) 485; Aubert de Vincelles (n 6) 94.

[8] This replaces the 'substance of the thing'. Paragraph 1 of old article 1110 provided that 'mistake is a ground of nullity of the contract where it bears on the very substance of the thing which is its subject-matter' (translation by Aubert de Vincelles (n 6) 95).

[9] Civ (3) 22 Oct 2013, pourvoi no 12-26.047, JCP 1014.115, note J Ghestin.

[10] O Deshayes, T Genicon, and Y-M Laithier, *Réforme du droit des contrats, du régime général et de la preuve des obligations* (2nd edn, LexisNexis: Paris, 2018) 218; G Chantepie and M Latina, *La réforme du droit des obligations, Commentaire théorique et pratique dans l'ordre du Code civil* (2nd edn, Dalloz: Paris, 2018) [305].

[11] Even where the mistake is made by the seller: (*L'affaire du Poussin*) Civ (1) 22 Feb 1978, D 1978.601; Civ (1) 13 Dec 1983, D 1984.340, note J-L Aubert; (*L'affaire du Verrou de Fragonard*) Civ (1) 25 May 1992, Bull civ I no 165.

[12] Civ (3) 21 June 1995, *Contrats, Conc, Consomm*, 1995, no 197; Civ (3) 28 Jan 2009, JCP 2009.I.138 no 16, note Y-M Serinet.

[13] Civ 27 April 1953, D 1953.444.

[14] Civ 13 Dec 1983 no 82-12237, Bull civ I no 293, JCP 1984.II.20186; CA Versailles 7 Jan 1987, D 1987.485, note J Ghestin.

been advised by the auctioneer's expert that it was the work of the Carracci school and not Nicolas Poussin, an artist of much greater renown. It was later acquired by the Louvre and exhibited as a Poussin, albeit there were differing views as to whether that was correct. The contract of sale was annulled for mistake because, at the time of the auction, the sellers had mistakenly believed that the painting definitely was not a Poussin whereas this was actually a possibility. Its artistic authorship was an essential quality.

*(ii) Mistake as to the other party*

The identity and characteristics of a contracting party can also be an essential quality.[15] Factors such as their profession, knowledge, experience, and creditworthiness can in certain contexts be decisive to the consent of the other. For example, artists and lawyers are often retained on the basis of their talent or expertise.

Where such a mistake occurs, the contract can be annulled. This is illustrated by a case relating to an arbitration settlement in which it became apparent that the arbitrator, a practising lawyer, had represented one of the parties to the arbitration in another context.[16] Since the other party had mistakenly believed that the arbitrator was independent, the *Cour de cassation* annulled the settlement. In another case it was held that there was an actionable mistake where a party entered into a contract erroneously believing the counterparty to be a business that specialized in publishing magazines when in fact it was a sole trader with no relevant experience.[17]

*(iii) Mistake as to motive*

In contrast, a mistake in a party's motives for entering a contract will generally not suffice. Motives are not an essential quality of the act of performance and ordinarily do not form part of the contract.[18] This serves to uphold legal certainty and safeguard the interests of the other party, which would be easily undermined if private reasoning that is inherently subjective could be relied upon to defeat the contract. There is therefore no actionable mistake where a family buys a house near to a school in the mistaken belief that doing so would automatically entitle their child to admission. The sale cannot be annulled as the mistake does not relate to an essential characteristic of the property but merely the motive for buying it.

There is an exception where a motive that is decisive to one or both parties has been brought within the contractual sphere and made an essential feature of the contract.[19] In the well-known 'Villa Jacqueline' case,[20] a villa with advertised grounds of 7,800 square metres was bought with the intention of subdividing the

[15] Article 1132; CA Rouen 4 March 1969, JCP 1969.II.15911, RTD civ 1969.762, note Y Loussouarn; Deshayes, Genicon, and Laithier (n 10) 222.

[16] Civ 16 July 1964, Gaz Pal 1964.2.371.

[17] St Denis, 6 Oct 1989, JCP 1990.II.21504.

[18] Civ (3) 24 April 2003, Bull civ III no 82, D 2004.450, note S Chassagnard, JCP 2003.II.10135, note R Wintgen, RDC 2003.42, note D Mazeaud, RTD civ 2003.699, note J Mestre and B Fages.

[19] Article 1135 of the Civil Code.

[20] Civ 23 Nov 1931 DP 1932.I.129, note L Josserand.

grounds into lots for sale. The sellers knew that this was a decisive consideration for buyers. In fact, the grounds were much smaller at 5,119 square metres, which rendered the scheme impractical. Finding that the motive of the buyer was essential and had been incorporated into the contract, the *Cour de cassation* annulled the contract. The size of the grounds was 'an essential property of the subject-matter of the contract' which had been entered into under a mistake that 'went to the very essence of the thing which was the subject-matter of the contract'.[21] In contrast, it was held in another case that there was no actionable mistake where a party entered into a contract to obtain tax advantages which did not materialize.[22] Even though the motive was known to the other party, it was not brought 'into the contractual sphere, elevating it to a condition of the contract'.[23]

Another exception relates to what are referred to in article 1135 as 'acts of generosity'. These are acts which include contracts in which performance moves from one party to the other but without any reciprocal performance. The paradigm is contracts of gift. A testamentary donation made in the mistaken belief that the beneficiary was the natural son of the donor,[24] and another made on the misapprehension that the donor had no heirs,[25] were therefore nullified for mistake. The basis for the exception is that a party who receives something but gives nothing in return is regarded as less deserving of legal certainty.[26]

#### *(iv) Mistake as to value*

A mistake as to the value of the subject-matter of the contract due to an erroneous valuation is also not actionable. There can therefore be no annulment of the contract where the seller has sold too cheaply or the buyer has bought too dearly. Its substantive content and economic balance are outside of the purview of the court. This is reflected in new article 1168 of the Code, which provides that 'in synallagmatic contracts, a lack of equivalence in the acts of performance of the parties is not a ground of nullity of the contract, unless legislation provides otherwise'. For a mistake as to value to result in annulment would contravene this provision.[27]

A distinction is drawn in article 1136 between erroneous valuations that are based on accurate information, for which there is no relief, and those that are based on a mistake as to an essential quality that in turn affects the value, which can lead to annulment. This is justified on the basis that, in the latter case, the error in the valuation is the direct consequence of a mistake as to an essential quality of the subject-matter.

[21] Translation in Beale, Fauvarque-Cosson, Rutgers, and Vogenauer (eds) (n 7) 526–7.

[22] Civ (1) 13 Feb 2001, Bull civ I no 31, JCP 2001.I.330 [5], note J Rochfeld, RTD civ 2001.352, note J Mestre and B Fages; Civ (3) 24 April 2003, no 01-17.458, Bull civ III no 82, RTD civ 2003.699, note J Mestre and B Fages.

[23] Ibid.

[24] Req 17 March 1812, D 1826.1.367.

[25] CA Paris 9 Feb 1867, S 1867.2.139.

[26] F Terré, P Simler, Y Lequette, and F Chénedé, *Droit civil: les obligations* (12th edn, Dalloz: Paris, 2018) [287]; Deshayes, Genicon, and Laithier (n 10) 226–7.

[27] Deshayes, Genicon, and Laithier (n 10) 229.

It has therefore been held that, where the seller of a painting was mistaken as to the identity of the painter and in consequence sold too cheaply, the sale can be annulled. The attribution of the painting was an essential quality of the subject-matter of the contract.[28] This was also true of a mistake as to the value of a piece of agricultural land which was thought to be cultivable immediately but in fact could not be.[29] In contrast, there was no actionable mistake where, despite having been provided with all relevant information, a person bought a life insurance policy that turned out to be financially disadvantageous.[30]

### (b) The mistake must be decisive

The second requirement is that the mistake is decisive to the consent of the mistaken party. In other words, but for the mistake, the mistaken party would not have entered into the contract or would have done so on substantially different terms.[31]

The decisive character of the mistake is assessed at the time that the contract was entered into and 'in the light of the person and of the circumstances in which consent was given'.[32] By 'the person' is meant the mistaken party. Relevant factors can include their age, profession, knowledge, personal background, experience, and expectations. As Deshayes, Genicon, and Laithier have explained, the court 'must dive into the intimate and personal psychology of the victim, which reflects … the traditional attachment of French law to the internal will (*volonté interne*) … It is forbidden to use the abstract average and normally diligent man as a reference.'[33]

On this basis, the *Cour de cassation* has refused to annul the employment contract of a person who had misleadingly used someone else's identity documentation in order to obtain the role where he would have been hired even using his own documentation.[34] The same verdict was reached in respect of a mistake as to the nationality of the counterparty. It could not be proven that, with knowledge of his true nationality, the mistaken party would have declined to enter into the contract.[35]

### (c) Inexcusable mistake and assumed risk

Two further requirements for nullifying a contract, which are often characterized as defences to a claim in mistake,[36] are set out in articles 1132 and 1133: the mistake must be excusable and must not relate to a known risk.

[28] As illustrated by the 'Poussin' cases considered earlier: CA Versailles 7 Jan 1987, D 1987.485, note J Ghestin.

[29] Soc 4 May 1956, D 1957.313, note P Malaurie. See also TGI Fontainebleau 9 Dec 1970, D 1971.89, note J Ghestin, and Com 7 Feb 1995, D 1996.5, note R Blasselle, RTD civ 1995.878, note J Mestre.

[30] Civ (2) 8 Oct 2009, no 08-18928, JCP 2009.574 no 12, note Y-M Serinet, RDC 2010.39, note T Genicon.

[31] Paragraph 1 of article 1130 of the Civil Code.

[32] Paragraph 2 of article 1130 of the Civil Code.

[33] Deshayes, Genicon, and Laithier (n 10) 210.

[34] Req 17 Jan 1911, DP 1911.5.61.

[35] Civ (1) 4 Jan 1980 Juriclass civ, fasc 1110.

[36] Deshayes, Genicon, and Laithier (n 10) 213.

*(i) Excusable mistake*

Where the mistaken party had enough information to avoid the mistake or could have done so without undue effort, they are regarded as having failed to take adequate precautions and therefore as negligent. The mistake is 'inexcusable' and cannot be the basis of a claim for nullity.[37]

Whether a mistake is excusable is assessed having regard to the characteristics of the mistaken party. Their age, profession, and area of competence or expertise[38] are all relevant. In one case, an art expert purchased a painting that was supposedly by a famous Russian artist. It was later shown to be a forgery. The sale was not annulled because the buyer's mistake was found to have been inexcusable. As an expert specializing in Russian art who had been allowed to inspect the painting before the auction, he had the expertise and opportunity to form his own view on its authenticity. The mistake owed to a failure in his assessment.[39]

*(ii) Assumed risk*

There is no mistake where a risk known to both parties relating to a quality of the subject-matter subsequently materializes. It is assumed by entry into the contract. As paragraph 3 of article 1133 states, 'acceptance of a risk about a quality of the act of performance rules out mistake in relation to this quality'. This is illustrated by the well-known 'Verrou de Fragonard' case,[40] in which a painting that was sold at auction in 1933 as 'attributed to Fragonard', a famous painter, was confirmed by experts in the 1970s to be authentic. On this basis, the seller's heirs sought to annul the contract of sale, arguing that the uncertainty as to the authenticity of the painting at the time of sale conveyed in the words 'attributed to' had been shown to be mistaken. Dismissing the claim, the *Cour de cassation* affirmed the Paris Court of Appeal's decision that, by these words, the auction house had identified that the painting might or might not be a Fragonard. By proceeding with the sale, each party had accepted that risk. It was therefore not open to the seller to complain when the risk materialized.

## (d) Whose mistake?

The mistake can be unilateral, that is, made by one party alone. It need not be shared by the other. However, both parties must know of the essential importance of the quality to which the mistake relates. What must be common to the parties is the knowledge that a particular feature was essential, not the mistake itself.[41]

[37] Article 1132 of the Civil Code; Deshayes, Genicon, and Laithier (n 10) 215.

[38] The mistaken party's status as a professional or expert does not necessarily prevent the mistake from being excusable: Civ (1) 8 Dec 2009, no 08-16.471, LDC 2010 no 68.13, note L Gallou; Civ (1) 14 Dec 2004, Bull civ I no 326, JCP 2005.I.141 no 1, note Y-M Serinet, RTD civ 2005.123, note J Mestre and B Fages.

[39] Civ (1) 9 April 2015 no 13-24772, D 2016.568. See also Soc 3 July 1990, Bull civ V no 329 D 1990.IR 1999, RTD civ 1991.316, note J Mestre.

[40] Civ (1) 24 March 1987, no 85-15736.

[41] Terré, Simler, Lequette, and Chénedé (n 26) [281].

The mistake can be made by either party. In a contract for the sale of goods, for example, it is not only a mistake of the buyer that can be actionable. So too can a mistake of the seller, for example the unwitting sale of a painting at an undervalue without realizing that it is the work of a famous painter.[42] This avoids a situation where 'those who have superior knowledge strip those who do not'.[43] Usually, however, seller mistakes are concerned with the value of performance or inexcusable. They therefore rarely give rise to nullity.

### (e) Remedies for mistake

The remedy for mistake—nullity—is also the remedy for all defects in consent.[44] Its effect is that the contract is deemed never to have existed.[45] There is also a right of restitution in respect of acts of performance which have already been carried out. This is set out in new articles 1352 to 1352-9.

There are two forms of nullity. The one that results from defects in consent is referred to in article 1130 as 'relative nullity'. According to new article 1179, relative nullity is available where 'the rule that is violated has as its sole object the safeguarding of a private interest'. 'Absolute nullity', in contrast, results from the violation of a rule that 'has as its object the safeguarding of the public interest'.[46] This distinction is relevant to who can seek the remedy. Relative nullity 'may be claimed only by the party that the legislation intends to protect [and] may be remedied by affirmation'.[47] A claim for absolute nullity is more widely available. It can be made 'by any person who can demonstrate an interest, as well as by the *ministère public* (the state)'.[48] Nullity for defects in consent can therefore only be sought by the party whose consent has been vitiated. This reflects an aim of confining the protection to the private interests of the parties.[49]

Where harm is caused to the mistaken party by a mistake that was induced by the negligence of the other party, extra-contractual damages can be claimed under article 1240 of the Civil Code in addition to,[50] or instead of,[51] nullity.[52] Damages will be awarded instead of nullity, for example, where the mistaken party would have entered into the contract despite the mistake but on different terms.

[42] Civ (1) 22 February 1978 D 1978. 601, note P Malinvaud; Civ (1) 28 Oct 2015, no 14-17893, *Contrats, Conc, Consomm*, 2016 comm 1, note L Leveneur.

[43] Terre, Simler, Lequette, and Chénedé (n 26) [283] citing J Ghestin and Malinvaud, D 1973.413. But see Chantepie and Latina (n 10) [307] for objections to this rule.

[44] Article 1130 of the Civil Code.

[45] Article 1178 of the Civil Code.

[46] Article 1179 of the Civil Code.

[47] Article 1181 of the Civil Code.

[48] Article 1180 of the Civil Code.

[49] 'Report to the President of the Republic relating to Ordonnance no 2016–131 of 10 February 2016 on the reform of contract law, the general regime and proof of obligations', JORF no 0035 of 11 February 2016, 16.

[50] Compensation for pure economic loss is available under article 1240; Civ (3) 9 July 2013 no 12-13.327, JCP 2014.115, note J Ghestin.

[51] Civ (1) 12 Nov 2009, no 08-14.563.

[52] Paragraph 4 of article 1178 of the Civil Code.

## 2 Fraud (*dol*)

**Civil Code**

Art. 1137.—Fraud is an act of a party in obtaining the consent of the other by scheming or lies.

The intentional concealment by one party of information, where he knows its decisive character for the other party, is also fraud.

**(2018 addition)**

*Nevertheless, it is not fraud for a party not to reveal to the other contracting party his assessment of the value of the act of performance.*

Art. 1138.—Fraud is equally established where it originates from the other party's representative, a person who manages his affairs, his employee or one standing surety for him.

It is also established where it originates from a third party in collusion.

Art. 1139.—A mistake induced by fraud is always excusable. It is a ground of nullity even if it bears on the value of the act of performance or on a party's mere motive.

The second defect in consent addressed in the Code is fraud. This involves dishonest behaviour. It requires that one party, as a result of the deceit of the other, enters into a contract under a false apprehension. The victim makes a mistake but not of their own accord. It is induced by the fraud, which vitiates their consent.[53]

Four conditions must be met for a claim in fraud: there is a deceptive act; it is intentional; it is perpetrated by the other contracting party; and it is decisive in the consent of the victim.

### (a) The deceptive act

As to the first requirement, what is and is not a fraud is explained in article 1137. This provides that the deceptive act can take the form of scheming (*manoeuvres*), lies, or concealment. Scheming is calculating behaviour that involves pretence (*mise en scène*). Some examples from the decided cases are a garage owner conveying a misleading picture of a used car by falsifying registration documents and the odometer reading;[54] feigning pregnancy to extort money from the supposed father;[55] and the concealment of a will that bequeaths property with a view to entering into an agreement with the beneficiary to obtain a share of the inheritance.[56]

[53] Terré, Simler, Lequette, and Chénedé (n 26) [295].
[54] Com 19 Dec 1961, D 1962.240; Civ (1) 31 Jan 1979, D 1979.IR288.
[55] Civ 17 April 1882, DP 82.5.163.
[56] Lyon 28 Nov 1932 S 1932.2.201, note Rodière, confirmed by Req 23 May 1933, DH 1933, 361.

A lie is a positive misleading statement. There is fraud by lying, for example, where the director of a bank certifies the good financial health of a customer even though its account shows significant indebtedness and is about to be closed for that very reason.[57] Another example is a false declaration of good health in order to obtain a lower insurance premium.[58]

Concealment includes fraud by silence, that is, dishonest non-disclosure. Having been well-established in the pre-reform cases despite not being referred to in the 1804 Code, this is now expressly recognized in the new Code. This formalizes what had come to be 'the most common form of pre-contractual fraud in the case law'.[59] Some examples are the concealment from the buyer of a house that the water in the well that supplied the house was not potable;[60] concealment that a house was in an area susceptible to flooding; and the omission by the seller of a business to disclose that his wife owned a competing business in the same neighbourhood.[61]

### (b) Intention to deceive

The second requirement is that the perpetrator of the fraud must intend to deceive the other party.[62] Where the perpetrator is themselves mistaken, there can be no intention to deceive and therefore no fraud.[63] Negligence is not enough.[64] Any claim for annulment or damages based on negligence should be made on the ground of mistake. It was therefore held that a settlement between a debtor and creditors in his bankruptcy could not be annulled for a careless failure by the debtor to disclose that some years previously he had bought two properties jointly with another person.[65]

An intention to deceive is a defining feature of fraud. It does not depend upon there being an anterior obligation to provide information. As such, it is distinguishable from breach of the obligation to inform in article 1112-1, which can only be made out where such an obligation exists.[66] Concealment can similarly be established irrespective of whether there is an anterior obligation to inform.[67] Where a non-disclosure is intentional and decisive to the consent of the other party, it will be fraudulent. A breach of the duty to inform in article 1112-1 can but will

57 Com 7 Feb 1983, Bill civ IV no 50 D 1984.IR 84.

58 Civ (1) 7 Oct 1998, JCP 1998.II.10185.

59 Deshayes, Genicon, and Laithier (n 10) 233.

60 Civ (3) 10 Feb 1999, Juris-Data no 1999-000659.

61 Com 20 June 1995, D 1995.IR.211. See also Civ (3) 29 Nov 2000, Bull civ III no 182; Civ (1) 10 May 1989, JCP 1989.II.21363, note D Legeais.

62 Article 1137 of the Civil Code.

63 Civ (1) 25 June 2015, nos 14-18.486 and 14-19.786.

64 Com 9 Feb 2016, no 14-23210, D 2016.420.

65 Req 27 Jan 1874, DP 1874.1.352.

66 See the section on the duty to provide information in Chapter 4, pp 63–6.

67 This is clear from the 'Report to the President' (n 49) 16 which states that 'concealment is codified (paragraph 2 of article 1137) without being subordinated to the existence of the obligation of information of article 1112-1, the emphasis being on the intention to deceive'. This contrasts with the position before the reforms: Civ (3) 9 Oct 2012 no 11-23869, D 2013.391, note S Amrani-Mekki and M Mekki; Civ (1) 4 June 2009 no 08-13480, D 2010.230, note S Amrani-Mekki.

not necessarily amount to concealment. It can also be negligent and unintentional, which does not amount to fraud. Articles 1137 and 1112-1 therefore do not correspond exactly,[68] with each having its own requirements.

### (c) The perpetrator of the fraud

The third requirement—set out in article 1138—is that the fraud originates from the party to the contract or his 'representative, a person who manages his affairs, his employee or one standing surety for him'.[69] It is not enough that the fraud is perpetrated by a third party, unless they have colluded in the fraud with the contracting party.[70] In one case, the *Cour de cassation* refused to nullify a guarantee in favour of a bank on the basis that the fraud was committed by the debtor, who was not a party to the guarantee, and there had been no collusion between the debtor and the guarantor.[71] It is, however, open to the victim of the fraud to seek extra-contractual damages from a fraudulent third party under new article 1240, pursuant to which 'any human action whatsoever which causes harm to another creates an obligation in the person by whose fault it occurred to make reparation for it'.

### (d) Decisive provoked mistake

The fourth and final requirement comprises two limbs: first, the deceptive act must have induced the other party to make a mistake; second, the mistake must have been decisive to their consent. Where there is fraud, the restrictions on the type of mistake that can vitiate consent in articles 1132 to 1136 do not apply. It does not matter that the mistake is inexcusable or that it relates to the value of the subject-matter or the motives of the parties. This is spelled out in article 1139. Mistakes that are induced by fraud can therefore give rise to nullity, even if naïve, negligent, or unrelated to the essential qualities of the act of performance.[72] In some circumstances, this can make obtaining relief for fraud easier than for mistake.[73]

There is an exception for non-disclosure of a valuation of the act of performance. According to paragraph 3 of article 1137, this cannot give rise to a claim in fraud. The exception is rooted in the unwillingness of French courts to interfere with the substantive content and economic balance of the contract, as embodied in new article 1168.[74] It is, however, confined to concealment and does not extend

[68] Deshayes, Genicon, and Laithier (n 10) 233–9; Terré, Simler, Lequette, and Chénedé (n 26) [300].

[69] Paragraph 1 of article 1138 of the Civil Code.

[70] Paragraph 2 of article 1138 of the Civil Code.

[71] See, for example, Civ (1) 26 Jan 1977, no 75-13.920, Bull civ I no 52.

[72] Civ (3) 21 Feb 2001, Bull civ III no 20, RTD civ 2001.353; see also Civ (1) 22 June 2004, RTD civ 2004.503, note J Mestre and B Fages; Civ (3) 12 Oct 2017, *Contrats, Conc, Consomm*, 2018, no 5; Deshayes, Genicon, and Laithier (n 10) 244.

[73] Aubert de Vincelles (n 6) 103.

[74] See above pp 90–1 on mistake as to value and Civ (1) 3 May 2000 Bull civ I no 131, JCP 2001. II.10510, note Jamin, Défrenois no 19, 1106, note Mazeaud and note Delebecque (*affaire des photographies de Baldus*); see Chapter 7 on unfair terms.

to mistakes as to value that are induced by positive acts such as lies and scheming, which can form the basis of a claim in fraud.[75]

The broad availability of relief for deliberately induced mistakes has been explained on the basis that an intention to deceive is particularly reprehensible and important to deter. This has however been criticized in academic commentary. Aubert de Vincelles, for instance, has argued that it is over-protective and allows the victim to be negligent and imprudent, especially in the context of fraudulent non-disclosure, where a business or professional is entitled to relief despite failing to carry out even the most 'elementary checks'.[76] She cites by way of illustration a case in which the buyer of a property and hotel business sought to nullify the sale for fraud because he was unaware that the hotel could not open by reason of not having the requisite authorization and a breach of health and safety rules. Relief was initially refused by the Aix-en-Provence Court of Appeal on the basis that the mistake was inexcusable 'given the professional character of the operation and the simple checks that the purchaser could have made with the seller which would have revealed the precise administrative situation of the business'. However, this decision was quashed by the *Cour de cassation* on the ground that 'fraudulent non-disclosure … always makes the mistake excusable'.[77] Aubert de Vincelles argues that such an outcome is undesirable, not all induced mistakes should be excusable and too much importance is given in the new Code to deceptive intent.[78]

As with other defects in consent, article 1130 requires that a mistake induced by fraud is decisive to the consent of the victim. It must be proven that, without the mistake, they would have contracted on substantially different terms or not at all.[79] The decisiveness of the fraud is assessed at the date on which the contract was entered, without regard to subsequent events. Account can, however, be taken of personal characteristics of the victim such as their age, level of intelligence, and profession, which is intended to protect weak and naïve parties who are more susceptible to scams.

### (e) Remedies

In common with other defects in consent, the victim of a fraud can claim that the contract is a nullity under article 1131. Since *dol* is an extra-contractual fault, the victim can also claim extra-contractual damages for loss. This is in addition to, or instead of, nullity.[80]

75 Chantepie and Latina (n 10) [327]–[327-1].
76 Aubert de Vincelles (n 6) 103 ff.
77 Civ (3) 21 Feb 2001, no 98-20.817, Bull civ III.20, D 2001.2702, note D Mazeaud.
78 Aubert de Vincelles (n 6) 103 ff.
79 Article 1130 and paragraph 1 of article 1137 of the Civil Code.
80 Civ (1) 14 Mar 1972, D 1972.653, note J Ghestin.

## 3 Duress (*violence*)

**Civil Code**

Art. 1140.—There is duress where one party contracts under the influence of a constraint which makes him fear that his person or his wealth, or those of his near relatives, might be exposed to considerable harm.

Art. 1141.—A threat of legal action does not constitute duress, except where the legal process is deflected from its proper purpose or where it is invoked or exercised in order to obtain a manifestly excessive advantage.

Art. 1142.—Duress is a ground of nullity regardless of whether it has been applied by the other party or by a third party.

**(2016 version)**

*Art. 1143.—There is also duress where one contracting party exploits the other's state of dependence and obtains an undertaking to which the latter would not have agreed in the absence of such constraint, and gains from it a manifestly excessive advantage.*

**(2018 version)**

Art. 1143.—There is also duress where one contracting party exploits the other's state of dependence in relation to him to obtain an undertaking to which the latter would not have agreed in the absence of such constraint, and gains from it a manifestly excessive advantage.

The third vitiating factor, *violence*, has never received significant attention in French law. It has been described as the 'defect in consent that is invoked least often in practice'[81] and one which 'has not enthused many academics either'.[82] However, this did not deter the drafters of the reforms, who made a number of changes in this area.

There is *violence*— 'duress' in the English translation of the Code used in this book[83]—where the victim enters into a contract as a result of one of two forms of illegitimate conduct on the part of the other party or a third party. These are the exertion of illegitimate pressure (articles 1140 to 1142) and the exploitation of some dependence on that party (article 1143). In both cases, the consent of the victim is neither free nor real. As with the other defects in consent, the remedy is annulment of the contract.

[81] Fabre-Magnan (n 7) [403].

[82] C Kennefick '*Violence* in the Reformed Napoleonic Code: The Surprising Survival of Third Parties' in J Cartwright and S Whittaker (eds), *The Code Napoléon Rewritten: French Contract Law after the 2016 Reforms* (Hart Publishing: Oxford, 2017) 109, 109.

[83] See the translation into English by J Cartwright, B Fauvarque-Cosson, and S Whittaker: <http://www.textes.justice.gouv.fr/art_pix/THE-LAW-OF-CONTRACT-2-5-16.pdf> (2016 version) and <http://www.textes.justice.gouv.fr/art_pix/Translationrevised2018final.pdf> (2018 version) accessed 1 September 2021.

### (a) Illegitimate pressure

Under article 1140, consent is vitiated where an illegitimate threat induces the victim to enter a contract out of fear that significant harm would otherwise be inflicted on his person or wealth, or those of their near relatives.

#### *(i) Illegitimate threats*

The threat must cause the victim to enter into the contract as the lesser of two evils. Both physical and economic threats are actionable.

A threat to exercise a right or bring legal proceedings is not duress unless there is an abuse of right.[84] It is an abuse to exercise a right for a purpose other than that for which it was conferred or in order to obtain a manifestly excessive advantage.[85] This was the case where a shoplifter agreed to pay 5,000 French francs as the price for the owner of the shop not to bring proceedings against her. This was much more than was necessary to compensate the loss caused by the theft, which was less than 3,000 francs.[86]

#### *(ii) The parties involved in duress*

Whether or not a threat amounts to duress is assessed by reference to the characteristics of the victim rather than the standard of a person of reasonable firmness and robustness. For example, where the victim was a widow who lived on her own and was inexperienced in business, these factors were all relevant in a finding that she had been illegitimately coerced to renounce her right to bid in an auction for the house in which she had always lived.[87]

The other contracting party does not necessarily have to be the maker of the threat; it can come from a third party.[88] This is justified as being necessary to protect the consensual basis of the contract. After all, a threat can be no less potent when made by a third party rather than by a contracting party.[89] It has, however, been criticized for undermining legal certainty (*sécurité juridique*)[90] and inconsistency with the rule in article 1138 that only a contracting party, not a third party, can commit an actionable fraud.[91] Some consider that the same rule should apply in respect of *violence*.[92]

[84] Civ (3) 17 Jan 1984, Bull civ I no 13; Paris, 12 Jan 2000, JCP 2000.II.10443; Civ (1) 3 Nov 1959, D 1960.2.1887, note G Holleaux RTD civ 1960.295, note by H and L Mazeaud; Soc 8 1984, no 82-14816, Bull civ V no 423.

[85] Article 1141 of the Civil Code.

[86] Cited in Beale, Fauvarque-Cosson, Rutgers, and Vogenauer (n 7) 607: CA Paris 31 May 1966, Gaz Pal 1966.2.194, RTD civ 1967.147, note J Chevallier.

[87] Civ (1) 3 Nov 1959 D 1960.2.187, translated in Beale, Fauvarque-Cosson, Rutgers, and Vogenauer (n 7) 606–7.

[88] Article 1142 of the Civil Code.

[89] Kennefick (n 82) 109.

[90] Ibid., 113–16; Chantepie and Latina (n 10) [334].

[91] Ibid.

[92] Chantepie and Latina (n 10) [334].

### (b) Abuse of a state of dependence

The second form of duress recognized in the Code—in new article 1143—is the abuse by one party of the other's dependence on them in order to obtain a manifestly excessive advantage. Unlike with the first form of duress, this does not involve illegitimate threats made by a person. The pressure on the victim is instead caused by external events that result in the victim being dependent on the abusive party and impelled to enter a contract with them to which they would not otherwise have agreed. To give two examples, a disadvantageous contract of employment might be entered by a person who is in severe financial difficulty. Or a driver might agree to a contract for roadside assistance at an exorbitant price immediately after a motorway accident where there is no other option, such that there is no competition which the roadside assistance provider exploits.

This was a new addition to the Code and was described by the drafters in the 'Report to the President of the Republic' as 'one of the essential innovations'.[93] In reality it had already been established in cases prior to the reforms. There was, however, a degree of tension with article 1111 of the 1804 Code, which envisaged only duress in the form of illegitimate threats made by a person. It did not refer to a party gaining a manifestly excessive advantage by exploiting the dependence of the other.[94] Now there is formal recognition of, and a clear framework for, *violence* being caused by the impersonal forces of circumstances.

There are three conditions that must be fulfilled for abuse of a state of dependence to be made out: first, a state of dependence; second, the constraint arising from the dependence is decisive to the consent of the victim in entering the contract; and third, the other party has exploited the dependence to gain a manifestly excessive advantage.

#### *(i) State of dependence*

A state of dependence arises where a party has lost autonomy in relation to the other party to the contract. It can be financial or psychological.[95] As the Report to the President explained, 'all situations of dependence are targeted'.[96] It is not necessary that the victim is objectively weak or vulnerable (for example, through old age).[97] What is important is that there is dependence on the other party. The requirement that the dependence relates specifically to the other party was added in 2018 during the parliamentary debates in respect of the ratifying law. In the 2016 version, the requirement of dependence was expressed in the abstract, which came to be viewed as uncertain and too broad.[98]

[93] 'Report to the President' (n 49) 18.
[94] Kennefick (n 82) 109–10.
[95] Terré, Simler, Lequette, and Chénedé (n 26) [321].
[96] 'Report to the President' (n 49) 16.
[97] This is the example given by Deshayes, Genicon, and Laithier (n 10) 257.
[98] Chantepie and Latina (n 10) [340].

*(ii) The determinative role of the state of dependence*

The constraint arising from the state of dependence must have been determinative of the consent of the victim. This is assessed, according to paragraph 2 of article 1130, with regard to their personal characteristics such as their age, gender, profession, and background.

*(iii) Abuse to gain of a manifestly excessive advantage*

The pressure of events is not, on its own, sufficient for duress. It will only qualify when exploited by the other party in order to gain 'a manifestly excessive advantage'. In a case concerning economic duress, the *Cour de cassation* explained that duress is 'an abusive exploitation of a situation of economic dependence to make a profit from the fear of evil which directly threatened a person's legitimate interests'.[99] What is required is, therefore, an abuse of the events.[100]

There was held to be duress where the captain of a stranded ship about to lose her cargo accepted an offer of a tow from a tug in return for 18,000 French francs, which was excessive. He was able to annul the agreement, having consented only 'under a fear caused by a considerable and present evil to person and property', which the tug operator had exploited.[101]

In contrast, there was no abuse where an employee assigned the intellectual property in her work to her employer, a publisher, out of fear of dismissal at a time when many of her colleagues were being made redundant. She was unable to show that her job was at risk or that her employer had used the threat of redundancy to coerce her.[102] Similarly, there is no abuse simply because the weaker party is in financial difficulty. This is illustrated by a case in which a contractor demanded 50,000 French francs more than the agreed price to complete the construction of a hotel. The hotelier claimed to have been coerced into accepting the demand by their financial difficulties and inability to endure the delay that finding another contractor would have involved. This was rejected by the Court of Appeal of Pau on the ground that 'economic difficulties of a business should not, of themselves, be considered a moral constraint [on contracting]'.[103]

'Manifestly excessive advantage' sets a high bar that is unlikely to be met easily, thus limiting the scope and significance of this form of duress.[104] This has been condemned as inefficient by some commentators, and the drafters described as 'hypocritical' for introducing the provision with one hand but then taking away with the other.[105] The contention in relation to the requirement reflects a somewhat

[99] Civ (2) 3 April 2002, D 2002.1860.

[100] Soc 5 July 1965, Bull civ V no 545; Civ (1) 30 May 2000, D 2000.879, note J-P Chazal, JCP 2001. II.10461.

[101] Req 27 April 1887, S 1887.1.372. See law no 67-545 of 7 July 1967 relating to events at sea (loi no 67-545 du 7 juillet 1967 relative aux événements de mer). See articles 10 and 15 of the Civil Code.

[102] Civ (1) 3 April 2002 no 00-12932, Bull civ I no 108.

[103] CA Pau 24 May 1983, RTDC 1984.708, note J Mestre.

[104] Deshayes, Genicon, and Laithier (n 10) 248–9.

[105] G Loiseau, 'Les vices du consentement' Contrats Concurrence Consommation 2016.5.

turbulent drafting history. It was absent from the draft of the article that was originally published. Indeed, at that stage, there was no need for the party exercising duress to gain a manifestly excessive advantage. Duress would therefore be established where one party abused the other's position of weakness to coerce them to enter into an agreement that they would not have entered in the absence of that coercion. This prompted expressions of serious misgivings from business representatives, for whom the original wording went beyond guarding against duress by protecting the consent of the parties. It was tantamount to a mechanism for the courts to interfere with the substance of the contract and rebalance the bargain. The requirement was inserted by the draftsmen in response to these concerns, thereby reining in the article.[106]

#### (c) Remedies

As with other defects in consent, the remedy for duress is the relative nullity of the contract.[107] The victim can also seek extra-contractual damages under article 1240 of the Civil Code.

## B Illegality

> Art. 6.—No one may, by private agreements, derogate from legislation concerning public policy and good morals.
>
> Art. 1102.—Everyone is free to contract or not to contract, to choose the person with whom to contract, and to determine the content and form of the contract, within the limits imposed by legislation.
>
> Contractual freedom does not allow derogation from rules which are an expression of public policy.
>
> Art. 1162.—A contract cannot derogate from public policy either by its stipulations or by its purpose, whether or not this was known by all the parties.

Another condition in article 1128 for a contract to be valid is that the contractual content is lawful.[108] The rules on legality of content are found in new articles 6, 1102, and 1162 of the Code. The combined effect of these provisions is to prevent the parties from contracting in a way that is contrary to the rules of public policy or good morals.

As a preliminary point, a notable change of terminology was made in this condition as part of the reforms. The word 'content' (*le contenu*) is entirely new, not

[106] Ancel, Fauvarque-Cosson, and Gest (n 2) [24.23–24.26].
[107] Article 1131 of the Civil Code.
[108] Article 1128 of the Civil Code.

having appeared in article 1108 of the 1804 Code, which is where the previous conditions for contractual validity were enumerated. These were consent, capacity, a defined object (*objet*) as the subject-matter of the contract, and a cause that was legal (*cause*).[109] Instead, as the drafters have acknowledged,[110] it was borrowed directly from the UNIDROIT Principles[111] and the Principles of European Contract Law (PECL)[112] for the purpose of replacing the long-standing conditions of *objet* and *cause* in the old article. This has given rise to considerable controversy.

## 1 The removal of the requirement of a legal *cause*

The removal of reference to legal *cause* and the introduction of the concept of contractual content have been amongst the most widely debated changes made by the reforms. Previously, a distinction was drawn between 'objective cause' (*cause objective*) and 'subjective cause' (*cause subjective*). The objective cause was the 'abstract' goal of the contract. This was the aim that could be determined simply from the terms of the contract rather than from the concrete circumstances in which the contract was made. It was usually the counter-performance promised by the other party and therefore the same, regardless of the category of contract. For example, in sale of goods contracts, invariably the *cause* of the seller was payment of the purchase price and the *cause* of the buyer was to acquire ownership of the goods. If there was no objective cause, the contract lacked reciprocity and was susceptible to annulment by the court. This was founded upon a belief that a contract must have a purpose—a *raison d'être*—in order to be valid, which meant that each party had to receive some benefit. Subjective cause, on the other hand, concerned the subjective reason that a party entered into a contract. This would differ for each contract, reflecting that parties enter into contracts for different reasons. In order for the contract to be valid, the subjective cause had to be lawful.

As will be explained in Chapter 7 on the regulation of unfair terms, the doctrine of *cause* had come to be regarded as problematic in France. This was mainly because the courts were finding in an increasingly broad range of circumstances that a contract had no objective cause in order to justify interfering with the agreed terms. It became a basis for rebalancing contracts that were perceived to be unfair. There was also concern that, as the notion was not widely used or known abroad, even in legal systems that have historically been influenced by French law, it risked diminishing the attractiveness of the Civil Code for international contracts.[113] For these reasons, *cause* was excised from the new Code.

[109] Articles 1131 to 1133 of the 1804 Civil Code.
[110] Ancel, Fauvarque-Cosson, and Gest (n 2) [25.71].
[111] Article 1.1 UNIDROIT Principles.
[112] Article 1:102 PECL.
[113] Ancel, Fauvarque-Cosson, and Gest (n 2) [25.74].

Although *cause* as a formal requirement has gone, it has been replaced with more specific rules that seem likely to allow the courts to reach similar solutions.[114] The concept of subjective cause has to a large extent re-appeared in new article 1162, which provides that a contract cannot derogate in its terms or aims from public policy. This is the focus of this section. Again, as will be shown in Chapter 7, the role of objective cause in regulating unfair terms is now performed by articles 1169 to 1170.[115]

It might therefore be thought to be surprising that the removal of *cause* as an essential ingredient of a valid contract has generated so much controversy. One important reason is undoubtedly that the doctrine had deep roots and was the subject of equally deep attachment in French contract law. This is discernible in some of the obituary-esque remarks written at the time of the reforms by mournful commentators, which included terms such as an 'emblem of the French Civil Code'[116] and 'culturally important'.[117] However, these points seem more ideological than substantive.[118] The changes made by the reforms were probably more semantic than real and in practice have made little difference.

## 2 Lawful contractual stipulations

The performance of the contract must not involve prohibited behaviour. One cannot contract to kill[119] or to alienate a fundamental freedom, for example the freedom to marry or to vote for a particular candidate in an election. Nor can the freedom to conduct business be disavowed except in relatively narrow circumstances. For example, non-compete covenants must be proportionate, justified, and limited in their geographical scope, duration, and subject-matter.[120]

A distinction is drawn in French law between matters which can be the subject of legal transactions (*choses et prestations dans le commerce*) and those which cannot (*choses et prestations hors du commerce*).[121] For example, there cannot be a binding contract for the sale of illicit drugs,[122] counterfeit items,[123] protected animal species, or body parts. A contract for the sale of a piece of tattooed skin for

[114] 'Report to the President' (n 49) 26.
[115] See Chapter 7, pp 137–43.
[116] R Boffa, 'Juste cause (et injuste clause)' D 2015.335.
[117] T Genicon, 'Défense et illustration de la cause en droit des contrats—à propos du projet de réforme du droit des contrats, du régime général et de la preuve des obligations' D 2015.1551.
[118] Contra Genicon (n 117).
[119] A Bénabent, *Droit des obligations* (18th edn, LGDJ: Paris, 2019) [170].
[120] Soc 9 Oct 1985, Bull civ V no 442; Civ (1) 25 May 1987, Bull civ I no 161.
[121] See old article 1128 of the 1804 Civil Code. The distinction is still used in the literature but does not feature in the new Civil Code. See, for example, Bénabent (n 119) [170]; Terré, Simler, Lequette, and Chénedé (n 26) [508]–[513].
[122] Com 16 May 2006, Bull civ IV no 124.
[123] Com 26 Oct 1999, Bull civ IV no 185.

a film was therefore held to be a nullity.[124] Contracts of surrogacy by which women agree to carry and give birth to the child of another are also void, whether or not gratuitous.[125]

## 3 Lawful aim of the contract

The purpose of the parties in entering into the contract must also be lawful. The focus here is on the subjective reasons of each party, which cannot be illicit or immoral. So, for example, whilst a contract to lease premises is ordinarily lawful, it has been held to be a nullity where the intended use of the premises was to counterfeit money and traffic drugs.[126] A loan agreement was similarly annulled where the purpose of the borrower was to establish a brothel.[127] These transactions were rendered unlawful by their context and purpose.

Where a contract is entered into for several reasons, it is sufficient that one of those reasons is unlawful for the contract to be a nullity.[128] According to article 1162, it is not necessary for the other party to be aware of the reason at the time of entering the contract. This is perceived as protecting the innocent party who is unaware of the motives of the other.[129] It is, however, necessary that the illegal or immoral purpose was determinative in the decision to enter the contract. If it was not determinative, the contract cannot be annulled. This prevents the innocent party from opportunistically seeking to escape from the contract by relying upon subsidiary motives that happen to be illegal or immoral, which would be to the detriment of contractual certainty.

The remedy for illegality is the nullity of the contract. Where specific clauses are illegal or immoral but the rest of the contract is not and can survive without those clauses, it is open to the court to nullify only the unlawful clauses.[130] The nullity is typically 'absolute' rather than 'relative'. This follows from new article 1179, which

[124] TGI Paris, 3 July 1969, D 1970.136; Civ (1) 23 Feb 1972, JCP 1972.II.17135.

[125] Only certain blood and organ donations in a medical context are permitted. Ass Plén 31 May 1991, D 1991.417; see the law of 29 July 1994 relating to the donation and use of elements and products of the human body, medically assisted procreation, and prenatal diagnosis (loi no 94-654 du 29 juillet 1994 relative au don et à l'utilisation des éléments et produits du corps humain, à l'assistance médicale à la procréation et au diagnostic prénatal) and article 16-5 of the Civil Code which provides that 'conventions with a view to confer patrimonial rights to the human body, its elements or its products, are null and void'.

[126] Soc 29 Oct 1957, Bull civ IV no 1027; 8 Jan 1964, D 1964.267.

[127] Soc 29 Oct 1957, Bull civ IV no 1027; 8 Jan 1964, D 1964.267; Civ (1) 1 Oct 1996, *Contrats, Conc, Consomm,* 1997, no 3, note L Leveneur; D 1997 Somm 171, note R Libchaber, RTD civ 1997.116, note J Mestre; Civ (1) 26 Sept 2012, pourvoi no 11-12941, RDC 2013.25, note J Rochfeld; Trib of Tarbes, 14 March 1899, S 900.2.219.

[128] Chantepie and Latina (n 10) [405].

[129] Ibid., [407].

[130] Soc 21 Oct 1960, JCP 1960.II.11886 cited and translated in Beale, Fauvarque-Cosson, Rutgers, and Vogenauer (n 7) 690.

provides that absolute nullity results from the violation of a rule that 'has as its object the safeguarding of the public interest'.[131] An unlawful contract or clause is injurious to society at large. As noted in the context of remedies for mistake, absolute nullity 'may be claimed by any person who can demonstrate an interest, as well as by the *ministère public*'.[132] This is in contrast with 'relative nullity', which is available only where 'the rule that is violated has as its sole object the safeguarding of a private interest' and can be claimed solely by 'the party that the legislation intends to protect'.[133]

Where a party has performed obligations under a contract, only for the contract to be nullified, this normally gives rise to a right to restitution. There are no exceptions in the Code for illegality or immorality, which implies that even a party that has rendered performance unlawfully or immorally can claim restitution. In practice, however, at least in the case of immoral contracts, the courts have applied the adage *nemo auditor propriam suam turpitudinem* ('nobody may be heard relying on his own wrongdoing') to avoid this consequence.[134] The effect is that, whilst the contract is nullified, the parties are barred from claiming restitution.[135] Somewhat counter-intuitively perhaps, the adage has not been applied where the contract is unlawful, such that parties that have rendered performance unlawfully have been able to claim restitution.[136]

## C Certainty of Subject-Matter

**Civil Code**

Art. 1163.—An obligation has as its subject-matter a present or future act of performance.

The latter must be possible and determined or capable of being determined.

An act of performance is capable of being determined where it can be deduced from the contract or by reference to usage or the previous dealings of the parties, without the need for further agreement.

Art. 1164.—In framework contracts it may be agreed that the price will be fixed unilaterally by one of the parties, subject to the requirement that the latter must provide the reason for the amount if it is challenged.

In the case of an abuse in the fixing of a price, a court may hear a claim for damages and, in an appropriate case, for the termination of the contract.

[131] Article 1179 of the Civil Code.
[132] Article 1180 of the Civil Code.
[133] Article 1181 of the Civil Code.
[134] Terré, Simler, Lequette, and Chénedé (n 26) [579] and all the references cited.
[135] J Bell, S Boyron, and S Whittaker, *Principles of French Law* (2nd edn, OUP: Oxford, 2008) 447.
[136] Civ (1) 27 Nov 1984, GP 1985.2 Pan jur 135, note F Chabas.

**(2016 version)**
*Art. 1165.—In contracts for the supply of services, in the absence of an agreement by the parties in advance of their performance, the price may be fixed by the creditor, subject to the latter's providing a reason for its amount if it is challenged. In the case of abuse in the fixing of the price, the court may hear a claim for damages.*

**(2018 version)**
Art. 1165.—In contracts for the supply of services, in the absence of an agreement by the parties in advance of their performance, the price may be fixed by the creditor, subject to the latter's providing a reason for its amount if it is challenged. In the case of abuse in the fixing of the price, the court may hear a claim for damages and, where appropriate, termination of the contract.

Art. 1166.—Where the quality of the act of performance is not determined or capable of being determined under the contract, the debtor must offer an act of performance of a quality which conforms to the legitimate expectations of the parties taking into account its nature, usual practices and the amount of what is agreed in return.

Art. 1167.—Where the price or any other element of a contract is to be determined by reference to an index which does not exist or has ceased to exist or to be available, the index is replaced by the index which is most closely related to it.

Certainty is another of the conditions stated at article 1128 for a contract to be valid.[137] The terms must be specified with sufficient precision and without any gaps in respect of essential elements of the act of performance, which cannot be held over to be ascertained by later negotiations. Two additional requirements must also be satisfied by the act of performance under new article 1163: first, it must be possible or exist; and second, it must be determined or capable of being determined.

## 1 The act of performance must be possible or exist

The act of performance must be possible[138] or exist at the time of formation, failing which the contract will be a nullity. This has been found, for example, in respect of contracts for the sale of an animal that turned out to be dead and a house that has been destroyed in a fire.[139] One exception relates to contracts for future performance,[140] for which it is enough that the act of performance will exist one day. For

[137] Paragraph 3 of article 1128 of the Civil Code.
[138] Paragraph 2 of article 1163 of the Civil Code.
[139] But if the subject-matter of the performance ceases to exist after the formation of contract, the contract remains valid.
[140] Paragraph 1 of article 1163 of the Civil Code.

example, the subject-matter of a contract can be an animal to be born in the future or a property to be built.

## 2 The act of performance must be determined or capable of being determined

The second condition is that the act of performance must be determined or capable of being determined. An act is determined where it can be identified and ascertained with precision. If it has not already been determined, it is enough that it is objectively possible to ascertain it.

According to paragraph 3 of article 1163, the act of performance is ascertainable where it is capable of being deduced from the contract or the usage or previous dealings of the parties. This will not be satisfied where there is a need for some further agreement, which was the case, for example, with a promise to 'give a reward'.[141] In contrast, where the parties stipulate a formula or mechanism by which the act of performance can be ascertained at a later date without their further involvement, it will be capable of being determined. This is exemplified by a term that is to be fixed by reference to an index or the decision of a third party.

It is not necessarily fatal that the contract is silent on the standard of quality that the act of performance must attain. There are a number of ways in which this can be determined and the contract rendered valid. For example, article 1166 provides that the promisor must offer an act of performance of a quality that conforms 'to the legitimate expectations of the parties taking into account its nature, usual practices and the amount of what is agreed in return'.

Similarly, article 1167 establishes a means of avoiding a contract being rendered a nullity where, due to unexpected circumstances, the index by reference to which the price or other elements of the contract are to be determined does not exist or ceases to exist or be available. It provides that 'the index is replaced by the index which is most closely related to it', which if necessary will be determined by the court.

The requirement that the act of performance be determined is subject to an exception for the contract price in 'framework contracts' and contracts for services.[142] In these contexts, it suffices that there is an agreement that one party should have a unilateral power to fix the price at a later date.[143] According to article 1111, a 'framework contract' (*contrats cadres*) is a contract 'by which the parties agree the general characteristics of their future contractual relations'. Its function is to lay

[141] Examples given by Bénabent (n 119) [158]; Com 28 Feb 1983, Bull civ IV no 86.

[142] Article 1165 of the Civil Code.

[143] This codifies the long-standing case law of the *Cour de cassation*: see Civ (1) 29 Nov 1994, no 91-21009, Bull civ I no 348; Ass Plén 1 Dec 1995, no 91-15578, 91-15999, 93-13688, and 91-1965.

the ground for one or (usually) more implementation contracts, which are typically entered into simultaneously with or subsequent to the framework contract and 'determine the modalities of performance'.[144] It is valid despite the absence of any stipulation as to the price because its purpose is only to provide a broad outline of the contractual relationship. The price and a range of other issues are left over to be covered in implementation contracts or otherwise as they arise.

In order to prevent abuse, contractual rights that enable a party to fix the price at a later date are regulated in the Code. According to articles 1164 and 1165, any such right must not be exercised abusively and, if called upon to do so, the beneficiary must give reasons justifying the price.[145] Where there has been abuse, the other party can seek compensation for loss and even the termination of the contract. It is not, however, open to the court to fix or revise the price.

## D Concluding Observations

Of the various reforms in respect of the validity of the contract, the new provisions on defects in consent and the removal of the old concept of *cause* are the main ones that stand out.

### 1 Defects vitiating consent

The number of articles on defects in consent has increased from nine in the 1804 Code to fifteen in the new Code. In most respects, the reforms simply codified rules that had been developed and applied in cases over the last two centuries.[146] Whilst by no means groundbreaking, this has resulted in articles that are more up-to-date and presented in a clear manner that is easier to read and more accessible, helping to fulfil one of the main overarching objectives of the reforms.[147]

Three features of the reformed articles in particular are notable for the light that they shed on the French conception of contract and make for interesting comparative analysis. The first is how defects in consent are presented in the Code. All three defects are brought together under a single heading, 'Defects in Consent', and a common regime in articles 1130 and 1131. This has been described as 'a significant contribution' that 'enhances the profound unity of the defects in consent'[148] in French law.

[144] Article 1164 of the Civil Code.

[145] Terré, Simler, Lequette, and Chénedé (n 26) [387]; Deshayes, Genicon, and Laithier (n 10) 313–16.

[146] Ancel, Fauvarque-Cosson, and Gest (n 2) [24.21]; Deshayes, Genicon, and Laithier (n 10) 206.

[147] But see Aubert de Vincelles (n 6) 99 who argues that by simply codifying existing rules the reformers failed to tackle a number of difficult questions in this area which therefore remain and there has been no improvement in contractual certainty.

[148] Chantepie and Latina (n 10) [294].

The UNIDROIT Principles take a similar approach, addressing in Chapter 3 on the Validity of Contracts what are referred to as 'grounds for avoidance'.[149] This is in contrast with English law, where defects are not generally regarded as forming a unified category. Mistake, misrepresentation, duress, and undue influence are considered as separate and specific doctrines and not usually grouped together as vitiating factors.[150] Cartwright has explained the reason to be that 'English law does not focus on the consent of the parties but views contract as an (objectively ascertained) agreement where each party has provided consideration for the other's promises in the agreement. The contract is a bargain between the parties giving effect to their agreement.'[151]

A second feature is the retention of the long-standing focus on the nature of the mistake (essential qualities, value, and motive) rather than its source (whether it is unilateral, common, or induced). For example, it is irrelevant whether the mistake is shared by both parties or unilateral, provided that it concerns an essential aspect of the contract.[152] What matters is that the contract reflects the agreement between the parties.[153]

This is also in contrast with English law,[154] which focuses not on consent but on the source of the mistake, in particular whether it is common to both parties or induced by the non-mistaken party. The doctrine of mistake is narrow. Only mistakes that are fundamental and shared by both parties are actionable. A party whose mistake is unilateral is unlikely to have a remedy except through the broader doctrine of misrepresentation, which applies where the mistake was induced by a false representation made by the other party,[155] whether innocently, negligently, or intentionally.[156] This provides greater contractual certainty. As Beale, Fauvarque-Cosson, Rutgers, and Vogenauer have explained:

[149] Articles 3.2.1 to 3.2.17 UNIDROIT Principles; see also 'Chapter 4: Validity' in the Principles of European Contract Law (PECL).

[150] J Cartwright, *Contract Law: An Introduction to the English Law of Contract for the Civil Lawyer* (3rd edn, Hart Publishing: Oxford, 2016) 159. See, however, H Beale (ed) *Chitty on Contracts* (34th edn, Sweet & Maxwell: London, 2021) Part 3, which now considers misrepresentation, duress, undue influence, and unconscionable dealings under the heading 'Grounds of Avoidance', and M Chen-Wishart, *Contract Law* (6th edn, OUP: Oxford, 2018), Part IV entitled 'Vitiating Factors' which considers misrepresentation and non-disclosure, mistake, frustration, duress, and unfairness. As Beale, Fauvarque-Cosson, Rutgers, and Vogenauer (n 7) 483 note, in practice the courts frequently treat them as parallel doctrines.

[151] Cartwright (n 150) 158.

[152] Beale, Fauvarque-Cosson, Rutgers, and Vogenauer (n 7) 525.

[153] Chantepie and Latina (n 10) [302]; Aubert de Vincelles (n 6) 94–5.

[154] For a detailed comparison of English and French law, see Beale, Fauvarque-Cosson, Rutgers, and Vogenauer (n 7) 483ff; Cartwright (n 150) 158 ff. See also PECL article 4:103; Draft Common Frame of Reference (DCFR) article II.-7:201; UNIDROIT Principles article 3.2.2. On mistake being imported into English textbooks from French law: see B Simpson, 'Innovation in Nineteenth Century Contract Law' (1975) 91 LQR 247.

[155] The representor can address the misrepresentation to a third party with the intention that it is passed on to the other party: *Commercial Banking Co of Sydney v RH Brown and Co* [1972] 2 Llyod's Rep 360.

[156] Aubert de Vincelles (n 6) 94.

> The common law places great emphasis on the appearance of the agreement, in order to protect the reasonable expectations of the other party... English law readily gives relief when one party has misled the other into entering the contract by giving incorrect information—even if this was done without fault. Relief is not under the doctrine of mistake but that of misrepresentation. In other words, the common law looks to the position of both parties and, with the limited exception of common mistake, insists on some misleading behaviour on the part of the other party before avoidance will be allowed.[157]

The third feature is the express recognition of fraudulent non-disclosure. This formally extends the boundaries of fraud and in so doing further strengthens the protection of consent. It has been said by Aubert de Vincelles to be a mechanism 'in the service of contractual loyalty ... [which] restricts certainty of transactions ... This is a balance desired and assumed by the reform.'[158]

The recognition of fraudulent non-disclosure is in line with a number of international contract instruments, such as PECL[159] and the UNIDROIT Principles,[160] but again diverges from the approach in English law, where silence alone cannot amount to fraud.[161] Only where there is some actual conduct that is false and induces the mistake is relief available through the doctrine of misrepresentation.[162]

## 2 The disappearance of the notion of *cause*

The removal of *cause* in order to reduce judicial meddling with contract terms and allay the misgivings of international users of French contract law was described by the drafters as sending 'a strong signal that French law is open towards comparative law and the European contract law harmonisation projects and seeks to promote certainty'.[163] It was, however, an exaggeration for some commentators to suggest that the doctrine is peculiar to French law and unknown in other jurisdictions. There are analogues in several articles of the Quebec Civil Code[164] and in the Italian Civil Code,[165] both of which have historically been influenced by French law. It is true that there is no such doctrine in international instruments such as the UNIDROIT Principles and the PECL or indeed in English law but, as in the

[157] Beale, Fauvarque-Cosson, Rutgers, and Vogenauer (n 7) 500 and 525.

[158] Aubert de Vincelles (n 6) 79.

[159] Article 4:107.

[160] UNIDROIT Principles article 3.2.5; see also DCFR article II.-7:205.

[161] Subject to certain exceptions in certain contracts in which there is a duty of disclosure, see *Chitty on Contracts* (n 150) [9-167]–[9-168].

[162] For a comparison on this topic, see Beale, Fauvarque-Cosson, Rutgers, and Vogenauer (n 7) 490; Aubert de Vincelles (n 6) 101.

[163] Ancel, Fauvarque-Cosson, and Gest (n 2) [25.74].

[164] Articles 1371, 1385, 1410, and 1411 of the Quebec Civil Code.

[165] Articles 1325 and 1343 to 1345 of the Codice Civile.

new Civil Code, some of the functions performed by *cause* can be found in other mechanisms.

In English law, it has been suggested that the doctrines of consideration, illegality, public policy, frustration, and the rules on unfair terms achieve some of the same solutions as *cause*.[166] This is partly true, although, at least in the context of the regulation of unfair terms, French law clearly goes further, as will be explained in Chapter 7.[167]

[166] B Markesinis, '*Cause* and Consideration: A Study in Parallel' 37(1) CLJ 53.
[167] See Chapter 7 on unfair terms.

# PART III

# THE CONTENT OF THE CONTRACT

# 6

# The Interpretation and Supplementation of Contracts

There are two distinct types of interpretation in French contract law. These are known as explanatory interpretation (*interprétation explicative*) and creative interpretation (*interprétation créatrice*).[1] *Interprétation explicative*—by which the court ascertains the meaning of the express terms of the contract—is the focus of the first part of this chapter and will be referred to simply as 'interpretation'. *Interprétation créatrice*—by which the court supplements the contract with a term to fill a gap where the contracting parties have omitted to address a material issue—is addressed in the second part of this chapter. It will be referred to as 'supplementation'. Both types of interpretation were the subject of revision in the reforms.[2]

## A Interpretation: *Interprétation explicative*

**Civil Code**[3]

Art. 1188.—A contract is to be interpreted according to the common intention of the parties rather than stopping at the literal meaning of its terms.

Where this intention cannot be discerned, a contract is to be interpreted in the sense which a reasonable person placed in the same situation would give to it.

Art. 1189.—All the terms of a contract are to be interpreted in relation to each other, giving to each the meaning which respects the consistency of the contract as a whole.

[1] A Etienney De Sainte Marie, '"L'interprétation créatrice": l'interprétation et la détermination du contenu du contrat', RDC 2015.166.

[2] Ibid. See also R Aikens, '"The Obscure, the Implied and the Illegal": English and French Approaches to the Interpretation of Contract, Implication of Terms and Contracts Affected by Illegality' in C Mitchell and S Watterson (eds), *The World of Maritime and Commercial Law: Essays in Honour of Francis Rose* (Bloomsbury Publishing: London, 2020) 215, 223–224.

[3] 'Ordonnance no 2016-131 du 10 février 2016 portant réforme du droit des contrats, du régime général et de la preuve des obligations', JORF no 0035 of 11 February 2016. The Ordonnance was translated into English by J Cartwright, B Fauvarque-Cosson, and S Whittaker: <http://www.textes.justice.gouv.fr/art_pix/THE-LAW-OF-CONTRACT-2-5-16.pdf> (2016 version) and <http://www.textes.justice.gouv.fr/art_pix/Translationrevised2018final.pdf> (2018 version) accessed 1 September 2021. The translations of the new articles contained in this book are theirs.

*The New French Law of Contract.* Solène Rowan, Oxford University Press. © Solène Rowan 2022.
DOI: 10.1093/oso/9780198810872.003.0006

> Where, according to the common intention of the parties, several contracts contribute to one and the same operation, they are to be interpreted by reference to this operation.
>
> Art. 1190.—In case of ambiguity, a bespoke contract is interpreted against the creditor and in favour of the debtor, and a standard-form contract is interpreted against the person who put it forward.
>
> Art. 1191.—Where a contract term is capable of bearing two meanings, the one which gives it some effect is to be preferred to the one which makes it produce no effect.
>
> Art. 1192.—Clear and unambiguous terms are not subject to interpretation as doing so risks their distortion.

Perhaps surprisingly, contractual interpretation has generally given rise to little interest in France.[4] In the words of one French academic lawyer, 'the articles of the Civil Code on interpretation are without a doubt those that have left commentators most indifferent'.[5] For another, 'these articles are well-known but seldom used and relatively little studied'.[6]

This apparent disinterest did not deter the drafters of the reforms, who considered that the principles of interpretation that prevailed prior to the reforms were in need of overhaul.[7] A key objective was to clarify the principles and eliminate articles that were regarded as redundant.[8] This saw the number of articles in the Code on interpretation reduced from nine to five, with new articles 1188 to 1192 replacing old articles 1156 to 1164.[9]

Three aspects of the law relating to interpretation were the particular focus of the reforms. These are the dichotomy between the subjective and objective approaches to interpretation; the power of the *Cour de cassation* to quash decisions of lower courts on issues of interpretation that distort the clear and precise meaning of a term (*dénaturation des clauses claires et précises*); and the application of the *contra proferentem* rule to the interpretation of standard form contracts.

[4] A number of the observations in this chapter on contractual interpretation in France and the impact of the reforms were addressed from a comparative perspective in S Rowan 'Problems of Contractual Interpretation: English and French Law Compared' [2020] LMCLQ 273.

[5] P Simler, 'Art 1188 à 1192–Fasc 10: Contrat—Interprétation du contrat—L'instrument: notion, normes, champ d'application' [2017] JCL [3].

[6] O Deshayes, 'Les directrices d'interprétation du Code civil: la cohérence des textes' RDC 2015.159, 159.

[7] See paragraph 5 of article 8 of the *Loi d'habilitation de l'ordonnance no 2016-131 portant réforme du droit des contrats du 10 février 2016*.

[8] 'Report to the President of the Republic relating to Ordonnance no 2016–131 of 10 February 2016 on the reform of contract law, the general regime and proof of obligations', JORF no 0035 of 11 February 2016, 11.

[9] Old articles 1158, 1159, 1160, 1163, and 1164 have not been retained in the new Civil Code.

## 1 The dichotomy between the subjective and objective approaches to interpretation

It is trite to say, and the Code recognizes, that a contract does not always reflect the shared intentions of the parties. According to paragraph 1 of new article 1188, the court should not simply give mechanical effect to the plain and ordinary meaning of the words that the parties have used. To the contrary, the common intention of the parties has precedence. This willingness to look beyond literalism when interpreting a contract has been explained by French commentators as based on good faith. For a contracting party to hide behind the literal meaning of a term in order to escape their true obligations would be inimical to this principle.[10]

### (a) The starting point: establishing the common subjective intention of the parties

At least as a starting point, French courts take a subjective approach to identifying the common intention of the parties. The aim is to ascertain their real and actual intention as at the time that the contract was formed.[11] This is consistent with the theory of the autonomy of the will (*théorie de l'autonomie de la volonté*).[12] Since contractual obligations are by their nature the product of mutual consent, the parties should only be bound if, and to what, they truly intend.[13] It is also thought to be fairer and to provide better justice than simply abiding by their declared intention, which would risk imposing obligations that do not reflect their actual intention and to which they did not agree. The search for the real intention of the parties has been described as the most fundamental and essential principle of interpretation[14] and the court as the 'servant of the will of the parties'.[15]

In order to ascertain the common subjective intention of the parties, the contract is interpreted in context and against the background of the surrounding circumstances.[16] The plain meaning of the words can be overridden.[17] As the Paris Court of Appeal has said:

[10] M Fabre-Magnan, *Droit des obligations, Contrat et engagement unilatéral* (5th edn, PUF: Paris, 2019) [630].

[11] Ass Plén 12 May 1989, JCP 1989.II.21322, note G Lyon-Caen; Civ (1) 2 March 1982, GP 1982.2 Pan 245.

[12] On this theory, see Chapter 2, p21; F Terré, P Simler, Y Lequette, and F Chénédé, *Droit civil, Les obligations* (12th edn, Dalloz: Paris, 2018) [606].

[13] A Bénabent, *Droit des obligations* (18th edn, LGDJ: Paris, 2019) [281].

[14] M-H Maleville, *Pratique de l'interprétation des contrats: étude jurisprudentielle* (PU de Rouen, 1995) [272]; B Gelot, *Finalité et méthodes objectives d'interprétation des actes juridiques* (LGDJ: Paris, 2003); P Simler, 'Art 1188 à 1192–Fasc 20: Contrat—Interprétation du contrat –La mise en œuvre: rôle respectif des juges du fond et de la Cour de cassation' [2017] JCL [23–4].

[15] Terré, Simler, Lequette, and Chénédé (n 12) [606].

[16] Civ (3) 14 Nov 1968, Bull civ III no 465; Civ (1) 2 Dec 1959, Bull civ I no 512; Civ (1) 19 Jan 1983, Bull civ I no 29; Maleville (n 14) [281].

[17] Com 1 May 1980, Bull IV no 197; Maleville (n 14) and the many examples given at [284]–[306].

> It is the role of the court to give effect to the real intention of the parties without limiting itself to terms which are inaccurate or inefficiently used, and in this search for their real intention, it is necessary, so as to understand the value and scope of the disputed terms, to take into account the context of the contract, the personality of the contracting parties and the circumstances surrounding the contract.[18]

As long as the common subjective intention of the parties is clear, there is no limit on the power of the court to correct mistakes in the language of a contract by interpretation. Unlike in certain other legal systems such as in England, the Code does not recognize a separate remedy of rectification.[19] There are however close similarities between correction by interpretation and rectification in all but name.[20]

The correction of a contract through interpretation is illustrated by a case[21] involving an insurance claim by a farmer under a permanent disability policy for the annual sum of 50,000 French francs. Although clearly stipulated in the policy, this sum was argued by the insurer to be incorrect, only 5,000 francs having been intended. The *Cour de cassation* affirmed the decision of the Toulouse Court of Appeal to 'interpret' the reference in the policy to 50,000 francs as actually meaning 5,000 francs, which the parties clearly intended should be the benefit payable. This could be deduced, amongst other things, from the amount of the premium and the average income earned by farmers in the same area as the claimant at the time the cover was taken out.

Another example is a case in which a contract contained a clause stating that disputes should be resolved by the 'Chamber of Commerce of Belgrade'.[22] There was no Chamber of Commerce in Belgrade but rather a Chamber of Commerce of Yugoslavia which was located in Belgrade. The clause was interpreted as referring to that institution.

### (b) The admissibility of evidence of pre-contractual and post-contractual conduct

There are no restrictions on the evidence that is admissible to ascertain the common subjective intention of the parties.[23] An expansive approach is also taken

[18] CA Paris 4 Nov 1955, Gaz Palais 1956.I.153; Civ (3) 14 Nov 1968, Bull civ III no 465; Civ (1) 2 Dec 1959, Bull civ I no 512; Civ (1) 19 Jan 1983, Bull civ I no 29.

[19] Maleville (n 14) [310] and [544]; S Vogenauer, 'Interpretation of Contracts: Concluding Observations' in A Burrows and E Peel (eds), *Contract Terms* (OUP: Oxford, 2007) 123, 136–42; N Jansen and R Zimmermann (eds), *Commentaries on European Contract Laws* (OUP: Oxford, 2018) 750–1; C Valcke, 'On Comparing French and English Contract Law: Insights from Social Contract Theory' (2009) 4 Journal of Comparative Law 69.

[20] Vogenauer, 'Interpretation of Contracts: Concluding Observations' (n 19) 136–42.

[21] Civ (1) 2 March 1982, GP 1982.2.

[22] Civ (1) 14 Dec 1983 Rev Arb 1984.439, note M-C Rondeau-Rivier.

[23] Subject to paragraph 1 of new article 1359 (old article 1341) of the Civil Code: 'A juridical act relating to a sum of money or value in excess of an amount fixed by decree must be proved by evidence in

to the 'context' and 'surrounding circumstances' that can be taken into account. Lower courts seised of issues of interpretation are able to have regard to what the parties said or did before[24] or after[25] the formation of contract, whether to each other or to third parties. Any pre-contractual correspondence between the parties,[26] even if only containing subjective statements of intention, is admissible, as are previous contracts entered into by the parties[27] or by one of the parties with a third party,[28] and documents that were generated contemporaneously with the formation of contract, whether by the parties or even third parties.

The willingness of French courts to rely upon evidence of pre-contractual conduct is illustrated by a case relating to the inception date of insurance coverage. There was ambiguity in the policy, which referred to two different dates, 17 and 21 August. Since the insured suffered loss on 18 and 19 August, this was a determinative issue. Affirming the decision of the Limoges Court of Appeal, the *Cour de cassation* held that cover was effective from the earlier date. This was based on a letter written on 16 August by the broker that had negotiated and placed the cover acknowledging receipt of confirmation from the insurer that all was in order and that the policy would start with immediate effect.[29]

Reliance on evidence of pre-contractual conduct is encouraged by the *Cour de cassation*. It is thought to provide a fuller picture of the background to the contract and to assist the court in establishing how the terms used by the parties should be understood, thereby enabling more precise justice. An analogy is often drawn by commentators with the interpretation of acts of parliament, where regard can be had to parliamentary preparatory works to discern legislative intention.[30]

Evidence of the post-contractual conduct of the parties is also admissible for the same reasons.[31] It has even been characterized by the Chambery Court of Appeal as 'the best source of interpretation',[32] inevitably shedding light on what they intended to agree. Being relied on only as evidence of the intention of the parties 'at the time the contract was formed', it does not permit the court to change the meaning of the contract.[33]

writing, whether privately signed or authenticated.' However, this article is narrow in scope; it does not apply to commercial contracts and relates only to evidence that the contract has been entered into, not evidence of the extent of the obligations agreed by the parties.

24 Civ (1) 18 Feb 1986, no 84-12.347 Bull civ I no 31.
25 Civ (1) 9 Nov 1993, Bull civ I no 317.
26 Com 15 May 1972, JCP 1974, II.17864; Civ (1) 21 April 1976, Bull civ I no 135.
27 Aix 18 April 1978, Bull Aix 1978/2.
28 Com 8 Dec 1987, Bull civ IV no 262; Maleville (n 14) [409].
29 Soc 27 Feb 1947, GP 1947.I.205; CA Paris 4 Nov 1955.
30 Maleville (n 14) [403]; T Ivainer, 'La lettre et l'esprit de la loi des parties' JCP G 1981.I.3023; Simler (n 5) [2].
31 Civ (1) 13 Dec 1988, no 86-19068; Com 4 March 1997, no 95-10.507 Bull civ IV no 61; Com 3 July 2001, RTD civ 2002, 293, note J Mestre and B Fages; Maleville (n 14) [411].
32 CA Chambery 18 Aug 1876, DP 1878.1.31.
33 Civ (1) 9 Nov 1993, Bull civ I no 317.

### (c) Objective methods of interpretation to ascertain the parties' common intention

Where the common subjective intention of the parties cannot be ascertained, French courts have been willing to take account of considerations that are objective in nature as an aid to interpretation. Examples include the nature of the contract,[34] commercial usage, and practices and customs in the relevant trade or profession.[35] There is also explicit reference in the Code to a number of factors that are objective in nature. These are the purpose of the contract, other terms of the contract, and common sense. Paragraph 1 of article 1189 states that 'terms should be interpreted in the light of the other terms of the contract and in a way that is consistent with the spirit and purpose of the contract as a whole'.[36] Where 'several contracts contribute to a single operation', paragraph 2 provides that they are to be interpreted by reference to the 'purpose of the whole operation'. According to article 1991, 'where a term is capable of bearing two meanings, a meaning which gives the term some effect should be preferred over one which does not'.[37]

The tenets that underpin articles 1189 and 1191 are coherency and effectiveness. Contracts should be interpreted so as to be coherent, effective, and in line with their purpose. There are many examples of the application of these principles in the cases.[38] One such case arose out of a clause in a commercial lease that prevented any assignment by the lessee 'to persons in the same trade' without the express consent of the lessor. The *Cour de cassation* affirmed the decision of the Paris Court of Appeal that, having regard to the nature of the contract, the surrounding clauses, and other contracts previously entered into by the parties, the word 'except' (*si ce n'est*) should be read into the clause. It was therefore interpreted as meaning that assignment required the consent of the lessor 'except [where the assignment is] to persons in the same trade'.[39] This resulted in an interpretation that was the very opposite of the literal meaning, which would have had the 'strange and unusual' effect of enabling the lessee to assign the lease without the consent of the lessor only where the assignee was in a different trade to the lessor.

Another example is a case in which a loan agreement stated that there would be 'an exemption of one year' from the payment of interest. It was argued by the borrowers that no interest at all was due in respect of that year whereas the lending bank contended that interest continued to accrue but only became payable after the year had ended. Finding for the bank, the Paris Court of Appeal stated that the *raison d'être* of the loan from the bank's perspective was to earn money through

[34] CA Paris 30 Sept 1983, GP 1984.1 Somm 176; CA 2 Dec 1985, GP 1986.1.214, note A Piedelièvre.
[35] Com 9 February 1976 JCP 1977.II.18598.
[36] Reproducing old article 1161 of the 1804 Civil Code.
[37] See old article 1157 of the 1804 Civil Code.
[38] For more examples, see Gelot (n 14) [147]–[148] and [157].
[39] Com 29 Nov 1965, Bull civ III no 612.

interest, which the borrowers could not realistically have expected would be foregone.[40]

A further illustration is a case involving a non-compete clause, by which the director of a business agreed not to take 'similar employment' in a competing business in a specific region for a period of one year. The *Cour de cassation* affirmed the lower court decision that this precluded him from taking the same position in a company that he had newly set up. In order to give full effect to the purpose of the clause, the word 'employment' could not just mean 'employed by a third-party business'.[41]

### (d) Recognition in the 2016 reforms of objective considerations in the interpretation process

Whilst French courts often take account of objective considerations, this is seldom done openly. Instead the exercise is characterized as a search for the subjective intention of the parties, based on the irrefutable premise that the parties must have intended that the contract would be coherent and effective.[42] Through this pretence, the courts claim to be ascertaining the subjective intention of the parties whilst in reality looking beyond it.[43]

The dogma that objective considerations are not relevant was controversial. Some have argued that an exclusively subjective approach to interpretation has limitations and this should be recognized openly. In reality, reliance on objective considerations is not only inevitable but widespread. It should therefore not be disguised. To claim that the parties have a common intention in all cases, or that it can always be identified, is a fiction. It would be preferable to accept that French law adopts a mixed or at least a more nuanced approach to interpretation, which would enhance transparency and certainty.[44]

These voices seem to have been heard by the drafters of the reforms. There is now formal recognition in the Code that, where the actual intention of the parties cannot be identified, the contract should be interpreted objectively.[45] This appears in paragraph 2 of new article 1188, immediately following the statement that the court should ascertain the common intention of the parties. It provides that 'where the intention cannot be discerned, a contract is to be interpreted in the sense which a reasonable person placed in the same situation would give it'. This acceptance that the French approach to interpretation draws upon a combination of subjective

[40] CA Paris 2 Dec 1985. For other examples, see Gelot (n 14) [147]–[148].
[41] Soc 5 Jan 1984, BRDA 1984/7.
[42] Gelot (n 14) [1]–[19]; Maleville (n 14) [443]; Deshayes (n 6) 163-5; Simler (n 5) [29].
[43] Deshayes (n 6).
[44] Gelot (n 14) [1]–[19]; N Martial-Braz, 'L'objectivation des méthodes d'interprétation: la référence à la "personne raisonnable" et l'interprétation *in favorem*' RDC 2015.193.
[45] G Chantepie and M Latina, *Le nouveau droit des obligations* (2nd edn, Dalloz: Paris, 2018) [503].

and objective factors serves to create greater transparency and certainty, two of the avowed aims of the reforms.

### (e) The influence of international contract law instruments and a rapprochement with English law?

Some commentators consider that the newly added paragraph was influenced by and brings the French approach to interpretation closer to English law,[46] which gives effect to the objective intention of the parties and ignores their subjective intention. In ascertaining this objective intention, the courts in England seek to establish what a reasonable person in the position of the parties would have understood by the term.[47] This is distilled from the contract, rather than any enquiry into their real intention as in France. The exercise is fundamentally objective in nature[48] and believed to bring about greater predictability, consistency, and certainty as to how the contract will be interpreted. This is of particular benefit to third-party assignees who, despite coming to the contract after it was formed and not being privy to what the parties truly intended, should nonetheless be able to ascertain its meaning.[49]

A corollary of the objective approach to interpretation in England is that evidence of subjective intention is irrelevant to ascertaining the intention of the parties. There is therefore no need to have regard to evidence of pre-contractual negotiations.[50] This is regarded as 'unhelpful'[51] since only in the final agreement is the common intention of the parties recorded.[52] Other justifications include that taking pre-contractual negotiations into account would mean that a significant volume of potentially relevant documentation might need to be reviewed to ascertain the subjectively intended meaning, which in litigation would add to the cost burden.[53] It would also create greater uncertainty and difficulty for practitioners advising on what a reasonable outside observer would have taken to have been the intention of the parties.[54]

Whilst making no reference to English law as a source of influence, the drafters were open in acknowledging that the new paragraph was directly 'inspired by the Principles of European Contract Law, the Draft Common Frame of Reference and the UNIDROIT Principles'.[55] It is in almost identical terms to the corresponding

[46] See, for example, Martial-Braz (n 44) [2]: 'This standard of reasonableness... is imported directly from our Anglo-Saxon friends.'

[47] *Investors Compensation Scheme v West Bromwich* [1998] 1 WLR 896 (HL) 912-3 (Lord Hoffmann); *Deutsche Genossenschaftbank v Burnhope* [1995] 1 WLR 1580 (HL) 1587 (Lord Steyn).

[48] *Deutsche Genossenschaftbank v Burnhope* [1995] 1 WLR 1580 (HL) 1587 (Lord Steyn).

[49] *Chartbrook v Persimmon* [2009] 1 AC 1101 (HL) [40] (Lord Hoffmann).

[50] Ibid.

[51] *Prenn v Simmonds* [1971] 1 WLR 1381 (HL) 1384 (Lord Wilberforce).

[52] Ibid.

[53] *Chartbrook v Persimmon Homes* (n 49) [41] (Lord Hoffmann).

[54] Ibid., [39] and [41].

[55] 'Report to the President' (n 8) 11.

provisions in each of these instruments. For example, article 4.1 of the UNIDROIT Principles provides that:[56]

> (1) A contract shall be interpreted according to the common intention of the parties.
> (2) If such an intention cannot be established, the contract shall be interpreted according to the meaning that reasonable persons of the same kind as the parties would give to it in the same circumstances.

The instruments establish a hierarchy between the different approaches to interpretation.[57] Priority is given to ascertaining the actual intention of the parties, which takes precedence. If this cannot be ascertained, only then does the court turn to objective factors.

### (f) The significance of the conflict between the objective and subjective approaches

Some commentators consider that this hierarchy and more generally the supposed conflict between the objective and subjective approaches to interpretation have no real practical significance. The primacy of subjective interpretation 'is confined to a very narrow group of cases [where] ... both parties ... intend to employ words in a distinctive sense which does not correspond to the meaning which the words reasonably bear' and the 'application of article 4.1(2) is the rule, whilst article 4.1(1) is the exception'.[58] As for the conflict, it 'rarely matters in practice and ... [it] is more or less irrelevant once it is acknowledged that the same interpretative criteria must be employed in establishing the "subjective" intention of the parties as well as the "objective" understanding of reasonable persons'.[59]

Whilst it is true that, in many cases, both the subjective and objective methods would lead to the same outcome, that is, to the interpretation of ambiguous terms in the same way, the differences of approach are nevertheless relevant in several respects. First, the formal bias towards the subjective approach explains why French

[56] Article 5:101 of the PECL and article II.–8:101 of the DCFR.

[57] Official Comments to article 4.1; see S Vogenauer in S Vogenauer (ed), *Commentary on the UNIDROIT Principles of International Commercial Contracts (PICC)* (2nd edn, OUP: Oxford, 2015) 578 ff.

[58] See also S Vogenauer in N Jansen and R Zimmermann (eds), *Commentaries on European Contract Law* (OUP: Oxford, 2018) 1153: 'mere programmatic points of departure from which European legal systems attempt to develop solutions that are predictable and ... fair'; H Kötz, *European Contract Law* (2nd edn, OUP: Oxford, 2017) 109–10 and 112: 'hardly matters at all today'; H Beale, B Fauvarque-Cosson, J Rutgers, and S Vogenauer (eds) *Ius Commune Casebook on European Contract Law* (3rd edn, Hart Publishing: Oxford, 2019) 727: the distinction is 'largely irrelevant, particularly since it is well established that the same criteria must be employed in establishing both the "subjective" intention of the parties and the "objective" understanding of reasonable persons'.

[59] Vogenauer, *Commentary on the UNIDROIT Principles of International Commercial Contracts* (n 57) 580.

law has a wide conception of 'interpretation' that covers not only the ascertainment of the meaning of express terms but also the correction of mistakes and, as will be explained,[60] the supplementation of the contract. Giving meaning to, correcting, and supplementing the express terms of the contract all form part of a single, unified exercise that strives to ascertain and implement the actual intention of the parties, whether expressed or otherwise. The search for this intention is the common thread running through these processes. Second, the difference in approach helps explain why evidence of pre- and post-contractual conduct is admissible in French law but not in some systems that adopt an objective approach. In English law, the exclusion of such evidence has been said to follow 'from the objective character of all contractual construction. The course of the negotiations cannot tell us what the contract objectively meant. It can tell us only what one or other or both of the parties subjectively thought or assumed or hoped that it meant.'[61] Third, and as will be explained in the next section, a consequence of the predominantly subjective approach in France is that issues of interpretation are regarded as questions of fact, whereas under the objective approach in England they are questions of law.

There is also deep attachment amongst French lawyers to subjective interpretation. A number of commentators have opined that the new arrangement of article 1188 upholds this attachment by enshrining the primacy of the actual intention of the parties over their declared intention.[62] This is based on the reference having been positioned at the head of the section of the reformed Code on interpretation, effectively over-arching the other provisions.[63] In contrast, the requirement in old article 1156 for the court to establish the subjective common intention of the parties did not have any greater importance than any other principles of interpretation in the 1804 Code.

Nor has there been any suggestion that paragraph 2 of article 1188 casts doubt on the primacy of the subjective approach. On the contrary, commentators have variously remarked that 'to abandon the subjective approach to interpretation … which has an essential role, has never seriously been considered';[64] 'nothing has supplanted the classical search for the subjective intention of the parties';[65] 'the search for the common intention continues to reign… and this is not to be regretted';[66] and 'article 1188 gives real primacy to the search for the common intention of the parties … and this hierarchy would not make sense if the court

[60] See below pp 130–4 on *interprétation créatrice.*

[61] Lord Sumption, 'A Question of Taste: The Supreme Court and the Interpretation of Contracts' (2017) 17 OUCLJ 301, 309–10.

[62] O Deshayes, T Genicon, and Y-M Laithier, *Réforme du droit des contrats, du régime général et de la preuve des obligations* (2nd edn, LexisNexis: Paris, 2018) 417–19; Chantepie and Latina (n 45) [502]–[503]; Terré, Simler, Lequette, and Chénédé (n 12) [608].

[63] Ibid.

[64] Simler' (n 5) at [3] and [9].

[65] Ibid., [24].

[66] Deshayes (n 6) 162: see also C Grimaldi, 'Paradoxes autour de l'interprétation des contrats' RDC 2008.207; A Cermolacce 'L'article 1159 du Code civil' RLDC 2004.7 no 302.

could freely choose its preferred method of interpretation'.[67] The subjective approach has even been described as 'sacrosanct'[68] and the 'one and only mandatory principle' of interpretation.[69]

## 2 *Dénaturation*

Another novel feature in the 2016 reforms is the introduction of an express provision on *dénaturation*. This is the power of the *Cour de cassation* to review on appeal the decision of a lower court in which a contract is interpreted in a way that distorts the meaning of a term that is clear and precise. In practice, however, the *Cour de cassation* rarely exercises this review power, which leaves the final determination of issues of interpretation almost exclusively in the hands of lower courts.

### (a) The codification of *dénaturation*

The ascertainment of the subjective intention of the parties is a factual question[70] and therefore exclusively a matter for the courts of first instance and lower appeal courts. It is not open to the *Cour de cassation* to review findings of fact. Its appellate jurisdiction is confined to ensuring that legal principles have been applied properly. The only exception is where the interpretation of a lower court distorts the clear and precise meaning of a term (*dénaturation des clauses claires et précises*), in which case the *Cour de cassation* can review the decision. This power is codified in new article 1192 in a negative statement that 'clear and unambiguous terms are not subject to interpretation as doing so risks their distortion'. As the terms admit of only one meaning and the intention of the parties is self-evident, there is no need or even room for interpretation. It is not for the court to disturb an allocation of risk that is clear or to impose a different bargain.[71] The power of the *Cour de cassation* to review a decision that strays into this terrain gives the parties confidence that their clear and unambiguous meaning will be applied.[72]

[67] Terré, Simler, Lequette, and Chénédé (n 12) [607] ff; A Etienney de Sainte Marie 'Les principes, les directives et les clauses relatives à l'interprétation' RDC 2016.384, 388.

[68] P Simler, 'Propos introductifs—A la recherche des frontières de l'interprétation' RDC 2015.146; Deshayes (n 6) 165; D Mazeaud, 'L'encadrement des pouvoirs du juge: l'efficacité des clauses relatives à l'interprétation' RDC 2015.187.

[69] Gelot (n 14) [315]. See also Deshayes (n 6) 163–5; Etienney De Sainte Marie (n 67); Mazeaud (n 68); Deshayes, Genicon, and Laithier (n 62) 417–9. E Rawach, 'La portée des clauses tendant à exclure le rôle des documents précontractuels dans l'interprétation du contrat' D 2001.223 [14]–[16]. Supporting this view: Civ (1) 20 Jan 1970 Bull civ I no 24.

[70] Terré, Simler, Lequette, and Chénédé (n 12) [616]: 'A question of fact decided sovereignly by the lower courts.'

[71] Vogenauer, 'Interpretation of Contracts: Concluding Observations' (n 19) 131; Simler (n 5) [5].

[72] 'Report to the President' (n 8) 11; Civ 4 May 1942 DC 1942.131, note J Besson; see also the many cases cited by Maleville (n 14) [241]–[243].

In practice, the *Cour de cassation* exercises this power very rarely[73] and lower court decisions on questions of interpretation are seldom overturned on appeal. Some degree of ambiguity can usually be identified in a clause, particularly when regard is had to the context, surrounding circumstances, and the contract as a whole. Only occasionally therefore can the meaning of a term be said to be so clear and precise that the power is engaged.[74] This is likely to mean that the impact of the codification of *dénaturation* is minimal. It is also for this reason and in the absence of any defining decisions or significant guidance from the *Cour de cassation* on matters of interpretation[75] that the subject has not generated nearly the same interest in France as in common law jurisdictions.[76]

### (b) Interpretation clauses to provide commercial certainty?

Whether and the extent to which lower courts take advantage of the narrow remit of the *Cour de cassation* in order to rewrite or distort contract terms is difficult to know. Any proper analysis is prevented by interpretation issues ultimately turning on the subjective intention of the parties, which is very much fact-specific and hard to second-guess from the brief judgments that are given by French courts. This itself can give rise to uncertainty and has been the subject of criticism.[77] Some have called for the *Cour de cassation* to be more vigorous in using *dénaturation* to review interpretation decisions of lower courts.[78] However, at least prior to the reforms, this had not led to any change of approach.[79] Perhaps more significantly, the calls were echoed by the drafters of the reforms.[80] It remains to be seen whether they will be heeded.

A possible means of enhancing transparency and certainty in the interpretation process would be for contracting parties to be able to contract out of, or adapt, the principles of interpretation in the Code. This would be effected through the insertion into the contract of an interpretation clause to direct or influence how the words used are understood and applied.[81]

[73] Simler (n 14) [51].

[74] Simler (n 14) [61]–[72].

[75] Cass Sect Reun, 2 Feb 1808, S chron, GAJC, t 2, no 160; D Tricot, 'Le juge: le contrôle de dénaturation et la liberté d'interprétation des conventions' RDC 2015.149.

[76] See, however, the workshop of the Revue des Contrats held in 2015: 'L'interprétation: une menace pour la sécurité des conventions?' RDC.2015.

[77] See Tricot (n 75) and the other papers published on the back of the workshop organized by the Revue des Contrats entitled 'L'interprétation: une menace pour la sécurité des conventions?' 1 RDC.2015.

[78] See Tricot (n 75) 150–1 and 153.

[79] Ibid.

[80] F Ancel, B Fauvarque-Cosson, and J Gest, *Aux sources de la réforme du droit des contrats* (Dalloz: Paris, 2017) [33.36].

[81] See Rawach (n 69); Mazeaud (n 68); Gelot (n 14) [258] ff; C Helleringer, 'Quand les parties font leur loi. Réflexion sur la contractualisation du pouvoir judiciaire d'interprétation' in M Xifaras and G Lewkowicz (eds), *Repenser le contrat* (Dalloz: Paris, 2009) 277; B Fauvarque-Cosson, 'Les nouvelles règles du Code civil relatives à l'interprétation des contrats: perspective comparative et internationale' RDC 2017.363.

It is clear from decisions of the *Cour de cassation* that the interpretation principles contained in the Code do not bind but instead serve as 'mere advice to judges... without mandatory character and not imposing absolute rules'.[82] They should be seen as akin to a 'tool box',[83] there to assist the court in identifying what the parties sought to achieve.[84]

One perceived benefit of enabling the parties to contract out of the interpretation principles in the Code or otherwise direct how the contract should be interpreted is that this would curtail or even exclude the broad powers of lower courts over interpretation issues. In turn this would reduce the scope for the court to depart from the meaning intended by the parties.[85]

The reforms were silent in relation to interpretation clauses. It is, however, difficult to see that there could be any fundamental objection to their use or enforceability, given that they are no more than an expression of the will of the parties and, after all, interpreting a contract is but a search for their intention. Any other analysis would seem to be at odds with the fundamental principle of freedom of contract.

Two particular types of interpretation clause warrant particular mention. The first is the entire agreement clause (*clause d'intégralité*), which typically provides that the obligations of the parties are entirely contained in the contract and any collateral or oral agreements or pre-contractual statements between the parties have no contractual or other effect. This is intended to prevent such agreements or statements as might be made from being taken into account in ascertaining the obligations of the parties. The second is the so-called priority clause (*clause de priorité*), which seeks to create a form of hierarchy between the terms of the contract or between the contract and other instruments made by the same parties. Such clauses are particularly prevalent in complex contractual relationships involving lengthy or multiple different contracts where there is an increased risk of conflict. By establishing an order of priority, the court is directed as to how the parties intend that any such conflict should be resolved.

There has been relatively little coverage of priority clauses in the case law but they have clearly been held to be valid in some cases.[86] Only in one case—a decision of the Paris Court of Appeal—does it appear that the impact of an entire agreement clause has been considered. There it was held that, in order to be effective, the clause must preclude evidence of pre-contractual negotiations and other extraneous documents from being relied upon to *interpret* the contract. It is

[82] Req 18 March 1807, S 1807, 1, 367; Req 16 February 1892, S 1893.1.409; Civ (1) 19 Dec 1995, Bull civ 1995 I no 466.

[83] Simler (n 68).

[84] C Grimaldi, 'La valeur normative des directives d'interprétation' RDC 2015.154 [4]; Simler (n 14) [37].

[85] Mazeaud (n 68).

[86] CA Paris 15 June 2005, RTD civ 2006 p111, note J Mestre; see also the cases cited by Mazeaud (n 68) and Rawach (n 69) 223; Gelot (n 14) [258] ff.

not sufficient that the clause precludes the reliance on such evidence to prove the *content* of the contract since this does not necessarily prevent reliance on the evidence in the interpretation process.[87]

The silence of the reforms in relation to interpretation clauses is in contrast with the international contract law instruments that served as the inspiration for some of the newly introduced articles of the Code on interpretation. An example is article 2:105 of the Principles of European Contract Law (PECL), which states that:[88]

> (1) If a written contract contains an individually negotiated clause stating that the writing embodies all the terms of the contract (a merger clause), any prior statements, undertakings or agreements which are not embodied in the writing do not form part of the contract.
>
> ....
>
> (3) The parties' prior statements may be used to interpret the contract. This rule may not be excluded or restricted except by an individually negotiated clause.

Under this provision, unless there is an express exclusion, evidence of pre-contractual negotiations is admissible in the interpretation process, which achieves a similar effect to the Paris Court of Appeal decision.

It has been lamented by some commentators that the reforms did not confirm the enforceability of interpretation clauses. This would have been conducive to transactional certainty.[89] As regards entire agreement clauses, which are commonly incorporated in international commercial contracts,[90] it would also have helped to fulfil one of the objectives of the reforms of increasing the attractiveness of French law to the international business community.[91] As it stands, the uncertainties as to their enforceability that existed before the reforms persist.

## 3 Standard form contracts and the *contra proferentem* rule

Prior to the 2016 reforms there was thought to be a pressing need for regulation of how standard form contracts are interpreted, with two issues giving rise to particular consternation. The first was whether it is realistically possible to ascertain any common subjective intention from standard terms. Some argued that this

[87] CA Paris 4 March 1980, Expertises, no 17, April 1980, 8.

[88] See also article 2.1.17 UNIDROIT Principles and article II.–4:104 of the Draft Common Frame of Reference (DCFR).

[89] Mazeaud (n 68); B Fauvarque-Cosson, 'L'interprétation du contrat: observations comparatives' RDC 2007.481.

[90] Ibid.

[91] Terré, Simler, Lequette, and Chénédé (n 12) [603]; Bénabent (n 13) [284]; Deshayes, Genicon, and Laithier (n 62) 417–9.

simply could not be done[92] since standard terms are by definition not negotiated and typically are simply imposed by the stronger party in the relationship. An approach to interpretation that is appropriate in the context of negotiated contracts is therefore unlikely to be suitable for standard terms. The second was that, on some occasions, different courts have interpreted the same clause in a standard form contract in different ways, giving rise to uncertainty.[93]

The solution of the drafters was to provide for the application of the *contra proferentem* rule. New article 1190 states that 'in case of ambiguity, a bespoke contract is interpreted against the creditor and in favour of the debtor, and a standard form contract is interpreted against the person who put it forward'. The practical effect is that the contract is interpreted against the party that introduces the standard terms rather than the other party.[94] It provides for an objective approach that does not look to the actual intention of the parties or the true meaning of their words but instead is concerned with rebalancing their obligations.[95]

The *contra proferentem* rule was already familiar in French law prior to the reforms, having appeared in other contexts in the 1804 Code such as in relation to sale contracts pursuant to old article 1602, as well as to consumer contracts under article L211-1 of the Consumer Code.[96] It is commonly justified on grounds of fairness, equity, and the protection of the weaker party, and also as incentivizing the party drafting the contract to do so with precision and clarity.[97] With the insertion of article 1190, the section of the Code on interpretation now specifically refers to standard form contracts. This is consistent with the stated aim of the reforms of designating provisions 'which only apply to standard form contracts'.[98]

In common with several of the other features that were introduced in the reforms, the new approach is in line with a number of international contract instruments. For instance, article 5:103 of the PECL states that 'where there is doubt about the meaning of a contract term not individually negotiated, an interpretation

[92] See, for example, T Revet 'L'uniformisation de l'interprétation: contrats types et contrats d'adhésion' RDC 2015.199.

[93] Terré, Simler, Lequette, and Chénédé (n 12) [616] citing Civ 28 Jan 1907, two decisions DP 1908, 1.5, S 1912.1.22. For the lack of intervention of the *Cour de cassation* in this area, see also: Com 24 Mars 1965, Bull civ III no 230; Civ (1) 21 May 1969, Bull civ I no 169; Civ (1) 28 Oct 1970, Bull civ I no 285; Chantepie and Latina (n 45) [508]; B Nicholas, *The French Law of Contract* (2nd edn, OUP: Oxford, 1992) 48–9; Revet (n 92) has shown that, through *dénaturation*, the *Cour de cassation* has on occasions imposed its own interpretation of clauses in standard form contracts but without acknowledging that it was doing so.

[94] It has long been recognized by the *Cour de cassation* that in some circumstances, the creditor is not the person who drafts the contract and that protection should be against the latter whose responsibility it is to draft a contract with clear and precise terms: Civ (1) 22 Oct 1974 Bull civ I no 271; Simler (n 5) [62]–[67].

[95] It is, therefore, objective in a different sense from article 1188 of the Civil Code.

[96] Although the impact of the rule differs in the consumer context as the *most* favourable interpretation for the consumer is to be adopted.

[97] Fauvarque-Cosson (n 81) and (n 89); Martial-Braz (n 44); Terré, Simler, Lequette, and Chénédé (n 12) [610].

[98] *Loi d'habilitation* (n 7).

of the term against the party who supplied it is to be preferred'. There are comparable rules in article 4.6 of the UNIDROIT Principles and article II. –8:103 of the Draft Common Frame of Reference (DCFR), albeit their scope extends to all unclear terms rather than being confined only to those that are contained in standard terms.

The greater prominence given to the *contra proferentem* rule by the reforms in France[99] is in contrast with England where, aside from in relation to exclusion clauses, the rule has repeatedly been criticized as unreliable and leading to potentially arbitrary outcomes.[100] It has been said to be 'in its death throes',[101] 'rarely, if ever, of any assistance,'[102] and 'very much a last refuge, almost an admission of defeat, when it comes to construing a document'.[103] The point has been reached where 'there are now only skeletal, if any remains'[104] of the rule. Its growing relevance in France might therefore surprise English contract lawyers.

## B The Supplementation of the Terms: *Interprétation créatrice*

What English lawyers regard as implying terms is known in France as *interprétation créatrice* and forms part of the broader process of interpreting the contract for the purpose of ascertaining the common subjective intention of the parties.[105] It is available where the parties have omitted to address a significant issue and enables the court to supplement the contract with a term to fill the resulting gap.[106] A supplementary obligation is therefore imposed on the parties, despite not being provided for in their contract.[107]

[99] Martial-Braz (n 44).

[100] *K/S Victoria Street v House of Fraser (Stores Management)* [2011] Ch 497 (CA) [68] (Lord Neuberger). On the role and relevance of the *contra proferentem* rule, see J McCunn, 'Contra Proferentem Rule: Contract Law's Great Survivor' (2019) 39 OJLS 483. McCunn argues that there is still a role for the rule in contract law today.

[101] Ibid.

[102] *K/S Victoria Street v House of Fraser* (n 100); McCunn (n 100).

[103] *BNY Mellon Corporate Trustee Services v LBG Capital No 1* [2016] UKSC 29 (SC) [53] (Lord Neuberger); McCunn (n 100).

[104] *Multiplex Construction (Europe) v Dunne* [2017] EWHC 3073 (TCC) [27] and see the other references in McCunn (n 100).

[105] Terré, Simler, Lequette, and Chénédé (n 12) [608]–[614]; P Malaurie, L Aynès, and P Stoffel-Munck, *Droit des obligations* (10th edn, LGDJ: Paris 2018) [772]; J Bell, S Boyron, and S Whittaker, *Principles of French Law* (2nd edn, OUP: Oxford, 2008) 329: 'the distinction between express and implied terms is not as pervasive a distinction as is found in English law… instead, the French starting point in determining the effects of a contract is to look into what was the common ('subjective') intention of the parties and in this respect no distinction needs to be drawn between what they expressly and what they impliedly agreed. Questions of what the parties agreed are treated as ones of interpretation, whether this relates to determining what was included within their agreement or what meaning should be attributed to words which they clearly did include.'

[106] Terré, Simler, Lequette, and Chénédé (n 12) [612]–[614].

[107] Rowan (n 4) 291–2; Aikens (n 2) 230–1; Bell, Boyron, and Whittaker (n 105) 329–32.

## 1 The sources of supplementary contractual obligations

The power of the court to supplement the contract is set out in new article 1194, which states that 'contracts create obligations not merely in relation to what they expressly provide, but also to all the consequences which are given to them by equity, usage or legislation'.

Of these three sources of supplementary obligations, equity (*équité*) is perhaps the most controversial. Over many years the *Cour de cassation* declined various invitations to supplement the terms agreed by the parties on this basis, holding that to do so would infringe upon their freedom of contract. In an 1876 decision, for example, it held that:

> in no circumstances, even if it would seem equitable to do so, should the court take into account the time and circumstances in order to modify the parties' contract and to substitute new terms for those that were freely agreed by the parties.[108]

On occasion the courts have, however, been willing to supplement contracts of certain types with general obligations that enhance the protection of one party. The two main examples are the obligation of safety (*obligation de sécurité*) in contracts for transportation, which requires the party providing the transportation services to protect the passenger against the risk of personal injury, and the obligation to provide information (*obligation d'information*), primarily in contracts for professional services, which requires the professional (*professionnel*) to inform the other contracting party about aspects of the service of which they are less likely to be aware.[109]

Usage (sometimes referred to as 'custom') involves supplementing the contract with a term in accordance with the practice of a particular trade or industry, to which both parties must belong,[110] or a course of prior dealing on particular terms, for example where an employer routinely makes bonus payments to employees on certain terms.[111] Whether there is such a custom is a matter of fact, which falls to the lower courts to determine.

Legislation that relates to particular categories of contracts[112] can also be a source of supplementary contractual obligations. Where a contract falls within a

[108] Cited and translated in Aikens (n 2) 230: Civ 6 March 1876, D 76.1193 1876.1.193, note A Giboulot.

[109] For example, a doctor is under an obligation to inform his patient about the risks involved in surgery: Civ (1) 19 April 1988 Bull civ I no 107; Civ (3) June 2010 Bull civ I no 128, D 2010.1522, note Sargos, RDC 2010.1235, obs Borghetti; Terré, Simler, Lequette, and Chénédé (n 12) [614] ff; Bénabent (n 13) [293–4].

[110] Com 18 Jan 1972 JCP 1972.II.17072.

[111] P Ancel, *Droit des obligations. Séquence 5—Contenu du contrat: par la volonté et au-delà de la volonté* (Dalloz: Paris, 2018) 210.

[112] See Chapter 3 on the classification of contracts, pp 44–51.

special category, thus becoming what is referred to as a *contrat spécial*,[113] it is automatically supplemented with obligations that apply to contracts in that category. These obligations are mostly capable of being modified or excluded by agreement between the parties (*lois supplétives*)[114] but some are mandatory and therefore incapable of exclusion (*lois impératives*). As Nicholas explained:

> The first step for a French court … is to 'qualify' or characterize the agreement before it. If the agreement falls within the limits of one of the special contracts, its contents will be largely determined by the appropriate *lois supplétives*. Even if it is 'qualified' as an innominate contract, its incidents will often be determined by reference to that one (or more) of the special contracts to which it is most analogous. The French starting-point is that the incidents of a contract are fixed by law, subject to the parties' power to vary them.[115]

As an example, the Civil Code contains over 100 articles that regulate contracts of sale, including forty-eight relating to the obligations of the seller (articles 1602 to 1649) and eight on those of the buyer (articles 1650 to 1657). Unless the parties have expressly stipulated obligations of the seller and the buyer in their contract, those set out in the Code will apply.

## 2 The relationship between supplementation and interpretation

There has been debate in France as to whether *interprétation créatrice* can properly be regarded as part of a broader exercise of contractual interpretation. A number of commentators have contended that it is not truly in the nature of interpretation and should instead be seen as a distinct process.[116] It has been argued that on no view can the supplementary obligation of safety (*obligation de sécurité*) in transportation contracts and the obligation of information (*obligation d'information*) in professional services contracts be attributed in all cases to a common subjective intention of the parties. Indeed the process does not involve any attempt to ascertain the meaning of terms that they have chosen.[117] On the contrary, it is usually indisputable that the parties did not intend or even think about such obligations,

[113] Ibid.

[114] Ancel, Fauvarque-Cosson, and Gest (n 80) [33.11].

[115] Nicholas (n 93) 49; see also B Nicholas, 'Rules and Terms—Civil Law and Common Law' (1973-1974) 48 Tul L Rev 946.

[116] Terré, Simler, Lequette, and Chénédé (n 12) [608]–[614]; Malaurie, Aynès, and Stoffel-Munck (n 105) [772].

[117] Etienney de Sainte Marie (n 1) [4]; Simler (n 5) [13] ff; Terré, Simler, Lequette, and Chénédé (n 12) [612]–[614]; Deshayes (n 6); Chantepie and Latina (n 45) [500]; P Catala, 'Interprétation et qualification dans l'avant-projet de réforme des obligations' in *Etudes offertes à G Viney* (LGDJ: Paris, 2008) 243; G Viney, P Jourdain, and S Carval, *Traité de droit civil, Les conditions de la responsabilité* (LGDJ: Paris, 2013) [458] ff.

which are imposed for policy reasons and often based on fairness. The process is entirely objective. It has even been described as 'forcing the contract' (*forcage du contrat*),[118] reflecting in graphic terms that it occurs independently of the subjective intention of the parties.

One reason that the supplementation of the contract with additional terms has been understood as a species of interpretation is that it was partly addressed in the section of the 1804 Code on interpretation. One oft-cited example is old article 1160, which provided that 'the contract must be supplemented by clauses which comply with usages'. Whilst this was capable of being linked to the intention of the parties, in substance it amounted to supplementing the contract with new terms.

The view that *interprétation créatrice* should be regarded as a distinct process was heeded in the 2016 reforms with the removal of what was old article 1160 that dealt with supplementation by custom from the section of the Code on interpretation.[119] The five surviving articles in that section relate principally to *interprétation explicative*, with *interpretation creátrice* addressed later in the Code at new article 1194.[120] This is consistent with the approach in international contract law instruments such as the PECL and the DCFR, which deal with the supplementation of terms separately from interpretation.[121] It is also more coherent, given that the two processes have distinct objectives and modes of operation.

The relationship between the supplementation of terms and interpretation has also been topical relatively recently in England, where the method of supplementing the contract is for the court to imply terms. A distinction is usually drawn between terms that are implied into individual contracts to give effect to the presumed but unexpressed intention of the parties (which are known as terms implied 'in fact') and those implied into all contracts of a particular type to give effect to a rule of law or public policy (known as terms implied 'in law').

There has recently been a debate in England as to whether the implication of terms and contractual interpretation are truly distinct or in substance part of the same process, albeit this related only to the implication of terms in fact, not in law.[122] In *A-G of Belize Telecom v Belize Telecoms Ltd*,[123] Lord Hoffmann expressed the view—redolent of the original understanding in France—that to imply a term in fact is essentially an exercise in interpretation. It involves discovering what the instrument means and giving effect to the intention of the parties as objectively ascertained.[124] There 'is only one question: is that what the instrument,

[118] L Josserand, obs under CA Lyon 7 Dec 1928 DP 1929.II.17; Etienney de Sainte Marie (n 1).

[119] Old article 1160 of the 1804 Civil Code.

[120] Old article 1135 of the 1804 Civil Code.

[121] International contract law instruments have taken different approaches to this question: articles 6:102 PECL and II.-9:101 DCFR are in the sections on the contents and effects of contract; note, however, that article 4.8 of the UNIDROIT Principles addresses the implication of terms but in the section on interpretation.

[122] R Hooley, 'Implied Terms After Belize' (2014) 73 CLJ 315, 325–6.

[123] [2009] 2 All ER 1127.

[124] Ibid., [16] (Lord Hoffmann).

read as a whole against the relevant background, would reasonably be understood to mean?'.[125]

Whilst the assimilation of interpretation with implication was welcomed in some quarters as enhancing 'the internal coherence of the law',[126] it has since been doubted by the Supreme Court. In *Marks and Spencer plc v BNP Paribas Securities Services Trust Co (Jersey) Ltd*,[127] whilst recognizing that the two processes share a number of characteristics, Lord Neuberger stated that they are distinct and should not be elided. The similarities include that both involve determining the scope and meaning of the contract and take similar factors into account,[128] including the words of the contract, the surrounding circumstances known to the parties, commercial common sense and what would be understood by the reasonable reader.[129] Ultimately, however, interpretation involves resolving ambiguities or inconsistencies in the express language used by the parties, whereas there is no such language to interpret where the court implies a term. As such, interpretation precedes any question of implication. Only where the court has decided what the parties have expressly agreed can consideration then be given as to whether a term should be implied.[130] Today the settled position seems to be that Lord Hoffmann's view should be treated as 'inspired discussion rather than authoritative guidance on the law of implied terms'.[131] Despite sharing the common aim of establishing the objective intention of the parties,[132] interpretation and implication remain 'two logically distinct exercises with separate rules'.[133]

[125] Ibid., [21] (Lord Hoffmann).

[126] *Stena Line Ltd v Merchant Navy Ratings Pension Fund Trustees Ltd* [2011] Pens LR 223, [36] (Arden LJ). *Belize* generated extensive discussion in academic literature. See, for example: D McLauchlan, 'Construction and Implication: In Defence of Belize Telecom' [2014] LMCLQ 203; PS Davies, 'Recent Developments in the Law of Implied Terms' [2010] LMCLQ 140.

[127] [2015] UKSC 72; [2016] AC 742.

[128] Ibid., [26] (Lord Neuberger).

[129] Ibid., [26]–[28] (Lord Neuberger).

[130] Ibid., [28] (Lord Neuberger).

[131] Ibid., [31] (Lord Neuberger).

[132] E McKendrick, *Contract Law* (13th edn, Basingstoke: Macmillan, 2019) 188.

[133] *Europa Plus SCA SIF v Anthracite Investments (Ireland) plc* [2016] EWHC 437 (Comm) [34] (Popplewell J).

# 7
# Unfair Terms and the Rebalancing of Contracts

As shown in Chapter 5 on the validity of the contract, French courts can review the way in which contracts are concluded and in certain circumstances will annul those that result from procedural unfairness. In contrast, substantive fairness, that is, the fairness of the actual content of the contract, is generally regarded as a matter for the parties rather than the courts. As Alfred Fouillée famously wrote, 'whatever is contractual is just' (*qui dit contractuel dit juste*).[1]

There are, however, important exceptions to this principle and on occasion the courts will interfere with unfair terms in the name of substantive fairness (*justice contractuelle*). This can happen where the contractual benefit purportedly conferred by the contract on one of the parties is 'illusory or derisory' (article 1169); a term deprives an 'essential obligation [of the contract] of its substance' (article 1170); or a non-negotiable term in a standard form contract 'creates a significant imbalance in the rights and obligations of the parties' (article 1171).

## A The Starting Principle: No Judicial Interference with the Content of the Contract

**Civil Code**[2]

Art. 1168.—In synallagmatic contracts, a lack of equivalence in the acts of performance of the parties is not a ground of nullity of the contract, unless legislation provides otherwise.

Article 1168 is the first of four new articles that regulate the equilibrium of the contract. It provides that an imbalance between the mutual performances required

[1] A Fouillée, *La science sociale contemporaine* (2nd edn, Librairie Hachette: Paris, 1885) 410.

[2] 'Ordonnance no 2016-131 du 10 février 2016 portant réforme du droit des contrats, du régime général et de la preuve des obligations', JORF no 0035 of 11 February 2016. The Ordonnance was translated into English by J Cartwright, B Fauvarque-Cosson, and S Whittaker: <http://www.textes.justice.gouv.fr/art_pix/THE-LAW-OF-CONTRACT-2-5-16.pdf> (2016 version) and <http://www.textes.justice.gouv.fr/art_pix/Translationrevised2018final.pdf> (2018 version) accessed 1 September 2021. The translations of the new articles contained in this book are theirs.

*The New French Law of Contract.* Solène Rowan, Oxford University Press. © Solène Rowan 2022.
DOI: 10.1093/oso/9780198810872.003.0007

under the contract is not a ground of nullity in synallagmatic contracts.[3] As long as the three requirements of article 1128—consent, capacity, and content which is lawful and certain—are present, the contract will be valid.[4] In the words of the 'Report to the President of the Republic', in which the drafters of the reforms explained the new articles, the 'equivalence of the performances of the parties is not a condition of the validity of the contract'.[5]

The parties are therefore free to determine the substantive content and economic balance of their bargain. That the bargain turns out to be bad for one of the parties is ordinarily irrelevant and no more a ground of nullity in France than in England, where the courts have shown no appetite to disturb what the parties have willingly agreed. It is similarly not open to French courts to rebalance the obligations of the parties. These limitations on judicial power over unfair terms are consistent with the principle of the autonomy of the will which, as noted in Chapter 2, holds that above all else contracts are regulated by the will of the parties, who are free to bind themselves to whomever and on whatever terms they decide, and the courts will give effect to their voluntarily created obligations.[6]

The rule that contracts do not have to be objectively fair or balanced in order to be valid is long-standing, uncontroversial,[7] and regarded as essential for legal certainty.[8] In the words of Pothier, it 'has been widely established for the security and freedom of commerce, which requires that one cannot easily go back on agreements. Otherwise we would not dare to make a contract for fear that the person with whom we have contracted might consider themselves harmed and bring a case against us.'[9]

Whilst new article 1168 does not establish a novel principle, it is nevertheless notable for two reasons. First, its position as the first of the four articles regulating the equilibrium of contractual obligations is 'symbolic',[10] enunciating at the outset the overarching principle of non-interference on the ground of substantive fairness. The three articles that follow (articles 1169 to 1171) merely stipulate exceptions to this principle. Second, the new formulation of the principle is clearer and more precise than in the former provision—old article 1118—which rather elusively stated that '*lésion* vitiates agreements only in certain contracts and with

[3] For a definition of synallagmatic contracts and more generally the classification of contracts, see Chapter 3 , pp 44–51.

[4] See Chapter 5.

[5] 'Report to the President of the Republic relating to Ordonnance no 2016–131 of 10 February 2016 on the reform of contract law, the general regime and proof of obligations', JORF no 0035 of 11 February 2016, 9.

[6] See the section on definition of contract in Chapter 3, pp 31–2.

[7] G Chantepie and M Latina, *La réforme du droit des obligations, Commentaire théorique et pratique dans l'ordre du Code civil* (2nd edn, Dalloz: Paris, 2018) [428].

[8] P Malaurie, L Aynès, and P Stoffel-Munck, *Droit des obligations* (10th edn, LGDJ: Paris, 2018) [519].

[9] R Pothier, *Traité des obligations I, Œuvres, vol. I* (Berville: Paris, 1821) 36–7. Translation by John Bell.

[10] O Deshayes, T Genicon, and Y-M Laithier, *Réforme du droit des contrats, du régime général et de la preuve des obligations* (2nd edn, LexisNexis: Paris, 2018) 325.

regard to certain persons, as will be explained in this same section'.[11] The term *lésion*, which unhelpfully was not defined, has now been replaced with a definition of the vitiating factor—'lack of equivalence in the acts of performance'—that is more meaningful and informative. New article 1168 also expressly articulates the principle of non-interference whereas old article 1118 somewhat focused only on the exceptions to it.[12] Lastly, the new article specifies that the principle applies to 'synallagmatic contracts', replacing the vague previous references to 'certain contracts' and 'certain persons'. These clarifications were intended to achieve greater accessibility and intelligibility, one of the main overarching aims of the reforms.[13]

## B The Exceptions to Article 1168: The Protection against Unfair Terms

Civil Code

Art. 1169.—An onerous contract is a nullity where, at the moment of its formation, what is agreed in return for the benefit of the person undertaking an obligation is illusory or derisory.

Art. 1170.—Any contract term which deprives a debtor's essential obligation of its substance is deemed not written.

(2016 version)

*Art. 1171.—Any term of a standard form contract which creates a significant imbalance in the rights and obligations of the parties to the contract is deemed not written.*

*The assessment of significant imbalance must not concern either the main subject-matter of the contract nor the adequacy of the price in relation to the act of performance.*

(2018 version)

Art. 1171.—In a standard-form contract, any term which is non-negotiable and determined in advance by one of the parties and which creates a significant imbalance in the rights and obligations of the parties to the contract is deemed not written.

The assessment of significant imbalance must not relate either to the main subject-matter of the contract nor to the adequacy of the price in relation to the act of performance.

[11] Article 1118 of the 1804 Civil Code: '*Lésion* does not vitiate agreements except in certain cases or with regard to certain persons, as shall be explained in this same section.'

[12] Deshayes, Genicon, and Laithier (n 10) 325.

[13] 'Report to the President' (n 5) 1.

Of the numerous exceptions to article 1168,[14] several existed before the reforms. These include what is now article 1149, which provides that 'mere substantive inequality of bargain' (*simple lésion*) can nullify 'day-to-day acts effected by a minor'; article 1844-1, pursuant to which a clause in a partnership agreement that entitles a partner to all of the partnership's profits or insulates a partner from all of its liabilities is deemed not written; and article 1674, which states that, in a contract for the sale of land, where the price received by the seller is less than five-twelfths of the market value, the seller can seek rescission of the contract and the buyer has the option of either returning the land and recovering the price or keeping the land and paying a supplement of the difference between the contract price and the market value minus one-tenth.[15]

The exceptions at articles 1169, 1170, and 1171 were newly introduced into the Civil Code by the reforms. According to the Report to the President, these provisions were intended to 'preserve the interests of the party which is the weakest'[16] and 'to guarantee substantive fairness (*justice contractuelle*)'.[17] As it has turned out, they have proved to be some of the most contentious. This is in no small part because they generalize and formalize exceptions that had been developed in cases decided before the reforms that were founded on the controversial doctrine of *cause*.[18]

## 1 Use of the doctrine of *cause* before the reforms to redress contractual imbalance

In order to expose both the genesis of, and the controversy surrounding, the new exceptions to article 1168, it is helpful to begin with an outline of the doctrine of *cause* from prior to the reforms. It will be recalled from Chapter 5[19] that the formal excision of this doctrine from the Civil Code was one of the most symbolic and widely discussed changes brought about by the reforms. Hitherto, a contract was only valid if it had a *cause* that was lawful. This was one of the four conditions set out in old article 1108 that had to be fulfilled for a contract to be valid, the others being consent, capacity to contract, and a defined object (*objet*) as the subject-matter of the contract.

[14] In addition to the examples cited in the text, see article 889 of the Civil Code; article L411-13 of the Rural Code; and article L131-5 of the Intellectual Property Code.

[15] Article 1681 of the Civil Code.

[16] 'Report to the President' (n 5) 3.

[17] Ibid., 9.

[18] Articles 1169 and 1170 of the Civil Code. P Stoffel-Munck, 'The Revolution in Unfair Terms' in J Cartwright and S Whittaker (eds), *The Code Napoléon Rewritten: French Contract Law after the 2016 Reforms* (Hart Publishing: Oxford, 2017) 145, 146.

[19] See the section on the removal of *cause* as a requirement in Chapter 5, pp 103–4 and 111–2.

A *cause* could be either objective or subjective. The 'objective cause' (*cause objective*) was the abstract goal of the contract. This was usually the counter-performance promised by the other party, which was typically the same within any given category of contract. For example, in sale of goods contracts, the *cause* of the seller was payment of the purchase price and the *cause* of the buyer was to acquire ownership of the goods. In the absence of an objective cause, the contract lacked reciprocity and was susceptible to being annulled by the court. The rationale was that a contract must have a purpose—a *raison d'être*—in order to be valid, which meant there had to be a minimum benefit for both parties. 'Subjective cause' (*cause subjective*) on the other hand, concerned the subjective reason that a party entered into a contract. This would differ for each contract, reflecting that parties enter into contracts for multitudinous reasons. In order for the contract to be valid, the subjective cause had to be lawful.

The doctrine of *cause* came to be regarded as problematic mainly because French courts were finding that a contract had no objective cause to justify interfering with the agreed terms in an increasingly broad range of circumstances. It was known for French courts to invoke the doctrine to annul contracts which had become bad bargains. In one familiar case, the *Cour de cassation* annulled a contract in which, although performance on both sides was still possible, it became apparent that the promisee's commercial rationale for entering the contract was unrealistic and his commercial aspirations for the contract were unachievable.[20] The doctrine also became a basis for rebalancing contracts that were perceived to contain unfair terms. As an example, in another well-known 'Chronopost' case, the doctrine was relied upon by the *Cour de cassation* to justify the striking down of exemption and limitation clauses where the promisor failed to perform a fundamental obligation of the contract and sought to rely on the clause to pay derisory compensation to the promisee.[21]

The virtues and shortcomings of the doctrine of *cause* were the subject of considerable debate. It was lauded by some as an instrument for promoting fairness and criticized by others as a judicial device for interfering with contractual terms. These controversies ultimately led to the formal removal of the doctrine from the new Civil Code. However, this was probably more semantic than real and in practice has made little difference. To a large extent the requirement of an objective cause has reappeared in new articles 1169 and 1170, which seek to ensure some degree of contractual fairness by enabling the court to interfere with the terms of a contract in certain circumstances. As the Report to the President recognized, 'the formal abandonment of the notion of cause, which has given rise to much debate, will allow France to move closer to the legislation of many foreign countries, while

[20] See the well-known *Video cassette* decision: Civ (1) 3 July 1996, D 1997.500 note P Reigné.

[21] See the well-known decision: Com 22 Oct 1996, D 1997.121 note A Sériaux; Com 30 May 2006, D 2006.1599, note X Delpech and D Mazeaud.

introducing in the law the various functions, including the rebalancing of the contract, which had been assigned to the doctrine of cause by the case law'.[22]

## 2 'Illusory or derisory' counter-performance

The spirit of objective cause can now be found in article 1169, which is the first of three newly introduced 'corrective measures to guarantee substantive fairness'.[23] It provides that the performance to be rendered by a party under an onerous contract[24] cannot be illusory or derisory. Every contract serves, or should serve, an economic purpose or usefulness. If the performance is illusory or derisory, then the contract is deemed to lack content and is a nullity.[25]

Whether the performance is illusory or derisory must be assessed objectively at the time the contract is made. It will be 'illusory' where it is not real or serious.[26] This was held to be the case for example, in respect of an insurance policy where, unbeknownst to the policy holder, the subject-matter of the insurance cover had already perished when the policy was taken out;[27] a promise to pay a debt that had already been discharged;[28] and a contract for the transfer of a permit that was non-transferable.[29]

The performance is 'derisory' where the benefit conferred is so small as to be insignificant. There must be an imbalance that is 'enormous to the point of rendering the contract useless'.[30] This is a fluid standard and the courts have a broad discretion. For instance, the *Cour de cassation* refused to annul the sale of a ring designed and sold by the celebrated jeweller Cartier for 100,000 French francs where its market value was 460,000 French francs.[31] Although low, the price was not insignificant. In contrast, a contract for the holiday rental of a bungalow in Corsica was annulled on the basis that the agreed price of 790 euros was derisory where the bungalow was in a prime location, the rental was for two weeks at the height of the holiday season, including half board for five people,[32] and the market price was 3,950 euros.

22 'Report to the President' (n 5) 2.
23 Ibid., 9.
24 On the definition of onerous contracts, see Chapter 3, pp47–8.
25 New article 1169 goes further than the doctrine of consideration in English law, under which a contract will not be enforced where there is a real lack of consideration. Unlike in France, it is not enough that the consideration is derisory or does not fulfil the subjective expectations of the parties when they entered into the contract. Consideration is assessed objectively. It must be sufficient but need not be adequate: *Chappell & Co v Nestlé* [1960] AC 87.
26 Deshayes, Genicon, and Laithier (n 10) 328; see also Chantepie and Latina (n 7) [435].
27 Civ (1) 27 Feb 1990 no 88-14.364, Bull civ I no 52.
28 Civ (1) 3 July 2013, no 12-16853, Bull civ III no 145.
29 Civ (1) 5 Dec 1995, Bull civ I no 445; see also Civ (1) 18 April 1953, D 1953.403.
30 Chantepie and Latina (n 7) [435]; Deshayes, Genicon, and Laithier (n 10) 328.
31 Civ 4 July 1995, no 93-16.198, Bull civ I no 303, D 1997.206, note A-M Luciani.
32 TGI Paris 4th Ch 1 sect 27 June 2017 no 17/07192 Gaz Pal 2018 no 1, 32, obs D Houtcieff. Cited in Deshayes, Genicon, and Laithier (n 10) 328–9.

## 3 Contract terms depriving one's essential obligation of its substance

Article 1170 states that any contract term which deprives a debtor's essential obligation of substance is deemed not written. Like article 1169, it codifies case law in which the courts invoked the doctrine of *cause* to rebalance the contract.[33] This was exemplified by decisions striking down limitation clauses that set recoverable compensation so low as to reduce the remedy for breach almost to nothing,[34] thus denuding the primary obligation of any meaningful content.

An example is the 'Chronopost' case.[35] A standard form delivery contract was entered into between the eponymous express courier company and the claimant business for the delivery within twenty-four hours of two letters that enclosed a proposal in response to a request for tender that had been issued by a third party. Chronopost failed to deliver the letters within the agreed time resulting in the proposal not being considered. When the business claimed compensation, Chronopost sought to rely on a clause limiting its liability to the cost of delivery, which was 122 French francs. The *Cour de cassation* held that this clause should be struck out:

> given that, acting as a specialist in rapid carriage, guaranteeing the reliability and speed of its service, Chronopost had undertaken to deliver the envelopes... within a specified period of time, and given the breach of that essential obligation, the clause limiting liability under the contract, which contradicted the scope of the undertaking given, was to be deemed not written.[36]

New article 1170 is significantly broader in scope than the doctrine of *cause*. It applies to any contract term so long as the other conditions of the provision are satisfied, not just limitation clauses. As Stoffel-Munck has noted, article 1170 'opens up a new, completely general, destiny for the formula of *Chronopost*... because it applies to all contracts, even those that are negotiated, and to all contract terms, without any restriction as to their nature'.[37]

The expansion from 'a simple solution of case law uniquely relating to a single type of clause to a highly generic and non-exclusive text'[38] has caused concern and dissension amongst commentators, as has the perceived vagueness and lack

33 'Report to the President' (n 5) 7.

34 Stoffel-Munck, 'The Revolution in Unfair Terms' (n 18) 148; *Faurecia II* (Com 29 June 2010 no 09-11841) unambiguously held that this mode of control can be exerted 'only' over limitation clauses.

35 Com 22 Oct 1996, D 1997.121, note A Sériaux.

36 Translation of Stoffel-Munck, 'The Revolution in Unfair Terms' (n 18) 147. See also H Beale, B Fauvarque-Cosson, J Rutgers, and S Vogenauer (eds), *Cases, Materials and Text on Contract Law, Ius Commune Casebooks for the Common Law of Europe* (3rd edn, Hart Publishing: Oxford, 2019) 821–2.

37 Stoffel-Munck, 'The Revolution in Unfair Terms' (n 18) 148–9.

38 Deshayes, Genicon, and Laithier (n 10) 334.

of definition in the drafting of article 1170. One recurring question is how should a court determine the essential obligation in a contract? This will be relatively straightforward for some contracts but less so with others.[39] The text of article 1170 also implies that there can be only one essential obligation whereas, in reality, complex contracts tend to be made up of several and in some cases many obligations that are essential to varying degrees.[40] There is similar uncertainty regarding the requirement that the essential obligation be deprived of its substance. Does this require the obligation to be deprived of all substance or only part of it?[41] The text does not provide any guidance as to how this is to be measured or determined.

It has been said that the most that can be understood from article 1170 is that the term 'must adversely affect what is at the heart of the contract and do so in a considerable way'.[42] However, this appears to be too simplistic and some potential clues as to its meaning are capable of being found in the pre-reform case law based on the doctrine of *cause*. As Stoffel-Munck has noted, 'a reading of this provision separated from its historical context renders these questions unanswerable. It is instead in the reports of cases and in academic writing that we shall find the knowledge necessary to begin to answer these questions, which is somewhat paradoxical when one recalls that the reform was aimed at making French law more accessible.'[43]

Factors that were relevant in pre-reform cases to whether a limitation clause deprives an essential obligation of its substance include the level at which the recoverable compensation was set, whether the term was negotiated, and whether the promisee had obtained a reduced price in return for accepting the term.[44] In the well-known *Faurecia II* case, for instance, the software company Oracle, having breached a contract to design and deliver an integrated IT software system, sought to rely on a limitation clause that set its liability in a small sum.[45] This was held to be valid because the contract, including the limitation clause, was the product of tough negotiations and the low limit on Oracle's liability was counterbalanced by a significant discount on the contract price and other benefits that moved from Oracle to the claimant, Faurecia. It therefore reflected and formed part of a broader allocation of risks between the parties.[46]

If the conditions of article 1170 are met, the term is deemed never to have existed. The rest of the contract survives, thus upholding the interests of the injured party against whom the offending term had been relied on.[47] This is reinforced by

[39] Malaurie, Aynès, and Stoffel-Munck (n 8) [602]; Stoffel-Munck, 'The Revolution in Unfair Terms' (n 18) 146–9.

[40] Deshayes, Genicon, and Laithier (n 10) 334–5.

[41] Stoffel-Munck, 'The Revolution in Unfair Terms' (n 18) 148–9.

[42] Deshayes, Genicon, and Laithier (n 10) 335.

[43] Stoffel-Munck, 'The Revolution in Unfair Terms' (n 18) 146–9.

[44] Beale, Fauvarque-Cosson, Rutgers, and Vogenauer (n 36) 822; Stoffel-Munck, 'The Revolution in Unfair Terms' (n 18) 149.

[45] *Faurecia II* (Com 29 June 2010 no 09-11841).

[46] See also Com, 3 Dec 2013, RDC 2014.176, note T Genicon.

[47] See, for example, Deshayes, Genicon, and Laithier (n 10) 339.

paragraph 2 of article 1184, which states that 'the contract is upheld where legislation deems a contract term not written'.

## 4 Unfair terms in standard form contracts

The protection against unfair terms has been further enhanced by the introduction of new article 1171. This deems not written any term in a standard form contract that is 'non-negotiable and determined in advance' and which 'creates a significant imbalance in the rights and obligations of the parties'. The significant imbalance cannot relate to the main subject-matter of the contract, nor the adequacy of the price. This rule has its origins in consumer protection law but now applies more broadly.

### (a) The changes to the wording of article 1171 in 2018

Whilst article 1170 was a source of controversy, this was largely confined to legal *doctrine* and pales in comparison to article 1171, which was perhaps the single most debated provision of the new Civil Code, both by commentators and the French legislature.[48] An issue of particular focus was that, in the formulation of article 1171 promulgated in 2016, it was unclear to which clauses the provision applied. It stated that:

> Art. 1171.—Any term of a standard form contract which creates a significant imbalance in the rights and obligations of the parties to the contract is deemed not written.
>
> The assessment of significant imbalance must not concern either the main subject-matter of the contract nor the adequacy of the price in relation to the act of performance.

This was so broad in scope that every term in a standard form contract that caused a significant imbalance in the rights and obligations of the parties would have effectively been struck out. There were fears that the article could be invoked widely, undermining contractual certainty.[49] Therefore, during the ratification process in 2018, its scope was restricted to terms in standard form contracts that are 'non-negotiable and determined in advance by one of the parties'.[50] Despite this, the protection afforded by article 1171 against unfair terms is still significantly more comprehensive than before the reforms when the jurisdiction of French courts

[48] Ibid., 340.

[49] See, for example, the criticism of Stoffel-Munck, 'The Revolution in Unfair Terms' (n 18) 157–65.

[50] Contracts entered into between 1 October 2016 and 30 September 2018 are subject to the wording promulgated in 2016: see Chapter 1 for the ratification process of the reforms.

over unfair terms was piecemeal except in respect of consumer contracts and competition law. There was no general power to strike down unfair terms and the types of provision that tended to be unfair, notably penalty clauses, exclusion and limitation clauses, and non-compete clauses, were regulated separately and discretely.[51] In article 1171, 'the legislator has generalised a disposition to counter abusive clauses'.[52]

### (b) The requirements for the application of article 1171

To determine if article 1171 applies or not, the court must establish whether the term is (i) in a standard form contract, (ii) non-negotiable and determined in advance by one of the parties, and (iii) the source of a significant imbalance in the rights and obligations of the parties.

Standard form contracts are defined in article 1110 as comprising 'a set of non-negotiable clauses which are determined in advance by one of the parties'. This is different from the original definition adopted in 2016, which required only a contract containing terms that had not been negotiated, regardless of whether they were negotiable or not.[53] It will be recalled from Chapter 3[54] that this was deprecated for being too broad and conferring protection unnecessarily on those who had the opportunity to negotiate but chose not do so.[55] It was revised and narrowed in 2018 when the Ratification Bill was before the French Parliament. The substituted definition aligns with the new wording of article 1171, in that protection is available only to a party who did not have the opportunity to negotiate.

Paragraph 2 of article 1171 provides guidance as to how the courts should approach the question of whether an imbalance in the rights and obligations of the parties is significant. Two matters are excluded from this assessment: the imbalance cannot relate 'to the main subject-matter of the contract nor to the adequacy of the price in relation to the act of performance'. Purely financial imbalances (*déséquilibres économiques*)[56] are therefore not reviewable, which is consistent with the general principle in article 1168 that a lack of equivalence in financial value is outside the corrective control of the court.[57] As Whittaker has explained, 'article 1171 is not to be used for the control of the core elements of the contract: it is a control of unfair *ancillary* matters rather than a control of the substantive fairness of the contract itself'.[58]

[51] *Photo Production Ltd v Securicor Transport Ltd* [1980] AC 827, 844–7 (Lord Wilberforce).
[52] Chantepie and Latina (n 7) [440].
[53] Deshayes, Genicon, and Laithier (n 10) 83.
[54] See the section on standard form contracts in Chapter 3, pp 50–1.
[55] Chantepie and Latina (n 7) [133]; Deshayes, Genicon, and Laithier (n 10) 81.
[56] Deshayes, Genicon, and Laithier (n 10) 353.
[57] Chantepie and Latina (n 7) [428].
[58] S Whittaker, 'Unfair Terms in Commercial Contracts and the Two Laws of Competition: French Law and English Law Contrasted' (2019) 39(2) OJLS 404, 422.

There are, however, questions that remain unanswered on how 'significant imbalance' should be assessed.[59] Is the disputed term to be analysed in isolation from other terms or as part of the contract as a whole? What is the threshold for a 'significant imbalance'? Neither the 2016 nor the 2018 versions of the article address these questions. One commentator has suggested that 'significant' connotes that the harmony between the parties must have been fundamentally disturbed, beyond the usual imbalance that is to be expected in most contracts.[60] This should be decided 'on the basis of a pragmatic assessment of the interests involved'.[61]

It has also been said that article 1171 simply assumes that the courts are equipped to make commercial judgements on when a term creates an imbalance. Stoffel-Munck has argued powerfully that it is questionable whether judges possess the necessary experience to make such judgements. In his view, there is doubt as to whether:

> ... a young recruit of 25 years of age who has known only the benches of the Faculty and the National Judicial College [or] ... an old veteran, who was first an investigating magistrate in criminal cases (*juge d'instruction*), then in family affairs, became responsible for enforcement (*juge de l'exécution*), has heard traffic accidents cases and then social affairs [will be equipped] to decide what a "significant imbalance" is in a business contract... [S]ince the fundamental nature of the mechanism [of article 1171] is to allow a judicial policing of contract terms left entirely to the discretion and wisdom of the judges, it becomes even more central to have confidence in their experience and their prudence.[62]

A contrasting view is that these difficulties in designating a precise threshold for 'significant imbalance' could actually enhance the usefulness of article 1171. The reasoning is that it is 'a legal ... concept that is sufficiently vague and adaptable to take into account the precise circumstances and specificities of the relevant contractual relationship'.[63]

### (c) Unfair terms in the Consumer Code and the Commercial Code

The drafters of article 1171 drew inspiration from pre-existing provisions that regulate unfair terms in the Consumer Code for consumer contracts and in the

[59] Chantepie and Latina (n 7) [446]–[447]; Deshayes, Genicon, and Laithier (n 10) 352.

[60] Chantepie and Latina (n 7) [447].

[61] Malaurie, Aynès, and Stoffel-Munck (n 8) [603].

[62] Stoffel-Munck, 'The Revolution in Unfair Terms' (n 18) 160–1. He contrasts this with article L442-1 of the Commercial Code: 'commercial law allocates disputes relating to the test of significant imbalance to well-chosen judges. For business contracts, it is "consular judges" (*juges consulaires*), that is to say, traders elected by their peers, which have jurisdiction at first instance. Their experience of the world is not only legal and, above all, not only in litigation. On appeal, only the Court of Appeal of Paris has jurisdiction, and familiarity with these cases is entrusted to a limited number of judges.'

[63] Deshayes, Genicon, and Laithier (n 10) 350.

Commercial Code for unfair competitive market practices.[64] In article 1171 they sought to extend similar protection to all contracting parties. This led to debate during the ratification process in 2018 as to the relationship between this proposed new article and these existing provisions.

*(i) Comparable provisions to article 1171 in other codes*

Some of the text of article 1171 was lifted directly from article L212-1 of the Consumer Code, which relates to contracts between professionals and consumers. It provides that:

> Any clause contained in a contract concluded between a professional and a consumer shall be regarded as unfair if its object or effect is to create, to the detriment of that person or consumer, a significant imbalance in the rights and obligations of the parties to the contract.
>
> . . . the unfairness of a clause shall be assessed by reference, at the time of conclusion of the contract, to all the circumstances attending the conclusion of the contract and to all the other terms of the contract. It shall also be assessed in the light of the clauses contained in another contract where the conclusion or performance of each of those two contracts is legally dependent on the conclusion or performance of the other.
>
> Assessment of the unfair nature of any clause within the meaning of the first paragraph shall relate neither to the definition of the main subject-matter of the contract nor to the adequacy of the price or remuneration as against the goods sold or the service offered, as long as the clause is drafted in plain, intelligible language.[65]

Article L212-1 of the Consumer Code and article 1171 of the Civil Code share a number of similarities: an obligation must create a significant imbalance in the rights and obligations of the parties for the provision to be engaged; core terms are not reviewable; and a term will be struck down if found to be unfair. One material difference relates to the types of terms that can be reviewed. Whereas article 1171 only concerns non-negotiable terms in standard form contracts, article L212-1 applies to all contract terms, whether in individually negotiable or standard form contracts.

Another analogue of article 1171 is article L442-1, I of the Commercial Code, which regulates unfair competitive market practices. It provides that:[66]

[64] F Ancel, B Fauvarque-Cosson, and J Gest, *Aux sources de la réforme du droit des contrats* (Dalloz: Paris, 2017) [25.91]; 'Report to the President' (n 5) 9.

[65] Translation in Beale, Fauvarque-Cosson, Rutgers, and Vogenauer (n 36) 846–7.

[66] Translation by S Whittaker. I am grateful to Simon Whittaker for bringing to my attention the three main changes brought by new article L442-1, I to old article L442-6, I, 2: first, the new article is broader in scope and now includes 'any person exercising production, distribution or service activities' whilst at the same time being restricted to situations where the activity is 'in the course of the

> The following behaviour by any person exercising production, distribution or service activities in the course of the commercial negotiation, conclusion or performance of a contract attracts responsibility in its perpetrator and obliges him to make reparation for the loss caused by this action:
> 1 obtaining or trying to obtain from the other party an advantage not corresponding to anything in return [to any contrepartie] or manifestly disproportionate having regard to the value of what is agreed in return;
> 2 subjecting or attempting to subject the other party to obligations creating a significant imbalance in the rights and obligations of the parties;

This applies to any commercial contract between traders[67] but in practice it has mainly been relied on in the mass distribution food sector to counteract the imbalance in negotiating power between large purchasers and their suppliers.[68] As with article 1171, the test is whether an obligation creates a significant imbalance in the rights and obligations of the parties. Its scope is however wider than article 1171 in that it is not restricted to standard form contracts, core terms are not excluded from review, and the substance of the bargain, including any financial imbalance, can be reviewed. Another significant difference is that the sanctions under article L442-1, I are broader than article 1171 in that the court has the power not only to order compensatory damages but also an injunction and a civil penalty.[69]

*(ii) Potential conflicts in unfair term regulations*

Article 1171 is part of the general law of contract and applies to all contracts without limitation, regardless of whether the parties are consumers or commercial parties. During the ratification process in 2018, this prompted considerable focus on the question of how the provision would operate alongside articles L212-1 of the Consumer Code and L442-1, I of the Commercial Code. Could the three provisions be invoked cumulatively or are they mutually exclusive?[70]

The French Parliament sought to settle this issue by supporting the view that article 1171 cannot be relied upon where the special provisions of the Consumer

commercial negotiation, conclusion or performance of a contract'; second, 'subjecting or attempting to subject the other party to obligations creating a significant imbalance in the rights and obligations of the parties' is drafted so as to apply only where 'the other party' (and not the 'commercial partner') suffers the imbalance; third, it expressly states that the courts can review the substance of the bargain between the contracting parties.

[67] CA 1 Oct 2004 no 13.16336; see Whittaker (n 58) 411–12.

[68] Stoffel-Munck, 'The Revolution in Unfair Terms' (n 18) 152–6.

[69] For more details (in English) on article L442-1 of the Commercial Code (old article L442-6, I, 2) see Whittaker (n 58) 410–18; Stoffel-Munck, 'The Revolution in Unfair Terms' (n 18) 152–6; Beale, Fauvarque-Cosson, Rutgers, and Vogenauer (n 36) 848–9.

[70] Stoffel-Munck, 'Le nouveau droit des obligations: les questions en suspens' in 'Le nouveau droit des obligations après la loi de ratification du 20 avril 2018' RDC June 2018 55; Beale, Fauvarque-Cosson, Rutgers, and Vogenauer (n 36) 849 ff.

Code or the Commercial Codes apply.[71] An amendment was proposed to this effect. Ultimately this was not adopted but only because the Minister of Justice considered that the parliamentary debates alone would be sufficient evidence of the legislative intention on the point.[72]

In practice, contracting parties who seek to challenge the fairness of contract terms are likely to prefer to rely upon article L212-1 of the Consumer Code or L442-1, I of the Commercial Code over article 1171 of the Civil Code. In contrast with the various uncertainties that attend article 1171, the role of article L212-1 of the Consumer Code in striking down unfair terms is well-settled. This is in part because it contains a list of terms that are either deemed to be unfair in all circumstances or presumed unfair.[73] No such guidance is provided in article 1171.

Similarly, article L442-1, I seems likely to be preferred over article 1171. One reason is that disputes relating to the fairness of competitive commercial practices are heard at first instance by elected tradesmen in specialist commercial courts (with appeals heard by judges drawn from a small pool in the Court of Appeal of Paris), rather than career judges in the civil courts. This brings greater certainty and the 'subjectivity of the assessment of significant imbalance is restrained by the drastic reduction in the number of judges with familiarity with it... [it] allows for more predictability'.[74]

Some have predicted that article 1171 will be invoked mainly in respect of contracts between individuals. This encompasses, for example, contracts made through online platforms such as Airbnb or involving professionals who are not treated as engaging in commercial activities such as independent self-employed individuals (*professions libérales*) including lawyers, accountants, and consultants.[75]

[71] 'Réforme du droit des contrats, du régime général et de la preuve des obligations: Discussion d'un projet de loi adopté par le Sénat', JORF 12 Dec 2017, 6358 <https://www.assemblee-nationale.fr/dyn/15/comptes-rendus/seance/session-ordinaire-de-2017-2018/seance-du-lundi-11-decembre-2017.pdf> accessed 1 September 2021; the general principle is that rules relating to special contracts take precedence over the general principles of the Civil Code as newly codified by paragraph 3 of article 1105 relating to nominate and innominate contracts: Chapter 3, pp 46–7.

[72] F Pillet, 'Rapport fait au nom de la commission des lois constitutionnelles, de législation, du suffrage universel, du Règlement et d'administration générale (1) sur le projet de loi, modifié par l'Assemblée Nationale, ratifiant l'ordonnance n° 2016-131 du 10 février 2016 portant réforme du droit des contrats, du régime général et de la preuve des obligations' (Sénat: no 247, 24 Jan 2018), 23 <https://www.senat.fr/rap/l17-247/l17-2471.pdf> accessed 1 September 2021.

[73] Articles R212-1 to R212-5 of the Consumer Code; Deshayes, Genicon, and Laithier (n 10) 342; Chantepie and Latina (n 7) [444]; Beale, Fauvarque-Cosson, Rutgers, and Vogenauer (n 36) 849 ff.

[74] Stoffel-Munck, 'The Revolution in Unfair Terms' (n 18) 152–6.

[75] Ibid.

## C Concluding Observations on Significant Aspects of the Reforms

The new rules in articles 1168 to 1171 are intended to protect weaker parties[76] and promote substantive fairness (*justice contractuelle*).[77] They have been described as 'innovative'[78] and a 'revolution',[79] and are widely thought of as 'reflecting a profound change of the spirit of French contract law'.[80] Chantepie and Latina, for instance, have said that they have 'real symbolic value... the legislator guarantees a balance to contracting parties who cannot negotiate contract terms'.[81] For Deshayes, Genicon, and Laithier, they appear to reflect a 'fragmentation in contract law between a modern law governing structurally imbalanced contracts' on the one hand and a 'classical law which continues to govern the traditional model of an egalitarian contractual relationship.[82]

Whilst mainly inspired by pre-existing French legislation on consumer contracts and unfair competitive market practices, article 1171 was also influenced by rules against unfair terms in several international contract law instruments.[83] Indeed it essentially reproduces article 4:110 of the Principles of European Contract Law (PECL).[84] There are some, albeit fewer, similarities with the corresponding provision in the UNIDROIT Principles, article 7.1.6, which states that 'a clause which limits or excludes one party's liability for non-performance or which permits one party to render performance substantially different from what the other party reasonably expected may not be invoked if it would be grossly unfair to do so, having regard to the purpose of the contract'. This affords protection that is more limited in some respects than article 1171 and broader in others. It is more limited in that there is no general control mechanism for unfair terms. Instead, it is confined to exclusion and limitation clauses. It does though apply to all contracts, whether negotiated or in standard form. There are also other complementary provisions in the UNIDROIT Principles under which unfair contract terms can be reviewed, namely article 2.1.20 (which prohibits 'surprising terms' contained in standard terms) and article 3.2.7 (which enables the avoidance of a contract or an individual term that unjustifiably gave one party an excessive advantage).

The protection against unfair terms in England is more limited than in French law. The courts are reluctant to disturb how the contracting parties have chosen to

[76] 'Report to the President' (n 5) 3.
[77] Ibid., 9.
[78] Stoffel-Munck, 'The Revolution in Unfair Terms' (n 18) 146.
[79] Ibid.
[80] Chantepie and Latina (n 7) [440]; Deshayes, Genicon, and Laithier (n 10) 354; Ancel, Fauvarque-Cosson, and Gest (n 64) [25.91].
[81] Chantepie and Latina (n 7) [445].
[82] Deshayes, Genicon, and Laithier (n 10) 354.
[83] Ancel, Fauvarque-Cosson, and Gest (n 64) [25.101].
[84] See also articles 8:109 of the PECL; II.-9:401 to II.-9:410 of the Draft Common Frame of Reference.

balance their competing interests and allocate risk. Precedence is given to the contract terms, which are usually enforced dispassionately and without judicial meddling. This is vaunted as promoting transactional certainty and predictability of outcome.[85]

There is no general jurisdiction for the court to invalidate contract terms based on concepts of reasonableness or unconscionability. This possibility was firmly dismissed, even in exceptional circumstances, in *Union Eagle Ltd v Golden Achievement Ltd*,[86] which Lord Hoffmann justified by reference to commercial certainty. He said that 'in many forms of transaction, it is of great importance that if something happens for which the contract has made express provision, the parties should know with certainty that the terms of the contract will be enforced'.[87] Similarly, the doctrine of fundamental breach, which shares parallels with article 1170 and was developed as a means of invalidating exclusion or limitation clauses for breaches of contract that were fundamental,[88] was rejected by the House of Lords in *Photo Production Ltd v Securicor Transport Ltd*.[89]

Any interference with unfair terms is exceptional and the rules are limited and piecemeal, mainly operating in the sphere of consumer contracts. The Consumer Rights Act 2015, which implements EU consumer protection regulations,[90] confers power on the court to control the fairness of 'non-core' terms where one of the parties to the contract is a consumer.[91] Whilst a proposal to extend the statutory protection for consumers to small businesses[92] was made by the Law Commission in 2002 on the ground that most are unsophisticated and akin to consumers, it did not achieve consensus support and was not implemented.

Outside the context of consumer contracts, only very specific terms such as exclusion or limitation clauses in standard form contracts[93] and penalty clauses can potentially be challenged.[94] Discrete protection is also afforded to address concerns about specific industry practices. This is the case for example in the grocery

[85] See, for example, *Golden Strait Corp v Nippon Yusen Kubishika Kaisha (The Golden Victory)* [2007] 2 AC 353 (HL) [1] (Lord Bingham). On the contentment of English lawyers with their contract law, see P MacMahon, 'The Englishness of English Contract Law' (paper on file with author, presentation at the LSE Law Department on 28 February 2020).

[86] [1997] AC 514 (PC).

[87] Ibid., 518.

[88] See, for example, *Karsales (Harrow) Ltd v Wallis* [1956] 1 WLR 936.

[89] [1980] UKHL 2 (HL).

[90] Council Directive (EC) 13/1993 of 5 April 1993 on unfair terms in consumer contracts. In that respect, there are similarities between the provisions of the CRA 2015 and article 1171.

[91] For example the Consumer Rights Act 2015, s 17 imposes a duty on the court to consider the fairness of a term in a consumer contract, so long as it has sufficient information to do so. This applies even if the parties have not raised the issue of its fairness.

[92] Those with fewer than ten employees.

[93] See the protection provided by the Unfair Contract Terms Act 1977, s 3 (liability for breach of contract).

[94] See *Cavendish Square Holding BV v Talal El Makdessi* [2015] UKSC 67 (SC) with its conjoined appeal *ParkingEye Ltd v Beavis* [2016] AC 172 (SC); it is also not possible to exclude liability for fraud.

sector where the UK Competition Commission identified that large retailers were using anti-competitive and unfair practices to transfer excessive risks or unexpected costs onto their suppliers.[95] The Groceries Supply Code of Practice[96] imposes general requirements of fair dealing and good faith on large grocery retailers in their relationships with suppliers, requiring that they conduct the relationships with good faith.[97]

In this way, any perceived need to correct unfairness is addressed discretely rather than with rules of general application. Such interventions are tailored to specific types of contract terms which have the potential to give rise to exploitation and particular concerns about industry practices. As Whittaker has summarized, English law does not generally allow contract terms to be reviewed on the basis of unfairness unless:

> a particular justification is established: in the type of economic relationship (consumer contracts), in the type of contract term (exemption clauses or penalty clauses) or owing to the particular type of contract or its market context. As regard the latter, where a market failure is established in a particular commercial sector, the UK has proved willing to adopt dedicated control measures to correct it, including the provision for complaints to be made of unfair trade practices by other traders. And, where such controls are put in place, fairness and good faith may be given a central role.[98]

This differs from the approach in French law, which imposes broader fetters on the general principles of freedom of contract and the binding force of contract in the interest of protecting weaker parties and promoting contractual justice.

[95] Whittaker (n 58) 428.

[96] Article 4 and Schedule 2 of the Competition Commission, The Groceries (Supply Chain Practices) Market Investigation Order 2009 (2009 Order).

[97] Paragraph 2 of the Groceries Supply Code of Practice: 'A Retailer must at all times deal with its Suppliers fairly and lawfully. Fair and lawful dealing will be understood as requiring the Retailer to conduct its trading relationships with Suppliers in good faith, without distinction between formal or informal arrangements, without duress and in recognition of the Supplier's need for certainty as regards the risks and costs of trading, particularly in relation to production, delivery and payment issue.' See Whittaker (n 58) 429.

[98] Whittaker (n 58) 434.

# PART IV

# THE REACH OF THE CONTRACT BEYOND THE CONTRACTING PARTIES

# 8

# The Effect of the Contract on Third Parties

Who can be bound by a contract? Who is able to take the benefit or be compelled to perform? Can a benefit be conferred or a burden imposed on a stranger to a contract? These questions concern the legal reach of contractual rights and obligations and are addressed in the section of the Civil Code entitled 'The Effects of Contracts as regards Third Parties'. This contains eleven articles (new articles 1199 to 1209), a significant increase on the five in the 1804 Code.[1] In the main, the new articles are not ground-breaking but simply codify established principles that over time have been developed in the case law, which as a result are presented with greater clarity.

## A The Starting Principle

**Civil Code**[2]
Art. 1199.—A contract creates obligations only as between the parties.

Third parties may neither claim performance of the contract nor be constrained to perform it, subject to the provisions of this section and those in Chapter III of Title IV.

Art. 1200.—Third parties must respect the legal situation created by a contract.

They may rely on it notably in order to provide proof of a fact.

Art. 1203.—A person is not able to undertake engagements in his own name except for himself.

The starting principle is that, ordinarily, only the parties to a contract can benefit from and be bound by its terms. They alone can enforce the rights and bear the burden of the obligations that they have created. It is not open to third parties to

[1] Old articles 1165 to 1167 dealt with the relative effect of the contract, the *action oblique* and the *action paulienne*; article 1119 provided that a promise made to a person for the benefit of another was not valid; article 1121 dealt with stipulations for the benefit of third parties (*stipulations pour autrui*).

[2] 'Ordonnance no 2016-131 du 10 février 2016 portant réforme du droit des contrats, du régime général et de la preuve des obligations', JORF no 0035 of 11 February 2016. The Ordonnance was translated into English by J Cartwright, B Fauvarque-Cosson, and S Whittaker: <http://www.textes.justice.gouv.fr/art_pix/THE-LAW-OF-CONTRACT-2-5-16.pdf> (2016 version) and <http://www.textes.justice.gouv.fr/art_pix/Translationrevised2018final.pdf> (2018 version) accessed 1 September 2021. The translations of the new articles contained in this book are theirs.

*The New French Law of Contract.* Solène Rowan, Oxford University Press. © Solène Rowan 2022.
DOI: 10.1093/oso/9780198810872.003.0008

demand performance. Nor can they be required to perform. This is set out in new articles 1199 and 1203 of the Code.

The principle is known as the 'relative effect of the contract' (*principe de l'effet relatif du contrat*) and has been described as 'one of the pillars of France's contractual temple'.[3] Its origins lie in Roman law[4] and in protecting the autonomy of third parties and their freedom from intrusion.[5] Commentators have explained that, 'at root, the principle of the relative effect of the contract channels freedom of contract, and correlatively, preserves the independence of each individual',[6] and that 'the contracting parties are sovereign, but they are only sovereign over themselves'.[7]

It would be wrong however to suppose that a contract has no effect on third parties. Although clearly not bound by a contract to which they have not agreed, third parties cannot simply ignore its existence. There is an obligation under article 1200 to 'respect the legal situation created by a contract'. This has a range of implications in practice. Foremost are that third parties cannot act inconsistently with contracts entered by others and can be subject to extra-contractual liability for consciously aiding, inducing, or otherwise contributing to a breach of a contract. It has been held by the *Cour de cassation* that 'anyone who, knowingly, helps another to break his contractual obligations commits a delictual fault towards the victim of the breach'.[8] The principle that a contract can have consequences but not obligations for third parties[9] is known as the 'opposability of the contract' (*principe de l'opposabilité du contrat*), which has been defined as 'the ability to set the contract up against third parties'.[10] This qualifies the principle of the relative effect of the contract.

[3] D Mazeaud, 'Contracts and Third Parties in the Avant-projet de réforme' in J Cartwright, S Vogenauer, and S Whittaker (eds), *Reforming the French Law of Obligations: Comparative Reflections on the Avant-projet de réforme du droit des obligations et de la prescription* (Hart Publishing: Oxford, 2009) 207, 210.

[4] Old article 1165 was directly inspired by the principle *res inter alios acta aliis neque nocere neque prodesse potest*: an act made between certain people cannot adversely affect the rights of other people who are not party to the act.

[5] F Terré, P Simler, Y Lequette, and F Chénédé, *Droit civil, Les obligations* (12th edn, Dalloz: Paris, 2018) [670]; S Vogenauer, 'The Effects of Contracts on Third Parties: The Avant-projet de réforme in a Comparative Perspective' in J Cartwright, S Vogenauer, and S Whittaker (eds), *Reforming the French Law of Obligations: Comparative Reflections on the Avant-projet de réforme du droit des obligations et de la prescription* (Hart Publishing: Oxford, 2009) 235, 237.

[6] Mazeaud (n 3) 210.

[7] J-L Aubert, Y Flour, and E Savaux, *Droit civil: Les obligations, l'acte juridique* (16th edn, Sirey: Paris, 2014) [422].

[8] Com 13 March 1979 no 77-13.518, Bull civ 100; AP 9 May 2008, RTD civ 2008.485, note B Fages; Civ (1) 12 Oct 2004, no 01-03.213.

[9] J-S Borghetti, 'The Effects of Contracts and Third Parties' in J Cartwright and S Whittaker (eds), *The Code Napoléon Rewritten: French Contract Law after the 2016 Reforms* (Hart Publishing: Oxford, 2017) 227.

[10] On the principle of 'opposability' of contracts, see ibid., 245–6, for whom it is regrettable that article 1200 does not refer explicitly to 'opposability'.

## B Enforceable Rights Conferred on Third Parties under Legislation

The parties to a contract may wish to confer a benefit or even an enforceable right to a benefit on a third party. These possibilities are recognized in the Code in a number of exceptions to the principle of the relative effect of the contract. Amongst the most notable are the 'stipulations for the benefit of a third parties' (*stipulations pour autrui*), 'direct action' (*action directe*), *action oblique*, and *action paulienne*.

### 1 Stipulations for the benefit of a third party

**Civil Code**

Art. 1205.—A person may make a stipulation for another person.

One of the parties to a contract (the 'stipulator') may require a promise from the other party (the 'promisor') to accomplish an act of performance for the benefit of a third party (the 'beneficiary'). The third party may be a future person but must be exactly identified or must be able to be determined at the time of the performance of the promise.

Art. 1206.—The beneficiary is invested with a direct right to the act of performance against the promisor from the time of the stipulation.

Nevertheless, the stipulator may freely revoke the stipulation as long as the beneficiary has not accepted it.

The stipulation becomes irrevocable at the moment when the acceptance reaches the stipulator or the promisor.

Art. 1207.—Revocation may be effected only by the stipulator, or, after his death, by his heirs. The latter may do so only after a period of three months has elapsed from the date when they put the third party on notice to accept the benefit of the promise.

If it is not accompanied with the designation of a new beneficiary, the revocation benefits the stipulator or his heirs, as the case may be.

Revocation is effective as soon as the third party beneficiary or the promisor becomes aware of it.

Where it is made by testament, it takes effect from the moment of the testator's death.

The third party who was initially designated is deemed never to have benefited from the stipulation made for his benefit.

> Art. 1208.—Acceptance may come from the beneficiary or, after his death, his heirs. It may be express or implied. It may take place even after the death of the promisee or the promisor.
>
> Art. 1209.—The stipulator may himself require the promisor to perform his undertaking towards the beneficiary.

A commonly deployed mechanism for conferring a right on a non-party to a contract is the stipulation for the benefit of a third party (*stipulation pour autrui*).[11] One contracting party, the promisor, promises to the other, who in this context is referred to as the stipulator, to render some performance for the benefit of a third-party beneficiary, who thereby acquires a directly enforceable right to the performance from the promisor.[12]

A classic example is a life insurance policy under which the insured pays a premium to the insurer under a policy that requires the insurer to pay the death benefit to one or more named beneficiaries in the event of the insured's death during the term of the policy. Although not themselves parties to the policy, the beneficiaries have a direct contractual right against the insurer in respect of the death benefit.

### (a) New articles 1205 to 1209 of the Civil Code

Five new articles—1205 to 1209—govern stipulations for the benefit of a third party. It is stated in article 1205 that this can be a future person, as long as that person is identified with precision or able to be identified at the time of performance of the promise. This optionality seeks to strike a balance between the need for legal certainty and commercial flexibility.[13]

There is no requirement that the beneficiary accepts the stipulation, that is, communicates to the promisor or the stipulator that they wish to avail themselves of the benefit.[14] From the moment the stipulation comes into existence, it is enforceable in their name. In practice, however, the beneficiary will often accept the stipulation. The reason is that, under article 1206, it can be revoked by the stipulator until they do so.[15] Acceptance puts an end to this possibility. This is referred to as 'consolidating' the right under the stipulation and can be done expressly or by implication by the beneficiary or their successors. It takes effect when the acceptance reaches either the promisor or the stipulator.[16]

[11] Ibid., 235; Mazeaud, 'Contracts and Third Parties in the Avant-projet de réforme' (n 3) 212.

[12] Article 1205.

[13] Vogenauer, 'The Effects of Contracts on Third Parties: The Avant-projet de réforme in a Comparative Perspective' (n 5) 245.

[14] Paragraph 1 of article 1206 of the Civil Code; Civ (1) 19 Dec 2000, Bull civ I no 98-14.105. Although the Code is silent on this point, it is clear that the beneficiary can also reject the stipulation: see O Deshayes, T Genicon, and Y-M Laithier, *Réforme du droit des contrats, du régime général et de la preuve des obligations* (2nd edn, LexisNexis: Paris, 2018) 500–01.

[15] Paragraph 2 of article 1206 of the Civil Code. See also, G Chantepie and M Latina, *La réforme du droit des obligations, Commentaire théorique et pratique dans l'ordre du Code civil* (2nd edn, Dalloz: Paris, 2018) [571]–[575]. Chantepie and Latina have said that the possibility of revocation prior to acceptance renders the right of the beneficiary 'precarious'.

[16] Article 1208 of the Civil Code.

A revocation is effective as soon as the beneficiary or the promisor becomes aware of it.[17] Its effect is that the beneficiary is deemed never to have benefited from the stipulation.[18] Where a new beneficiary is not designated in the revocation, it 'benefits the stipulator or his successors'.[19]

The beneficiary can enforce the stipulation against the promisor,[20] as can the stipulator, who has a parallel right of enforcement under article 1209. This enables the stipulator to require the promisor to perform by seeking specific enforcement, which might occur for example where the third-party beneficiary cannot afford to sue the promisor.

### (b) Omissions from the new articles on stipulations for third parties

Although article 1209 only provides for specific enforcement, it is clear that the stipulator can also seek other remedies on behalf of the beneficiary such as termination and damages for the losses suffered by the beneficiary.[21] The article does not, however, address what should happen where the beneficiary and the stipulator both seek to enforce the stipulation but claim different remedies. No indication is given as to whom or what remedy should have priority. As under the old Code, it appears to be left to the court to determine the most appropriate remedy.

There are two other questions on which the Code is silent. The first is whether the stipulator can impose obligations on the beneficiary as part of a stipulation. Prior to the reforms, it had been held that the stipulator could attach obligations to the stipulation, to which the beneficiary would be taken to consent by accepting the stipulation. A beneficiary who was unwilling to accept the obligations could renounce the stipulation, thus rejecting both the rights and the obligations.[22] The effect was to safeguard against third parties being subjected to obligations against their will. This principle was not codified in the reforms but nonetheless appears likely to continue to apply.[23]

The second issue on which the new Code is silent is whether a promisor sued by a beneficiary can raise defences, for example set-offs, counterclaims, limitation periods, and exclusions, that would have been available to the promisor in an action brought by the stipulator. Prior to the reforms, it was uncontroversial that the promisor could do so[24] and the silence of the reforms on the point suggests that this remains the case.

[17] Paragraph 3 of article 1207 of the Civil Code.

[18] Paragraph 5 of article 1207 of the Civil Code.

[19] Paragraph 2 of article 1207 of the Civil Code.

[20] Paragraph 1 of article 1206 of the Civil Code.

[21] The stipulator can claim damages for their own loss. See Deshayes, Genicon, and Laithier (n 14) 502. Civ (1) 29 March 1989, Bull civ I no 142; A Bénabent, *Droit des obligations* (18th edn, LGDJ: Paris, 2019) [262].

[22] Civ (1) 1 Dec 1987, Bull civ I no 353, D 1989 Somm 233, note Aubert; Bénabent (n 21) [258]; Borghetti, 'The Effects of Contracts and Third Parties' (n 9) 236.

[23] Borghetti, 'The Effects of Contracts and Third Parties' (n 9) 236.

[24] Com 25 March 1969 no 66-14054, Bull civ IV 118.

## 2 Direct action in payment (*action directe en paiement*)

**Civil Code**

Art. 1341-3.—In cases determined by legislation, a creditor may sue directly to obtain satisfaction from a debtor of his own debtor.

The direct action in payment is a mechanism that allows a third party who is owed money to bring a claim in debt in their own name and on their own account against a person who owes a debt to their own debtor. The following are examples: the right of a landlord to require direct payment from a sub-tenant of rent due under the sub-lease in order to satisfy arrears of rent of the main tenant (new article 1753); in an agency relationship, the right of a principal to claim against the sub-agent in respect of the duties that the agent was required under the agency contract to undertake (new article 1994); in a construction context, the right of a sub-contractor to claim payment directly from the project manager in respect of work undertaken by the sub-contractor (article 12 of law no 75-1334 of 31 Dec 1975);[25] and the right of a person who has suffered loss to sue the insurer of the person who is liable in respect of the loss (article L124-3(1) of the Insurance Code).

In contrast with stipulations for the benefit of third parties, the right of the third party to sue and obtain payment does not arise out of a contract entered into by others for their benefit. Rather, it is laid down in legislation as a method of enforcement. The third party is able to garnish the rights of the beneficiary of the contract as a means of enforcing their own rights against the beneficiary, who is their debtor under a separate contract.[26] By stepping into the shoes of the debtor, the third party is able to enforce a contract between the debtor and another, who is required to pay the third party directly. At no point does the payment enter the hands of the debtor and thereby become available to be disposed of by the debtor or enforced against by their other creditors.

The right of the third party under a direct action in payment is subject to three limitations. First, the third party can recover no more than the amount owing under their contract with the debtor. So, for example, in a sub-lease, the landlord cannot recover more from the sub-lessee than the amount of rent that is outstanding from their tenant, even if the rent payable under the sub-lease exceeds the rent under the head-lease. Second, the third party cannot recover a greater amount than is owed to their own debtor. In the sub-lease example, the landlord cannot obtain more than the rent payable under the sub-lease, even if that falls short of the rent that is

[25] *Loi* no 75-1334 du 31 décembre 1975 relative à la sous-traitance.

[26] As Mazeaud 'Contracts and Third Parties in the Avant-projet de réforme' (n 3) 214 has put it, 'the third party becomes the holder of a right of his own not because the contracting parties have decided that he should have it without his knowledge, but because legislation has provided that he should have it'.

outstanding from their tenant. Lastly, all defences and exclusions that are available in respect of the debtor's claim can also be raised against the third party.[27]

## 3 *Actions obliques*

**Civil Code**

Art. 1341-1.—Where a debtor's failure in the exercise of his patrimonial rights and actions compromises the rights of his creditor, the latter may exercise them on behalf of the debtor, with the exception of those which belong exclusively to the debtor personally.

The *action oblique*, which is prescribed in new article 1341-1, is another form of third-party claim. It enables a third party, again in their capacity as a creditor, to claim against their debtor, who is the beneficiary of rights under a contract. The purpose is to preserve their ability to enforce their own rights against their debtor in circumstances where it would otherwise be prejudiced by the failure of a debtor to enforce rights against their own debtors.[28] Acting on behalf of the debtor, the third party brings an *action oblique* to exercise the rights of the debtor against them.

The *action oblique* is more widely available than the direct action in payment. This is because, unlike the direct action, it is not confined to situations prescribed by legislation. However, it is not nearly as advantageous in practice.[29] The third party, despite going to the trouble of bringing the action, does not thereby become entitled to the proceeds. Nor does the third party have priority over the debtor's other creditors, all of whom have equal standing in asserting their claims. This is because the third party is acting not in their own right but exercising the rights of the debtor, as if the debtor had brought the action.[30]

Two conditions must be satisfied for a third party to rely on the *action oblique*.[31] First, the debtor of the third party must be inactive in enforcing their own rights.[32] The reason for their inactivity is irrelevant and need not be reprehensible. Second, the debtor's inactivity must compromise and imperil the rights of the third party. If, for example, the debtor has sufficient funds to satisfy the third party's claim even despite their failure to exercise rights under the contract, the third party cannot rely on the *action oblique* and must sue the debtor in the conventional way.[33] It is not, however, necessary for the third party to prove that the debtor is bankrupt or

[27] Bénabent (n 21) [267].

[28] Deshayes, Genicon, and Laithier (n 14) 802–04.

[29] Chantepie and Latina (n 15) [920].

[30] And for this reason, the third party is subject to all the defences and limitations that are contained in the contract between their debtor and their sub-debtor: Civ (1) 9 Oct 1991, Bull civ I no 250.

[31] Deshayes, Genicon, and Laithier (n 14) 802–04.

[32] Civ (3) 7 March 1968, Bull civ III no 87; Civ (3) 20 Dec 1994, Bull civ III no 225.

[33] Bénabent (n 21) [803]; Civ (1) 17 May 1982, Bull civ I no 176.

insolvent.[34] All that must be shown is a risk of insolvency or that the third party's rights are imperilled. In practice, the courts adopt an expansive approach to the concept of peril, which must result from 'the deliberate will of the debtor not to exercise his right'.[35]

### 4 *Actions pauliennes*

**Civil Code**

Art. 1341-2.—A creditor may also sue in his own name to obtain a declaration that acts made by the debtor in fraud of his rights may not be set up against him. In the case of non-gratuitous acts, he can do so only if he establishes that the third party contracting with the debtor knew of the fraud.

Lastly, the *action paulienne* enables a third party, again in the capacity of creditor, to challenge a transaction that their debtor has entered with another party in a fraud on their rights. If the action succeeds, the fraudulent transaction is declared ineffective against the third party. It must be shown that the debtor sought to put assets beyond reach,[36] preventing the third party from recovering their due. Unhelpfully, fraud is not defined in the Code. It was previously the position that the debtor had to intend to harm the third party, but there have since been cases in which it was held to be sufficient that the debtor knew that their actions were prejudicial to the third party's rights.[37] Where fraud is proven, the impugned action is invalidated and the debtor's counterparty in the fraudulent transaction is deprived of any entitlement under the contract.[38]

## C Court-Made Exceptions to the Principle of Relative Effect

Over time the courts have created a number of other exceptions to the relative effect of contract which are not addressed in the reformed Code. Third parties that suffer loss as a result of a breach of contract can in some circumstances sue the defaulting party for compensation, despite not being a party to the contract. As will be shown later in this chapter, in some cases the remedy for the third party is based on contractual liability and in others on extra-contractual liability. A unifying feature of these cases is that the court seeks to protect the third party where no remedy would otherwise be available.

[34] Civ (1) 28 May 2002, Bull civ I no 145.
[35] Civ (1) 23 May 2006 no 05-18.065, Bull civ 2006.I.263.
[36] Deshayes, Genicon, and Laithier (n 14) 807–09.
[37] P Malaurie, L Aynès, and P Stoffel-Munck, *Droit des obligations* (10th edn, LGDJ: Paris, 2018) [1141]–[1148].
[38] Chantepie and Latina (n 15) [925]–[926].

Despite being limited in nature, these exceptions have been controversial. Some argue that, in the absence of any privity of contract, it should not be open to the third party to claim in respect of a breach of the contract. The question of whether the claim is in contract or extra-contractual is also thorny for a number of reasons. One is the rule of *non-cumul*, which prevents the victim of a wrong from suing for extra-contractual liability where the basis of the claim is the breach of a contractual obligation.[39] To allow third parties to make an extra-contractual claim based on a breach of contract is inconsistent with the rule. It also enables third parties to bypass the defences and exclusions in the contract that were agreed by the contracting parties.[40] Another arises from the availability in France of compensation for pure economic loss where the liability is extra-contractual. This gives rise to the risk of the defaulting party being liable to third parties in ways and amounts that are unforeseeable.[41]

The most common exceptions—the implied stipulation for the benefit of a third party, the direct action in liability, and the possibility of a third party making an extra-contractual claim against a contracting party for breach of contract—will now be considered in turn.

## 1 Implied stipulations for the benefit of a third party (*stipulations pour autrui implicites*)

In some cases, French courts have implied stipulations for the benefit of a third party, even though there is no reference to the third party in the contract. This has served to give a contractual remedy to a third party who is thought to be deserving of protection but is unable to make an extra-contractual claim or would achieve a more advantageous outcome by suing in contract than for extra-contractual liability.[42]

Stipulations have been implied, for instance, in contracts for the carriage of goods,[43] and persons,[44] and for the supply of blood.[45] In one well-known case, a passenger on a train fell onto the track and died. Since there was no evidence that

[39] See Chapter 1 on the rule of non-cumul within the law of obligations, pp 17–8; Civ, 11 Jan 1922 S 1924.1.105, note R Demogue GAJC no 182. On the rule of *non-cumul* generally, see Terré, Simler, Lequette, and Chénédé (n 5) [897]; Malaurie, Aynès, and Stoffel-Munck (n 37) [1141]–[1148].

[40] Civ (1) 7 June 1995, no 93-13.898, Bull civ I no 249, D 1996 395, note D Mazeaud; Chantepie and Latina (n 15) [570]; Bénabent (n 21) [269]–[271].

[41] Borghetti, 'The Effects of Contracts and Third Parties' (n 9) 249–53.

[42] S Whittaker, 'Privity of Contract and the Law of Tort: The French Experience' (1995) 15 OJLS 327, 337.

[43] Civ 21 November 1978, JCP 1980.I.19315, note P Rodière. Translated in H Beale, B Fauvarque-Cosson, J Rutgers, and S Vogenauer (eds) *Cases, Materials and Text on Contract Law, Ius Commune Casebooks for the Common Law of Europe* (3rd edn, Hart Publishing: Oxford, 2019) 1274–6.

[44] Civ 6 Dec 1932, DP 1933.I.137, note L Josserand. Translated in Beale, Fauvarque-Cosson, Rutgers, and Vogenauer (n 43) 1277–8.

[45] Civ 2, 17 Dec 1954, D 1955.269, note M Rodière, JCP 1955.II.8490, note R Savatier; Civ (2) 20 Oct 2005, RTD civ 2006.122, note P Jourdain.

the railway company had been negligent, his widow and children were unable to claim based on extra-contractual liability. However, damages were awarded for the breach of a strict contractual obligation to carry passengers safely.[46] It was held that the passenger, on purchasing a ticket, had impliedly contracted on behalf of his wife and children, giving them a direct contractual action against the company.

Implied stipulations have been contentious in a number of respects. They rely on the contracting parties having intended to benefit the third party, but this is hypothetical and often entirely fictitious. The potential exposure for the defaulting party is difficult to predict or quantify. It is also thought to be objectionable for there to be civil liability based only on the 'strong social policy of granting maximum protection to the innocent dependents of fatally injured victims of accidents'[47] and a 'desire to make up for what [is] felt to be a deficiency of tort law'.[48]

The courts appear to have heeded these criticisms and over time have limited the types of contract into which stipulations can be implied, thereby narrowing the range of third parties able to benefit from them. In the case of contracts of carriage, for example, only close relatives who are owed a legal duty of support by the passenger can do so.[49] This has led to reliance on implied stipulations steadily declining over time, which has also been enabled by extra-contractual protection for third parties improving.[50]

## 2 Direct action in liability (*action directe en responsabilité*)

In some contexts, the courts have extended the scope of the direct action in payment in article 1341-3, which was considered earlier in this chapter, beyond debt claims in order to enable third parties to bring a claim in contract in respect of defective products.

One such context in which this has occurred is back-to-back contracts for the sale of goods that turn out to be defective where ownership of the goods is transferred under the chain of contracts on multiple successive occasions. Typically the goods are sold by the original manufacturer to an initial buyer, who in turn sells to another party, and there may be several more such sales. The ultimate buyer of the goods is treated as having the same contractual rights of action against the manufacturer as the initial buyer.[51] Another context is where defective materials

[46] Civ 6 Dec 1932, DP 1933.I.137, note L Josserand. Translated in Beale, Fauvarque-Cosson, Rutgers, and Vogenauer (n 43) 1277–8.

[47] Beale, Fauvarque-Cosson, Rutgers, and Vogenauer (n 43) 1278.

[48] Ibid., 1281.

[49] Civ 24 May 1933, DP 1933.I.137, note L Josserand; Civ (2) 23 Jan 1959, D 1959.281, note R Rodière.

[50] Terré, Simler, Lequette, and Chénédé (n 5) [897].

[51] Civ (1) 9 Oct 1979, Bull civ I no 241; Civ (3) 28 March 1990, Bull civ III no 93.

are used in the construction of a building, which was contracted or later purchased by a third party.[52] Despite the absence of a direct contractual nexus, the third party can claim in contract against the manufacturer and the contractor. As Mazeaud has explained, a 'third party has the ability to rely upon a contract concluded by others ... [his] right to damages if his action succeeds constitutes an extension and a projection of the contractual right of the [initial] party'.[53]

In a well-known construction case, a building contractor bought insulation material from the manufacturer for use in the construction of a property. The material had a latent defect which led to corrosion in water pipes in the property. Although unable to make an extra-contractual claim against the manufacturer because the limitation period had expired, the employer was able to sue in contract, where the limitation period was longer.[54]

This has been justified by the *Cour de cassation* on the basis that the right to sue and obtain relief stays with the defective goods. Where the material is incorporated into a building during construction works, it 'attaches' to the property and thereafter can move from the original buyer through the chain of later buyers of the property as an 'accessory' of the property (*la théorie de l'accessoire*). One implication of the right to sue attaching in this way is that the exception can only apply where the original and subsequent contracts involve the sale of goods (that have been incorporated or not into a building).[55] As regards contracts for the provision of services which does not involve the sale of goods, third parties are only able to bring an extra-contractual claim.[56]

Since it is the same right of action that is transferred through the chain of contracts, it remains subject to all the limitations as under the initial contract.[57] The defaulting party therefore continues to be able to raise any exclusion clause and other defences that would have been available in a claim by the initial buyer.[58] There is no scope for third parties to bypass or vary the initial contract[59] and any claim 'should not be subject to different, and potentially more favourable, conditions than actions by the other contracting party'.[60]

[52] In the context of building contracts, see articles 1792 ff and 2224 to 2226 of the Civil Code and article 1641 relating to the liability for latent defects; see also Whittaker (n 42).

[53] Mazeaud, 'Contracts and Third Parties in the Avant-projet de réforme' (n 3) 221–2.

[54] See cases cited in Beale, Fauvarque-Cosson, Rutgers, and Vogenauer (n 43) 1329: Ass Plén 7 Feb 1986, no 84-15.189 Bull AP no 2; Civ (3) 26 May 1992, Bull civ III no 168; Civ (1) 23 June 1993, Bull civ I no 226.

[55] It was held in the well-known 'Besse' decision that an employer does not have a direct contractual claim against a subcontractor for defective work (Ass Plén 12 July 1991 no 90-13602, Bull AP no 5) translated and commented by Beale, Fauvarque-Cosson, Rutgers, and Vogenauer (n 43) 1331–3.

[56] For a criticism of this, see Bénabent (n 21) [269]–[271].

[57] Ass Plén 7 Feb 1986, JCP 1986.II.20616, note P Malinvaud.

[58] Civ (1) 7 June 1995, no 93-13.898, Bull civ I no 249, D 1996 395 note D Mazeaud.</INT>

[59] Ibid.; Chantepie and Latina (n 15) [570]; Bénabent (n 21) [269]–[271].

[60] Borghetti, 'The Effects of Contracts and Third Parties' (n 9) 249–53.

## 3 Actions in extra-contractual liability by third parties for breach of contract

There are also cases in which the *Cour de cassation* has allowed a third party that has suffered loss as a result of a breach of contract to bring an extra-contractual claim against the defaulting party despite not being a party to the contract. In a controversial 2006 case, the *Assemblée Plénière* of the *Cour de cassation* held that a 'third party to a contract may invoke a failure in contractual performance on the basis of extra-contractual liability where this failure has caused him harm'.[61] It is not necessary that the breach of contract constitutes the commission of a separate wrong against the third party, who only needs to suffer loss as a result of the breach. There is a synergy between the contractual fault and the extra-contractual fault by which the third party is able to rely on the breach of contract as a fault that gives rise to extra-contractual liability. It 'allow[s] a complete stranger to rely on contractual performance'[62] and make a claim on the basis that a breach of contract has occurred and caused loss.

The decision is contentious for two main reasons. First, as Borghetti has explained, 'the solution constitutes a serious breach of the principle of relative effect laid down in new article 1199, insofar as it enables the third party to obtain, in the form of damages, a benefit which the proper performance of the contract would have afforded them, even if it was merely the hope of gain. To a certain extent, it therefore makes the third party a creditor of the party in breach.'[63] Second, by making an extra-contractual claim, the third party is able to circumvent any exclusions and limitations in the contract and thus 'have his cake and eat it,'[64] but at considerable perceived unfairness to the defaulting party.

To the disappointment of commentators, amongst whom there is consensus in favour of legislative intervention to reverse this decision,[65] it was not addressed in the reforms. Instead it was held over to be dealt with in the reform of civil liability, which has been ongoing since 2016. Article 1234 of the 2017 Reform Bill on Civil Liability[66] would pare back the decision and require the third party to establish

[61] Ass Plén 6 Oct 2006, RTD civ 2006.115, obs P Jourdain. On this topic, see C Grimaldi, 'Toute faute contractuelle est une faute délictuelle, mais encore faut-il s'entendre sur le préjudice réparable!' RDC 2007.563; P Ancel, 'Faut-il faire avec?' RDC 2007.538; P Stoffel-Munck, 'La relativité de la faute contractuelle' RDC 2007.587; G Wicker, 'La sanction délictuelle du manquement contractuel ou l'intégration de l'ordre contractuel à l'ordre juridique général' RDC 2007.593.

[62] P Stoffel-Munck, 'Liability of Contracting Parties Towards Third Parties' in J-S Borghetti and S Whittaker (eds), *French Civil Liability in Comparative Perspective* (Hart Publishing: Oxford, 2019) 55, 59.

[63] Borghetti, 'The Effects of Contracts and Third Parties' (n 9) 249–53.

[64] Beale, Fauvarque-Cosson, Rutgers, and Vogenauer (n 43) 1333.

[65] Chantepie and Latina (n 15) 496; Borghetti 'The Effects of Contracts and Third Parties' (n 9) 249–53; Stoffel-Munck, 'Liability of Contracting Parties Towards Third Parties' (n 62).

[66] Ministère de la Justice, *Projet de réforme de la responsabilité civile* (13 March 2017), <http://www.justice.gouv.fr/publication/Projet_de_reforme_de_la_responsabilite_civile_13032017.pdf>; translated from French into English by S Whittaker in consultation with J-S Borghetti:, *Reform Bill on Civil*

that the breach of contract satisfies the requirements for extra-contractual liability. It also provides that a claim in contract could be made where the third party has a 'legitimate interest' in the performance of the contract. The draft article states as follows:

> Where non-performance of a contract causes harm to a third party, the latter can claim reparation of its consequences from the debtor only on the basis of extra-contractual liability, and subject to that third party's establishing one of the actions giving rise to liability targeted by Section II of Chapter II.
>
> Nevertheless, a third party who has a legitimate interest in the proper performance of a contract can equally invoke, on the basis of contractual liability, a contractual failing where the latter has caused him harm. The conditions and limitations on this liability which are applicable in the relations between the contracting parties may be set up against him. Any contract term which limits the contractual liability of a party to the contract in relation to a third party is deemed not written.[67]

This proposal has proved to be contentious. If interpreted broadly, it could be understood as giving a 'third party victim of the non-performance an option between contractual liability and delictual liability'.[68] The legitimate interest exception has been described as 'highly debatable' and 'hardly limit[ing] the scope of this contractual liability'.[69] Criticism has also been made of the failure to establish any hierarchy between the extra-contractual claim referred to in the first paragraph and the contractual claim in the second.[70]

The reform of civil law is still ongoing and whether, and if so when, a set of proposals will be put before the French Parliament has for some time been a source of uncertainty. Against this background, in 2020, several senators put forward a proposal to amend article 1234.[71] This would require a third party wishing to bring a claim in contract to prove not only a legitimate interest but also that they have no other right to obtain a remedy. Whether this is adopted remains to be seen. In the

*Liability* (March 2017), <http://www.textes.justice.gouv.fr/art_pix/reform_bill_on_civil_liability_march_2017.pdf> accessed 1 September 2021.

[67] Translation in Beale, Fauvarque-Cosson, Rutgers, and Vogenauer (n 43) 1334.

[68] Ibid.; for further criticism of article 1234, see Borghetti, 'The Effects of Contracts and Third Parties' (n 9) 249–53; J-S Borghetti, 'La responsabilité des contractants à l'égard des tiers dans le projet de réforme de la responsabilité civile' D 2017.1846; but see also M Leveneur, 'Une solution convaincante pour l'engagement de la responsabilité des contractants par les tiers. A propos de l'article 1234 du projet de réforme de la responsabilité civile' JCP G 2017.1182; Stoffel-Munck, 'Liability of Contracting Parties Towards Third Parties' (n 62).

[69] Beale, Fauvarque-Cosson, Rutgers, and Vogenauer (n 43) 1335.

[70] Stoffel-Munck 'Liability of Contracting Parties Towards Third Parties' (n 62).

[71] Several senators who were impatient to see reforms enacted put forward proposals amending the 2017 reforms: '23 propositions pour simplifier la vie des Français en facilitant la réparation des dommages' (Sénat: 22 July 2020) <www.senat.fr/presse/cp20200722a.html> accessed 1 September 2021.

meantime, French courts can be expected to continue to apply the decision, as was illustrated by a decision of the *Assemblée Plénière* in 2020 reaffirming it.[72]

## D Concluding Observations

The reforms did not contain any significant innovations in respect of the relationship between third parties and the contract. In the main the focus was on codifying established principles without significant modification. A number of points can nonetheless be made. The first is that the drafters recognized the importance of third-party rights in the significant expansion of the number of articles, as compared with the 1804 Code. This has generally been welcomed on the basis that the Code 'addresses the topic head-on',[73] 'aims to take the bull by the horns',[74] and recognizes that 'there are relationships between the contract and third parties which the law cannot ignore ... [since] the relationship [that a contract] establishes between the parties is liable continuously to affect other relationships'.[75]

Second, the drafters sent a clear message that the principle of relative effect remains pivotal in France. Given how liberally exceptions to the principle have been created, to the point that it is questionable whether the principle is still meaningful, this may come as something of a surprise.[76] The law governing the effect of the contract on third parties has been characterized as a 'French paradox'[77] and attributed by some to judicial attempts to reconcile opposing considerations. In the words of Mazeaud, these are 'the individualistic dimension of contracts on the one hand (which allows the channelling of the freedom of the contracting parties) and their economic and social dimension on the other (which lead, under certain conditions, to the extension of the factual and obligational effects of contracts to third parties)'.[78]

From a comparative perspective, the importance of the principle of relative effect, the proliferation of exceptions to the principle, and the growing number of articles on third-party rights are all in contrast with the main international contract law instruments. Neither the Principles of European Contract Law (PECL)[79] nor

[72] Ass Plén 13 Jan 2020 no 17-19.963: Doctrin'Actu Jan 2020, art 115, note A Nivert.

[73] Borghetti 'The Effects of Contracts and Third Parties' (n 9) 227.

[74] Ibid., 229.

[75] Ibid., 228.

[76] See Vogenauer, 'The Effects of Contracts on Third Parties: The Avant-projet de réforme in a Comparative Perspective' (n 5) 268: 'The ostensible reinforcement of the principle is hollow.'

[77] Borghetti, 'The Effects of Contracts and Third Parties' (n 9) 253.

[78] Mazeaud, 'Contracts and Third Parties in the Avant-projet de réforme' (n 3) 209.

[79] In the PECL, relative effect is assumed as the starting point. Both the PECL and the UNIDROIT Principles allow the creation of third-party rights. Article 6:110 (Stipulation in Favour of a Third Party) Principles of European Contract Law:

(1) A third party may require performance of a contractual obligation when its right to do so has been expressly agreed upon between the promisor and the promisee, or when such

the UNIDROIT Principles make any reference to the principle. The UNIDROIT Principles, for example, state only that third-party rights can be created by contract.[80] There is a solitary mention of the principle of relative effect in the commentary on article 5.2.1, which states that 'usually contracts are intended by the parties to create rights and obligations between themselves. In such cases only the parties will acquire rights and duties under the contract'. There were divergent views in the Working Group that drafted the UNIDROIT Principles as to whether or not relative effect should be referred to in the main text. This was favoured by the members of the Group from Romanist legal systems but 'ultimately rejected because it was feared that emphasizing the principle of relativity too strongly might constitute an obstacle to the future development of the law in this area'.[81] The resulting contrast with French law is striking.

There is also divergence with the approach in England,[82] where the principle of relative effect resides in the doctrine of privity of contract, under which 'only a person who is a party to a contract can sue on it'[83] and third parties cannot be burdened by a contract made by others. This is founded on the requirement of consideration,[84] which dictates that only a party that provides consideration can acquire and enforce rights under a contract.

English law has been much slower than French law to create a formal mechanism that allows for the enforcement of third-party rights under contract. The privity rule was resolutely applied until the enactment of the Contract (Rights of

agreement is to be inferred from the purpose of the contract or the circumstances of the case. The third party need not be identified at the time the agreement is concluded.

(2) If the third party renounces the right to performance the right is treated as never having accrued to it.

(3) The promisee may by notice to the promisor deprive the third party of the right to performance unless:

(a) the third party has received notice from the promisee that the right has been made irrevocable, or

(b) the promisor or the promisee has received notice from the third party that the latter accepts the right.

80 The section on 'Third Party Rights' (articles 5.2.1 to 5.2.5) contains provisions addressing the validity and enforceability of contracts that confers rights on third parties, the requirements that must be satisfied in order to create such contracts, and the rights and obligations of the promisor, the promisee, and the third-party beneficiary.

81 S Vogenauer, 'Commentary on article 5.2.1 of the UNIDROIT Principles' in S Vogenauer (ed), *Commentary on the UNIDROIT Principles of International Commercial Contracts (PICC)* (2nd edn, OUP: Oxford, 2015) 659.

82 For a comparison of the French and English rules, see Vogenauer, 'The Effects of Contracts on Third Parties: The Avant-projet de réforme in a Comparative Perspective' (n 5) 236; Borghetti, 'The Effects of Contracts and Third Parties' (n 9).

83 'Only a person who is a party to a contract can sue on it'; *Dunlop Pneumatic Tyre Co Ltd v Selfridge and Co Ltd* [1915] AC 847, 853 (HL) (Viscount Haldane LC).

84 *Tweddle v Atkinson* [1861] 1 B & S 393 (QB).

Third Parties) Act 1999, with exceptions only rarely made by the courts where to allow a third party to benefit would avoid injustice.[85]

The 1999 Act provides that contracting parties can agree, both expressly or by implication, to confer an enforceable right on a third party in a way that is similar to the stipulation for the benefit of a third party in French law. Even then, however, the position of third parties under English law is notably weaker in a number of respects. For example, the circumstances under which the right can be implied are more limited because the Act requires as a minimum a contractual term 'that purports to confer a benefit'[86] on the third party; the Act imposes more burdensome requirements as to the identifiability of the third party;[87] and a promisee can recover in respect of their own losses but not those of the third party. This is in contrast with the right of the stipulator under article 1209 to obtain specific performance whilst also claiming damages from the promisor for breach of the promise.

Similarly, in many situations where French law has permitted third parties to claim in contract, the only option under English law is a claim in tort, which is subject to restrictive rules on the recovery of pure economic loss.[88] For instance, where there are back-to-back contracts for the sale of goods, unlike in France, the ultimate purchaser can bring a contractual claim only against their direct counterparty and not parties lower down the chain. The option of falling back on a tortious claim can be more apparent than real because the courts have refused to impose a duty of care where this would be inconsistent with the contractual structure put in place by the parties and undermine the privity principle.[89]

[85] For judicial criticisms of the privity doctrine, see *Darlington BC v Wiltshier Northern Ltd* [1995] 1 WLR 68 (CA); *Scruttons Ltd v Midland Silicines Ltd* [1962] AC 446 (HL) 473 (Lord Reid); *Woodar Investment Development Ltd v Wimpey Construction UK Ltd* [1980] 1 WLR 277 (HL) 300 (Lord Scarman); *Swan v Law Society* [1983] 1 AC 598 (HL) 611 (Lord Diplock). Isolated exceptions were made to the privity rule through mechanisms such as trusts, assignment, agency, and specific performance (*Beswick v Beswick* [1968] AC 58 (HL) and in tort (*White v Jones* [1995] 2 AC 207 (HL) and property law. In certain situations, the courts also allowed a contracting party to sue for damages for a third party's loss (*Linden Gardens Trust Ltd v Lenesta Sludge Disposals Ltd* [1994] 1 AC 85 (HL); *Darlington Borough Council v Wiltshier Northern* [1995] 1 WLR 68 (CA); *Alfred McAlpine Construction Ltd v Panatown Ltd* [2001] 1 AC 518 (HL).

[86] Contract (Rights of Third Parties) Act 1999, s1(1)(b).

[87] Ibid., s1(3); Vogenauer, 'The Effects of Contracts on Third Parties: The Avant-projet de réforme in a Comparative Perspective' (n 5) 250; Beale, Fauvarque-Cosson, Rutgers, and Vogenauer (n 43): see Chapter 8 on 'The Effect of the Contract on Third Parties'; Borghetti, 'The Effect of Contracts and Third Parties' (n 9) 250, concludes that 'as a result, many cases in which French courts imply a stipulation for the benefit of a third party would not create an enforceable right in the third party under English law'.

[88] For construction disputes, and the distinction between pure economic loss and loss that is consequent on property damage, see *Spartan Steel & Alloys Ltd v Martin & Co (Contractors) Ltd* [1973] QB 27 (CA); *D&F Estates Ltd v Church Commissioners for England and Wales* [1989] 1 AC 177 (HL); *Aswan Engineering Establishment Co v Lupdine Ltd* [1987] 1 WLR 1 (CA); *Anns v Merton London Borough Council* [1978] AC 728 (HL); *Murphy v Brentwood District Council* [1991] 1 AC 393 (HL); and the controversial *Junior Books Ltd v Veitchi Co Ltd* [1983] 1 AC 520 (HL). For a thorough distinction on this topic, see Stoffel-Munck, 'Liability of Contracting Parties Towards Third Parties' (n 62); Beale, Fauvarque-Cosson, Rutgers, and Vogenauer (n 43) 1295–6.

[89] *Simaan General Contracting Co v Pilkington Glass Ltd (No 2)* [1988] QB 756; *Scruttons Ltd v Midland Silicones Ltd* [1962] 1 AC 446 (HL).

Another difference is that in English law, a breach of contract does not automatically give rise to a claim in tort. The defaulting party must owe an independent and recognized duty of care to the third party.[90] However, where the loss is economic in nature, the circumstances in which such a duty will be recognized are very limited.[91] These include negligent misstatements by specially skilled and knowledgeable professionals who assume responsibility for the provision of information that is reasonably relied upon by the victim,[92] and the negligent performance of services by professionals who are aware that the services are for the benefit of third parties.[93]

[90] Stoffel-Munck, 'Liability of Contracting Parties Towards Third Parties' (n 62).

[91] Ibid.

[92] *Hedley Byrne & Co Ltd v Heller & Partners Ltd* [1964] AC 465 (HL); *Smith v Eric S. Bush* [1990] 1 AC 831 (HL); *Caparo v Dickman* [1990] 2 AC 605 (HL).

[93] *White v Jones* [1995] 2 AC 207 (HL) and in particular Lord Browne-Wilkinson's statement at 271: where a lawyer fails to fulfil the duties of care entrusted to him by his client in carrying out his last wishes.

# PART V
# FAILURE TO PERFORM

# 9
# Failure to Perform Due to Unforeseen Circumstances

Performance is sometimes rendered impossible or more difficult as a result of unforeseen events that cannot be imputed to the party subject to the obligation to perform. In these circumstances, their failure to perform attracts different remedial consequences than does breach of contract (considered in Chapter 10), reflecting the absence of fault.[1]

A distinction is drawn in French contract law between unforeseen events that render performance impossible, whether permanently or temporarily, and those that render performance extremely difficult or onerous. Force majeure, provided for in new articles 1218, 1351, and 1351-1 of the Civil Code, is relevant to the first situation. The new doctrine of *imprévision* in article 1195, which gives the court broad powers to adjust the contract and is one of the major innovations in the 2016 reforms, is relevant to the second.

## A Performance That Is Impossible: Force Majeure

**Civil Code**[2]

Art. 1218.—In contractual matters, there is force majeure where an event beyond the control of the debtor, which could not reasonably have been foreseen at the time of the conclusion of the contract and whose effects could not be avoided by appropriate measures, prevents performance of his obligation by the debtor.

If the prevention is temporary, performance of the obligation is suspended unless the delay which results justifies termination of the contract. If the prevention is permanent, the contract is terminated by operation of law and the parties

[1] As will be shown in Chapter 10, pp 225–8, in French law breach of contract is considered as a wrong and the defaulting party is regarded as being at fault for not performing.

[2] 'Ordonnance no 2016-131 du 10 février 2016 portant réforme du droit des contrats, du régime général et de la preuve des obligations', JORF no 0035 of 11 February 2016. The Ordonnance was translated into English by J Cartwright, B Fauvarque-Cosson, and S Whittaker: <http://www.textes.justice.gouv.fr/art_pix/THE-LAW-OF-CONTRACT-2-5-16.pdf> (2016 version) and <http://www.textes.justice.gouv.fr/art_pix/Translationrevised2018final.pdf> (2018 version) accessed 1 September 2021. The translations of the new articles contained in this book are theirs.

*The New French Law of Contract.* Solène Rowan, Oxford University Press. © Solène Rowan 2022.
DOI: 10.1093/oso/9780198810872.003.0009

are discharged from their obligations under the conditions provided by articles 1351 and 1351-1.

Art. 1351.—Impossibility of performing the act of performance discharges the debtor to the extent of that impossibility where it results from an event of force majeure and is definitive unless he had agreed to bear the risk of the event or had previously been given notice to perform.

Art. 1351-1.—Where the impossibility of performance is a result of the loss of the thing that is owed, the debtor who has been given notice to perform is still discharged if he proves that the loss would equally have occurred if his obligation had been performed. He must, however, assign to the creditor his rights and claims attached to the thing.

The principle of *ad impossibilia nemo tenetur*, meaning that nobody is held to the impossible, has long been of central importance in French contract law. Impossibility is primarily understood and expressed through the concept of force majeure. To the layperson, this is familiar as an event that disrupts the natural order of things, for example a catastrophic meteorological phenomenon, a riot, a civil war, or a pandemic.[3] In practice performance may also be rendered impossible by events that are far less dramatic in nature. Whether such events constitute force majeure will depend on a number of factors and is assessed on a case-by-case basis.[4]

## 1 Characterization of force majeure

The drafters sought to clarify and bring greater certainty to force majeure by introducing a new definition in article 1218. No definition had been provided in the 1804 Civil Code and, to add to the resulting ambiguity, it appeared alongside the closely related concepts of 'fortuitous event' (*cas fortuit*) and 'extraneous cause' (*cause etrangère*), which unhelpfully were also undefined.[5] The doctrine therefore fell to be developed by the courts.[6] So emerged three conditions that the event

[3] See F Lichère, F Akoka, A Meynier-Pozzi, and V Lamy, 'Crise sanitaire et contrats publics, une approche de sociologie juridique' AJDA 2021.1425. Also Ordonnance no 2020-316 of 25 March 2020 relating to the payment of rent, water, gas, and electricity bills of professional premises of companies whose activity is affected by the spread of the Covid-19 pandemic (Ordonnance no 2020-316 du 25 mars 2020 relative au paiement des loyers, des factures d'eau, de gaz et d'électricité afférents aux locaux professionnels des entreprises dont l'activité est affectée par la propagation de l'épidémie de covid-19).

[4] P Malaurie, L Aynès, and P Stoffel-Munck, *Droit des obligations* (10th edn, LGDJ: Paris, 2018) [952]. See also, P-H Antonmattel, *Contributions à l'étude de la force majeure* (LGDJ: Montpellier, 1993).

[5] Although this remains true of the Civil Code today, see Malaurie, Aynès, and Stoffel-Munck (n 4) [952]; compare G Chantepie and M Latina, *La réforme du droit des obligations, Commentaire théorique et pratique dans l'ordre du Code civil* (2nd edn, Dalloz: Paris, 2018) [618–619] [617].

[6] The definition, in particular the requirement of externality, was questioned by commentators and varied by the *Cour de cassation* on several occasions at the beginning of the twenty-first century. For a full explanation, see Chantepie and Latina (n 5) [618]–[619].

preventing performance must satisfy, which are now enshrined in the article.[7] These are that the event must (i) be reasonably unforeseeable; (ii) result in insurmountable consequences; and (iii) be beyond the control of the party that is under the obligation to perform. The conditions are cumulative and each must be satisfied for force majeure to be established.

### (a) A reasonably unforeseeable event

Force majeure can have a multitude of different causes. These include: acts of nature;[8] third parties;[9] the promise; or the State.[10] It had long been recognized in the cases that, in order to qualify, an event had to be unforeseeable at the time the parties entered into the contract. If it could be foreseen, the promisor would effectively have promised to perform in the knowledge that this would, or might not, be possible, which would amount to a fault.[11]

The unforeseeability requirement is qualified in article 1218 by a standard of reasonableness. Only an event that could not have been reasonably foreseen will suffice. This is assessed objectively, having regard to the circumstances of the contract and the characteristics of the event but not the personal characteristics of the parties.[12] In practice the court has considerable latitude for decision.[13] The operation of the requirement can be illustrated through three cases involving France's state-owned railway company, the SNCF, each relating to its duty to maintain the safety of passengers. In the first case, an attempt by a passenger to board a moving train was held by the *Cour de cassation* to be foreseeable and not force majeure[14] since the SNCF is 'regularly confronted by such behaviour'.[15] Similarly, in the second case, the assault of a passenger aboard a train did not qualify as force majeure because this too was foreseeable and indeed could have been avoided by the implementation of appropriate security measures.[16] In contrast, in the third case,

[7] Malaurie, Aynès, and Stoffel-Munck (n 4) [953]–[956]. Chantepie and Latina (n 5) [618]–[621].

[8] Civ (3) 11 May 1994, Bull civ III no 74.

[9] Civ (1) 23 June 2011, no 10-15.811, Bull civ I 123; Ch Mixte 4 Feb 1983, Bull civ no 1 and 2 RTD civ 1983.549, note G Durry; Civ (1) 24 Jan 1995, Bull civ I no 54. But see Civ (1) 7 March 1966, Bull civ I no 166.

[10] Civ (3) 1 June 2011, pourvoi no 09-70.502.

[11] A *Droit des obligations* (18th edn, LJDJ: Paris, 2019) [348].

[12] Chantepie and Latina (n 5) [620]. Previously, the personal circumstances of the promisor were taken into account in some cases. See, for example, Malaurie, Aynès, and Stoffel-Munck (n 4) [955] citing Com 3 Oct 1989, Bull civ IV no 346 RTD civ 1990.87, note P Jourdain; Civ (1) 26 Jan 1971, Bull civ I no 27; Civ (3) 30 Nov 1983, Bull civ III no 253.

[13] B Fauvarque-Cosson, 'Does Review on the Ground of *Imprévision* Breach the Principle of the Binding Force of Contracts?' in J Cartwright and S Whittaker (eds), *The Code Napoléon Rewritten: French Contract Law after the 2016 Reforms* (Hart Publishing: Oxford, 2017) 187, 197; L Aynès, 'Le contrat, loi des parties' [2005] Cahiers du Conseil Constitutionnel, Dossier: Loi et Contrat, no 17 <https://www.conseil-constitutionnel.fr/nouveaux-cahiers-du-conseil-constitutionnel/le-contrat-loi-des-parties> accessed 1 September 2021.

[14] Civ (2) 3 March 2016, pourvoi no 15-12.217.

[15] Ibid.

[16] Civ (1) 12 Dec 2000, Bull civ I no 323, D 2001.1650, note C Paulin.

the fatal stabbing of a passenger on a train did amount to force majeure[17] since it was unforeseeable. It was also unavoidable,[18] in that there was nothing that the SNCF could have done to prevent it.

### (b) An event whose effects could not be avoided by appropriate measures

The impossibility of performance must be objectively insurmountable or unavoidable.[19] This is commonly referred to as *irresistibilité*,[20] connoting that it cannot be prevented or overcome. An unforeseeable event that renders performance devoid of interest[21] or more costly will not suffice. Nor can force majeure apply to payment obligations,[22] since 'it is never impossible to transfer money'.[23] It is therefore not available where the promisor is simply in financial difficulty.[24]

If there is an alternative way to perform, non-performance cannot be excused on grounds of force majeure since performance is possible. As with the foreseeability requirement, this is assessed objectively[25] and the courts have broad scope for decision. There are a number of illustrations of the requirement in the cases. For example, a strike by sailors was held not to be force majeure for a contract to transport pilgrims to the Holy Land by sea where air travel was an available alternative.[26] The Gulf War did not prevent a travel agency from organizing a holiday in Morocco, which was not involved in the conflict although holidaymakers were advised to exercise a heightened level of prudence.[27] A drought-affected farmer could not claim to be excused from an obligation to supply agricultural products which could be sourced on the open market.[28]

### (c) An event 'beyond the control of the promisor'

The force majeure event must be outside the sphere of control of the promisor. A party cannot rely on the acts of those under their control to establish force majeure. An employer therefore cannot contend that the acts of an employee are

[17] Civ (1) 23 June 2011, pourvoi no 10-15811, D 2011.1817, obs I Gallmeister.

[18] Ibid.

[19] For a criticism of the wording of the provision that suggests that it is the consequences of the event, and not the event itself, that must be unavoidable, see Chantepie and Latina (n 5) [621].

[20] Ibid.; Bénabent (n 11) [347]; Malaurie, Aynès, and Stoffel-Munck (n 4) [954].

[21] Com 23 Jan 1968, JCP 1968.III.15422; but see Civ (3) 19 April 1972, D 1973.205, note H Souleau, and Civ (1) 10 Feb 1998, D 1998.539, note D Mazeaud.

[22] Com, 16 Sept 2014, pourvoi no 13-20306, D 2014.2217, note J Francois RDC 2015.21, note Y-M Laithier.

[23] Chantepie and Latina (n 5) [622]. See also, O Deshayes, T Genicon, and Y-M Laithier, *Réforme du droit des contrats, du régime général et de la preuve des obligations* (2nd edn, LexisNexis: Paris, 2018) 538.

[24] Soc Feb 1996, D 1996.633, note C Puigelier.

[25] However, there have been instances of the personal circumstances of the promisor being taken into account. See, for example, Civ (3) 19 April 1972, Bull civ III no 247, D 1973.205, note H Souleau; CA Orléans, 25 Oct 1973, D 1974.66, note H Souleau.

[26] Com 12 Nov 1969, Bull civ IV no 327.

[27] Civ (1) 8 Dec 1998, Bull civ I no 346, JCP G 1999.II.10106.

[28] Bénabent (n 11) [347]; Com 4 Jan 1980, Bull civ IV no 6.

beyond their control, nor can building contractors disavow responsibility for failures of their materials, techniques, or sub-contractors.[29]

Whether an event is outside the sphere of control is a factual question that is assessed on a case-by-case basis.[30] For instance, industrial strikes, even where unforeseeable and their effects unavoidable,[31] are ordinarily not force majeure, being internal to the affected employer.[32] A distinction can, however, be drawn where a strike results from circumstances that are genuinely external to, and outside the sphere of, control of the employer, for example a government decision to freeze pay in a particular industry. Where such a decision affects a nationalized sector as a whole, the event will ordinarily be beyond the control of an employer within the sector and can constitute force majeure.[33]

## 2 The effects of force majeure

### (a) No liability for damages

If force majeure is established, the defaulting party cannot be liable in damages for the failure to perform. It is for the injured party to bear any resulting losses. This is an exception to the general rule that damages can be claimed where non-performance or a delay in performance has occurred. It is recognized in article 1231-1, which states that 'a debtor is condemned, where appropriate, to the payment of damages either on the ground of the non-performance or a delay in performance of an obligation, unless they justify this on the ground that performance was prevented by force majeure'.

By way of example, the tenant of a property destroyed by a force majeure event was held to be unable to claim compensation for the cost of finding alternative accommodation. Similarly, an employer cannot recover from an absent employee the cost of hiring a temporary replacement.[34]

### (b) Discharge from obligations

A distinction is drawn in paragraph 2 of article 1218 between a temporary prevention of performance, in which case performance is merely suspended, and permanent prevention, which results in the contract being discharged entirely.

[29] See, for example, Civ (3) 17 May 1983, Bull civ III no 115; Chantepie and Latina (n 5) [619].

[30] Chantepie and Latina (n 5) [619].

[31] Civ (1) 20 Oct 2008, pourvoi no 07-17.134, Bull civ I no 234.

[32] But see Civ (1) 6 Oct 1993, JCP G 1993.II.22154.

[33] Civ (1) 24 Jan 1995 pourvoi no 92-18.227, Bull I no 4 D 1995, note G Paisant. Translated and analysed in H Beale, B Fauvarque-Cosson, J Rutgers, and S Vogenauer (eds), *Cases, Materials and Text on Contract Law, Ius Commune Casebooks for the Common Law of Europe* (3rd edn, Hart Publishing: Oxford, 2019) 1177–8; Civ (1) 7 March 1966, Bull civ I no 166; Malaurie, Aynès, and Stoffel-Munck (n 4) [957].

[34] See the examples given by Bénabent (n 11) [357].

*(i) Temporary impossibility (*impossibilité temporaire*): suspension*
Where the impossibility to perform is temporary and time is not of the essence, the affected obligation is suspended for the duration of the impossibility. The contract therefore remains in force and the party subject to the obligation to perform is relieved of the obligation only temporarily. This codifies a principle recognized since the end of the nineteenth century, which is sometimes referred to as 'temporary force majeure' (*force majeure temporaire*).[35]

*(ii) Permanent impossibility (*impossibilité totale*): termination by operation of law*
The parties are discharged from their obligations where the impossibility is permanent. An employer was therefore held to be entitled to terminate the employment contract of an employee who was unable to work for a prolonged period of time due to ill health.[36] Similarly, a tenant may validly terminate a lease where the landlord needs to undertake substantial repairs rendering the property uninhabitable for a protracted duration.[37]

Termination of the contract occurs automatically without any need for permission from the court. The parties are released from their obligations with retroactive effect, unless the contract is one of successive performance, meaning that performance is fragmented and in instalments.[38] In that case, the termination discharges obligations to render future performance only.[39]

There has been criticism of paragraph 2 of article 1218 for failing to explain how significant must be the obligation that is impossible to perform for termination to occur. Commentators have presumed that the entire contract is automatically terminated, even if the prevention relates to a minor aspect of the contract taken as a whole. Deshayes, Genicon, and Laithier,[40] as well as Chantepie and Latina,[41] have argued that a more balanced solution would have been to allow for a reduction in the price where the failure to perform is minor, with the right to terminate reserved for failures that are 'sufficiently serious'. This would have been consistent with article 1223, which enables the victim of a breach of contract to accept the defective performance at a reduced price, and article 1224, which allows termination for 'sufficiently serious' breaches.[42]

According to article 1351, a contract will only be terminated for permanent impossibility to the extent that it cannot be performed. This addresses the situation

[35] See Chantepie and Latina (n 5) [623].
[36] Bénabent (n 11) [353]. Compare, for example, Soc 25 Jan 1984, Bull civ V no 33.
[37] Paragraph 3 of article 1724 of the Civil Code.
[38] Successive contracts are defined at article 1111-1 of the Civil Code, see the section on classification in Chapter 3, pp 44–51.
[39] Bénabent (n 11) [354]–[356] (3). For example, if a lease is terminated following the destruction of the rented premises, termination applies prospectively only: article 1722.
[40] Deshayes, Genicon, and Laithier (n 23) 539.
[41] Chantepie and Latina (n 5) [624].
[42] Ibid.

where some form of permanent impossibility has arisen but partial performance is nonetheless possible. The party is released to the extent of the impossibility. This is subject to exceptions where they have agreed to bear the risk of the event[43] or where they were given notice to perform the affected obligation before the force majeure event occurred but failed to do so. From the latter exception there is a carve-out in article 1351-1 where the impossibility results from the loss of the thing that is owed. In that case the performing party can nevertheless be discharged by showing that, even if they had performed, the loss would have occurred anyway. In other words, for the carve-out to apply, there must be no causal link[44] between non-performance and the loss, which would still not have been avoided if the obligation had been duly performed.

## B *Imprévision*

Civil Code
Art. 1195.—If a change of circumstances that was unforeseeable at the time of the conclusion of the contract renders performance excessively onerous for a party who had not accepted the risk of such a change, that party may ask the other contracting party to renegotiate the contract. The first party must continue to perform his obligations during renegotiation.

In the case of refusal or the failure of renegotiations, the parties may agree to terminate the contract from the date and on the conditions which they determine, or by a common agreement ask the court to set about its adaptation. In the absence of an agreement within a reasonable time, the court may, on the request of a party, revise the contract or put an end to it, from a date and subject to such conditions as it shall determine.

Force majeure has no application where there is an unforeseeable change of circumstances that renders performance more difficult or costly but not impossible. The affected party must instead turn to the new doctrine of *imprévision* in article 1195. This confers broad powers on the court to revise or terminate the agreement in order to promote substantive fairness (*justice contractuelle*).

The introduction of *imprévision* is amongst the most significant and controversial changes made in the reforms. Its effect is to reverse the principle enunciated by the *Cour de cassation* in the well-known 'Canal de Craponne'[45] case that the

[43] This is commonly achieved through a warrant that performance will occur.
[44] Deshayes, Genicon, and Laithier (n 23) 915.
[45] Civ 6 March 1876, 1876.1.193, note A Giboulot translated in Beale, Fauvarque-Cosson, Rutgers, and Vogenauer (n 33) 1213–4. The case concerned a contract entered into in 1567 still in force in 1876!

contract should be applied in accordance with its terms and neither the passage of time nor changes in circumstances can justify the court inserting new terms that have not been agreed by the parties. It was stated to be 'no part the function of the courts, however equitable it may seem to them, to modify the parties' agreements in the light of changing time and circumstances or to substitute new terms in the place of those freely accepted by the parties'.[46] This was rationalized on the basis of the binding force of contract, which is 'general and absolute'.

The principle had, however, come under increasing strain, particularly in moments of economic instability and with the increasing prevalence of long-term contracts, which by their nature are more vulnerable to changes of circumstances. It had already been attenuated to some extent by the emergence and enforcement of hardship clauses and the recognition of the right of unilateral termination of contracts of indeterminate duration.[47] In some cases, the courts had also invoked good faith to adjust contract terms in the interest of fairness.[48]

There were opposing views on whether the principle should be reversed. This is reflected in the divergence between the two major reform projects that preceded the 2016 reforms. The 'Catala proposals' would have maintained the Canal de Craponne tradition, seeing *imprévision* as superfluous since the parties can themselves provide for unforeseen circumstances, if they so desire. In contrast, an *imprévision* mechanism was proposed by the 'Terré project'. It was said to be conducive to contractual fairness and largely inspired by article 6:111 of the Principles of European Contract Law (PECL).[49]

The drafters of the reforms justified the introduction of *imprévision* in the 'Report to the President of the Republic' in the following terms:

> France is one of the last countries in Europe not to recognise the theory of *imprévision* as a moderating factor of the binding force of the contract. Its enshrinement inspired by comparative law as well as European harmonisation projects make it possible to combat major contractual imbalances arising during performance, in according with the objective of contractual fairness sought by the Ordonnance.[50]

[46] Ibid.

[47] Contracting parties have in practice used so-called indexation clauses, benchmarking clauses and hardship clauses to redistribute the risk of unforeseen circumstances occurring. See, for example: Malaurie, Aynès, and Stoffel-Munck (n 4) [762]; Bénabent (n 11) [307]; F Terré, P Simler, Y Lequette, and F Chénedé, *Droit civil: les obligations* (12th edn, Dalloz: Paris, 2018) [647–8].

[48] Soc 25 Feb 1992, D 1992.390, note M Defossez; Com 29 June 2010, RDC 2011.1.34, note E Savaux.

[49] See Terré, Simler, Lequette, and Chénedé (n 47) [632].

[50] 'Report to the President of the Republic relating to Ordonnance no 2016–131 of 10 February 2016 on the reform of contract law, the general regime and proof of obligations', JORF no 0035 of 11 February 2016, 12.

However, this did not put an end to the discussion. During the parliamentary debates in respect of the Ratification Bill in 2018, the Senate sought to excise article 1195 from the new Civil Code.[51] It did so out of concern that *imprévision* would undermine legal certainty and encourage litigation. Ultimately, the Senate and the *Assemblée Nationale* agreed that the article should be retained but on the basis that the court would only be able to revise the contract by unilateral request as a last resort once the parties had attempted to reach agreement on the anterior solutions of renegotiation, termination, and adaptation.[52] The Senate was however successful in excluding financial contracts and securities transactions from the scope of the doctrine, as these contracts involve a significant degree of speculation.[53]

## 1 Necessary conditions for *imprévision*

With the exception of financial contracts and securities transactions, *imprévision* applies to all contracts. In practice it is most likely to be relevant where performance takes place over an extended period of time.[54] Three cumulative conditions must be satisfied. These are (a) an unforeseeable change in circumstances; (b) the risk of which had not been accepted by the party subject to the obligation to perform; and (c) performance has become excessively onerous as a result.

### (a) An unforeseeable change in circumstances

The first condition is that, at the time of entering into the contract, the parties could not have foreseen the change in circumstances. If it was or could have been foreseen, they were at liberty to provide for it and should not be entitled to protection.[55]

Any event can render performance excessively onerous. It need not be of a particular type. As commentators have noted, its breadth enables the court to take into account:

> all types of event whether legal (adoption of a new law), economic (establishment of a customs barrier), financial (stock market crash), societal (war), environmental (ecological catastrophe), technological (development of a new technology rendering a product obsolete), or even natural (earthquake).[56]

[51] Chantepie and Latina (n 5) [522].
[52] Ibid.
[53] See the securities and financial transactions referred to in article L211-1 (I to III) of the Monetary and Financial Code as to which see article L211-40-1 of that Code; A Couret, H Le Nabasque, M-L Coquelet, T Granier, D Poracchia, A Raynouard, A Reygrobellet, and D Robine, *Droit financier* (3rd edn, Dalloz: Paris, 2019) [1150].
[54] Bénabent (n 11) [304].
[55] A widely made point, see, for example, Malaurie, Aynès, and Stoffel-Munck (n 4) [764].
[56] Chantepie and Latina (n 5) [524].

Commentators have criticized the uncertainty generated by the high level of abstraction and lack of detail relating to the requirement. The article does not specify whether the unforeseeability must relate to the actual occurrence or the gravity of the event. Nor is it stated how foreseeability is to be determined. The consensus amongst commentators is that the test is an objective one.[57] A greater source of uncertainty is an apparent discrepancy in the test for foreseeability between force majeure and *imprévision*. In relation to force majeure the requirement is qualified in article 1218 by a standard of reasonableness. However, no equivalent qualification appears in article 1195 in respect of *imprévision*. There is no clear explanation for this difference and views differ on its effect. One suggestion is that 'the mechanism of *imprévision* would be available only if the circumstance was *radically* unforeseeable and not only *reasonably* foreseeable'.[58] Others consider that the interpolation of a standard of radicalness in place of reasonableness goes too far.[59]

### (b) No acceptance of the risk of such a change

There can be no *imprévision* where the risk of the change in circumstances occurring has been assumed by the party affected. In that case the right to call upon article 1195 is deemed to have been waived.[60]

The assumption of risk can be express or implied. It will be express where provided for in terms in the contract itself. This is illustrated by a provision that precluded any adjustment of the contract price to take account of fluctuations in the price of the materials that were needed for performance.[61] It will be implied where inherent in the nature of the contract but not spelled out expressly. In a fixed-price construction contract, for example, it is implicit that the builder assumes, and the employer is insulated from, the risk of a rise in the price of materials.[62]

It is possible that the courts will be sceptical of contract terms that purport to exclude or narrow the role of *imprévision*. Such provisions might be strictly interpreted,[63] perhaps to be given effect only in respect of risks that are expressly identified.[64] It seems likely that some more sophisticated parties will seek to sidestep the possibility of judicial resistance by agreeing to exclude article 1195.[65] This should be permissible because *imprévision*[66] is not stated in the Civil Code to be a matter of public policy (*d'ordre public*). It is therefore non-mandatory and can be disapplied by agreement. The parties should, therefore, be free to contract out

[57] Ibid.; Deshayes, Genicon, and Laithier (n 23) 445.
[58] Chantepie and Latina (n 5) [524].
[59] Terré, Simler, Lequette, and Chénedé (n 47) [638].
[60] Deshayes, Genicon, and Laithier (n 23) 452.
[61] Terré, Simler, Lequette, and Chénedé (n 47) [641].
[62] Ibid.
[63] Ibid.
[64] Deshayes, Genicon, and Laithier (n 23) 453.
[65] Ibid.
[66] The same is true of force majeure. The parties can contract out of article 1218 and provide their own definition of force majeure and its effects.

of the article or limit or modify its effect.[67] In relation to standard form contracts (*contrats d'adhésion*), this is subject to article 1171. As a result, if the party that has assumed the risk has little bargaining power and there is a significant imbalance between the parties,[68] the clause will be sanctioned as abusive.[69]

### (c) Excessively onerous performance

The third condition is that the unforeseeable change in circumstances results in performance being excessively onerous for one of the parties. 'Excessively onerous' is not defined but appears to connote at least some degree of extremity and more than a financial burden that is unexpected and unwelcome. This is consistent with the Report to the President, which refers to 'major contractual imbalances' between the parties.[70]

There is also a lack of guidance on how excessive onerousness should be assessed. It appears to be an objective test.[71] According to Stoffel-Munck, it should be understood as 'a negative cost / benefit ratio [ … ] characterised by the difference between the value of what was provided and what was received.'[72] Whatever the correct approach, the court is likely to have broad scope for decision as to whether the condition is satisfied on the given facts.

## 2 Effects

The effect of satisfying the three conditions is to unlock the cascading options set out in article 1195. These begin with consensual renegotiation, failing which the parties can agree to terminate or request that the court adapts the contract. If neither of these options can be agreed within a reasonable time, the last resort is either judicial revision or termination, both by unilateral request. The latter options are only available in exceptional circumstances and are the most controversial.

### (a) Renegotiation

Pursuant to paragraph 1 of the article, the party for whom performance has become excessively onerous should first seek to renegotiate the contract with the other party. Since the powers of the court are only enlivened in the absence of an agreement within a reasonable time, this initial requirement appears to be mandatory.[73]

67 Civ (3) 31 Oct 2006, Bull civ III no 212.

68 Chantepie and Latina (n 5) [525].

69 Com 8 July 1981, Bull civ IV no 312, RTD civ 1982.426, note G Durry; Fauvarque-Cosson, 'Does Review on the Ground of *Imprévision* Breach the Principle of the Binding Force of Contracts?' (n 13) 199; Malaurie, Aynès, and Stoffel-Munck (n 4) [764].

70 'Report to the President' (n 50) 12.

71 Terré, Simler, Lequette, and Chénedé (n 47) [638].

72 P Stoffel-Munck 'Imprévision et la réforme des effets du contrat' RDC hors-série, 2016.30.

73 Terré, Simler, Lequette, and Chénedé (n 47) [643].

During any renegotiations, the contract remains in force and the affected party must continue to perform their obligations, even though excessively onerous. The premise is that the changed circumstances are not so onerous as to prevent performance entirely, which would qualify as force majeure and engage articles 1218, 1351, and 1351-1.

It is unclear whether the other party must accede to a request for renegotiation. There is no express requirement in the article to do so. On that basis, some commentators have contended that there is no obligation to renegotiate and a refusal to do so cannot be wrongful.[74] This would however dilute the right to request renegotiation, which would barely differ from the notional right of any contracting party to seek to renegotiate at any time. Another view is that, if the three conditions of article 1195 are satisfied, a refusal to negotiate without grounds could be abusive[75] and a breach of the duty to act in good faith.[76] This seems more convincing. The parties are subject to a duty to cooperate in performance, which necessitates a minimum standard of conduct when responding to a request to renegotiate and in any renegotiations.

### (b) Termination or judicial revision by common agreement

If the request for renegotiations comes to naught, according to paragraph 2 of the article, the parties may agree to terminate the contract or to ask the court to revise it. The right to terminate is merely a restatement of article 1193, which provides that a 'contract can be modified or revoked only by the parties' mutual consent' and recognition of the reality that a contract can be terminated by agreement at any time, which is known by the Latin formulation *mutuus dissensus*.[77]

### (c) Judicial termination or revision by unilateral request

The real innovation in the article is the new powers of the court to revise or terminate the contract at the request of one of the parties. This has been described as an 'ideological rupture with the old law'[78] and was the particular focus of the Senate's opposition to *imprévision*. The reality is that, aside from these powers, the parties have always been able to agree any of the cascading options at any stage during the life of their contract. None of the three conditions of the article is a prerequisite for doing so. By directing the parties to consider renegotiation, termination, and judicial revision before a unilateral request can be made to the court, the article seems merely to encourage the parties to try to find common ground[79]

[74] Chantepie and Latina (n 5) [528].

[75] Fauvarque-Cosson, 'Does Review on the Ground of *Imprévision* Breach the Principle of the Binding Force of Contracts?' (n 13) 202.

[76] Ibid.; Malaurie, Aynès, and Stoffel-Munck (n 4) [764].

[77] Malaurie, Aynès, and Stoffel-Munck (n 4) [757].

[78] Terré, Simler, Lequette, and Chénedé (n 47) [634].

[79] The 'Report to the President' (n 50) 12 explains that *imprévision* is intended to 'play a preventive role: the risk of destruction or revision of the contract by the court should encourage the parties to negotiate'. See also, Fauvarque-Cosson (n 13) 191.

rather than take their chances with involving the court.[80] For the beneficiary of the change in circumstances, it may be preferable to renegotiate than run the risk of the court amending or terminating the contract. As with nuclear weapons, to borrow Deshayes, Genicon, and Laithier's analogy, the effect is more theoretical than practical.[81]

The powers of the court are couched in broad terms and the article gives no guidance as to how they should be exercised. It is therefore unclear whether the court is entirely at liberty to revise or terminate the contract or some constraints apply. As Malaurie, Aynès, and Stoffel-Munck have rhetorically asked, if 'presented with a request to revise the contract, can the judge opt for termination instead, or vice versa'?'[82] This seems permissible on a strict reading of the article but would be a radical departure from the will of the parties.

Article 1195 is also silent on how the contract should be modified if the court decides to do so. This is in contrast with the Lando principles and the Terré project, which both proposed guidance. The former envisaged that the court would 'distribute effectively between the parties the profits and losses resulting from the change in circumstances'. In the latter, the court was required to 'adapt the contract in consideration of the legitimate expectations of the parties', which introduces the subjective wishes of the parties into the exercise.[83] The absence of any guiding principle appears to leave the court with generous decision-making autonomy, with the potential for unpredictable outcomes.

## C Concluding Observations

The most notable of the reforms relating to changes of circumstances is indubitably the introduction of *imprévision* in article 1195. In the words of the drafters, the purpose was to 'encourage the parties to "save" the contract where its performance becomes difficult'.[84] This is consistent with the bias that pervades French contract law for performance over the discharge of the contract, which will be developed in Chapter 10.

The article also seeks to promote substantive fairness (*justice contractuelle*), one of the main general objectives of the reforms. According to the Report to the

[80] Fauvarque-Cosson, 'Does Review on the Ground of *Imprévision* Breach the Principle of the Binding Force of Contracts?' (n 13) 191; Deshayes, Genicon, and Laithier (n 23) 437; C Pédamon 'The paradoxes of the theory of *imprévision* in the new French law of contract: a judicial deterrent?' (Winter 2017) (12) Amicus Curiae, 15 <https://westminsterresearch.westminster.ac.uk/download/5fd1f14711f47ce6763eb35ad6af62589a799a58a019051f7a50f1aeee29d8c6/206738/Amicus%20Curiae%20112%20-%20Catherine%20Pédamon%20-%20Published%20version.pdf> accessed 1 September 2021.

[81] Deshayes, Genicon, and Laithier (n 23) 4.

[82] Malaurie, Aynès, and Stoffel-Munck (n 4) [764].

[83] Terré, Simler, Lequette, and Chénedé (n 47) [644].

[84] F Ancel, B Fauvarque-Cosson, and J Gest, *Aux sources de la réforme du droit des contrats* (Dalloz: Paris, 2017) [25.131].

President, the aim was to redress 'major contractual imbalances that arise during performance, in accordance with the objective of contractual justice pursued by the Ordonnance'.[85] As with article 1171, which protects against unfair terms, it serves as a counterweight to the principle of the binding force of contract.[86] A balance is sought between holding parties to the agreed terms and fairness.

The ultimate responsibility for establishing this balance is entrusted to the court. Its powers over the contract have been strengthened and are now considerable. Article 1195 has been said by one of the drafters, Fauvarque-Cosson, to embody the values and philosophical underpinnings of French contract law. In her words, it ensures 'the taking into account of ethics in the life of business. The traditional conception of the judge, a simple servant of the contract, gives way to a new "contractual morality" based on good faith and fairness'.[87]

Not everyone shares this enthusiasm for the expansion of the powers of the court. For some commentators, the previous, less-interventionist regime had the advantage of encouraging contracting parties to combine in dealing with the risk of unforeseen circumstances. Stoffel-Munck, for example, regards the article as a subordination of freedom and individual responsibility 'to the providential intervention of the judge'.[88] The Senate also criticized the provision when considering whether to ratify the decree. It expressed misgiving as to whether the extraordinary jurisdiction conferred on the court would improve either the attractiveness or the commerciality of French law, which was another aim of the reforms. The Report of the Senate stated as follows:

> Our fear is to see the judge become a regulator of the contract and to police contracts to the detriment of freedom of contract and the autonomy of the will… the reinforcement of the role of the judge is a source of uncertainty and is a negative symbol for the attractiveness of French law… in the case of article 1195 on unforeseen circumstances, the judge almost becomes a contracting party himself.[89]

[85] 'Report to the President' (n 50) 12.

[86] Fauvarque-Cosson, 'Does Review on the Ground of *Imprévision* Breach the Principle of the Binding Force of Contracts?' (n 13) 188–9.

[87] Ibid., 188.

[88] Stoffel-Munck (n 72) 30.

[89] S Houlié 'Rapport fait au nom de la commission des lois constitutionnelles, de la législation et de l'administration générale de la République sur le projet de loi, modifié par le Sénat en deuxième lecture, ratifiant l'ordonnance no 2016-131 du 10 février 2016 portant réforme du droit des contrats, du régime général et de la preuve des obligations' (Assemblée Nationale: no 429, 29 Nov 2017) <https://www.assemblee-nationale.fr/dyn/15/rapports/cion_lois/l15b0429_rapport-fond> accessed 1 September 2021; F Pillet, 'Rapport fait au nom des lois constitutionnelles, de législation, du suffrage universel, du Règlement d'administration générale (1) sur le projet de loi ratifiant l'ordonnance no 2016-131 du 10 février 2016 portant réforme du droit des contrats, du régime général et de la preuve des obligations' (Sénat: no 33, 11 Oct 2017) <https://www.senat.fr/rap/l17-022/l17-0221.pdf> accessed 1 September 2021.

The Senate fought hard but ultimately unsuccessfully for the removal of these powers. It did, however, take comfort from contracting parties being able to contract out of article 1195.

One particular concern is that, as noted repeatedly during the course of the preceding analysis of *imprévision*, the new article contains several terms that are drafted at a high level of abstraction yet not always defined. This leaves open a number of fairly fundamental questions. For instance, must the change of circumstances be outside of the control of the parties? Does 'unforeseeable' mean 'reasonably unforeseeable'? What does 'excessively onerous' mean? This leaves considerable room for interpretation and attendant uncertainty.[90] It will fall to the courts to give content to their new powers. Only when this happens will the new face of French law become clearer.[91]

As a further complication, article 1195 applies only to contracts entered into after 1 October 2016. The old law continues to apply to contracts entered into prior to that date, as well as where the parties expressly exclude article 1195 from later agreed contracts. This has been described as moving from 'a system of opt-out to opt-in'.[92]

The inspiration for article 1195 was equivalent provisions in other European jurisdictions[93] and international contract law instruments. This was expressly acknowledged by the drafters in a number of contexts. In the Report to the President, they said as follows:

> Article 1195 of the Civil Code is one of the most striking illustrations of the phenomena of hybridisation across legal families and is also a testimony to legal pluralism within Europe. It draws its inspiration from the European and international environment, whilst differentiating itself from them in several respects.[94]

Both the UNIDROIT Principles and the PECL contain provisions on force majeure[95] and hardship which require or enable renegotiation.[96] The court has jurisdiction to rebalance the contract to take account of changed circumstances which have rendered performance 'excessively onerous' (PECL), or 'more onerous', and 'fundamentally alter the equilibrium of the contract' (UNIDROIT Principles).

[90] Stoffel-Munck (n 72).

[91] D Fenouillet, 'Les valeurs morales' RDC 2016.589; J Cartwright and S Whittaker 'Introduction' in J Cartwright and S Whittaker (eds), *The Code Napoléon Rewritten: French Contract Law after the 2016 Reforms* (Hart Publishing: Oxford, 2017) 10–11.

[92] Deshayes, Genicon, and Laithier (n 23) 437.

[93] Ancel, Fauvarque-Cosson, and Gest (n 84) [25.141]; paragraph 313(1) of the Bürgerliches Gesetzbuch (The German Civil Code BGB); article 1467 of the Italian Civil Code.

[94] 'Report to the President' (n 50) 12; see also Ancel, Fauvarque-Cosson, and Gest (n 84) [25.141].

[95] Article 8:108 (Excuse Due to an Impediment) of the PECL; article 7.1.7 (Force majeure) UNIDROIT Principles.

[96] Article 6:111 (Change of Circumstances) of the PECL; article 6.2.2 (Hardship) UNIDROIT Principles.

There is no similar rule in English law. Unless a right to terminate arises, only the narrow doctrine of frustration can rescue a party that is unable to point to a force majeure or an undue hardship clause. A contract may be frustrated where performance has become impossible, illegal, or 'something radically different from that which was in the contemplation of the parties'.[97] This sets a high bar and that in practice is rarely met. On the few occasions where the doctrine does apply, the contract is discharged. There is no power for the court to adapt it. Nor can frustration give rise to a right to render partial performance or performance being suspended for a limited duration, in contrast with French law. There is 'an "all or nothing" approach' with the parties either released or bound and therefore liable for non-performance.[98]

The rationale underpinning the English law approach is that contracting parties should not be relieved 'of the normal consequences of imprudent bargains'.[99] It is open to them to provide for and allocate the risk of unexpected events, which they are better placed to do than the court. If they omit to do so, the losses will generally lie where they fall. In either case, the uncertainties that attend entrusting the court with questions that are fundamentally commercial are avoided.[100]

These divergences reflect conflicting approaches to broader, more fundamental questions of principle. In English law the vanishingly narrow scope for avoiding the contract even in the face of unforeseen circumstances reveals a deep attachment to contractual certainty. The courts are unwilling to disturb the allocation of risk agreed between the parties, who are permitted to escape from their obligations only in exceptional circumstances. This is in contrast with the promotion of contractual fairness and adaptability in the face of economic and commercial vicissitudes in French law.

Whether article 1195 ultimately threatens contractual certainty will depend on whether (and if so how) the courts in France exercise the new powers. Again, in the view of Fauvarque-Cosson, there is no cause for concern. Drawing upon the experience in countries where *imprévision* has longer lineage, she has expressed confidence that the courts will use the powers conscientiously and with moderation. It is by no means the first occasion on which they have been called upon to exercise wide powers to adapt imbalanced contracts. In her words, if 'French courts bear [the imperative of legal certainty] in mind this will encourage them to exercise the

[97] *Davies Contractors Ltd v Fareham Urban District Council* [1956] AC 696 (HL); *Ocean Tramp Tankers Corp v V/O Sovfracht (The Eugenia)* [1964] 2 QB 226 (CA).

[98] Beale, Fauvarque-Cosson, Rutgers, and Vogenauer (n 33) 1185.

[99] *Pioneer Shipping Ltd v BTP Tioxide Ltd (The Nema)* [1982] AC 724 (HL).

[100] E McKendrick, *Contract Law, Text, Cases, and Materials* (9th edn, OUP: Oxford, 2020) 740–2. Although English law has in some situations implied a term that the contract was terminable: *Staffordshire AHA v South Staffs Waterworks* [1978] 1 WLR 138.

powers conferred by article 1195 with the utmost caution, a caution which they have already shown when similar powers were conferred on them in 1975 in relation to penalty clauses'.[101] Whether this proves true remains to be seen. As Beale, Fauvarque-Cosson, Rutgers, and Vogenauer caution, 'the future application of article 1195 of the Code civil will be anything but a long quiet river'.[102]

[101] Fauvarque-Cosson, 'Does Review on the Ground of *Imprévision* Breach the Principle of the Binding Force of Contracts?' (n 13) 205.

[102] Beale, Fauvarque-Cosson, Rutgers, and Vogenauer (n 33) 1213.

# 10
# Remedies for Breach of Contract

**Civil Code**[1]
**(2016 version)**
*Art. 1217.—A party towards whom an undertaking has not been performed or has been performed imperfectly, may:*
- *refuse to perform or suspend performance of his own obligations;*
- *seek enforced performance in kind of the undertaking;*
- *request a reduction in price;*
- *provoke the termination of the contract;*
- *claim reparation of the consequences of non-performance.*

*Sanctions which are not incompatible may be combined; damages may always be added to any of the others.*

**(2018 version)**
Art. 1217.—A party towards whom an undertaking has not been performed or has been performed imperfectly, may:
- refuse to perform or suspend performance of his own obligations;
- seek enforced performance in kind of the undertaking;
- obtain a reduction in price;
- provoke the termination of the contract;
- claim reparation of the consequences of non-performance.

Sanctions which are not incompatible may be combined; damages may always be added to any of the others.

New article 1217 sets out the remedies available to the injured party for breach of contract. These are to refuse to perform or suspend performance of their own obligations, to enforce performance, to reduce the contract price, compensation for

[1] 'Ordonnance no 2016-131 du 10 février 2016 portant réforme du droit des contrats, du régime général et de la preuve des obligations', JORF no 0035 of 11 February 2016. The Ordonnance was translated into English by J Cartwright, B Fauvarque-Cosson, and S Whittaker: <http://www.textes.justice.gouv.fr/art_pix/THE-LAW-OF-CONTRACT-2-5-16.pdf> (2016 version) and <http://www.textes.justice.gouv.fr/art_pix/Translationrevised2018final.pdf> (2018 version) accessed 1 September 2021. The translations of the new articles contained in this book are theirs.

*The New French Law of Contract*. Solène Rowan, Oxford University Press. © Solène Rowan 2022.
DOI: 10.1093/oso/9780198810872.003.0010

loss, and to terminate the contract. There are separate articles in the Civil Code for each remedy.

The choice between remedies for which the conditions are satisfied is unfettered. Any remedies that are not incompatible can be combined. The remedial regime is non-hierarchical, no remedy being superior or subsidiary to the others.[2] However, as will be shown, French law favours performance and saving the contract. This is apparent in the principles governing each remedy. It can also be seen in the requirement upon the injured party, before claiming any remedy, to give notice to the defaulting party that performance must be effected within a reasonable time (*mise en demeure*). This gives the defaulting party warning that relief will be sought and an additional opportunity to perform.

It is in relation to remedies for breach of contract that the 2016 reforms were most innovative. Several remedies were newly introduced or formally recognized, the scope for obtaining certain remedies without a court order was expanded, and some remedies were made subject to standards of reasonableness and proportionality. The articles on remedies were also reorganized. Having previously been dispersed across the 1804 Code,[3] they are now grouped together in a single section of the new Code and in a more logical order. This was intended to be clearer, easier to read, and more accessible, which were among the principal aims of the reforms.

## A Withholding Performance to Incentivize Performance: The *Exception d'Inexécution*

**Civil Code**

Art. 1219.—A party may refuse to perform his obligation, even where it is enforceable, if the other party does not perform his own and if this non-performance is sufficiently serious.

Art. 1220.—A party may suspend the performance of his obligation as soon as it becomes evident that his contracting partner will not perform his obligation when it becomes due and that the consequences of this non-performance are sufficiently serious for him. Notice of this suspension must be given as quickly as possible.

[2] Y-M Laithier, 'Les sanctions de l'inexécution du contrat' in 'Réforme du droit des contrats: quelles innovations?' RDC Hors-série, 2016.39; T Genicon, 'The *Exception d'Inexécution*' in J Cartwright and S Whittaker (eds), *The Code Napoléon Rewritten: French Contract Law after the 2016 Reforms* (Hart Publishing: Oxford, 2017) 291.

[3] The most well-known being articles 1137, 1142, 1143, 1144, 1147, 1149, 1150, 1151, 1152, 1184, 1226, 1231.

New articles 1219 and 1220 lay down the *exception d'inexécution*. This is a self-help remedy that is very well-established in France. It enables the injured party to withhold performance where the counterparty fails to perform their obligations. Often referred to as 'legitimate contractual self-defence',[4] it is relied on by the injured party in defence to a claim in respect of their non-performance.

By its nature, the *exception d'inexécution* is mainly relevant in bilateral contracts where the reciprocal obligations are interdependent and concurrent. It is temporary and provisional, suspending but not extinguishing the obligation to perform. The parties therefore remain bound by the contract. In the event that the defaulting party resumes performing, the injured party must reciprocate. If, however, the default continues, the injured party must decide whether to resort to other remedies, for example, specific enforcement, termination, or a price reduction.

## 1 Overview

Article 1219 states that a party can refuse to perform, even though performance is due, where the other party does not adhere to their side of the contract and the breach is sufficiently serious. This codifies and confirms the general application of the *exception*. There was no equivalent provision in the 1804 Code but only rules that applied to specific contracts.[5] However, the new article is in line with well-established French case law. Over a century ago the *Cour de cassation* recognized that a contracting party can suspend the performance of some or all of their obligations where the other party fails to perform.[6] This has since evolved into an established and uncontroversial principle. As examples, the tenant of rented premises is entitled to withhold rent where the landlord refuses to carry out repairs that prevent enjoyment of the premises,[7] and a seller may refuse to deliver goods where the buyer fails to pay the purchase price.[8]

A further, more novel innovation in the reforms is the introduction, in article 1220, of the anticipatory *exception d'inexécution*. This enables the injured party to suspend their performance as soon as it becomes clear that the counterparty will not perform their obligations when they are due and the consequences of breach would be sufficiently serious. Its effect is that performance can be withheld, even if a breach has not yet occurred.

4 Genicon, 'The *Exception d'Inexécution*' (n 2) 291.

5 Articles 1613 and 1653 of the Civil Code in the context of sale contracts.

6 French courts traditionally grounded the remedy in the notion of *cause*. Each obligation was the *cause* of the other, such that where one was not performed, this justified the non-performance of the other: Civ (1) 27 Dec 1961, Bull civ I no 360.

7 Civ (3) 21 Nov 1990, Bull civ III no 238; Civ (3) 21 Dec 1987, Bull Civ III no 212, 15 Dec 1993, D 1994.462, note Stork; Civ (3) 11 May 1995, Bull civ III no 60.

8 Civ (3) 21 Nov 1990, Bull civ III no 238; Civ (3) 21 Dec 1987, Bull Civ III no 212, 15 Dec 1993, D 1994.462, note Stork; Civ (3) 11 May 1995, Bull civ III no 60.

The *exception d'inexécution*, whether conventional or anticipatory, is thought to have three main advantages. First, it is a quick and efficient means of incentivizing performance, relying on deprivation of the reciprocal performance due under the contract as a means of bringing the defaulting party into line. It is a potentially powerful response to the breach that can usually be achieved at little or no cost and without resort to one of the more serious and potentially definitive remedies of specific enforcement and termination. It also seeks to promote performance and uphold the contract, which is at the heart of the remedial system in France, as will be seen throughout this chapter. Second, it provides the injured party with a defence and justification for not performing their obligations. Lastly, it minimizes the loss arising from the breach. The injured party can cease spending time and money on the failing contract, thus preventing or limiting any further deterioration in their position.

## 2 Necessary conditions for the *exception d'inexécution*

According to article 1219, two conditions must be satisfied in order for the *exception d'inexécution* to be invoked: the counterparty must have failed to perform an obligation under the contract and the breach must be sufficiently serious. Caution must be exercised by the injured party in both respects because to suspend performance without proper justification will ordinarily constitute a breach of contract for which the counterparty might seek to claim compensation or other relief.

Whether a breach qualifies as 'sufficiently serious' is a question of fact to be determined by a lower court judge without scope for review by the *Cour de cassation* (*pouvoir souverain des juges du fond*). No definition of this threshold is provided in the new article, which as a result has been criticized for vagueness.[9] Based on cases decided prior to the reforms, it has been interpreted by a number of commentators as meaning that the breach cannot be venial.[10]

That the breach is sufficiently serious is also a requirement in termination for breach (new articles 1224 to 1230 of the Civil Code).[11] This parallel has been lamented by several commentators[12] on the basis that termination is an altogether more serious remedy, putting an end to the contract, whereas the *exception d'inexécution* seeks to incentivize performance and avoids the need for resort to termination. In a system that strives to protect performance and uphold the contract, these objectives should be facilitated, not made hard to attain. It has therefore been argued by some to be undesirable for the *exception* to be subject to the same

[9] Genicon, 'The *Exception d'Inexécution*' (n 2) 294 ff.

[10] See, for example, O Deshayes, T Genicon, and Y-M Laithier, *Réforme du droit des contrats, du régime général et de la preuve des obligations* (2nd edn, LexisNexis: Paris, 2018) 541–3.

[11] See below, pp 213–22.

[12] In very strong terms by Genicon, 'The *Exception d'Inexécution*' (n 2) 294–304.

threshold requirements as termination.[13] A further criticism that has been made is that the victim of a breach who would prefer to rely on the *exception* but is unwilling to take the risk that the breach is sufficiently serious may be driven to bring a claim for specific enforcement, which is not subject to the same requirement. This has been said to be unwelcome because specific enforcement is more definitive and severe.[14]

Article 1219 is silent on whether the *exception d'inexécution* is also subject to a requirement of proportionality. However, it can be inferred that this was intended by the drafters since the 'Report to the President'—the document in which the new articles are explained—states that 'the *exception* can only be used as a means of pressure in a proportionate manner'.[15] This would be in line with cases prior to the reforms in which it was held that the suspension had to be proportionate to the nature and extent of the breach.[16]

A related question is whether the *exception d'inexécution* can only be invoked by a party acting in good faith. Despite being well-established in pre-reform cases, this requirement is similarly not mentioned in article 1219 but referred to in the Report to the President.[17] This states that relying in bad faith on the *exception* where the breach is insignificant is an abuse and can give rise to liability.[18] The drafters may have thought that it was unnecessary to be any more explicit in the article itself since good faith is already very prominent in the reforms, for example newly appearing in the 'Introductory Provisions' section of the Civil Code at article 1104. However, the issue is not free from doubt and this uncertainty has drawn criticism, in part on the basis that it is all the more important in a self-help remedy for there to be as much clarity as possible as to the threshold requirements.[19]

Article 1220 imposes other conditions in respect of the anticipatory *exception d'inexécution*. First, in contrast with the conventional *exception*, it is the consequences of the non-performance for the promisee that must be sufficiently serious, not the breach itself. For some commentators, this is a more difficult condition to satisfy and something of an oddity, particularly since a serious breach may not necessarily have serious consequences. By requiring that the promisee be significantly affected, it is possible that the drafters sought to provide further protection to the promisor where the remedy is invoked anticipatorily.[20]

[13] Deshayes, Genicon, and Laithier (n 10) 541–3; G Chantepie and M Latina, *La réforme du droit des obligations, Commentaire théorique et pratique dans l'ordre du Code civil* (2nd edn, Dalloz: Paris, 2018) [629]; Genicon, 'The *Exception d'Inexécution*' (n 2) 302.

[14] Chantepie and Latina (n 13) [629].

[15] 'Report to the President of the Republic relating to Ordonnance no 2016–131 of 10 February 2016 on the reform of contract law, the general regime and proof of obligations', JORF no 0035 of 11 February 2016, 15.

[16] Chantepie and Latina (n 13) [629]. Compare Civ (3) 7 July 1982, Bull civ III no 168 and Civ (3) 21 Nov 1990 Bull civ III no 238.

[17] 'Report to the President' (n 15) 14–15.

[18] Ibid., 15.

[19] Genicon, 'The *Exception d'Inexécution*' (n 2) 301–04.

[20] Chantepie and Latina (n 13) [630].

Second, it must be 'evident' that the promisor will not perform their obligation by the due date. Mere suspicion or risk of breach will not do. This protects the promisor, who after all has not actually committed a breach and for whom being deprived of the promised counter-performance may have significant negative consequences.[21]

Third, formal notice of the suspension of performance must be given to the promisor 'as soon as possible'. There is, however, no need for the notice to set out the grounds that are relied upon, which is required for self-help termination[22] and would have been more protective of the promisor.[23] He would have had a written statement of the reasoning of the promisee and thereby been better placed to challenge the suspension or alternatively assuage the concerns that prompted it.[24]

## B Enforced Performance in Kind

In sub-section 2 of the new Civil Code under the heading 'Enforced Performance In Kind' are set out the remedies that compel the defaulting party either *personally* to perform their contractual obligations (referred to herein as 'specific enforcement') or to pay *a third party* to do so in replacement or substitution of the promised performance (referred to as 'replacement').

### 1 Specific enforcement: compelling the defaulting party to perform (*exécution forcée en nature*)

**Civil Code**

Art. 1124.—A unilateral promise is a contract by which one party, the promisor, grants another, the beneficiary, a right to have the option to conclude a contract whose essential elements are determined, and for the formation of which only the consent of the beneficiary is missing.

Revocation of the promise during the period allowed to the beneficiary to exercise the option does not prevent the formation of the contract which was promised.

A contract concluded in breach of a unilateral promise with a third party who knew of its existence, is a nullity.

[21] Genicon, 'The *Exception d'Inexécution*' (n 2) 310 considers that the drafters must have been concerned in particular to protect companies that are in financial distress, potentially even on the brisk of insolvency, for which the anticipatory *exception d'inexécution* may have serious negative consequences.
[22] Article 1226 of the Civil Code.
[23] Chantepie and Latina (n 13) [630].
[24] See article 7.3.4 of the UNIDROIT principles; Deshayes, Genicon, and Laithier (n 10) 483.

(2016 version)

*Art. 1221.—A creditor of an obligation may, having given notice to perform, seek performance in kind unless performance is impossible or if there is a manifest disproportion between its cost to the debtor and its interest for the creditor.*

(2018 version)

Art. 1221.—A creditor of an obligation may, having given notice to perform, seek performance in kind unless performance is impossible or if there is a manifest disproportion between its cost to the debtor acting in good faith and its interest for the creditor.

Art. 1341.—A creditor has the right to performance of the obligation; he may compel the debtor to perform under the conditions provided by legislation.

Nearly all obligations are specifically enforceable in French law. An injured party can enforce both monetary and non-monetary obligations in most circumstances.[25] It is a very effective remedy, to a large extent because French courts are prepared to deploy significant means in order to give effect to the contract.

### (a) The formal recognition of specific enforcement as a remedy

New articles 1217 and 1221 both provide that, upon breach, the injured party can seek specific enforcement of the contract. This has been a central remedy in French law for many years and was widely available before the reforms, despite an apparent conflict in the 1804 Civil Code on the point. Specifically, the stipulation in paragraph 2 of old article 1184 that the injured party could compel the defaulting party to perform where performance was still possible[26] appeared at odds with the emphasis on damages to the exclusion of other remedies in old article 1142, which stated that 'every obligation to do or not to do gives rise to liability in damages in cases of non-performance by the promisor'. In practice, however, the apparent precedence given to damages was always construed restrictively. The courts consistently found that damages did not have to be the main or only remedy. Article 1142 was instead interpreted narrowly, as being confined to obligations of a personal character which could not be specifically enforced.[27] This approach is adopted in the new Civil Code, confirming specific enforcement as a broadly available and central remedy in France, which is an article of faith amongst French lawyers.[28]

[25] The enforcement of monetary obligations is dealt with separately at article 1341 of the Civil Code but this merely affirms what article 1221 provides in respect of non-monetary obligations.

[26] See also article 1228 of the 1804 Civil Code and article 1 of law 9 July 1991 on the reform of civil enforcement procedures (loi no 91-650 du 9 juillet 1991 portant réforme des procédures civiles d'exécution).

[27] Civ 20 Jan 1953, JCP 1953.II.7677, note P Esmein.

[28] Chantepie and Latina (n 13) [636]; Y-M Laithier, 'Exécution Forcée en Nature' in J Cartwright and S Whittaker (eds), *The Code Napoléon Rewritten: French Contract Law after the 2016 Reforms* (Hart Publishing: Oxford, 2017) 281.

### (b) The specific enforcement of monetary obligations

The specific enforcement of monetary obligations is enshrined in new article 1341, which confirms that the right of the injured party to performance under new article 1221 extends to debt claims,[29] leaving unaltered the position prior to the reforms.[30] It is an unfettered right, in that the contract price can be claimed in preference to other remedies such as compensatory damages and termination.[31] There does not appear to be any discretion in the court as to the appropriateness of the remedy. As the *Cour de cassation* held in one case, 'a creditor always has the right to prefer the payment of the price to an award of damages or termination of the contract'.[32]

An example is a case in which a student entered into a contract with a teaching institution to receive long-distance classes over a six-year period. He had to pay an enrolment fee of thirty francs and thirty-five monthly course fees of forty francs. Nine months after starting the course, he sought to terminate the contract. The *Cour de cassation* quashed the refusal of the lower court to order payment of the monthly fees for the remaining twenty-six months of the term, holding that the institution was entitled to recover the entire balance of the fees.

One means by which the injured party can be impeded in recovering the contract price is the *délai de grâce*.[33] Where the defaulting party is in financial difficulty, new article 1343-5 of the Civil Code confers a discretion on the court to extend time for payment of the sum due by up to two years. It states in its first three paragraphs as follows:

[29] See also paragraph 1 of article L111-1 of the Code of Civil Enforcement Procedures.

[30] Laithier, 'Exécution Forcée en Nature' (n 28) 269.

[31] Deshayes, Genicon, and Laithier (n 10) 638 have questioned whether the proportionality requirement in article 1221 of the Civil Code applies to the specific enforcement of monetary obligations. If it were to do so, the injured party may not be entitled to the agreed price where termination and compensatory damages would be adequate remedies and significantly less costly to the defaulting party. The requirement is not referred to in article 1341, suggesting that it does not apply. For P Malaurie, L Aynès, and P Stoffel-Munck, *Droit des obligations* (10th edn, LGDJ: Paris, 2018) [1136], even after the reforms, the injured party can prefer payment of the price over damages or termination. Some authors do not refer to any limitation on the right to obtain payment: F Terré, P Simler, Y Lequette, and F Chénedé, *Droit civil: les obligations* (12th edn, Dalloz: Paris, 2018), and Chantepie and Latina (n 13). See also Laithier, 'Exécution Forcée en Nature' (n 28) 269. It therefore appears that the limitation is understood by French lawyers not to apply in this context.

[32] Civ (1) 9 July 2003, JCP 2004.I.163, no 4, obs G Viney; RTD civ 2003.709, obs J Mestre and B Fages; M Fabre-Magnan, *Droit des Obligations, Contrat et engagement unilateral* (2nd edn, PUF: Paris, 2010) [215]. See, however, Com 22 Oct 1996, Bull civ IV no 260. This decision has been rationalized on the ground that the lower court had accepted, albeit wrongly, that the contract could be terminated unilaterally by the promisor: RTD civ 1997.123, obs J Mestre and P Jourdain 439; D 1997 Somm 173, obs R Libchaber.

[33] A Sériaux, 'Réflexions sur les délais de grâce', RTD civ 1993.789; Laithier, 'Exécution Forcée en Nature' (n 28) 267–8. For a detailed account in English on the *délai de grace*, see S Whittaker, 'A Period of Grace for Contractual Performance?' in M Andenas et al. (eds), *Liber Amicorum Guido Alpa, Private Law Beyond the National Systems* (British Institute of International and Comparative Law: London, 2007).

> Taking into account the situation of the debtor and the needs of the creditor, a court may defer payment of sums that are due, or allow it to be made in instalments, for a period no greater than two years.
>
> By a special, reasoned decision, a court may order that sums corresponding to deferred instalments shall bear interest at a reduced rate (not lower than the legal rate of interest) or that any payments made will first be allocated to repayment of capital.
>
> The court may make these measures subject to the debtor effecting acts appropriate to facilitate or to secure payment of the debt.

A *délai de grâce* usually takes the form of an order allowing deferred payment or payment in instalments.[34] Its effect is to postpone the right of the injured party to enforce the debt, allowing more time for the defaulting party to raise the amount owing.[35] Performance is therefore delayed, not excused.[36] This is justified on grounds of fairness[37] and beneficence to the defaulting party who is unable to fulfil a payment obligation despite acting in good faith.[38] It also serves to promote the performance of the contract, with late performance thought to be preferable to no performance at all.[39]

The potential for a *délai de grâce* to prejudice the interests of the injured party is limited by a requirement that the court, when exercising the discretion, balance their needs with those of the defaulting party. It is also open to the court to require the defaulting party to take steps to facilitate or guarantee the payment of the debt.

### (c) The specific enforcement of non-monetary obligations

French courts similarly show little hesitation in granting the specific enforcement of non-monetary obligations. It is a remedy that is available to the injured party as of right[40] and extremely broad in scope.[41] The defaulting party can be compelled to perform in a wide array of circumstances.

#### *(i) The wide availability of specific enforcement: practical examples*

The breadth of the availability of specific enforcement in French law can be demonstrated by surveying some common types of contract. Perhaps the most ubiquitous is the contract for the sale of goods, which is specifically enforceable. The nature of

[34] Whittaker, 'A Period of Grace for Contractual Performance?' (n 33) 1097.

[35] J Mestre, 'Réflexions sur l'abus de recouvrer sa créance' in *Mélanges offerts à Pierre Raynaud* (Dalloz-Sirey: Paris, 1985) [14].

[36] E Perru, L'impayé (LGDJ: Paris, 2005) [491]; Whittaker, 'A Period of Grace for Contractual Performance?' (n 33) 1092–3 and 1098.

[37] Laithier, 'Exécution Forcée en Nature' (n 28) 267.

[38] Sériaux, 'Réflexions sur les délais de grâce' (n 33) 795.

[39] Whittaker, 'A Period of Grace for Contractual Performance?' (n 33) 1098.

[40] Laithier, 'Exécution Forcée en Nature' (n 28) 263.

[41] Ibid., 262.

the goods, and whether they are unique, is irrelevant. There is no duty to mitigate[42] and the remedy cannot be refused solely on the basis that substitute performance is possible. In one illustrative case, the Dijon Court of Appeal ordered the performance of a contract for the sale of computer equipment in circumstances where the equipment that had originally been supplied did not conform to specification. The vendor was required to provide a replacement.[43]

Building contracts are also specifically enforceable. In many cases builders have been ordered to rectify work that does not conform to contractual specification.[44] By way of example, the remedy was granted in respect of a contract to construct a chalet.[45] The *Cour de cassation* has also quashed a decision refusing to order the demolition and reconstruction of buildings which, in breach of contract, were built out of conformity with contractual specification.[46]

The possibility that an order for specific enforcement might require a high degree of supervision does not seem to have caused the same concern in France as in England, with potential difficulties in ensuring compliance passing without mention in the literature on the topic. This can also be inferred from the willingness of French courts to order specific enforcement both of building contracts and where the effect of the order is to require the defaulting party to carry on a business. For example, in a case arising out of the oil crisis in the 1970s, an airline discontinued flights on a route between two towns which had been rendered financially onerous because of significant increases in the price of aviation fuel. This amounted to a breach by the airline of a contract with the Chamber of Commerce of one of the towns that the route would be kept open. The *Cour de cassation* affirmed the decision of the Besançon Court of Appeal to order specific enforcement. Despite the change in global economic circumstances, the fulfilment of the obligation remained possible.[47]

*(ii) The specific enforcement of negative promises*

The breach of a negative promise is equally widely restrained in France. In one case, for instance, the *Cour de cassation* quashed the refusal by the Lyon Court of Appeal to order that leased premises, which had been altered in breach of a negative obligation not to modify them during the demise, be restored to the condition in which they had been prior to the lease. That the premises had actually been improved

[42] See section 4(b) of this chapter on the absence of mitigation in French law; S Le Pautremat, 'Mitigation of Damages: A French Perspective' (2006) 55 ICLQ 205.

[43] Dijon 19 Sept 1989, Juris-Data no 1989-049228; Colmar 18 Oct 1972, D 1973.496, note M Cabrillac and A Seube. See S Whittaker, *Liability for Products: English Law, French Law and European Harmonisation* (OUP: Oxford, 2005) 69–86.

[44] See, for example, Civ (3) 3 May 2001, Bill civ III no 56; Civ (3) 11 May 2005, RDC 2005.323, note D Mazeaud.

[45] Civ (3) 3 May 2001, Bull civ III no 56.

[46] See, for example, Civ (3) 11 May 2005, RDC 2005.323, note D Mazeaud.

[47] Com 31 May 1976, Bull civ IV no 186.

by work undertaken by the tenant was held to be immaterial.[48] Nor would it have made any difference had the landlord been contemporaneously aware that the work was being undertaken, or that he had made no protest.[49]

The new Civil Code does not contain a specific article that provides for the defaulting party to undo the effects of a breach. This is in contrast with old article 1143, which provided that 'a promisee can request that what has been done in breach of the obligation be destroyed; and he can request authorisation to destroy it himself at the expense of the defaulting promisor'.[50] The Code now only provides, in new article 1222, for the latter type. This enables the injured party to obtain court approval to destroy a non-compliant subject-matter of the contract and claim the cost of doing so from the defaulting party.[51] It is, however, widely understood that the injured party can, as before the reforms, seek in court that the defaulting party themselves undo the breach.[52]

*(iii) Situations in which specific enforcement of non-monetary obligations will not be ordered*

There are three situations in which specific enforcement is unavailable in French law. The first is where performance is impossible.[53] This might occur, for example, where the subject-matter of the contract has already been purchased by a bona fide third party.[54] The second is where specific enforcement would result in involuntary servitude, such as in a contract for the provision of personal services. It has therefore been refused in respect of a contract in which an artist was commissioned to paint and deliver a picture.[55] The third is where there is a 'manifest disproportion' between the cost of performance to the defaulting party and the interest of the injured party in obtaining it.[56]

This exception is new and amongst the most notable changes made by the reforms. Previously, the courts did not have any discretion as to whether to grant specific enforcement. An order could not be resisted on grounds of unreasonableness or disproportionality. Nor was there an undue hardship bar, meaning that the remedy could be obtained even at the financial ruin of the defaulting party.[57]

[48] Civ (3) 25 Jan 1995, Bull civ III no 29; see also Civ (3) 3 April 1996, Bull civ III no 91; Civ (1) 14 Oct 1964, D 1964.710; Civ (1) 26 June 1967, D 1967.673; Civ (3) 15 Feb 1978, D 1978.IR.414; Civ (3) 23 May 1978, Bull civ III no 213; Civ (3) 30 June 1993, Bull civ III no 105.

[49] Civ (3) 27 Mar 1991, Bull civ III no 106.

[50] P Simler, *Fasc 10—Contrats et obligations—Classification des obligations—Distinction des obligations de donner, de faire et de ne pas faire* (LexisNexis Jurisclasseur: Paris, 2011) [113]–[125]; Terré, Simler, Lequette, and Chénedé (n 31) [781].

[51] Chantepie and Latina (n 13) [636].

[52] Ibid., [640]; Deshayes, Genicon, and Laithier (n 10) 555.

[53] Article 1221 of the Civil Code.

[54] Lyon 17 Feb 1995, Juris-Data no 1995-049787.

[55] Civ 14 March 1900, D 1900, D 1900.I.489; Civ 20 Jan 1953, JCP 1953.II.7677, note P Esmein.

[56] Article 1221 of the Civil Code.

[57] Civ (3) 3 Dec 1969, Bull civ III no 2.

This gave rise to some controversial and arguably surprising outcomes. In one case, a building company constructed a house that turned out to be thirteen inches beneath the height required in the contractual specifications. The Aix-en-Provence Court of Appeal found that the breach did not relate to an essential term of the contract and that the house was fit for purpose. It therefore declined the invitation to order that the house be demolished and rebuilt. This decision was quashed by the *Cour de cassation*: the injured party was entitled to compel the defaulting party to perform its obligations to the letter.[58]

In another case, the Aix-en-Provence Court of Appeal was found to have erred in refusing to order that a swimming pool built with three rather than the contractually specified four steps should be modified where the absence of the step did not impede access to the pool.[59] Similarly, the *Cour de cassation* quashed a decision that a builder should not be compelled to make modifications to a house which, in breach of contract, had been constructed slightly out of alignment with the specified dimensions. It held that it was irrelevant that the difference between the work done and the work required was minimal.[60]

Whilst the new exception was introduced in response to these decisions, it has divided opinion amongst commentators. Some have welcomed the more moderate approach,[61] arguing that to seek to enforce performance at all costs is an abuse of right (*abus de droit*).[62] In contrast, those who favour the strict availability of specific enforcement have raised concerns that it is inconsistent with the binding force of contract and allows promises to be broken with impunity for no other reason than that the cost of performing is too high.[63] Mekki, for instance, has said that the new exception is:

> ... too close to the solutions in common law systems. Enforced performance is a formidable weapon to encourage the promisor to perform. This exception sends a dangerous message to those promisors who might be tempted to breach their

[58] Civ (3) 11 May 2005, RDC 2005.323, note D Mazeaud.

[59] Civ (3) 17 Jan 1984, RTD civ 1984.711, translated in H Beale, B Fauvarque-Cosson, J Rutgers, and S Vogenauer (eds), *Cases, Materials and Text on Contract Law, Ius Commune Casebooks for the Common Law of Europe* (3rd edn, Hart Publishing: Oxford, 2019) 927.

[60] Civ (3) 17 Nov 1977, Bull Civ III no 392.

[61] Commentators who criticised these decisions include Y-M Laithier, *Étude comparative des sanctions de l'inexécution du contrat* (LGDJ: Paris, 2004) [315]ff; G Viney, 'Exécution de l'obligation, faculté de remplacement et réparation en nature en droit français' in M Fontaine and G Viney (eds), *Les sanctions de l'inexécution des obligations contractuelles, études de droit comparé* (Bruylant: Bruxelles and LGDJ: Paris, 2001) 107.

[62] See the 'Report to the President' (n 15) 15 which refers to the theory of abuse of right in relation to this new exception.

[63] M Mekki, 'Les remèdes à l'inexécution dans le projet d'ordonnance portant réforme du droit des obligations, Gazette Palais 30/4/2015; Terré, Simler, Lequette, and Chénedé (n 31) [778]; T Genicon, 'Contre l'introduction du "coût manifestement déraisonnable" comme exception à l'inexécution forcée en nature' Droit & Patrimoine 2014.63; O Tournafond and J-P Tricoire, 'Les contrats de construction face aux nouvelles orientations du droit des contrats' RDI 2016.391.

> contract, particularly in construction contracts ... We expect the exception to be confined to abusive claims.[64]

To prevent the exception from being invoked abusively, new article 1221 was amended at the ratification stage in 2018 to require that the defaulting party must be acting in good faith for it to apply. This was intended to remove the possible incentive for a party to commit a breach of contract deliberately with a view to arguing, in bad faith, that the cost of enforced performance is manifestly disproportionate to the interest of the injured party in obtaining the remedy.[65]

No guidance is provided in the reforms either as to the factors that are relevant to assessing the interest of the injured party or the meaning of 'manifest disproportion'. Commentators have anticipated that relevant factors are likely to include the seriousness of the breach, the extent of the injured party's loss, the level of difficulty obtaining the promised performance elsewhere, whether the injured party would themselves be in breach of a separate contract with a third party (for example where there are back-to-back contracts) and the risk of under-compensation if compensatory damages were awarded.[66] As for 'manifest disproportion', there is consensus that it must be blatant, in the sense of 'certain, evident and flagrant',[67] which serves to limit the scope of the exception.[68]

Whether the exception will have a significant practical impact remains to be seen. It is widely expected to be interpreted narrowly by French courts, which historically have been liberal in ordering specific enforcement.[69] Such an approach would certainly be welcomed by French commentators, for whom enforced performance should only be refused in extreme cases. In the words of Deshayes, Genicon, and Laithier, 'the exception is not a principle that is in competition with the binding force of contract and the general availability of specific enforcement... It would be a mistake to infer that specific enforcement will be ruled out every time compensatory damages are adequate to fulfil the expectations of the injured party.'[70] The same is true where a replacement can be obtained in the marketplace or the cost of the remedy is high. They have also said that 'this limitation is meant to operate at the margin',[71] and is 'exceptional' in character.[72]

As well as introducing this exception, the reforms also removed a limitation on the scope of specific enforcement that existed before the reforms. The remedy was unavailable for 'unilateral promises to contract'. As explained in Chapter 4, this is

[64] Mekki (n 63).
[65] Deshayes, Genicon, and Laithier (n 10) 550–1; Chantepie and Latina (n 13) [638].
[66] Deshayes, Genicon, and Laithier (n 10) 555; Laithier, 'Exécution Forcée en Nature' (n 28) 285.
[67] Chantepie and Latina (n 13) [638].
[68] Deshayes, Genicon, and Laithier (n 10) 555.
[69] Chantepie and Latina (n 13) [639]; Deshayes, Genicon, and Laithier (n 10) 485–8.
[70] Deshayes, Genicon, and Laithier (n 10) 549.
[71] Ibid.
[72] Laithier, 'Exécution Forcée en Nature' (n 28) 263.

a pre-contractual agreement whereby the promisee is given an exclusive right, exercisable for a defined period of time, to conclude a contract on set terms.[73] One example is an exclusive option to purchase real property (*promesse unilatérale de vente*), in respect of which specific enforcement was refused if, in breach of that contract, the promisor sold the property to a third party. The beneficiary of the unilateral promise was confined to damages.[74] This outcome attracted criticism[75] on the basis that unilateral promises to contract are fully constituted contracts, from which it was argued to follow that they should be specifically enforceable.

The reforms abolished this limitation. According to paragraph 2 of new article 1124, where a unilateral promise to contract is revoked during the period allowed for the beneficiary to exercise their right, thus breaching that contract, this does not prevent the formation of the promised contract. The beneficiary can seek specific enforcement.[76] This reinforces the effectiveness and certainty of the unilateral promise.[77]

*(iv) The enforcement of specific enforcement orders*

The effectiveness of specific enforcement in France is given considerable assistance by a separate, ancillary enforcement mechanism known as the *astreinte*. This is a court order made alongside and in support of an order for the specific enforcement of a contractual obligation that requires positive action. It prescribes a period of time—usually in days, weeks, or months—for each of which the promisor is in default, they will be liable to pay a monetary penalty to the injured party.

The *astreinte* is a means of coercing the promisor to comply with a specific enforcement order. Whilst the promisor is not physically compelled to perform, in that they are at liberty not to comply, that will give rise to a liability to pay an ever increasing penalty. This is set at a level that is in proportion to their financial means although, in order to be effective, it will generally be greater than the advantage that they stand to gain from non-performance.[78] In practice, the resulting pressure is usually effective to bring about performance because the liability will otherwise quickly become substantial. Failure is rare since no one's wealth can hold out indefinitely.

The nature of the *astreinte* is unequivocally punitive. It is granted *in terrorem* on the premise that 'it is necessary to frighten, almost terrorise, to incite

[73] See Chapter 4, pp 81–2.

[74] Civ (3) 15 Dec 1993, D 1994.507, note F Benac-Schmidt. Note the move towards the wider availability of specific enforcement in relation to pre-emption agreements before the reforms: Ch Mixte 26 May 2006, no 03-19376, Bull mixt no 4, D 2006.1861, note P-Y Gautier, note D Mainguy, D 2006.2638, obs S Amrani-Mekki and B Fauvarque-Cosson, RTD civ. 2006.550, obs J Mestre and B Fages.

[75] M Fabre-Magnan, 'Le mythe de l'obligation de donner' RTD civ 1996.85, 101 ff; D Mazeaud, JCP 1995.I.22366.

[76] 'Report to the President' (n 15) 6.

[77] Ibid.

[78] C Hugon, 'Regard sur le droit des voies d'exécution' RDC 2005.183, 193.

performance'.[79] Two particular features reinforce the punitive effect. First, it is not an insurable risk. Second, in assessing the final sum to be paid, the court will take account of any abusive persistence in non-compliance or bad faith on the part of the defaulting party.[80]

There is also provision for situations in which performance is required urgently. In a procedure for interim relief known as *référé*, where the existence of an obligation is beyond serious question, a *juge des référés* can order the defaulting party to perform, even before finally determining the case. For positive obligations, there is a special kind of *référé*, called the *référé-injonction de faire*.[81]

### (d) The reasons for the wide availability of specific enforcement

A range of justifications have been advanced for the wide availability of specific enforcement. The first is the binding force of contract (*principe de la force obligatoire du contrat*) or *pacta sunt servanda*, meaning that one must perform that which one has promised.[82] The bond created by the voluntary will of the parties can only be given full effect by remedies that compel performance.[83]

It is also often argued that the preference in France for specific enforcement is partly attributable to a perception that damages are an inferior remedy for breach of contract.[84] They subvert the principle that contractual obligations have binding force and, by their nature, are incapable of providing the injured party with full satisfaction or fulfilment of their expectations. These deficiencies inevitably follow from the acceptance, tacit in any award of damages, that the injured party will not receive the promised performance.[85] This is portrayed as a 'favour' to the contract-breaker, and damages as an unsatisfactory stopgap for the injured party.[86]

Specific enforcement is also argued to reinforce transactional security. To prefer damages over compelling performance is for many French commentators tantamount to making obligations optional. Specific enforcement promotes trust between contracting parties and in the market more broadly. It is essential for the orderly functioning of the economy that 'promises [are] kept'.[87]

Lastly, a view held by many French commentators is that damages risk under-compensation.[88] They are also inefficient in deterring breach. Instead, performance

[79] Ibid.
[80] Civ (1) 20 Oct 1959, Bull civ I no 419.
[81] Paragraph 2 of article 809 of the Code of Civil Procedure.
[82] W Jeandidier, 'L'exécution forcée des obligations contractuelles de faire' RTD civ 1976.700.
[83] N Molfessis, 'Force obligatoire et exécution: un droit à l'exécution en nature?' RDC 2005.37.
[84] Laithier, 'Exécution Forcée en Nature' (n 28) 262.
[85] Ibid.
[86] D Tallon, 'Dommages et intérêts et exécution en nature. Quelques observations entre la common law et le droit français' JT 1985.601, 602: 'if there is an idea deeply rooted in the legal conscience, it is that only specific performance fully satisfies the injured promisee'.
[87] P Brun, 'Le droit de revenir sur son engagement' Droit & Patrimoine 1998.79, 78.
[88] Laithier, 'Exécution Forcée en Nature' (n 28) 262.

should be encouraged at all costs. As Mazeaud and Chabas put it, 'if compulsion did not exist, many promisors would breach their undertakings'.[89]

## 2 Obtaining performance from a third party: 'replacement'

**Civil Code**

Art. 1222.—Having given notice to perform, a creditor may also himself, within a reasonable time and at a reasonable cost, have an obligation performed or, with the prior authorisation of the court, may have something which has been done in breach of an obligation destroyed. He may claim reimbursement of sums of money employed for this purpose from the debtor.

He may also bring proceedings in order to require the debtor to advance a sum necessary for this performance or destruction.

In the remedy of replacement (*faculté de remplacement*), the defaulting party is required to indemnify the injured party in respect of the cost of employing a third party to perform the obligation that has been breached. It is hybrid in nature, in that it has characteristics of specific enforcement and compensatory damages. The injured party obtains an equivalent of the promised performance but the defaulting party is liable only to pay a monetary sum.[90]

Before the reforms, there was a debate as to the true nature of replacement. It was thought by some commentators to be closer to specific enforcement than damages.[91] This has now implicitly been confirmed by article 1222[92] being positioned in the section of the new Civil Code on enforced performance in kind (*exécution forcée en nature*), immediately after article 1221, which establishes the centrality of specific enforcement. That said, from a common law perspective, it more closely resembles compensatory damages[93] in that the injured party obtains substitute performance as if an award of damages on the cost of cure basis has been made.

[89] H L Mazeaud and F Chabas, *Lećons de droit civil, Obligations, Théorie générale* (9th edn, Montchrestien: Paris 1998) [931].

[90] S Whittaker, 'Performance of Another's Obligation: French and English Law Contrasted' in D Johnston and R Zimmerman (eds), *Unjustified Enrichment: Key Issues in Comparative Perspective* (CUP: Cambridge, 2002) 433, 450.

[91] See, for example, G Viney, 'Exécution de l'obligation, faculté de remplacement et réparation en nature en droit français' in M Fontaine and G Viney (eds), *Les sanctions de l'inéxecution des obligations contractuelles, Etudes de droit comparé* (Bruylant: Bruxelles and LGDJ: Paris, 2001) 107, 188 ff.

[92] Even if, as Laithier, 'Exécution Forcée en Nature' (n 28) 272 and 281 recognizes, the characterization of replacement as enforced performance in kind 'is not self-evident' and 'technically debatable'.

[93] On the differences between replacement in English and French law see S Whittaker, 'Les sanctions de l'inexécution des contrats. Droit anglais' in M Fontaine and G Viney (eds), *Les sanctions de l'inexécution des obligations contractuelles, Études de droit comparé* (Bruylant: Bruxelles and LGDJ: Paris, 2001) 977, 1011–14; Laithier, 'Exécution Forcée en Nature' (n 28) 263.

Replacement is a particularly appropriate remedy where specific enforcement has become impossible or where the injured party no longer wishes to obtain performance from the defaulting party, for instance because of a loss of trust. It is commonly invoked in building contracts to replace the original contractor so that unfinished work may be completed or defective work cured.[94]

Whilst the 1804 Civil Code already provided for replacement in old articles 1143 and 1144, two new features were introduced in the reforms. First, there is now no need for the injured party to seek court approval in order to obtain replacement performance. This is a significant departure from the position under old article 1144, in which the court approval process was a safeguard against the perceived risk of the defaulting party being ousted from the contract arbitrarily.[95] As with termination under that code,[96] the court would verify that the defaulting party was refusing or unable to perform, thereby protecting their 'interest in performing'.[97]

Only exceptionally could the injured party proceed without court approval, for instance where there was urgency.[98] As a concession to commercial exigencies, this was also possible in the context of commercial contracts of sale. The vendor could sell the subject-matter of the contract to a third party or the purchaser could buy a replacement where their counterparty failed to perform.[99] This exception has been extended to all contracts. Obtaining replacement performance should therefore now be simpler and quicker. This is also congruous with the formal recognition in the reforms of self-help termination which, as explained below in the section on termination, enables an injured party to terminate the contract without first obtaining court approval.[100]

There are several requirements in article 1222 that counter-balance the curtailment of the role of the court and operate to protect the defaulting party. First, as with other remedies, replacement is conditional upon the injured party serving a notice on the defaulting party that performance must be effected within a reasonable time. Only where the refusal or failure persists can the injured party enter into a substitute contract.[101] Second, there is a requirement of reasonableness, which is intended to guard against abuse. Replacement must occur 'within a reasonable time and at a reasonable cost'. Article 1222 is silent on the criteria to be

[94] For example, Civ (1) 18 Jan 1956, Bull civ I no 34; Civ (1) 8 Oct 1962, Bull civ I no 400; Civ (3) 17 July 1973, Bull civ III no 485; C Atias and J Debeaurain, 'L'abandon du chantier de construction' D 1990 Chron 291.

[95] Soc 5 June 1953, D 1953.601; Civ (3) 20 Mar 1991, RTD civ 1991.735, obs J Mestre.

[96] See below, pp 217–8.

[97] Whittaker, 'Performance of Another's Obligation: French and English Law Contrasted' (n 90) 452; A Pinna, *La mesure du préjudice contractuel* (LGDJ: Paris, 2007) [368].

[98] Civ 2 July 1945, RTD civ 1946.39, obs J Carbonnier; Civ 7 Dec 1951, RTD civ 1952.242. The requisite level of 'urgency' is greater than in the case of the *référé*.

[99] D Plantamp, 'Le particularisme du remplacement dans la vente commerciale' D 2000 Chron 243.

[100] See section 1(b) of this chapter on self-help termination.

[101] Laithier, 'Exécution Forcée en Nature' (n 28) 264; Chantepie and Latina (n 13) [639]; M Faure-Abbad, 'Article 1222: la faculté de remplacement' RDC 2015.784.

applied in assessing reasonableness. It has been interpreted by commentators as analogous with the proportionality requirement in article 1221 relating to specific enforcement. There should therefore be a similar exercise in balancing the interests of the parties, in particular 'checking that the costs incurred by the defaulting party are not exorbitant, and that the injured party does not obtain, by means of indirect performance, a more valuable counter-performance than the one originally due'.[102]

Third, the court nonetheless retains an important role. As an exception to the self-help nature of replacement, the injured party is not permitted without court approval to have 'something... destroyed' to reverse the effects of the breach.[103] For example, where a building has been built in breach of a restrictive covenant, the injured party must obtain court approval in order to destroy it. The rationale is to prevent the remedy from being abused, which the drafters considered to be particularly important in view of the potentially 'irremediable character' of reversal.[104] It is also for the court to determine any claim brought by the defaulting party challenging a replacement[105] or by the injured party to recover the cost of a replacement and compensatory damages for any additional losses.

The text of article 1222 provides that the injured party 'may' have the obligation performed by a third party, thus conferring a right but without imposing any duty to enter into a substitute transaction. This is consistent with the absence of a duty to mitigate in French law, which is explained below.[106] The injured party can therefore 'prefer direct enforced performance in kind by his debtor (under article 1221) rather than seek a substitute solution himself'.[107]

## C Price Reduction

**Civil Code**
**(2016 version)**
*Art. 1223.—Having given notice to perform, a creditor may accept an imperfect contractual performance and reduce the price proportionally.*

*If he has not yet paid, the creditor must give notice of his decision to reduce the price as quickly as possible.*

[102] Laithier, 'Exécution Forcée en Nature' (n 28) 264; Chantepie and Latina (n 13) [639].
[103] On whether this applies to the reverse of the breach of a negative promise only, see Deshayes, Genicon, and Laithier (n 10) 555–6.
[104] 'Report to the President' (n 15) 15.
[105] Laithier, 'Exécution Forcée en Nature' (n 28) 281.
[106] See section 4(b) of this chapter on the absence of mitigation in French law.
[107] Laithier, 'Exécution Forcée en Nature' (n 28) 264.

(2018 version)
Art. 1223.—In the case of imperfect performance of the act of performance, the creditor, having given notice to perform and where he has not yet paid for all or part of the act of performance, may notify the debtor as quickly as possible of his decision to reduce its price proportionally. Acceptance by the debtor of the creditor's decision to reduce the price must be made in writing.

Where he has already paid, and in the absence of an agreement between the parties, the creditor may claim a reduction in price in court.

The remedy of price reduction was introduced as part of the reforms in new article 1223 of the Civil Code. It enables the injured party to accept performance that falls short of the contractually agreed standard but at a lower price. The reduction must be in proportion to the shortcomings in the performance. In practice this computes as the difference in value between the promised performance and the performance that was actually rendered.

In the Report to the President, the remedy is described as a middle ground between the *exception d'inexécution* and termination.[108] It differs from the *exception d'inexécution* in that the outcome is permanent, and from termination in that the contract remains on foot, albeit on new terms. Since the contract is treated as having been performed in accordance with those terms, it is no longer possible for the injured party to claim damages to compensate for the defect in performance, which is effectively spent.[109]

The injured party must give notice of the reduction as promptly as possible, upon which the defaulting party has an opportunity to rectify the breach. Where some or all of the price has not yet been paid, the reduction is self-help in nature and does not require any court approval. If, however, the price has already been paid, the remedy can only be granted by the court, absent agreement between the parties.

Introducing this remedy on a general basis was one of the more significant innovations in the reforms. In the 1804 Code, it was only available for certain specific contracts.[110] The other means of obtaining a price reduction, albeit an indirect one, was to claim damages to compensate for the defective performance.[111] Now the injured party can obtain a price reduction directly and unilaterally.

Unlike in the context of the *exception d'inexécution* and termination, there is no stipulation that the breach must be sufficiently serious or satisfy some other threshold requirement. Any breach, even a minor one, would appear to suffice.[112]

108 'Report to the President' (n 15) 15.

109 But the injured party can claim compensatory damages for other losses caused by the breach.

110 See articles 1617, 1619, and 1644 of the Civil Code; see also the well-established practice of *réfaction* in commercial law by which the court can adjust the price in certain circumstances: Req 23 May 1900, DP 1901.1.129; article 50 of the Vienna Convention on Contracts for the International Sale of Goods (CISG).

111 Deshayes, Genicon, and Laithier (n 10) 564.

112 Criticized in E Savaux, 'Article 1223: la réduction du prix' RDC 2015.3 [7]. But see Deshayes, Genicon, and Laithier (n 10) 559.

Whether or not to accept the defective performance at a reduced price is entirely a matter for the injured party.[113] This is implicit in the reference in article 1223 to their 'decision'. It cannot be imposed by the defaulting party or the court.[114] The alternative for the injured party is to seek other relief.

Whilst the onus is on the defaulting party to institute court proceedings in order to dispute the principle or the quantum of a price reduction made by the injured party, they do, however, benefit from protections against possible abuse by the injured party which counter-balance the absence of any requirement for prior court approval. These are the requirements for the injured party to give notice of the price reduction and that the reduction be proportionate.

The addition of price reduction to the remedial armoury of the Civil Code has been welcomed by commentators.[115] It is seen as a way of 'saving' a contract that has been defectively performed but still has value to the parties and of avoiding the altogether more severe sanction of termination.[116] In circumstances where the alternative remedy of compensatory damages would not achieve full compensation or is not available, it offers another way of adequately remedying the breach.[117]

The criticisms of article 1223 in the academic literature are twofold. First, the drafting is said to be clumsy. This afflicted the 2016 version of the article acutely[118] and its perceived obscurity led to fairly extensive amendment during the ratification process in 2018. However, the revised text remains unclear. One particular source of confusion is the reference to the defaulting party accepting the price reduction in writing.[119] If price reduction is to be a self-help remedy, as the drafters stated was their intention in the Report to the President,[120] it is puzzling and arguably contradictory that the defaulting party should be able to accept it.[121] It is, however, apparent from the parliamentary debate during ratification that this was intended not as a requirement but instead as a means of ensuring that the defaulting party does not subsequently try to dispute the reduction.[122] A written acceptance

[113] H Barbier, 'L'exécution et la sortie du contrat' RDC Hors-série June 2018.40, 42–3; Deshayes, Genicon, and Laithier (n 10) 562.

[114] Deshayes, Genicon, and Laithier (n 10) 562.

[115] See, however, Savaux (n 112); H Lecuyer, 'L'inexécution du contrat', Contrats, Concurrence Consommation no 5 May 2016 [15].

[116] Deshayes, Genicon, and Laithier (n 10) 558; Lecuyer (n 115); Mekki (n 63).

[117] Y-M Laithier, 'Les règles relatives à l'inexécution des obligations contractuelles' in 'Projet d'ordonnance portant réforme du droit des contrats, du régime général et de la preuve des obligations. Observations et propositions de modifications' JCP 2015, no spécial, 47, 53.

[118] Barbier (n 113) 42–3.

[119] Deshayes, Genicon, and Laithier (n 10) 563.

[120] 'Report to the President' (n 15) 15.

[121] Barbier (n 113) 42–3.

[122] S Houlié, 'Rapport fait au nom de la commission des lois constitutionnelles, de la législation et de l'administration générale de la République sur le projet de loi, modifié par le Sénat en deuxième lecture, ratifiant l'ordonnance no 2016-131 du 10 février 2016 portant réforme du droit des contrats, du régime général et de la preuve des obligations' (Assemblée Nationale: no 429, 29 Nov 2017) <https://www.assemblee-nationale.fr/dyn/15/rapports/cion_lois/l15b0429_rapport-fond> accessed 1 September 2021; F Pillet, Rapport fait au nom de la commission des lois constitutionnelles, de législation, du suffrage universel, du Règlement et d'administration générale (1) sur le projet de loi, modifié par

serves as evidence that the defaulting party has formally renounced to challenge the price reduction at a later point in time.[123]

Second, some commentators have argued that the safeguards for the defaulting party are inadequate. It would have been preferable to require the injured party to specify their grounds for reducing the price and method of calculating the reduction. Such a requirement, which is a feature of self-help termination, would disincentivize resort to the remedy without good reason and enable the defaulting party to challenge it on a more informed basis.[124]

## D Termination

Termination releases the parties from their contract and puts an end to their relationship. It is addressed in a new section of the Civil Code comprising seven articles that together deal with the termination process, the jurisdiction of the court when termination is sought or challenged, and the effects of the remedy.[125]

Such coverage contrasts markedly with the 1804 Code, which did not contain a comprehensive termination regime. There was only one provision on the remedy—article 1184—of which paragraph 1 provided for the retroactive termination of the contract where the defaulting party failed to perform; paragraph 2 conferred an election on the injured party between performance, if still possible, and termination with damages; and paragraph 3 stated that, if electing to terminate, the injured party had to apply to court for an order discharging the contract.

The absence of more comprehensive coverage in the Civil Code led to the principles on termination being developed mainly in the cases, not always with coherent or predictable results.[126] By introducing a specific section on termination, the reforms have sought to address some of these issues, which is consistent with their broader aim of bringing greater clarity and certainty.

Many of the new provisions simply codify solutions developed in the cases. However, one notable change is the abolition of the principle that termination can only be ordered by the court and the concomitant formalization of the optionality between court-ordered termination and termination by notice. The termination

l'Assemblée Nationale, ratifiant l'ordonnance no 2016-131 du 10 février 2016 portant réforme du droit des contrats, du régime général et de la preuve des obligations' (Sénat: no 247, 24 Jan 2018) <https://www.senat.fr/rap/l17-247/l17-2471.pdf> accessed 1 September 2021; Barbier (n 113) 42–3.

[123] Deshayes, Genicon, and Laithier (n 10) 563; Chantepie and Latina (n 13) [643].

[124] Chantepie and Latina (n 13) [643].

[125] S Rowan, 'Termination for Contractual Non-performance' in J Cartwright and S Whittaker (eds), *The Code Napoléon Rewritten: French Contract Law after the 2016 Reforms* (Hart Publishing: Oxford, 2017) 317: the following section reproduces many of the findings of this article.

[126] T Genicon, *La résolution du contrat pour inexécution* (LGDJ: Paris, 2007) [1]–[2] who describes termination as a 'mechanism [that is] troubled in its application' and the law on termination as giving rise to 'fundamental questions [that are] devoid of clear solutions' (citing with agreement E Savaux in his note on Cass civ (3) 30 April 2003, Defr 2003 art 37810 no 91, 1175).

regime that emerges will be examined through the study of three particular features: the different methods of terminating a contract; the role of the court in the process; and the legal effects of termination.

## 1 The different methods of terminating a contract

**Civil Code**

Art. 1224.—Termination results either from the application of a termination clause, or, where the non-performance is sufficiently serious, from notice by the creditor to the debtor or from a judicial decision.

Art. 1225.—A termination clause must specify the undertakings whose non-performance will lead to the termination of the contract.

Termination may take place only after service of a notice to perform which has not been complied with, unless it was agreed that termination may arise from the mere act of non-performance. The notice to perform takes effect only if it refers expressly to the termination clause.

Art. 1226.—A creditor may, at his own risk, terminate the contract by notice. Unless there is urgency, he must previously have put the debtor in default on notice to perform his undertaking within a reasonable time.

The notice to perform must state expressly that if the debtor fails to fulfil his obligation, the creditor will have a right to terminate the contract.

Where the non-performance persists, the creditor notifies the debtor of the termination of the contract and the reasons on which it is based.

The debtor may at any time bring proceedings to challenge such a termination. The creditor must then establish the seriousness of the non-performance.

Art. 1227.—Termination may in any event be claimed in court proceedings.

New article 1224 lists three methods of terminating a contract: the exercise of a contractual right to terminate contained in a termination clause; self-help termination; and court-ordered (or judicial) termination.

### (a) Termination clauses

The first method is termination pursuant to a contractual right. Where a contract contains a termination clause that is engaged by a breach, the injured party can terminate the contract and deploy their resources elsewhere without requiring court approval. Such provisions have long been upheld in French law despite not being recognized expressly in the 1804 Code.

New article 1225 lays down two conditions for exercising a contractual right to terminate. First, the termination clause must identify specifically the contract terms which, if breached, will engage the right. Second, unless the clause states otherwise, termination is only possible after the defaulting party has been served with a notice to perform (*mise en demeure*). This notice must contain a clear reference to the termination clause. Both of these conditions existed in uncodified form before the reforms.[127]

Although article 1225 is silent on the point, it is well-established that the right to terminate must be exercised in good faith.[128] Attempts to invoke termination clauses in bad faith have historically been rejected by the courts. In one case, the *Cour de cassation* refused to enforce a termination clause in a lease, which the lessor had sought to terminate abruptly for non-payment of rent, despite not having complained about the breach for eleven years.[129] Another example is a refusal by the *Cour de cassation* to enforce a termination clause that had been invoked more than six years after the default had occurred.[130]

### (b) Self-help termination

An injured party can terminate a contract under new article 1226 where the breach is 'sufficiently serious', simply by notifying the defaulting party.[131] In this way, the contract is brought to an end without an order of the court. This represents a break with the traditional requirement in paragraph 3 of article 1184 of the 1804 Code that termination should be by judicial order. It was introduced to enable the injured party to terminate more quickly, easily, and inexpensively.

Although the introduction of a process for self-help termination has been described as one of most noteworthy changes to the Code brought by the reforms,[132] it is not entirely new. Previously it was possible to terminate without recourse to the court where the breach was so serious (*comportement grave*) that for the contract to continue was extremely difficult or impossible. This was known as 'unilateral termination' and emerged in several decisions of the *Cour de cassation*, becoming an alternative to judicial termination in more extreme cases.[133]

Unilateral termination was, however, seen by many simply as an exception to judicial termination, which was very much the principal method of terminating a contract for breach. This was compounded by the cases on unilateral termination being relatively sporadic, meaning that its scope and impact in practice was uncertain.[134] Formal recognition in the Code, not as an exception but rather as an option on equal footing with judicial termination, clearly elevates its status.

[127] Civ (3) 3 Oct 2007, Bull civ III no 94.

[128] Civ (1) 14 Mar 1956, Bull civ I no 133; Civ (3) 25 Jan 1983, Bull civ III no 21, RTD civ 1985.163, note J Mestre.

[129] Com, 7 Jan 1963, Bull civ III no 16.

[130] Civ (1) 31 Jan 1995, D 1995.389, note C Jamin.

[131] Article 1226 of the Civil Code.

[132] Chantepie and Latina (n 13) [653].

[133] Civ (1) 13 Oct 1998, Bull civ I no 300, D 1999.198, note C Jamin; Com 10 Feb 2009, pourvoi no 08-12415.

[134] L Leveneur, 'La résolution unilatérale' Revue de Droit d'Assas (2010) 88. Between 1998 and 2009 Leveneur counted six cases in which unilateral termination for serious breach was recognized.

*(i) Sufficiently serious breach*

What constitutes a breach that is 'sufficiently serious' to warrant self-help termination is not clear. The *Cour de cassation* refrained from giving guidance in cases prior to the reforms and there is no definition in the new articles. Whether the breach crosses the necessary threshold is decided in each case by a lower court judge, which is not subject to review by the *Cour de cassation* (*pouvoir souverain des juges du fond*). By way of illustration, a sufficiently serious breach was established and a unilateral termination upheld where an anaesthetist committed a series of professional failings over a period of fifteen years, including refusing to perform surgery and treating patients with brutality.[135] Another concerned a food producer repeatedly supplying food that was unfit for human consumption and dangerous to health.[136]

The lack of guidance as to what constitutes a 'sufficiently serious' breach to justify termination has been deprecated by some commentators.[137] Leaving the issue to be resolved by lower courts does little to promote certainty. The question is one of enormous practical relevance since, in deciding whether or not to terminate, an injured party will usually need to be confident in their assessment of the risk of a successful challenge. One option might have been for the reforms to adopt the factors that have been taken into account in previous cases.[138] These include the consequences of the breach,[139] whether the contract would still serve its intended purpose,[140] the nature of the contract,[141] whether the failure to perform is total or only partial,[142] and the behaviour of the contracting parties, in particular any evidence of good or bad faith.[143] Spelling out these factors would by no means have eliminated all uncertainty but it would nonetheless have been helpful.

The drafters might also have drawn upon elucidation in the Principles of European Contract Law (PECL) and the UNIDROIT Principles of the types of breach that justify termination.[144] Under the PECL, the right arises in respect of breaches that are 'fundamental'.[145] According to article 8:103 PECL, these occur in three situations: where strict compliance with the obligation breached is of the

[135] Civ (1) 13 Oct 1998, Bull civ I no 300, D 1999.198, note C Jamin.

[136] Civ (1) 24 Sept 2009, pourvoi no 08-14524.

[137] Deshayes, Genicon, and Laithier (n 10) 575–6.

[138] C Jamin, 'Les conditions de la résolution du contrat: vers un modèle unique?—Rapport français' in M Fontaine and G Viney (eds), *Les sanctions de l'inéxecution des obligations contractuelles, études de droit comparé* (Bruylant: Bruxelles and LGDJ: Paris, 2001) 451, 464–9; Genicon, *La résolution du contrat pour inexecution* (n 126) [426] ff.

[139] See, for example, Civ (1) 24 Feb 1970, Bull civ I no 362; Civ 30 Nov 1949, RTD civ 1950.18,3 note H and L Mazeaud.

[140] Genicon, *La résolution du contrat pour inexécution* (n 126) [438] ff.

[141] See, for example, Com 11 April 1995, *Contrats, Conc, Consomm*, 1995, no 125, note L Leveneur.

[142] Civ (1) 4 Jan 1995, Bull civ I no 14.

[143] Civ (3) 29 April 1987, RTD civ 1987.536, note J Mestre; Civ (3) 3 June 1992, GP 1992.II.656, note J-P Barbier.

[144] Article 8:103 of the PECL and article 7.3.1 of the UNIDROIT Principles.

[145] Article 9:301 of the PECL.

essence of the contract; or the breach substantially deprives the injured party of what they expected to receive under the contract unless the result was not foreseen or reasonably foreseeable by the defaulting party; or the breach is intentional and gives the injured party reason to believe that it cannot rely on the other party's future performance. Similar criteria appear at article 7.3.1 of the UNIDROIT Principles, with the additional stipulation that the court should also have regard to whether the defaulting party would suffer disproportionate loss if the contract was terminated.[146]

*(ii) Conditions for unilateral termination*

New article 1226 sets two conditions for the injured party to be able to terminate the contract without a court order. First, except where there is urgency, they should inform the defaulting party by notice that performance must be effected within a specified period of time (*mise en demeure*), which must be reasonable. The notice must contain a clear statement that, if the defaulting party fails to comply, the injured party will have the right to terminate. Second, if the defaulting party remains in breach at the end of the designated period, the injured party must serve a further notice stating that the contract is at an end and the grounds of termination.

These conditions are intended to counter-balance the curtailment of the role of the court and protect the defaulting party, who is given both an additional opportunity to perform and a statement of the grounds relied upon by the injured party, enabling an informed assessment of the merits of a challenge to the termination and assisting in the preparation of any such challenge.

Article 1226 expressly provides for a defaulting party that wishes to challenge a termination to do so by bringing court proceedings. In that case, the burden of proving that the breach was sufficiently serious to justify termination is on the injured party.[147] Therefore, whilst it is the defaulting party who sues for wrongful termination, it is for the injured party to prove that they had the right to terminate, not for the defaulting party to disprove.

### (c) Judicial termination

Termination can also be claimed as a form of relief in court. Historically, this was the principal means of terminating a contract in France. The long-standing rule in article 1184 of the 1804 Code was that the injured party had to apply to court for an order discharging the contract, subject to certain exceptions. It was not possible unilaterally to treat the breach as terminating the contract; only the court could make that decision.

The prominent role of the court served to protect both the defaulting party and the contract itself. To enable contracting parties to free themselves from their

[146] Article 7.3.1 of the UNIDROIT Principles.
[147] Article 1226 of the Civil Code.

obligations without a court order was seen as irreconcilable with the key principle of the binding force of contract (*principe de la force obligatoire du contrat*)[148] and contractual morality (*moralisme contractuel*).[149] As the guardian of both, the court would ascertain whether the contract could be saved[150] and ensure that termination was the last possible resort.[151]

This supervisory role was also regarded as necessary protection for the interests of the defaulting party.[152] Requiring the injured party to bring proceedings in order to terminate ensured that there was a process for verifying that any attempt to oust the defaulting party from the contract was legitimate and not arbitrary.[153] The court would ensure that their interests, which were 'of prime importance',[154] were upheld and not defeated lightly.[155]

Following the reforms, judicial termination is simply one of three options available to the injured party that are listed in article 1224. That it is last in the list, after contractual and self-help termination, might be interpreted as sending a symbolic message that what was once the norm now no longer has primacy and could even be thought of as the least attractive option of the three.

As to the kind of breach that justifies judicial termination, article 1224 states that the non-performance must be 'sufficiently serious'. This substantially codifies the position that had emerged in the French case law prior to the reforms, which was that the breach must be serious for the contract to be terminated.[156] As noted in the context of self-help termination, the meaning of 'sufficiently serious' is left unexplained. There are no rules or guidance for determining whether a breach crosses this threshold. As was true before the reforms, it is a question to be resolved by the lower court judge hearing the case (*pouvoir souverain des juges du fond*).[157] There is no scope for review by the *Cour de cassation*, which has on many occasions disclaimed any desire to interfere with the exercise of this *pouvoir souverain*.

[148] Y Lequette, 'La résolution unilatérale du contrat aux risques et périls des créanciers' Revue de droit des affaires, 2003.149.

[149] C Jamin, 'Les sanctions unilatérales de l'inexécution du contrat: trois idéologies en concurrence' in *L'unilatéralisme et le droit des obligations* (Economica: Paris, 1999) 71, 72–3; J Ghestin, 'La résolution pour inexécution (en droit français)' in *Il contratto inadempiuto* (G Giappichelli: Turin, 1999) 109, 111.

[150] R Cassin, 'Réflexions sur la résolution judiciaire des contrats pour inexécution' RTD civ 1945.12, [2].

[151] Jamin, 'Les conditions de la résolution du contrat: vers un modèle unique? (n 138) 482. For a criticism of this view, see Genicon, *La résolution du contrat pour inexécution* (n 126) [539].

[152] Terré, Simler, Lequette, and Chénedé (n 31) [795–6]; J Rochfeld, 'Résolution et exception d'inexécution' in P Rémy-Corlay and D Fenouillet (eds), *Les concepts contractuels français à l'heure des Principes du droit européen des contrats* (Dalloz: Paris, 2003) 216.

[153] Introductory comments of J Rochfeld in *Avant-Projet de Réforme du Droit des Obligations (Art 1101 à 1386 du Code civil) et du Droit de la Prescription (Art 2234 à 2281 du Code Civil) under the direction of P Catala, 22 Sept 2005* (Paris, Documentation française, 2006).

[154] Genicon, *La résolution du contrat pour inexécution* (n 126) [511].

[155] Whittaker, 'A Period of Grace for Contractual Performance?' (n 33) 1104.

[156] See, for example, Civ (1) 12 Mar 1956, D 1956, 302; Civ (1) 15 July 1999, Bull civ I no 245.

[157] Civ 27 Nov 1950, Gaz Pal 1951.1.132.

Good faith is also relevant in the context of judicial termination. The court can refuse to order termination where the remedy is sought in bad faith. It has repeatedly been held that termination 'can only be granted if the injured party acts in good faith',[158] and should be rejected 'if his behaviour is tainted with bad faith',[159] or the request for termination 'can be characterised as disloyal speculation'.[160]

## 2 The new role of the court in the termination process

**Civil Code**

Art. 1228.—A court may, according to the circumstances, recognise or declare the termination of the contract or order its performance with the possibility of allowing the debtor further time to do so, or award only damages.

Where the court is seised of an issue of whether a contract should be terminated, either by the injured party seeking judicial termination or the defaulting party challenging self-help or contractual termination, the court essentially has two options: to uphold the termination or to reject it and instead compel performance of the contract.[161]

### (a) Where termination is justified

In proceedings brought by the defaulting party challenging an attempt to terminate, the court must ascertain whether the remedy is justified or wrongful. If the conditions for contractual or self-help termination in articles 1225 and 1226 respectively have been met such that the termination is justified, the court will *recognize* that the contract has been brought to an end. Where the injured party successfully claims that the contract should be terminated by way of judicial termination, the court will *declare* that the contract is at an end.

### (b) Wrongful termination

If termination is not justified, because the breach is not sufficiently serious in the case of judicial or self-help termination, or the conditions for a contractual right to terminate are not met, the court can reject the remedy and instead compel performance. In that case, the contract remains on foot. The court can also grant the defaulting party a period of grace (*délai de grâce*) in which to perform or, where the attempted termination was wrongful and has caused loss, an award of compensatory damages.

158 CA Poitiers, Civ (1) 4 July 2006, Juris-data no 2006-313835.
159 Ibid.
160 CA Paris, 22 Dec 1873 cited in Genicon, *La résolution du contrat pour inexécution* (n 126) [505].
161 Article 1228 of the Civil Code.

Compelling performance is not a new remedy. It was available prior to the reforms[162] and fits with the remedial framework of French law, which favours performance and saving the contract. Where a party that claims to have been the victim of a breach wrongfully terminates, this itself amounts to a breach. The roles are then reversed, with the party that initially was alleged to be in default becoming entitled to the remedies in the Code for breach of contract. These include specific enforcement where performance is still possible.[163]

Although a powerful and onerous remedy, compelling performance is justified in France on the basis that it is the only effective way of deterring the defaulting party from attempting to terminate without good cause.[164] It therefore serves to uphold the binding force of contract (*principe de la force obligatoire du contrat*).[165] A party that is minded to breach knows that they can in any event be ordered to perform. In many cases this should extinguish or at least reduce the temptation. The alternative of allowing the injured party to terminate and pay damages is seen as tantamount to conferring a right to opt out of contractual obligations, which is inimical to the binding force of contract.[166] As Mazeaud has explained, 'giving your word has a symbolic value which is priceless'.[167] In the same vein, Stoffel-Munck has observed that if wrongful termination could be remedied in damages alone rather than by an order requiring performance, the injured promisee would be able 'to atone for a sin with money'.[168]

However, this is not to say that the interests of the defaulting party are entirely disregarded. To the contrary, the court has the power to grant a period of grace for the performance of their obligations. It is well-established that there is a wide discretion not only as to whether to allow a grace period but also over its duration,[169] on which there is no limit except that, once ordered, the period cannot be renewed.[170] The *Cour de cassation* rarely interferes.

In exercising its discretion, the court must be satisfied that the defaulting party is acting in good faith.[171] If there is bad faith, the protection of the court is unlikely to be available. It is also required to take account of the interests of the injured party

162 Com 18 Nov 2008, RDC 2009.484, note D Mazeaud; Civ (1) 29 May 2001, RTD civ 2001.590, note J Mestre and B Fages.

163 P Stoffel-Munck, 'Le contrôle a *posteriori* de la résiliation unilatérale' Droit & Patrimoine 2004.106.

164 Civ (1) 20 Feb 2001, D 2001 somm 3239, note D Mazeaud; Com 18 Nov 2008, RDC 2009, 484, note D Mazeaud; D Mazeaud, 'L'introduction de la résolution unilatérale pour inexécution—Rapport français' RDC 2010, 81; J Mestre, 'Rupture abusive et maintien du contrat', RDC 2005, 99.

165 Mestre, 'Rupture abusive et maintien du contrat' (n 164).

166 See section B on the important role of enforced performance.

167 Com 18 Nov 2008, RDC 2009, 484, note Mazeaud.

168 Stoffel-Munck (n 163).

169 The prerogative was previously conferred by paragraph 3 of article 1184 of the 1804 Civil Code.

170 Civ (1) 19 Dec 1984, Bull civ I no 343.

171 Y-M Laithier, 'The French Law of Remedies for Breach of Contract' in N Cohen and E McKendrick (eds), *Comparative Remedies for Breach of Contract* (Hart Publishing: Oxford, 2005) 103, 121.

and their likely loss in the event that more time to perform is granted. The aim is to strike a balance between the interests of both parties.

Where performance is impossible or inappropriate, the only potentially remaining remedy is compensatory damages.[172] The injured party is compensated for losses that result from the breach and the wrongful termination.[173]

## 3 The effects of termination

**Civil Code**

Art. 1229.—Termination puts an end to the contract.

Termination takes effect, according to the situation, on the conditions provided by any termination clause, at the date of receipt by the debtor of a notice given by the creditor, or on the date set by the court or, in its absence, the day on which proceedings were brought.

Where the acts of performance exchanged were useful only on the full performance of the contract which has been terminated, the parties must restore the whole of what they have obtained from each other. Where the acts of performance which were exchanged were useful to both parties from time to time during the reciprocal performance of the contract, there is no place for restitution in respect of the period before the last act of performance which was not reflected in something received in return; in this case, termination is termed resiling from the contract.

Restitution takes place under the conditions provided by articles 1352 to 1352-9.

Art. 1230.—Termination does not affect contract terms relating to dispute-resolution, nor those intended to take effect even in the case of termination, such as confidentiality or non-competition clauses.

The effects of termination are dealt with in new articles 1229 and 1230. In article 1229 the main effect, regardless of the method of termination chosen by the injured party, is stated to be that the contract is brought to an end. This occurs at different points in time, depending on the method: it is at the time specified in the termination clause where a contractual right to terminate is exercised; upon receipt by the defaulting party of the injured party's termination notice in the case of self-help termination; and on the day stipulated by the court or, if there is no such a date, the date on which proceedings were commenced, in the case of judicial termination.

[172] Article 1228 of the Civil Code.

[173] As Pinna (n 97) has shown in his monograph on the assessment of damages, lower courts assess damages so as to compensate the injured party for his loss of the bargain; S Rowan, *Remedies for Breach of Contract: A Comparative Analysis of the Protection of Performance* (OUP: Oxford, 2012) 96.

According to article 1229, where the performance rendered before termination has been useful to both parties, termination—known in this context as *résiliation*—brings an end to the contract for the future only, without any restitution. The breach is remedied through compensatory damages. This contrasts with the position where only performance in full would be useful. In that case, termination—known as *résolution*—results in the contract being dissolved and restitution and counter-restitution of any money or property transferred.

This maintains the traditional distinction in French law[174] between *résolution* and *résiliation* but with a change to how it operates.[175] It was previously drawn by reference to whether the performance under the contract was continuous or in instalments on the one hand or instantaneous on the other. *Résolution* discharged *ab initio* contracts whose performance was instantaneous (*contrats à exécution instantanée*), thus having retroactive effect. *Résiliation* was available for contracts where performance was continuous or in instalments (*à exécution successive*) and discharged only obligations to render future performance. The rationale for the distinction operating in this way was that, for continuous or instalment contracts that had been partly performed, restitution and counter-restitution would be too difficult or undesirable where the parties had been intended to receive some performance under the contract prior to the time that termination supervened. The reforms shift the focus away from the nature of the contract onto whether the performance already rendered has actually been useful to the parties. As a result, *résolution* and *résiliation* can now apply equally to contracts whose performance is continuous, in instalments or instantaneous.[176]

The last of the seven new provisions on termination—article 1230—codifies the uncontroversial principle that the remedy does not affect rights and obligations under the contract that are intended to have effect after the contract has been brought to an end. As examples, dispute resolution clauses, confidentiality or non-competition clauses remain effective.

## 4 No anticipatory breach of contract or termination

There is no provision for anticipatory breach of contract in the new Code.[177] Unlike in England and various international instruments, it is simply not recognized in French law. The injured party therefore cannot terminate or seek specific

[174] The distinction is somewhat controversial: T Genicon, '"Résiliation" et "résolution" dans le projet d'ordonnance portant réforme du droit des contrats' JCP.G 2015.1605.

[175] For a criticism of this distinction and terminology, see ibid.

[176] 'Report to the President' (n 15) 16.

[177] Forms of 'anticipatory termination' (*résolution anticipée*) were countenanced in previous reform projects: see article 111 or article 169 of the Terré Project (F Terré, *Pour une réforme du droit des contrats* (Dalloz: Paris, 2008) and the first version of the Ministry of Justice project in 2008.

enforcement or damages before the promised performance is due.[178] This is true even where the defaulting party has renounced their obligations or disabled themselves from performing. At that stage, neither renunciation nor impossibility amount to a breach. It follows that the promisee does not have any immediate right of action in either case. Only when the time for performance occurs can this arise and the remedy be claimed.[179]

The absence of anticipatory breach in French contract law has been attributed to the policy of encouraging the performance of contractual obligations.[180] Even where the promisor clearly states an unwillingness or inability to perform at some future time, there will usually be a prospect of that changing before their performance is due, which should not be given up on. Any chance of the contract being performed, however remote, is enough to justify precluding the injured party from terminating. In the interest of contractual security,[181] it is important that the contract is given every possible opportunity of being performed.

It is worth noting in passing that the introduction of a right to terminate the contract before performance is due would not have been entirely inapposite in France. There would have been consistency with new article 1220, which provides for the anticipatory *exception d'inexécution*. This enables a contracting party to suspend the performance of an obligation as soon as it becomes evident that the other party will not perform by the due date, if the consequences of breach are sufficiently serious.[182] The upshot is that performance can be suspended before it becomes due, even if the contract cannot be brought to an end.

## E Compensation for Loss

**Civil Code**

Art. 1231.—Unless non-performance is permanent, damages are due only if the debtor has previously been put on notice to perform his obligation within a reasonable time.

Art. 1231-1.—A debtor is condemned, where appropriate, to the payment of damages either on the ground of the non-performance or a delay in performance of an obligation, unless he justifies this on the ground that performance was prevented by force majeure.

[178] Laithier, *Étude comparative des sanctions de l'inexécution du contrat* (n 61); S Whittaker, 'How Does French Law Deal with Anticipatory Breaches of Contract?' 45 (1996) ICLQ 662, 662.

[179] See Whittaker (n 178) 662.

[180] For other possible reasons, see ibid., 663.

[181] Genicon, *La résolution du contrat pour inexécution* (n 126) [314] ff.

[182] Mekki (n 63) 1344 who argues that the risk of breach justifies the suspension of performance but not that the entire contract is brought to an end.

The 2016 reforms did not amend in any significant respect the articles of the Civil Code relating to compensatory and agreed damages. Both forms of liability were held over by the drafters to be addressed together with extra-contractual liability by a later and broader project to reform civil liability in France.[183] As the Report to the President stated:

> Contractual liability cannot be reformed in isolation from extra-contractual liability: it is generally accepted that, fundamentally, these two forms of liability are mechanisms of the same nature, resting on the existence of an action giving rise to liability, harm, and a causal relationship between the two. Only differences of regime distinguish between them, based essentially on the special character of the action giving rise to liability in the contractual context.[184]

The result is that, apart from some terminological changes and reordering, the reforms left the rules on compensation unchanged. This has been a source of regret for several commentators. In the words of Deshayes, Genicon, and Laithier:

> Despite the considerable practical significance of this remedy and the laconic articles of the 1804 Code, new article 1231 and those that follow… merely reproduce the old provisions. This is a missed opportunity… The lacuna is all the more regrettable since specific enforcement is now less readily available than was previously the case.[185]

This regret has surely been compounded because, at the time of writing (June 2021), the proposed reform of civil liability has stalled. It is presently unclear whether it will be enacted and if so when and in what form. What follows is therefore an analysis of the original articles in the 1804 Code that were replicated and re-numbered in the 2016 reforms and continue to apply. Reference will also be made to some of the main changes and innovations contemplated by the proposed reforms, which could potentially be introduced in the future.

The focus of this section is on the following key aspects of the law relating to compensation: the concept of 'contractual fault'; the measure of damages; the availability of damages for non-pecuniary loss; the limits on the right to recover

[183] Ministère de la Justice, 'Projet de réforme de la responsabilité civile' (13 March 2017), <http://www.justice.gouv.fr/publication/Projet_de_reforme_de_la_responsabilite_civile_13032017.pdf>; English translation by S Whittaker and J-S Borghetti, Reform Bill on Civil Liability (March 2017), <http://www.textes.justice.gouv.fr/art_pix/reform_bill_on_civil_liability_march_2017.pdf≥ accessed 1 September 2021.

[184] 'Report to the President' (n 15) 17; Translation of Whittaker, 'A Common Framework for Civil Liability?' Chapter 2 in J-S Borghetti and S Whittaker (eds), *French Civil Liability in Comparative Perspective* (Hart Publishing: Oxford, 2019) 21.

[185] Deshayes, Genicon, and Laithier (n 10) 591; see also B Haftel, 'La responsabilité contractuelle' RDC 2017, 143.

compensatory damages; and agreed damages. Punitive and restitutionary damages, which have generated significant debate in France, are also considered.

## 1 'Fault' as the basis of contractual liability

Article 1231-1 enunciates the principle that where a party fails to perform or is late in performing a contractual obligation, and their non-performance is not the result of force majeure, they must pay damages to the other party. Although the article refers to 'non-performance', in practice the term 'contractual fault' (*faute contractuelle* or *inexécution fautive*) is widely used to describe the breach of a contractual duty. This is on account of contractual liability traditionally being understood in France as grounded in the notion of fault.[186]

The origins of this notion in a contractual context have been traced to Jean Domat and Robert-Joseph Pothier. In 'Les Lois Civiles dans leur Ordre Naturel', Domat elucidated a general principle of civil fault comprising delictual and contractual fault.[187] The breach of a contractual obligation was classified as a contractual fault which may give rise to damages.

In some respects, however, 'fault' is a misnomer. The reality is that both fault-based and strict contractual obligations are known in French law, as is apparent in the well-established distinction that is drawn between *obligations de moyens* and *obligations de résultat*. This was inspired by the groundbreaking analysis of the eminent jurist René Demogue in the 1920s.[188] An *obligation de moyens* requires the promisor to exercise reasonable care in performing the obligation but without any necessity to achieve a particular result. Liability therefore turns on whether reasonable care was exercised and, as such, is fault-based. In contrast, an *obligation de résultat* is a contractual obligation to bring about a contemplated result. The promisor will be in breach where the result is not achieved, despite exercising reasonable care and indeed making every possible effort to perform.[189]

One notable aspect of the distinction between *obligations de moyens* and *obligations de résultat* is in the burden of proof. For an *obligation de moyens*, the injured party must prove fault on the part of the promisor, who can resist liability by showing that they acted diligently in performing the obligation. The standard is

[186] The word 'fault' was also absent from the key provisions of the 1804 Civil Code on breach of contract and remedies. R Rodière, 'Une notion menacée: la faute ordinaire dans les contrats' RTD civ (1954) 201; A Tunc, 'Force majeure et absence de faute en matière contractuelle' RTD civ (1945) 17; P Esmein, 'Le fondement de la responsabilité contractuelle rapprochée de la responsabilité délictuelle' RTD civ (1933) 627.

[187] J Domat, *Les Lois Civiles dans leur Ordre Naturel, le Droit Public, et Legum Delectus* (Rollin et fils: Paris, 1713)No VIII to X of Section II, of Title V of Book III.

[188] R Demogue, *Traité des Obligations en Général* (Rousseau: Paris, 1923-1933)Book V, no 1237.

[189] Note that the most stringent type of obligation is the obligation of guarantee (*de garantie*) for which liability is absolute and the promisor cannot be excused from a failure to perform even by proving that it was due to an external cause.

an objective one; it is the standard to be expected from a reasonable person. This is in contrast with the *obligation de résultat*, where the injured party needs only to prove that the contractually agreed outcome has not been achieved. The onus then shifts to the promisor to demonstrate that this results from an external cause (*cause étrangère*). It will not suffice to show that appropriate diligence has been exercised.[190]

Although the promisor cannot escape from liability in respect of an *obligation de résultat* by exercising reasonable care, somewhat counterintuitively, their conduct is nonetheless described by French lawyers in terms of fault. A failure to comply with the obligation is referred to as a 'contractual fault' (*faute contractuelle*), as is also a breach of an *obligation de moyens*. In an attempt to justify this potentially confusing usage, *obligations de résultat* have been explained as giving rise to a presumption of fault. In reality, however, any such presumption is irrebuttable and liability is strict. The references to fault are otiose and obscure the true standard of liability.

It is not always straightforward to determine where, and on what grounds, the line between obligations *de moyens* and *de résultat* is drawn. In some cases, the standard is clear from the Civil Code. For instance, according to article 1992, the liability of agents is fault-based. In contrast, article 1792 provides that the liability of builders is strict. The standard might also be specified in the contract itself.[191]

The nature of the obligation is often suggestive of whether liability is strict or fault-based.[192] For example, obligations to give (*obligations de donner*)[193] are indubitably *obligations de résultat*. A supplier of goods engages to achieve a specific result, that is, the delivery of the goods.[194] Obligations not to do (*obligations de ne pas faire*) are also *obligations de résultat*, in that an abstention is by its nature a result that is ordinarily capable of being guaranteed.

A category of obligation that is less susceptible to simple classification is the obligation to do (*obligation de faire*). Either strict or fault-based liability may apply to such obligations, many of which straddle what is an uncertain border between the

[190] Demogue's division of contractual obligations as being *de moyens* or *de résultat* has been adopted and developed extensively by French courts. Both types of obligation have been sub-divided into two further categories, namely 'diminished' (*attenuées* or *allégées*) and 'intensified' (*aggravées* or *renforcées*). *Obligations de résultat* are *atténuées* or *aggravées; obligations de moyens* are *allégées* or *renforcées*. In the case of *obligations de résultat atténuées*, the promisor can avoid liability by showing that they have not committed a fault and their conduct adheres to the standard of the reasonable person. For *obligations de résultat aggravées*, the promisor bears the consequences of a *cause étrangère*. In *obligations de moyens allégées*, the promisor will only be liable for gross negligence (*faute lourde*). This is in contrast with *obligations de moyens renforcées*, for which the promisor must prove that they were particularly diligent.

[191] See S Rowan, 'Fault and Breach of Contract in France and England: Some Comparisons' (2011) 22(4) European Business Law Review, 467.

[192] Terré, Simler, Lequette, and Chénédé (n 31) [846].

[193] The distinction between obligations to give, to do, or not to do of the 1804 Code has disappeared in the reformed Code but remains helpful in practice.

[194] Under article 1138 of the Civil Code, the transfer of title to property is effective immediately upon the exchange of consent by the parties to the contract.

two standards. In deciding whether an obligation to do is *de moyens* or *de résultat*, the courts are guided by certain factors.[195] These include, for instance, the uncertainty and risk involved in performance. An obligation that involves no particular risk and requires only diligent conduct in order to reach the desired outcome is more likely to be an *obligation de résultat*. In contrast, contractual activities with uncertain parameters tend to be *obligations de moyens*. So it is that a lawyer must use reasonable care and skill in the conduct of litigation but does not promise to win.[196] The uncertainty is both as to what will have to be done and as to whether it will achieve the desired outcome.[197]

Several explanations have been proffered as to why contractual fault remains part of the French contract law lexicon even though liability can be strict. These include the relative lack of intellectual demarcation between contract law and extra-contractual liability in France, both being regarded academically as part of the wider law of obligations,[198] the French conception of contract being wedded to the idea of performance, and breach of contract being considered as blameworthy and disloyal.[199]

Some commentators have advocated ending the fiction that contractual liability is fault-based and even the complete removal of fault from the lexicon. The thrust of their objection is that whether the obligation breached is *de moyens* or *de résultat*, the defining common feature is that the promised performance has not been rendered and the defaulting party has failed to fulfil their promise. It is this feature rather than fault that should be captured in the nomenclature.

Tallon, for example, argued forcefully that in a contractual setting fault is prone to confuse and creates a false parallel with fault in extra-contractual liability.[200] The unitary concept of 'civil fault' comprising both contractual and extra-contractual fault leads to an 'evanescence' of the contractual regime by the extra-contractual regime, as well as undue prominence for compensatory damages and a corresponding neglect of other equally important contractual remedies such as specific enforcement.[201] On this basis, Tallon advocated the substitution of fault with the more neutral concept of non-performance (*inexécution*).

[195] G Marton, 'Obligations de résultat et obligations de moyens' RTD civ (1935) 33.

[196] Civ (1) 15 Oct 1985, Bull civ I no 257, RTD civ (1986) 759, note Huet; Civ (1) 24 June 1997, JCP 1997.IV.1816.

[197] Other factors include whether the promisor is remunerated or the promisee plays an active or a passive role in performance: see Rowan (n 191) 467.

[198] G Treitel, *Remedies for Breach of Contract: A Comparative Account* (Clarendon Press: Oxford, 1988) 8; F Lawson, 'Fault and Contract—A Few Comparisons' (1975) 49 Tul LR 295, 307–9.

[199] C Radé, 'L'impossible divorce de la faute et de la responsabilité civile' D (1998) 301, 304–5; D Tallon, 'Pourquoi parler de faute contractuelle?' in *Droit civil, procédure, linguistique juridique, Ecrits en hommage à Gérard Cornu* (PUF: Paris, 1994) 429, 432 citing A Sériaux, *Droit des obligations* (PUF: Paris, 1992) no 59: '[disloyalty] is the correct term given that the essence of the contract is loyalty to the other party'.

[200] D Tallon, 'L'inexécution du contrat: pour une autre présentation' RTD civ 1994.223; D Tallon, 'Pourquoi parler de faute contractuelle?' in *Droit civil, procédure, linguistique juridique, Ecrits en hommage à Gérard Cornu* (PUF Paris, 1994) 429.

[201] Tallon, 'L'inexécution du contrat: pour une autre présentation' (n 200) 223.

In a similar vein, Rémy has argued in two controversial articles that contractual fault and Demogue's distinction between *obligations de moyens* and *obligations de résultat* are at the root of a false amalgam between the functions of extra-contractual and contractual damages.[202] Unlike in extra-contractual liability, damages in contract should not be understood as a device for compensating loss suffered. Instead, their exclusive function is to enable the injured party to obtain equivalent performance (*exécution par équivalent*),[203] which is achieved by payment of an amount that is commensurate with the monetary value of the promised performance. The compensation of loss resulting from a breach of contract, for instance consequential loss, is a matter for extra-contractual liability. On this basis, the notion of contractual liability is said to be a 'false concept' which ought to be abandoned.

However, despite these strongly made objections from eminent sources, the majority of French commentators favour retaining contractual fault and liability alongside their extra-contractual equivalents. This is also the approach taken in the Reform Bill on Civil Liability which does not engage with whether the term 'contractual fault' should be expunged. Indeed, there is no reference at all to the standard of liability or how it is defined. If the project is enacted, fault therefore seems likely to remain relevant. As Deshayes, Genicon, and Laithier have said, 'it is probable that [contractual] fault retains its traditional role; it is a concept to which French lawyers are attached'.[204] This is because 'the *Projet de réforme* proclaims its loyalty to the ... model ... [that] civil liability is above all based on breach of a duty which is imposed by the law and, accordingly, it is the defendant's fault or unlawful act which occupies a central place'.[205]

## 2 The measure of damages

**Civil Code**

Art. 1231-2.—In general, damages due to the creditor are for the loss that he has incurred or the gain of which he has been deprived, with the following exceptions and qualifications.

[202] P Rémy, 'La "responsabilité contractuelle": histoire d'un faux concept' RTD civ 1997.323; P Rémy, 'Critique du système français de responsabilité civile' Droit et Cultures 1996.31. See also P Le Tourneau and L Cadiet, *Droit de la responsabilité des contrats* (4th edn, Dalloz: Paris, 1996) [220] ff and [1481] ff.

[203] For a more detailed explanation of this debate, see S Whittaker, 'A Common Framework for Civil Liability' and Y-M Laithier, 'The Relationship between Contractual and Extra-Contractual Liability as between Parties to a Contract' in J-S Borghetti and S Whittaker (eds), *French Civil Liability in Comparative Perspective* (Hart Publishing: Oxford, 2019) 15–36 and 37–54.

[204] Deshayes, Genicon, and Laithier (n 10) 593.

[205] Y-M Laithier, 'The Relationship between Contractual and Extra-Contractual Liability as between Parties to a Contract' (n 203) 75. Many commentators have argued that the distinction has become too complex and should not be codified: Terré, Simler, Lequette, and Chénédé (n 31) [858]; Chantepie and Latina (n 13) [678].

The aim of damages is to provide the injured party with the sum of money that is necessary to put them in the position in which they would have been had the contract been performed.[206] New article 1231-2, which substantially reproduces old article 1149, provides that the injured party is entitled to damages in respect of 'the loss that they have incurred and the gain of which they have been deprived'. Compensation should be full (*principe de réparation intégrale du préjudice*) and commensurate with the loss suffered (*tout le préjudice mais rien que le préjudice*).

Despite the clarity of these propositions, the principles governing the assessment of compensatory damages are not always easy to ascertain.[207] It generally falls to the courts of first instance and lower appeal courts to determine the loss that has been suffered and quantify an appropriate award, with no scope for review by the *Cour de cassation* (*pouvoir souverain d'appréciation des juges du fond*).[208] Its appellate jurisdiction is confined to ensuring that the principle of 'full compensation' has been properly applied. Since lower courts are not required to justify their awards or use any specific methods of assessment, it has very limited scope for intervening.[209]

Despite the general opacity of French judicial reasoning,[210] it is well-established that the two principal measures of damages are cost of cure and diminution in value.[211] In the context of building contracts,[212] both measures are frequently claimed.[213] The court has a broad power to decide between them, although in the name of full compensation, there is a general aversion to going behind the preference of the injured party, whose election is usually respected.[214] Cost of cure

[206] For an example of an express affirmation by a French court of this proposition, see Civ (3) 9 Jan 1991, Bull civ III no 12.

[207] See Pinna (n 97) [75]–[85]; T Ivainer, 'Le pouvoir souverain du juge dans l'appréciation des indemnités réparatrices' D 1972 Chron 7; P Jourdain, 'Les dommages-intérêts alloués par le juge. Rapport français' in M Fontaine and G Viney (eds), *Les sanctions de l'inexécution des obligations contractuelles, Etudes de droit comparé* (Bruylant: Bruxelles and LGDJ: Paris, 2001) 263; C Boismain, 'Etude sur l'évaluation des dommages-intérêts par les juges du fond' PA 2007 no 39.7.

[208] Pinna (n 97); but see L Thibierge, 'La mesure des dommages-intérêts: question de fait ou question de droit? Libres réflexions au travers du prisme de la minimisation du préjudice' RDC 2019.193.

[209] Civ (2) 11 July 1983, Bull civ II no 153; Civ (1) 4 Dec 1974, D 1974.IR.54.

[210] This opacity has been criticized by commentators, in particular G Viney and P Jourdain, *Traité de droit civil, Les effets de la responsabilité* (3rd edn, LGDJ: Paris, 2010) [63]–[66]; Ivainer (n 207). Note that the Catala proposals sought to make the assessment regime clearer. See in particular, article 1374 and articles 1380 to 1380-2 of the Catala proposals, which gave guidance as to the basis of assessment only where the choice is between the cost of replacement and the cost of repair, not where it is between the cost of cure and the diminution in value measures of damages.

[211] Pinna (n 97) [92]–[122]; Viney and Jourdain (n 210) [95].

[212] Note that there are different regimes of liability for building contracts. These include the *garantie décennale*, *garantie biennale*, and *garantie de parfait achèvement* of articles 1792 ff and 2270 of the Civil Code, as well as general contractual liability. For a summary in English, see Whittaker, *Liability for Products: English Law, French Law and European Harmonisation* (n 43) 104–8. This distinction has no material relevance in relation to the measure of damages.

[213] See generally P Jourdain, 'La réparation des dommages immobiliers et l'enrichissement de la victime' Rev Droit Immob 1995.51; P Malinvaud and P Jestaz, *Droit de la promotion immobilière* (7th edn, Dalloz: Paris, 2004) [101] ff; M Zavaro, *La responsabilité des constructeurs* (LexisNexis Litec: Paris, 2005) 101.

[214] Pinna (n 97) [135]–[137]; Viney and Jourdain (n 210) [95]; Y-M Laithier, *Étude comparative des sanctions de l'inexécution du contrat* (n 61) [394]. For exceptions to the rule, see Pinna (n 97) [141] ff.

damages have not been refused on the ground of unreasonableness or disproportionality. Nor would either of these factors appear to have a bearing on whether particular harms or costs qualify as loss. The *Cour de cassation* has generally taken the view that it is irrelevant to the assessment of damages that the cost of repair is high[215] or significantly in excess of the original contract price.[216]

In one notable pre-reform case, the *Cour de cassation* upheld the decision of the Angers Court of Appeal to award the cost of demolishing and reconstructing a house which, in breach of contract, had been built just over a metre beneath the agreed height. It was irrelevant that the house was fit for purpose.[217] In another case, the *Cour de cassation* quashed the refusal of the Montpellier Court of Appeal to award damages to remedy the non-conformity of a roof to contractual specification, despite the roof being perfectly adequate.[218]

The intention of the injured party to reinstate would also appear to be irrelevant. On numerous occasions the *Cour de cassation* has reaffirmed that compensation is not dependent on the injured party having cured or intending to cure the breach.[219]

The unfettered availability of cost of cure damages is at variance with the conditional availability of the analogous remedy of replacement under article 1222. It will be recalled that—in common with cost of cure damages—replacement involves a monetary award to enable the injured party to obtain substitute performance, subject however to a requirement that this occur 'within a reasonable time and at a reasonable cost'. The injured party must therefore act reasonably when claiming the cost of replacement under article 1222 but not the cost of cure under article 1231-1.

For remedies that achieve substantially the same outcome to have such divergent threshold requirements is surprising, particularly since the injured party has an entirely free choice of remedy under article 1217.[220] This circle might have been squared and the absence of any restrictions on the availability of cost of cure damages counterbalanced if the injured party was under a general requirement to take reasonable steps to mitigate their loss. As is explained in more detail below,[221] however, no such duty presently exists in French law and, whilst one is proposed in the pending Reform Bill on Civil Liability, it is unclear whether, and if so when, this

[215] Civ (3) 11 Jan 1984, Rev Droit Immob 1984.191; Civ (3) 9 Dec 1975, JCP 1976.IV.43; Pinna (n 97) [137].

[216] Civ (1) 12 Oct 1961, Bull civ I no 455.

[217] Civ (3) 5 Dec 1979, JCP 1981.II.19605. See also Civ (3) 6 May 1981, Juris-Data no 1981-001783.

[218] Civ (3) 22 Oct 2002, Rev Droit Immob 2003.95.

[219] Civ (2) 28 April 1975, RTD civ 1976.150, obs G Durry; Civ (2) 31 Mar 1993, RTD civ 1993.838, obs P Jourdain; Civ (3) 2 Dec 2003, Juris-Data no 2003-021391; Civ (1) 26 May 1993, Juris-Data no 91-18.750; Civ (3) 10 Jan 1984, Rev Droit Immob 1984.191, obs P Malinvaud and B Boubli; Y Chartier *La réparation du préjudice* (Dalloz: Paris, 1983) [472].

[220] Laithier, 'Exécution Forcée en Nature' (n 28) 264; Haftel (n 187) [14].

[221] See section 4(b) on the absence of mitigation in French law.

will be enacted.[222] Therefore, at least for the time being and quite possibly beyond, it seems likely that the incongruity between these remedies will remain, with the distortive effect of cost of cure damages being consistently favoured over replacement, all other things being equal.

Whether the drafters of the reforms addressed their minds to this incongruity is unclear. It has, however, been extensively discussed by commentators, drawing considerable criticism. This is reflected in the following rhetorical question posed by Laithier: 'is it possible to assess the damages at the level of the cost of repair or replacement where the magnitude of this cost partly explains the refusal of enforced performance in kind? Would it be legally or economically coherent to accept this limitation in respect of performance in kind but to refuse it in calculating the amount of damages?'.[223]

## 3 The compensation of non-pecuniary loss

Not all harm caused by a breach of contract will necessarily involve a diminution in the financial position of the injured party. Non-pecuniary loss (*dommage moral*) such as frustration, distress, injury to feelings, annoyance, and loss of reputation can all result from a breach, yet there is no subtraction from the wealth of the injured party.

Compensation for non-pecuniary loss is widely available in France.[224] This is well-established—albeit after some initial hesitation and despite the use of the words 'loss' and 'gain'—in new article 1231-2, replicating article 1149 of the 1804 Code, which on one interpretation might be taken to suggest financial detriment.[225] Indeed such is the consensus that there would not appear to be any real academic debate on the point[226] or notable exceptions. Even supposed difficulties of quantification are regarded as unconvincing,[227] particularly as awards are generally modest in amount.

The rationale is full compensation,[228] which requires that any and every loss resulting from a breach of contract should be compensated. This applies equally

[222] Article 1263 of the Draft Reform Project of Civil Liability; see J-S Borghetti, 'Faut-il distinguer les dommages et intérêts compensatoires des dommages et intérêts en lieu et place de la prestation?' RDC 2016.787 [19]–[26].

[223] Laithier, 'Exécution Forcée en Nature' (n 28) 284; See also Borghetti, 'Faut-il distinguer?' (n 222) [18]–[20].

[224] For a comparison of English and French law in this area, see B Jackson, 'Injured Feelings Resulting from Breach of Contract' (1977) 26 ICLQ 502.

[225] See, for example, Paris 27 Mar 1873, DP 1874.2.129.

[226] For example, a few pages in C Larroumet, *Droit civil, Les obligations, Le contrat* (5th edn, Economica: Paris, 2003) vol 3; five pages in H L Mazeaud and A Tunc, *Traité théorique et pratique de la responsabilité civile délictuelle et contractuelle* (6th edn, Montchrestien: Paris, 1965) vol 1.

[227] Larroumet (n 226) [653].

[228] Ibid.

where the object of the contract is to obtain a non-financial advantage. Damages have therefore been ordered against a tour operator for mental distress suffered by customers as a result of the inadequate organization of a holiday,[229] and in another case where the deficient provision of information regarding visa requirements led to the cancellation of a holiday.[230]

Compensation for non-pecuniary loss is also available where the object of the contract is to obtain a financial advantage and the injured party suffers injury to feelings as an incidental consequence of the breach. For example, damages for non-pecuniary loss are available for the wrongful dismissal of an employee in a manner that is harsh and humiliating. This is illustrated by a case in which an employee was wrongfully dismissed after asking for a short period of leave in order to get married. The Paris Court of Appeal made an award of 2,000 euros for the resulting mental distress.[231] Similarly, the Rennes Court of Appeal has ordered damages in favour of a wrongfully dismissed employee as compensation for a 'destabilising first professional experience'.[232]

## 4 Limits on compensation of loss

**Civil Code**

Art. 1231-3.—A debtor is bound only to damages which were either foreseen or which could have been foreseen at the time of conclusion of the contract, except where non-performance was due to a gross or dishonest fault.

Art. 1231-4.—In the situation where non-performance of a contract does indeed result from gross or dishonest fault, damages include only that which is the immediate and direct result of non-performance.

In order to avoid overcompensation, French law imposes a number of boundaries on the recovery of compensatory damages for breach of contract.[233] One of the main limiting principles is remoteness. However, the doctrine of mitigation of loss, which has an important role in English law, does not exist in France.

### (a) Remoteness

Pursuant to new article 1231-3,[234] the defaulting party must compensate only those consequences of non-performance that were either foreseen or could have

[229] Paris 24 March 1998, Juris-Data no 1998-020665.
[230] Lyon 16 May 2002, Juris-Data no 2002-205304. For other examples see Jackson (n 224) 510 ff.
[231] Paris 27 Sept 2006, Juris-Data no 2006-314146.
[232] Rennes 8 Sept 2005, Juris-Data no 2005-280803.
[233] B Nicholas, *French Law of Contract* (2nd edn, Clarendon Press: Oxford, 1992) 231–2.
[234] Its predecessor before the 2016 reforms was article 1150 of the 1804 Civil Code.

been foreseen by the parties when the contract was concluded.[235] What must be foreseen is the type and extent of the loss resulting from non-performance.[236] The remoteness rule is justified on the ground that the defaulting party should only be liable for the risks that they assumed on entering into the contract.[237] How the parties have chosen to allocate risks in the contract should be respected.

Where the breach is dishonest or deliberate or amounts to gross negligence, the remoteness rule is disapplied. The liability of the defaulting party therefore extends to all consequences flowing from the breach. Neither reliance on exclusion and limitation clauses, nor insurance is permitted.[238]

The approach of French courts has been to construe deliberate breach expansively. An intention to cause harm (*intention de nuire*) is not necessary and it is sufficient that the defaulting party wilfully refuses to perform an obligation.[239] It is therefore not unusual for compensation to be ordered in respect of all of the consequences flowing from a breach.

In one noteworthy case, full compensation was ordered against the vendors of a flat for their deliberate failure, in breach of the contract of sale, to treat an infestation satisfactorily prior to the transfer of the property. Their decision, in order to save money, to resort to an inexpensive treatment, which turned out to be substandard, was a sufficient basis for full compensatory liability.[240] Similarly, an airline which overbooked flights and was therefore unable to accommodate all of the passengers to whom tickets had been sold was held to have committed a deliberate breach. By reference to old article 1150, which is now article 1231-3, the airline was ordered to compensate the passengers who were denied boarding for *all* losses arising out of the breach, and was debarred from relying upon a limitation clause.[241]

Several explanations have been advanced to justify the inapplicability of the remoteness principle for deliberate or dishonest breaches of contract. The foremost is that deliberate or dishonest breach is reprehensible and therefore deserving of harsher treatment.[242] It has been argued by Chartier to be so serious that the defaulting party should be deprived of any protection, including the indulgence of remoteness.[243] The exception has also been explained as being grounded in

[235] For a criticism of article 1231-3 in a previous draft, see S Carval, 'Limitation de la responsabilité contractuelle au dommage prévu ou prévisible' RDC 2015.790; article 1251 of the Draft Reform Project of Civil Liability adopts the same rule as article 1231-3.

[236] Terré, Simler, Lequette, and Chénédé (n 31) [831]–[833]; Chantepie and Latina (n 13) [683].

[237] Ibid.

[238] See article L113-1 of the Insurance Code.

[239] Civ 4 Feb 1969, D 1969.601, note J Mazeaud; Com 19 Jan 1993, JCP 1993.IV.711. For the specific areas of insurance, transport, and road accidents, see Viney and Jourdain (n 210) [618]–[626-2].

[240] Civ (3) 10 Feb 1999, Juris-Data no 1999-000659.

[241] Paris 15 Sept 1992, D 1993.98, note P Delebecque.

[242] See, for example, Mazeaud and Chabas (n 89) [2376]; B Starck, H Roland, and L Boyer, *Obligations—Contrats* (5th edn, Litec: Paris, 1995) [1446] and [1449].

[243] Y Chartier, *La réparation du préjudice* (Dalloz: Paris, 1983) [76].

good faith, reflecting the will of the legislature to deter parties from deliberately breaching their contractual obligations, which is regarded as an act of bad faith.[244]

The denial of the protection afforded by the remoteness principle and exclusion and limitation clauses to those who commit deliberate and dishonest breaches of contract also applies where there is gross negligence (*faute lourde*).[245] This was originally a judge-made exception to the remoteness principle but was codified in new article 1231-3 as part of the reforms.[246] Breaches that involve gross negligence may be unintentional but they are nevertheless particularly serious and usually involve negligence that is exceptional in nature. In the words of the *Cour de cassation*, they are epitomized by 'negligence of extreme gravity denoting the inaptitude of the promisor to perform his contractual obligation'.[247] It is this gravity that justifies the alignment of gross negligence with deliberate or dishonest breach.

In assessing the seriousness of a breach, French courts have taken into consideration a range of factors. These include the difficulty involved in performance, the means[248] and aptitude[249] of the defaulting party, the frequency and number of breaches,[250] the consequences of breach for the injured party,[251] and whether the breach is of a fundamental term.[252] As an example, an airline which failed to transport a parcel for twelve days without any justification was found to have committed gross negligence.[253] A similar finding was made in respect of a delivery company that used manifestly inappropriate material to transport a machine, thereby causing damage.[254] French courts have generally shown little hesitation in characterizing negligence as 'gross', taking a markedly expansive approach.[255] It has even been found in respect of a delivery company whose employee drove ten km/h above the authorized fifty km/h speed limit.[256]

[244] G Brière de L'Isle, 'La faute dolosive, tentative de clarification' D 1980 Chron 133, 135; D Nguyen Thanh-Bourgeais, 'Contribution à l'étude de la faute contractuelle: la faute dolosive et sa place actuelle dans la gamme des fautes' RTD civ 1973.497 [20].

[245] See, for example, Com 25 Mar 1963, D 1964.17, note R Rodière; Civ (1) 22 Nov 1978, JCP 1979.II.19139, note G Viney; Com 11 July 1995, Bull civ IV no 215. In contrast with deliberate faults, serious faults are insurable: Com 7 April 1987, Bull civ IV no 83.

[246] See articles 1366 and 1382-2 of the Catala proposals.

[247] Com 17 Dec 1951, Bull civ IV no 396; Com 26 Feb 1985, RTD civ 1986.773, obs Huet.

[248] Nguyen Thanh-Bourgeais (n 244) 511; Viney and Jourdain (n 210) [611]. See Civ (3) 22 April 1980, D 1980.IR.486.

[249] The standard to be attained will be more exacting if the promisor is a professional: Civ (1) 22 Nov 1978, JCP 1979.II.19139, note G Viney; Civ (1) 11 Oct 1966, JCP 1967.II.15193, note A de la Pradelle.

[250] For example, Com 3 April 2001, Bull civ IV no 70.

[251] Viney and Jourdain (n 210) [612].

[252] Civ (1) 18 Jan 1984, JCP 1985.II.20372, note J Mouly. See, however, Ch Mixte 22 April 2005, JCP 2005.II.10066, note G Loiseau; Com 21 Feb 2006, RDC 2006.694, obs D Mazeaud.

[253] Ass Plén 30 June 1998, JCP 1998.I.1311.

[254] Com 13 Nov 1990, Bull civ IV no 271.

[255] Viney and Jourdain (n 210) [610]–[612]; note that there has been an increasing tendency on the part of French courts to characterize breach as 'gross'.

[256] Com 28 June 2005, JCP 2005.II.10150, note E Tricoire.

### (b) No loss mitigation in French law

Notwithstanding early conceptual support from eminent French legal theorists such as Domat[257] and Pothier,[258] there is no general requirement upon the victim of a breach of a contractual or extra-contractual duty to mitigate their loss in the Civil Code.[259] This has been attributed at least in part to the mitigation principle not having reached a sufficient degree of abstraction to warrant inclusion by the time of the original codification exercise in 1804.[260] Since then, it has made only occasional appearances in discrete areas such as leases,[261] insurance,[262] and the international sale of goods.[263]

At a practical level, it was perhaps inevitable that French courts would nevertheless be faced with disputes in which an apparent failure to mitigate is invoked as a defence to a claim for damages. A review of relevant authorities, which mainly relate to extra-contractual liability, reveals that notions of mitigation have indeed surfaced intermittently, albeit French lawyers have never thought in terms of there being a 'duty' to mitigate.[264] Instead, the concept has been addressed obliquely under a variety of judicial guises, which has served to divert attention away from the potential relevance of mitigation.

The duty to mitigate has been considered in France, 'if at all, as an aspect of the need for a causal link'.[265] As an example in an extra-contractual context, where the victim of a car accident closed his business for several months in order to recover from his injuries, the Montpellier Court of Appeal refused to make an award in respect of the resulting economic loss on the basis that it was not an inevitable consequence of the accident. As soon as the victim had recovered his intellectual

[257] J Domat, *Les lois civiles dans leur ordre naturel* (Rollin et fils: Paris, 1745) vol 1 [162].

[258] R Pothier, *Traité des obligations* (Debure, Rouzeau-Montaut: Paris Orléans, 1764) vol 3 [162]. See also the support of R Demogue, *Traité des obligations en général* (Rousseau: Paris, 1923-1933) vol 6.

[259] See generally, S Le Pautremat, 'Mitigation of Damage' (n 42) 205; Y-M Laithier, 'La *Cour de cassation* refuse d'imposer au créancier le devoir de minimiser le dommage' RDC 2010.52; O Deshayes, 'L'introduction de l'obligation de modérer son dommage en matière contractuelle—Rapport français RDC 2010.1139; Y-M Laithier, 'Les sanctions de l'inexécution du contrat' RDC 2016 no Hors-série 39; Haftel (n 185) 143; Borghetti, Faut-il distinguer? (n 222) 787; O Deshayes, '"Existe-t-il un devoir de minimiser son dommage en matière contractuelle?" —Une question mal posée' RDC 2014.27; L Thibierge, 'La mesure des dommages-intérêts: question de fait ou question de droit? Libres réflexions au travers du prisme de la minimisation du préjudice' RDC 2019.193; G Viney, 'La victime n'est pas tenue de limiter son préjudice dans l'intérêt du responsable' RDC 2015.24

[260] A Michaud, 'Mitigation of Damage in the Context of Remedies for Breach of Contract' (1984) 15 RGD 293, 338; B Hanotiau, 'Régime juridique et portée de l'obligation de modérer le dommage dans les ordres juridiques nationaux et le droit du commerce international' RDAI 1987.393, 398; A Laude, 'L'obligation de minimiser son propre dommage existe-t-elle en droit privé français?' in *Faut-il moraliser le droit français de la réparation du dommage? (à propos des dommages et intérêts punitifs et de l'obligation de minimiser son propre dommage)* (*Colloque*) PA 2002 no 232.55, 55–6.

[261] See article 1760 of the Civil Code.

[262] See article L172-23 of the Insurance Code.

[263] See articles 75 and 77 of the United Nations Convention on Contracts for the International Sale of Goods (1980), which has been in force in France since 1988.

[264] Nicholas (n 233) 231–2.

[265] Ibid.

and managerial capability, he should have hired a replacement employee for the remaining period of his absence to run the business.[266] His omission to do so broke the causal link between the accident and the loss that arose from the closure of the business.

Finding a break in the causal chain is not the only way in which French courts have reduced the recovery of victims of breaches of contractual or extra-contractual duties for passivity in the face of accruing losses. In several personal injury cases, the refusal of minor surgery or other medical treatment that is potentially remedial and involves minimal risk has been held to be a fault (*faute de la victime*), justifying a reduction in the award.[267]

In a further notable case, the Versailles Court of Appeal invoked the doctrine of remoteness to achieve the same end, holding that a trader who had been supplied with defective products in breach of contract should have found a solution to limit the detriment flowing from the breach. Any damage resulting from their failure to do so was held to be unforeseeable by the parties at the time the contract was executed and therefore irrecoverable.[268]

The civil law notion of good faith has also been called upon to perform a similar function to mitigation in the context of a debt claim.[269] In a case that came before the Paris Court of Appeal, the injured party had declined to exercise a contractual option to serve a break notice to terminate a contract under which the defaulting party was significantly in arrears of payment. Dismissing his claim in respect of debts that accrued thereafter, the court held that to allow the contract to continue in such circumstances was an act of bad faith, by which the claimant effectively aggravated his own loss.[270]

The possibility of the disparate case law hinting at a latent mitigation principle in French law being united into a formal duty to mitigate was ended by the *Cour de Cassation*, initially in respect of extra-contractual liability and later contractual liability. This began with two decisions—both delivered on 19 June 2003[271]—in which the victim of a wrong was held not to have to mitigated their loss. In the words of the court, the wrongdoer 'should compensate the victim for all the losses flowing from the wrong and the victim is under no obligation to limit their loss

[266] Montpellier 9 Dec 1965, D 1967.477, note P Azard.

[267] Crim 3 July 1969, JCP 1970.II.16447, note R Savatier; Crim 30 Oct 1974, D 1975.178, note R Savatier. See, however, Civ (2) 19 March 1997, RTD civ 1997.675, obs P Jourdain, in which the *Cour de cassation* affirmed that, pursuant to article 16-3 of the Civil Code, 'except as provided by law, no one can be forced to undergo a surgical operation'.

[268] Versailles 26 Nov 1986, Gaz Pal 1987.II.402.

[269] Under English law, mitigation does not have any role in debt claims.

[270] Paris 22 June 2001, D 2002.843, note P-J Coulon.

[271] Civ (2) 19 June 2003 (Dibaoui c/Flamand), D 2003.2396; Civ (2) 19 June 2003 (Xhauflaire c/ Decrept), D 2003.2396. Reaffirmed on many occasions in the context of extra-contractual liability, for example Civ 3, 10 July 2013, no 12-13851; Civ 2, 26 Mar 2015, no 14-16011.

in the interest of the wrongdoer'.[272] This has since been reaffirmed on several occasions.[273]

The duty was then rejected by the *Cour de cassation* in a contractual context in conspicuously identical terms to the 2003 decisions. This symmetry was widely interpreted as being deliberate and intended to sound the death knell for any form of duty to mitigate in French law. The case concerned defective construction work that had caused subsidence in the basement of a house. Temporary supportive beams that were installed by the builder were then stolen, causing further damage that necessitated the demolition and reconstruction of the house. The builder argued that this should have been prevented by the owner of the house providing replacement structural support after the theft, rather than simply ignoring the issue and leaving the house abandoned over several months. Citing old article 1149, which is now article 1231-2, the *Cour de cassation* rejected this argument, holding that the defaulting party was liable to compensate all of the losses flowing from the breach, which the injured party was not under any duty to limit.[274]

True to the characteristically laconic style of its judgments, the *Cour de cassation* has never given a detailed explanation for rejecting the duty to mitigate. There is, however, no doubt as to the important role of the principle of full compensation and the inviolable aim of returning the victim as closely as monetarily possible to the position in which they would have been had the wrong not been committed.[275] Mitigation appears to be regarded by the court as conceptually incompatible with this principle, hence its insistence that the wrongdoer should be liable for *all of the losses* flowing from the wrong. Anything less would be under-compensatory and therefore inadequate.

A further possible reason has been put forward in academic commentary on the issue. It has been argued that the initial fault of the wrongdoer should entitle the victim to remain passive in the face of accumulating losses, without prejudicing their right to full compensation.[276] Any requirement to take positive action would compound the inconvenience caused by the breach and represent a further unacceptable encroachment on their freedom of action in a situation that is not of their own making.[277] It would be burdensome and unjust to require the victim to

[272] 'Attendu que l'auteur d'un accident est tenu d'en réparer toutes les conséquences dommageables; que la victime n'est pas tenue de limiter son préjudice dans l'intérêt du responsable.'

[273] Civ (3) 5 Feb 2013, no 12-12126; Civ (2) 25 Oct 2012, no 11-25511; Civ (3) 2 July 2014, no 13-17599.

[274] Civ (3) 10 July 2013, no 12-13851. For an earlier decision, see Civ (3) 19 May 2009 RDC 2010.1 52, note Y-M Laithier.

[275] See section E2 above on the measure of damages; Civ (2) 4 Feb 1982, JCP 1982.II.19894, note J-J Barbiéri.

[276] H Muir Watt, 'La modération des dommages en droit anglo-américain' in *Faut-il moraliser le droit français de la réparation du dommage? (à propos des dommages et intérêts punitifs et de l'obligation de minimiser son propre dommage)* (*Colloque*) PA 2002 no 232.45.

[277] On this point, see the note of E Rosenfeld and C Bouchez on Civ (2) 19 June 2003, Gaz Pal 2003.I.281; J-L Aubert, 'La victime peut-elle être obligée de minimiser son dommage?' RJDA 2004.355;

advance money to mitigate the ensuing losses without any certainty of being compensated.[278] To do so would be tantamount to a role reversal in which the equities shift in favour of the wrongdoer, for whose benefit the victim would effectively be put to work,[279] and would subordinate justice and fundamental values to economic interests.[280]

Surprisingly, and indeed somewhat remarkably in view of the unbending approach of the *Cour de cassation*, the Reform Bill on Civil Liability that is pending in France contains two provisions—articles 1237 and 1263—that would introduce a duty to mitigate into French law in both a contractual and an extra-contractual context. They provide that:

> Art. 1237.—Expenses incurred by a claimant in order to prevent the imminent occurrence of harm or to avoid its getting worse, as well as in order to reduce its consequences, constitute a repairable loss as long as they were reasonably undertaken.
>
> Art. 1263.—Except in the case of personal injuries, damages are reduced where the victim did not take safe and reasonable measures, notably having regard to his ability to pay, appropriate to avoid an increase in his own loss.[281]

Despite these proposals, the *Cour de cassation* has not shown any sign of changing tack. This is apparent, for example, from a decision in 2020[282]—some three years after the publication of the reform proposals—relating to a contract for the sale and maintenance of a catamaran that proved to be defective. Overturning the decision of the Paris Court of Appeal, it held that the buyer could recover damages in respect of losses that resulted from the vessel being in repair, and therefore unavailable, for a prolonged period that would have been avoided if the buyer had arranged for the vessel to be repaired promptly. The buyer was not under any obligation to repair the catamaran and was entitled to compensation for all the losses flowing from the breach.

P Jourdain, 'Rapport Introductif' in *Faut-il moraliser le droit français de la réparation du dommage? (à propos des dommages et intérêts punitifs et de l'obligation de minimiser son propre dommage)* (Colloque) PA 2002 no 232.1.

[278] See Rosenfeld and Bouchez (n 277); Aubert (n 277).

[279] See the notes of J-P Chazal D 2003.2326 and Y Dagorne-Labbé PA 2003 no 261.17 on Civ (2) 19 June 2003; P-Y Gautier, 'Contre Bentham: l'inutile et le droit' RTD civ 1995.820, 824.

[280] Gautier (n 279); G Viney, 'Rapport de synthèse' in *Faut-il moraliser le droit français de la réparation du dommage? (à propos des dommages et intérêts punitifs et de l'obligation de minimiser son propre dommage)* (*Colloque*) PA 2002 no 232.66.

[281] Ministère de la Justice, *Projet de réforme de la responsabilité civile* (13 March 2017), <http://www.justice.gouv.fr/publication/Projet_de_reforme_de_la_responsabilite_civile_13032017.pdf>; translated from French into English by S Whittaker in consultation with J-S Borghetti: *Reform Bill on Civil Liability* (March 2017) <http://www.textes.justice.gouv.fr/art_pix/reform_bill_on_civil_liability_march_2017.pdf≥ accessed 1 September 2021.

[282] Com 23 Sept 2020 no 15-28.898.

## 5 Agreed damages clauses

**Civil Code**

Art. 1231-5.—Where a contract stipulates that the person who fails to perform shall pay a certain sum of money by way of damages, the other party may be awarded neither a higher nor a lower sum.

Nevertheless, a court may, even of its own initiative, moderate or increase the penalty so agreed if it is manifestly excessive or derisory.

Where an undertaking has been performed in part, the agreed penalty may be reduced by a court, even of its own initiative, in proportion to the advantage which partial performance has procured for the creditor, without prejudice to the application of the preceding paragraph.

Any stipulation contrary to the preceding two paragraphs is deemed not written.

Except where non-performance is permanent, a penalty is not incurred unless the debtor was put on notice to perform.

It has long been recognized in France that liquidated damages and penalty clauses are valid. A liquidated damages clause fixes the amount of compensation payable in respect of a breach of contract, serving to minimize possible uncertainties relating to the quantum of liability that may otherwise require litigation to resolve.[283]

Penalty clauses impose liability that goes beyond compensation and aim to deter breach and coerce performance.[284] Their effectiveness derives from the ever-present threat of sanction for breach. This was justified by one of the drafters of the original Civil Code as an 'excellent expression of morality in forcing people to perform the obligations that they have undertaken'.[285]

### (a) Bringing together the articles of the Civil Code

As part of the reforms, all of the pre-existing articles on agreed damages and penalties were grouped together in a single provision, new article 1231-5, in the sub-section on loss compensation. This diverges from the 1804 Code, in which they were relative strangers. The enforceability of liquidated damages clauses was recognized in paragraph 1 of old article 1152 in the section on 'Compensatory Damages'. This stated that 'where the contract provides that the defaulting party should pay a specific sum as compensatory damages, the other party may not be awarded a

[283] P Delebecque, *Fasc 22: Régime de la réparation—Modalités de la réparation—Règles particulières à la responsabilité contractuelle—Clause pénale* (LexisNexis Jurisclasseur: Paris, 2005) [4].

[284] Article 1231-5 of the Civil Code; article 1284 of the Reform Bill on Civil Liability.

[285] P-A Fenet, *Recueil complet des travaux préparatoires du code civil* (Videcoq: Paris, 1836) vol 13, 324; Mazeaud (n 164) [92]–[151]; G Paisant, 'Dix ans d'application de la réforme des articles 1152 et 1231 du Code Civil relative à la clause pénale (Loi du 9 juillet 1975)' RTD civ 1985.647; Com 5 April 1994, JCP 1995.II.22384, note Y Dagorne-Labbé.

greater or lesser sum'. Penalty clauses were addressed much later in the Code, in old article 1226 in a section entitled 'Obligations with Penalty Clauses',[286] which provided that 'a penalty clause is a provision by which a party, so as to ensure performance of the contract, binds himself to something in case of non-performance'.

The decision to situate both of these provisions in the section of the Code dealing with compensation has puzzled some commentators.[287] It has been suggested that the drafters might have been seeking either to blur the distinction between liquidated damages clauses and penalty clauses or even to put an end to the enforceability of penalty clauses. The deletion from new article 1231-5 of the reference to the coercive aim of penalty clauses that appeared in old article 1226 ('to ensure performance of the contract') was argued to reinforce this view.[288]

If true, this would be surprising. New article 1231-5 uses the term 'penalty' in several places and perpetuates the power of the court to vary the amount of an excessive penalty. There is also nothing in the Report to the President or other materials published by the drafters to suggest they sought to abrogate the enforceability of penalty clauses or even dilute their force. To the contrary, article 1231-5 is described simply as bringing together the two articles.[289] It is therefore unlikely that such a drastic change was intended.

### (b) The power of the court to vary agreed damages clauses

Liquidated damages and penalty clauses are not impervious to judicial intervention. As a result of a reform made in 1975, French courts have the power to modify an agreed amount of damages downwards or upwards.[290] In the reformed Civil Code, paragraph 2 of article 1231-5 provides that 'a court may, even of its own initiative, moderate or increase the penalty so agreed if it is manifestly excessive or derisory'. In relation to part-performed obligations, paragraph 3 of article 1231-5 adds that 'the agreed penalty may be reduced by a court, even of its own initiative, in proportion to the advantage which partial performance has procured for the creditor'.

This judicial power of moderation is regarded in France as necessary to ensure the protection of weaker contracting parties, particularly consumers. It was introduced as part of a broader wave of consumer protection measures in reaction in particular to the proliferation of standard term contracts such as hire purchase and rental agreements, which were thought to be ripe for abuse by the unscrupulous.[291] At the time, draconian clauses requiring payment of extortionate sums on

[286] According to Viney and Jourdain (n 210) [229], and Mazeaud (n 164) [516].

[287] Chantepie and Latina (n 13) [687]; Deshayes, Genicon, and Laithier (n 10) 596–7.

[288] Chantepie and Latina (n 13) [687].

[289] F Ancel, B Fauvarque-Cosson, and J Gest, *Aux sources de la réforme du droit des contrats* (Dalloz: Paris, 2017) [24.121]; 'Report to the President' (n 15) 17.

[290] Although courts also have the power to modify clauses upwards, this power is rarely used. The Catala proposals suggested that this possibility should be removed.

[291] On this point, see E Alfandari, 'Le contrôle des clauses pénales par le juge' JCP 1971.I.2395.

the occurrence of a breach were not uncommon. The power enables the court to regulate potentially abusive clauses.

Whilst the coercive force of penalty clauses has undoubtedly been eroded by the scope for the court to vary agreements on damages,[292] it has not been extinguished. The parliamentary debates that preceded the 1975 reform are instructive, demonstrating that the legislature intended only to curtail the abuse of penalty clauses, not to cast doubt on their legitimacy or bring an end to their deterrent role.[293] On several occasions, their 'salutary deterrent character' was underlined.[294] This has also been recognized by the *Cour de cassation*, which has characterized penalty clauses as a permissible 'means of forcing the parties to perform'.[295]

Judicial decisions that pre-date the 2016 reforms show that the deterrent and punitive functions of penalty clauses are still very much alive. First, the exercise of the power to reduce the stipulated sum is considered to be exceptional and facultative.[296] The word 'manifestly' in article 1231-5 makes clear that the power is to be used exceptionally,[297] whilst the term 'may' points to a discretion rather than an obligation to intervene.[298] It follows that the defaulting party can never be confident that the court will be persuaded to order a reduction in the sum payable, thus preserving the deterrent and intimidatory effects of the penalty clause.[299]

Second, where a court exercises the power, it must explain the decision to do so with rigour. The *Cour de cassation* will carefully scrutinize any decision by a lower court that damages agreed by the parties should be reduced. As the Reims Court of Appeal found on one occasion, it is not sufficient that the stipulated sum is 'a little high'; it must be manifestly excessive.[300] Where, however, the court decides not to exercise the power, it need not give reasons. The power to reduce the agreed sum is, after all, to be exercised exceptionally. A strict application of the terms agreed by the parties remains the norm.[301]

Third, the manner in which courts approach the question of whether an agreed sum is 'manifestly excessive' leaves little room for doubt that the coercive role of penalty clauses continues. Although whether a clause is manifestly excessive will

[292] G Paisant, *Répertoire civil Dalloz, La clause pénale* (Dalloz: Paris, 2003) [19].

[293] Mazeaud (n 164) [144].

[294] J Foyer, *Exposé des motifs* (JOAN *Annexes* no 1365; JOAN 17 May 1975) 2861–2 cited by Mazeaud (n 164) [143].

[295] Civ (1) 3 Jan 1985, Bull civ I no 4; Com 27 Mar 1990, D 1990.390, note E-S de la Marnierre; Com 5 July 1994, Bull civ IV no 253.

[296] Paisant (n 292) 650; F Chabas, 'La réforme de la clause pénale (L No 75-597 du 9 juillet 1975)' D 1976 Chron 229, 234.

[297] Chabas (n 296) 234.

[298] For example, Soc 11 Dec 1991, RJDA 1992.322; Mazeaud (n 164) [139]; B Boccara, 'La réforme de la clause pénale: conditions et limites de l'intervention judiciaire' JCP 1975.I.2742, [33]; S Sanz, 'La consécration du pouvoir judiciaire par la loi du 9 juillet 1975 et ses incidences sur la théorie générale de la clause pénale' RTD civ 1977.268, 277–8.

[299] Mazeaud (n 164) [138]; Paisant (n 292) [19].

[300] Ch Mixte 20 Jan 1978, Bull civ no 1.

[301] Civ (1) 23 Feb 1982, Bull civ I no 85; Civ (1) 12 July 2001, Bull civ I no 218.

be assessed as at the date of judgment,[302] the subjective intention of the parties when they entered into the contract are taken into account. According to the *Cour de cassation*, 'while the stipulated penalty may be apprehended both as a means of forcing the parties to perform and as an agreed pre-estimate of future loss, its amount can, in both cases, be reduced by the judge, who must, in assessing its excessive character, take into account its aim'.[303] It follows that if the stipulated sum was clearly intended by the parties to have a deterrent effect, this will inform the approach of the court.

The intentions of the parties are far from the only factor relevant to whether an agreed sum is manifestly excessive. Consideration may also be given to the nature of the contract, existing professional usages, the bargaining position of the parties and, perhaps most obviously, the disproportion between the actual loss suffered and the amount of the stipulated sum.[304] In order to qualify as manifestly excessive, any disproportion should be extreme[305] or an obvious abuse of the coercive function of penalty clauses.[306] It is not sufficient that the stipulated sum does not match the actual loss suffered by the injured party. In the words of the Nice Tribunal de Grande Instance, 'such an interpretation would remove the efficacy of agreed sums, the precise aim of which is to ensure that the promisor will perform by threatening him with a sanction'.[307] Even where the promisee has suffered no loss at all, it does not necessarily follow that the agreed sum should be regarded as 'manifestly excessive'.[308]

Fourth, should a court decide to reduce an agreed sum, the reduction will not, as a general rule, completely deprive the award of coercive effect. The *Cour de cassation* has held that the award should not be reduced beneath the level of loss suffered and need not be capped at the amount of actual loss.[309] Reductions of manifestly excessive penalties rarely[310] have the effect that the remaining element of the award is purely compensatory, diluting or removing their potency.[311] In many cases, the agreed sum will be reduced to 'somewhere in between the actual loss suffered by the injured promisee and the level above which it has a manifestly excessive character'.[312] It is also not unusual for only the excess to be removed.[313] In short, French law permits all but the most extravagant clauses.

[302] Civ (1) 19 Mar 1980, Bull civ I no 95, 10 Mar 1998, RTD civ 1999.97, obs J Mestre.

[303] Civ (1) 3 Jan 1985, Bull civ I no 4; Com 27 Mar 1990, D 1990.390, note E-S de la Marnierre.

[304] Viney and Jourdain (n 210) [254]–[257]; Com 11 Feb 1997, RTD civ 1997.654, obs J Mestre.

[305] Delebecque (n 283) [121].

[306] Viney and Jourdain (n 210) [256].

[307] TGI Nice 19 July 1977, Rev Jur Com 1978.265, note E-M Bey; Douai 10 March 1976, RTD 1977.338, note G Cornu; Versailles 13 Oct 1989, D 1989.IR.301.

[308] Soc 21 Mar 1978, Bull civ V no 218; Mazeaud (n 164) [582].

[309] Com 23 Jan 1979, Bull civ IV no 30; Com 29 Jan 1991, Bull civ IV no 43.

[310] For an example of a decision which has reduced the agreed sum to a level which is purely compensatory, see Paris 18 Jan 1983 D 1983.IR.420, note Y Serra. See also Viney and Jourdain (n 210) [264].

[311] Com 23 Jan 1979, Bull civ IV no 30; Paris 12 July 1983, D 1983.IR.430; Paisant (n 292) [83].

[312] Com 21 July 1980, Gaz Pal 1980.I.207; TGI Angers 17 May 1977, Gaz Pal 1977.II.394.

[313] Paris 20 June 1995, D 1995.IR.187; Sanz (n 298) 278.

## 6 Punishment and restitution as other functions of damages?

The enforcement of penalty clauses indicates that deterrence and punishment are present in the French law of remedies, despite not being formally recognized objectives. This is also implied by the disapplication of the remoteness rule resulting in larger awards of damages where wrongful conduct is deliberate, and by the *astreinte*, a monetary sanction for non-compliance with court orders that is explained in the section of this chapter on specific enforcement.[314]

A number of commentators have argued that the role of deterrence and punishment should be formalized and developed in contexts where the existing array of civil remedies is too weak.[315] The paradigm is profitable wrongs, against which the protection afforded by compensatory damages and the criminal law is presently inadequate.

### (a) Profitable wrongs

A common denominator of profitable wrongs is that the 'beneficial consequences for the wrongdoer would not be undone by the simple reparation of any harm which it has caused'.[316] The wrongdoer must intend that, even taking into account any liability to compensate the losses that flow from the wrong, they will make a profit or save money.[317] Such wrongs have been characterized in France as 'morally condemnable',[318] 'morally shocking',[319] 'socially and economically harmful',[320] and 'unacceptable'.[321]

Two elements are thought to be particularly objectionable. First, that one party can infringe the private rights of the other, simply by paying compensation;[322]

[314] S Carval, *La responsabilité civile dans sa fonction de peine privée* (LGDJ: Paris, 1995) [18]–[19]; A Jault, *La notion de peine privée* (LGDJ: Paris, 2005) [36]–[41]; Rowan, *Remedies for Breach of Contract* (n 173) 44–5.

[315] Carval, *La responsabilité civile dans sa fonction de peine privée* (n 314) [18]–[19]; Jault (n 314).

[316] G Viney, 'Exposé des motifs: Sous-titre III. De la responsabilité civile (Article 1340 à 1386)' in *Avant-projet de réforme du droit des obligations et de la prescription: Rapport remis au garde des Sceaux* (La Documentation française: Paris, 2006) 159, 168.

[317] D Fasquelle, 'L'existence de fautes lucratives en droit français' LPA 20 November 2002 no 232 27, 30; G Viney, 'Projet de réforme du droit des obligations: les Éléments clés en matière de droit de la responsabilité' Revue Lamy Droit Civil 2005 no 22.

[318] F Graziani, 'La généralisation de l'amende civile: entre progrès et confusions' D 2018.428; J Meadel, 'Faut-il introduire la faute lucrative en droit français?' LPA 17 April 2006 no 77, 6; Y-M Laithier, 'Le prononcé de dommages-intérêts punitifs en cas de faute lucrative' in N Ferrier and A Pélissier (eds), *L'entreprise face aux Évolutions de la responsabilité civile* (Economica: Paris, 2012) 117, 117–18.

[319] Fasquelle (n 317) 28; P Jourdain, 'Rapport introductif' in 'Faut-il moraliser le droit français de la réparation du dommage? (À propos des dommages et intérêts punitifs et de l'obligation de minimiser son propre dommage)' LPA 20 November 2002 no 232, 3–4; M Chagny, 'La notion de dommages et intérêts punitifs et ses répercussions sur le droit de la concurrence—Lectures plurielles de l'article 1371 de l'avant-projet de réforme du droit des obligations' JCP G 2006.I.149.

[320] E Dreyer, 'La sanction de la faute lucrative par l'amende civile' D 2017.1136; B Javaux, 'L'amende civile, entre sanction pénale et punitive damages?' JCP G 2019.6.152.

[321] Graziani (n 318).

[322] On the negative perception of efficiency theories in the French legal community, see, for example, P Malinvaud, 'Le "contenu certain" du contrat dans l'avant projet 'chancellerie' de code des obligations'

second, that they do so intentionally with the calculation of making a gain.[323] The outrage lies in the deliberateness of the wrongdoing and the disregard of the law and the rights of the other. Both are violated with impunity and in exploitation of a deficiency in the available remedies.

On this basis, commentators have argued[324] that any financial incentives to break the law for profit should be neutered. These arguments have been met with general support from those tasked with reforming French contract and tort law but without any clear agreement on the most appropriate solution. Several proposals to introduce punitive damages, gain-based damages and, more recently, civil penalties into French law have come to naught.

### (b) Proposals for punitive damages, gain-based damages, and civil penalties

#### *(i) Punitive damages*

The introduction of punitive damages[325] was considered in the 'Proposals for Reform of the Law of Obligations and the Law of Prescription', commonly referred to as the 'Catala proposals'.[326] These proposals were made in 2005 against the background of the bicentenary of the Civil Code. Aimed at revising the articles of the Code relating to the law of contract, civil liability, unjust enrichment, and prescription, they were considered by many to be the most ambitious attempt to reform the core areas of French private law since the creation of the Civil Code in 1804.[327] Draft article 1371 provided as follows:

D 2008, 2551; P Ancel and others, 'Points de vue convergents sur le projet de réforme du droit des contrats' JCP 2008 I 213; D Mazeaud, D 2001, 3239.

[323] Dreyer (n 320).

[324] See Carval, *La responsabilité civile dans sa fonction de peine privée* (n 314); Graziani (n 318); J Prorok, 'L'amende civile dans la réforme de la responsabilité civile. Regard critique sur la consécration d'une fonction punitive Générale' RTD civ 2018.327.

[325] S Rowan, 'Comparative Observations on the Introduction of Punitive Damages in French Law' in J Cartwright, S Vogenauer, and S Whittaker (eds), *Reforming the French Law of Obligations, Comparative Reflections on the Avant-projet de réforme du droit des obligations et de la prescription ('the Avant-projet Catala')* (Hart Publishing: Oxford, 2009) 325. See also the proposal of the Béteille Law of 9 July 2010 (proposition de *loi* no 657 portant réforme de la responsabilité civile), which provided for punitive damages to be introduced for deliberate faults with a view to gain, subject to an upper limit of twice the amount of the compensatory damages awarded: <https://www.senat.fr/leg/ppl09-657.html> accessed 1 September 2021.

[326] *Avant-Projet de Réforme du Droit des Obligations (Art 1101 à 1386 du Code civil) et du Droit de la Prescription (Art 2234 à 2281 du Code Civil)* under the direction of P Catala, 22 September 2005 (Documentation Française, 2006) translated into English by J Cartwright and S Whittaker: at <www.justice.gouv.fr/art_pix/rapportcatatla0905-anglais.pdf> accessed 1 September 2021. See also generally J Cartwright, S Vogenauer, and S Whittaker (eds), *Reforming the French Law of Obligations: Comparative Reflections on the Avant-projet de réforme du droit des obligations et de la prescription ('the Avant-projet Catala')* (Hart Publishing: Oxford, 2009).

[327] S Vogenauer, 'The *Avant-projet de réforme*: An Overview' in J Cartwright, S Vogenauer, and S Whittaker (eds), *Reforming the French Law of Obligations: Comparative Reflections on the Avant-projet de réforme du droit des obligations et de la prescription ('the Avant-projet Catala')* (Hart Publishing: Oxford, 2009) 3.

> A person who commits a manifestly deliberate fault, and notably a fault with a view to gain, can be condemned in addition to compensatory damages to pay punitive damages, part of which the court may in its discretion allocate to the Public Treasury. A court's decision to order payment of damages of this kind must be supported with specific reasons and their amount distinguished from any other damages awarded to the victim. Punitive damages may not be the object of insurance.

The scope of the draft article was wide, encompassing both contractual and extra-contractual liability and applying regardless of the motives of the defaulting party. All 'manifestly deliberate faults', of which 'fault with a view to gain' was just one example, would have been caught and potentially subject to the remedy. It would also have been available where the wrongdoer acted not for profit but maliciously.[328]

The draft article generated much interest and comment. Reactions were mixed, with many endorsing the proposed introduction of punitive damages[329] and others more circumspect. A recurrent concern was that there would be undeserved windfalls and the seminal principle that compensation should be full and commensurate with the loss suffered (*principe de la réparation intégrale*) would be infringed.[330] There were also fears of litigation floodgates opening, as well as of arbitrariness and excess in the quantum of damages awards as in the United States.[331] Another criticism was that there was insufficient guidance as to the circumstances in which part of the punitive award should be directed to the state and in what proportion.[332]

*(ii) Gain-based damages*

Whilst the Catala proposals were never enacted, draft article 1371 proved to be the trigger for wider discussion and analysis of how best to tackle profitable wrongs. The criticisms made of punitive damages resulted in gain-based damages being proposed as an alternative by a competing reform project led by a group of

[328] This would avoid a criticism made by English commentators of Lord Devlin's second category in *Rookes v Barnard* [1964] AC 1129 (HL) that it does not allow punitive damages to be awarded where the wrongdoer acts not for profit but maliciously: *Broome v Cassell* [1972] AC 1027 (HL) 1088 per Lord Reid, who thought that the distinction between greed and malice could be justified only by reference to authority. See also Lord Nicholls in *Kuddus v Chief Constable of Leicestershire Constabulary* [2001] UKHL 29, [2002] 2 AC 122 [67].

[329] J-S Borghetti, 'Punitive Damages in France' in H Koziol and V Wilcox (eds), *Punitive Damages: Common Law and Civil Law Perspectives* (Springer: New York, 2009) 55.

[330] M Behar-Touchais, 'L'amende civile est-elle un substitut satisfaisant à l'absence de dommages et intérêts punitifs?' LPA 2002, 36; Borghetti, 'Faut-il distinguer? (n 222) [47]; Prorok (n 324).

[331] S Carval, 'L'amende civile' in 'Avant-projet de loi portant réforme de la responsabilité civile, Observations et propositions de modifications' JCP suppl 25 July 2016 42, [7]; Javaux (n 320); Borghetti, 'Faut-il distinguer?' (n 222) citing L Engel, 'Vers une nouvelle approche de la responsabilité. Le droit français face à la dérive américaine' Esprit 1993.

[332] 'Rapport du groupe de travail de la *Cour de cassation* sur l'avant-projet de réforme du droit des obligations et de la prescription' 15 June 2007. See also S Rowan, 'Reflections on the Introduction of Punitive Damages for Breach of Contract' (2010) 30 OJLS 495.

academic lawyers. In their draft article 120, they proposed that 'in case of deliberate breach, the injured promisee may be awarded [instead of compensatory damages] all or some of the profit resulting from the breach'.[333]

This was met with broad approbation[334] as a less drastic and more proportionate solution, but there were also concerns that it would be too weak. As it would be limited to gains accruing from the wrongful conduct, a party tempted to commit a profitable wrong might form the view that they have little to lose. With the punitive and deterrent effects removed, at worst they would be deprived of their ill-gotten gains.[335]

*(iii) The latest proposal: civil penalties*

As a middle ground between punitive damages and gain-based damages,[336] the mechanism proposed in the most recent reform project in 2017, albeit only for extra-contractual liability and not contractual liability, is the civil penalty (*amende civile*). Draft article 1266-1 provides as follows:

> In extra-contractual matters, where the author of the harm has deliberately committed a fault with a view to gain or making a saving, a court may, at the request of the victim or the *ministère public* (the state) and by specially reasoned decision, order payment of a civil penalty.
>
> This penalty is proportionate to the seriousness of the fault, the financial means of the wrongdoer, and the profit gained from the wrongful conduct.
>
> The penalty cannot be more than tenfold the amount of the profit gained.
>
> If the wrongdoer is a corporation, the penalty can be up to 5% of the amount of the highest turnover before tax made in France in the tax years since the year preceding that when the fault was committed.
>
> This penalty is directed to the financing of a compensation fund related to the nature of the harm suffered or, failing this, to the public treasury.
>
> It is not insurable.

Civil penalties are already made in various contexts in France.[337] The aim is to deter and punish conduct that is reprehensible but insufficiently serious for criminal liability. This includes the breach by state officials of certain public duties;[338]

[333] Article 120, Terré Reform Project.

[334] R Mesa, 'L'opportune consécration d'un principe de restitution intégrale des profits illicites comme sanction des fautes lucratives' D 2012.2754; Carval, 'L'amende civile' (n 331). See also Z Jacquemin, 'Pour une reconnaissance de la spécificité contractuelle dans les effets de la responsabilité' RDC 2016.808; Laithier, 'Le prononcé de dommages-intérêts punitifs en cas de faute lucrative' (n 318) 117; Y-M Laithier, 'Clause pénale et dommages et intérêts incitatifs' in C Jamin (ed), *Droit et Économie des contrats* (LGDJ: Paris, 2008) 141.

[335] Prorok (n 324).

[336] *Projet de réforme de la responsabilité civile* (n 281).

[337] Behar-Touchais (n 330); Jault (n 314) [402]; Borghetti, 'Faut-il distinguer? (n 222) [18]–[21].

[338] Article 50 of the Civil Code.

bringing court proceedings abusively;[339] and demolishing a building without the requisite permission.[340]

In proposing civil penalties, the drafters sought to achieve a compromise between punitive and gain-based damages.[341] Whilst less severe than punitive damages, a civil penalty will usually hurt the defaulting party more than gain-based damages, partly through being calculated by reference to the gravity of the fault. This may be much higher than the profit made from the wrong, as well as being high in absolute terms.[342]

Since payment is made into a designated fund set up to counteract at a general level the negative consequences of the wrongful conduct, the victim is not benefited directly.[343] This is faithful to the cardinal principle that the victim should not be awarded any more than is necessary to compensate their loss[344] and also to the overarching purpose of civil liability in France, which is the reparation of wrongs.[345]

The application of draft article 1266-1 to extra-contractual liability but not contractual liability was justified by the drafters on the basis that contracting parties can incorporate a penalty clause in their contract if they wish to deter and punish breach. There were also fears that to import civil penalties into a contractual setting was too radical and might deter international businesses from opting for French law as their governing law in cross-border contracts.[346]

The exclusion of breach of contract from the draft article is, however, surprising when seen in the context of the proposals in the two previous projects. It is also an about-turn from an earlier draft of the article, which did not contain any such exclusion. The reality is that breaches are committed with a view to making a gain or a saving, which is perceived in France as objectionable. It seems questionable to exclude breach of contract simply to keep deterrence and punishment out of contract law unless agreed otherwise. As mentioned earlier, both are already present in French contract law, for example in the disapplication of the remoteness rule for deliberate breaches.[347] Specific enforcement, which has a central role in the

[339] Article 32-1 of the New Code of Civil Procedure.

[340] Articles L430-2 and L430-9 of the Urban Code.

[341] *Projet de réforme de la responsabilité civile* (n 281).

[342] Dreyer (n 320); Prorok (n 324).

[343] Carval, 'L'amende civile' (n 331) 42; *Projet de réforme de la responsabilité civile* (n 281).

[344] Borghetti, 'Faut-il distinguer? (n 222) [50]; Dreyer (n 320) [13]; Prorok (n 324); Graziani (n 318); M Cappelletti, 'Comparative Reflections on Punishment in Tort Law' in J-S Borghetti and S Whittaker (eds), *French Civil Liability in Comparative Perspective* (Hart Publishing: Oxford, 2019) 329.

[345] Borghetti, 'Faut-il distinguer? (n 222) [47]; *Projet de réforme de la responsabilité civile* (n 281); Prorok (n 324); Graziani (n 318).

[346] S Carval, 'Le projet de réforme de la responsabilité civile', JCP 2017.401; J-S Borghetti, 'Un pas de plus vers la réforme de la responsabilité civile: présentation du projet de réforme rendu public le 13 mars 2017' D 2017.770; T d'Alès and L Terdjman, 'L'introduction envisagée de mécanismes répressifs dans le droit de la responsabilité civile: le Rubicon sera-t-il franchi?' AJ Contrat 2017.69.

[347] See pp 198–208; S Rowan, 'Reflections on the Introduction of Punitive Damages for Breach of Contract' (2010) 30 OJLS 495.

remedial framework in France, also deters breach and can seem punitive in some circumstances in view of its broad and relatively unrestricted availability.

Only the pre-contractual period, which is governed by extra-contractual principles, is within the scope of draft article 1266-1. This is already subject to several significant rules that regulate the conduct of the parties, as explained in Chapter 4.[348] Article 1112 of the Civil Code requires that negotiations must be conducted in good faith and article 1112-1 imposes a general duty to provide information (*devoir d'information*). Under the proposed reforms, a party who fails to disclose information, for example with a view to making a gain or a saving, faces not only the threat of compensatory liability, but also exposure to a civil penalty.[349]

## F Conclusion

Four features of the reforms in particular have cast a new complexion on the French law of remedies. These are the introduction of notions of reasonableness and proportionality; the expansion of self-help relief; the prioritization of performance in kind; and the inspiration drawn by the drafters from external influences.

### 1 The introduction of standards of reasonableness and proportionality

Reasonableness and proportionality are now requirements of several remedies. Specific enforcement, replacement, price reduction, and termination[350] are all newly subject to these standards. This is a significant change and strikes a fairer balance between the parties. Extreme outcomes that subjugate the interests of the defaulting party to those of the injured party can now more easily be avoided. To that extent French law seems likely to be more attractive to commercial parties—one of the main aims of the reformers.

### 2 The expansion of self-help powers

Several self-help powers were introduced or formalized as part of the reforms. The right of the injured party to obtain relief unilaterally is now a feature of withholding performance, replacement, price reduction, and termination. No longer the only arbiter of remedies for non-performance, the court has a much reduced

[348] See Chapter 4 and the section on pre-contractual negotiations, pp 59–66.
[349] Prorok (n 324).
[350] Through the requirement of a sufficiently serious breach at article 1224.

role. Indeed, unless the defaulting party brings proceedings to challenge the exercise of a remedy, it is entirely absent from the process.[351]

Empowering the injured party in this way has undoubtedly made the French remedial regime less rigid and more flexible, and therefore more commercially attractive. It is now possible for the victim of a breach to take responsive action (in some contexts pre-emptively) more easily, quickly, and inexpensively. A failed or distressed contract can be abandoned and resources reallocated to other opportunities more readily, minimizing the losses of both parties. This can only serve their commercial interests.

It remains to be seen whether this assists in achieving the objectives of making French law more competitive and influential abroad, attracting foreign investors, and incentivizing the preference of French law as the governing law in commercial contracts.[352] In some aspects, the new powers are obscure and lack guidance.[353] This is all the more significant given that they can be exercised unilaterally. Faced with the unwelcome adversities of a breach of contract, the injured party needs to be able to evaluate their options and the risk of a self-help remedy being challenged. Leaving uncertainties to be resolved by lower courts does little to promote confidence in the remedy.

This concern is particularly acute in the context of termination. The absence of guidance as to what constitutes a breach that is 'sufficiently serious' to justify termination under article 1224 is a cause of real uncertainty. This is accentuated by the prospect that, if the remedy is exercised wrongfully, the injured party will themselves be exposed to possible claims for breach. Another source of uncertainty is the power of the court to resurrect a contract that has been formally terminated. This exposes the parties to the potential vagaries inherent in judicial discretion.

There is also inconsistency between the new self-help powers. The anticipatory *exception d'inexécution* in new article 1220 enables the promisee to suspend their own performance as soon as it becomes evident that the other party will not perform by the due date, if the consequences of breach are sufficiently serious.[354] There is, however, no equivalent right to terminate anticipatorily, even though this would have been consonant with the *exception*. Performance can therefore be suspended before becoming due but the contract cannot be brought to an end.

[351] It is therefore argued that it is inaccurate to say, as some commentators have (see, for example, N Ancel, 'Le juge et les remèdes à l'inexécution du contrat' RDC 2016.408) that the role of the court has not been reduced but simply shifted to determining whether termination is justified or wrongful.

[352] J Cartwright has sought to look at the strengths and weaknesses of French contract law. His conclusion was that the considerable powers of French courts, which have been reinforced in the reform, would discourage foreign professionals from choosing French law to govern their contracts: see J Cartwright, 'Un regard anglais sur les forces et faiblesses du droit français des contrats' RDC 2015.691.

[353] See the discussion on replacement above, [cross-refer].

[354] See Mekki (n 63) 1344 who argues that the risk of breach justifies that performance be suspended, not that the whole contract be brought to an end.

## 3 The strong protection afforded to performance

Despite the moderating force of the new standards of reasonableness and proportionality and the greater flexibility of the new self-help powers, the reformed law of remedies is still very protective of performance and the agreement of the parties. This is apparent in various aspects of the new regime. One is the general requirement upon the injured party to give notice before seeking a remedy that performance must be effected within a reasonable period of time (*mise en demeure*). This affords the defaulting party additional time and opportunity to perform. The effect is to give 'priority to performance'[355] over other remedies, constraining at least initially their freedom of action.

A second aspect is that there is formal recognition of the broad availability and cardinal role in the French remedial regime of specific enforcement, which now also extends to unilateral agreements. This confirms that the remedy is available for the very large majority of contracts. There is consensus that this status should not be negated significantly by the new 'manifestly disproportionate' limitation. It is therefore likely to remain at the heart of the entire remedial system for breach of contract.

Third, the damages regime in France is generous to the injured party. Non-pecuniary loss generally sounds in damages, in line with the principle of full compensation. There is no duty to mitigate, out of a concern not to burden the injured party with responsibility for reducing the liability of the defaulting party.

Lastly, termination remains a remedy of last resort. An injured party who wishes to terminate, whilst now able to do so unilaterally, will nevertheless encounter material impediments. These include the requirements to provide reasons in the notice to terminate and to prove that the breach is sufficiently serious. The adjudicative role of the court may now depend upon the termination being disputed but, when seised, it still has wide powers that favour saving the contract. Even when terminated, a contract can be resurrected or the defaulting party given more time to perform through the award of a grace period. The emphasis is on upholding performance rather than encouraging or even being passive in the face of an attempt to terminate. As between terminating the contract and compelling its performance, French law clearly favours the latter.

## 4 External influences

A number of commentators have noted, without enthusiasm, that the reforms move the French law of remedies closer to the common law.[356] This can be seen

[355] Borghetti, 'Faut-il distinguer? (n 222) [10]–[11].

[356] Mekki (n 63); Terré, Simler, Lequette, and Chénédé (n 31) [128]; N Martial-Braz 'L'objectivation des méthodes d'interprétation: la référence à la "personne raisonnable" et l'interprétation in favorem'

in several respects through a comparison with English law. The first relates to the new limitations on the availability of specific enforcement and replacement. In England, specific performance will generally be refused where it would cause undue hardship to the defaulting party[357] or give rise to cost that is wholly out of proportion to the benefit to the injured party.[358] The courts also have regard to any hardship that might be occasioned to third parties.[359]

Similarly, monetary relief that enables the injured party to obtain substitute performance from a third party, known as cost of cure damages, is subject to a requirement of reasonableness and proportionality.[360] When out of proportion to the benefit that would accrue to the injured party, it is regarded as unduly burdensome and refused.[361] This avoids undue hardship for the defaulting party. It has also been rationalized by reference to the principle of loss mitigation[362] and the interest in preventing economically wasteful conduct.[363]

Second, the formal recognition of self-help remedies, in particular termination, embraces a right of unilateral action that is long established in England[364] where, in the context of termination, it is triggered by a breach that is repudiatory. The injured party has an election between terminating and affirming the contract.[365] An election to terminate is exercised autonomously, without any need for an order from the court.[366] This does not, however, mean that the court has no role to play. As under the French reforms, a defaulting party who wishes to challenge an attempt to terminate can do so by bringing proceedings. It is for the court to determine whether the contract was terminated effectively. In many cases, ancillary issues as to the consequences of termination and, in particular, competing claims to compensatory damages also need to be determined.

However, the parallels between French and English remedies should not be overstated. There remain notable differences. For example, in England, specific relief is not even close to being comprehensively available. Whilst orders for the payment

RDC 2015.193 [2]: 'This standard of reasonableness… is imported directly from our Anglo-Saxon friends.'

357 *Francis v Cowcliffe* [1976] 33 P & CR 368 (Ch); *Patel v Ali* [1984] Ch 283; *Wedgwood v Adams* [1843] 49 ER 958 at 960 (Lord Langdale MR).

358 *Tito v Waddell (No 2)* [1977] Ch 106, 325–8 (Megarry V-C); *Co-operative v Argyll* [1998] AC 1 (HL).

359 Rowan, *Remedies for Breach of Contract* (n 173) 142.

360 *Radford v De Froberville* [1977] 1 WLR 1262 (Ch) 1270 (Oliver J); *Ruxley Electronics and Construction Ltd v Forsyth* [1996] AC 344 (HL).

361 C Webb, 'Performance and Compensation: An Analysis of Contract Damages and Contractual Obligation' (2006) 26 OJLS 41, 63; *Ruxley Electronics* [1996] 353 (Lord Bridge) and 373 (Lord Lloyd).

362 G Treitel, *An Outline of the Law of Contract* (6th edn, OUP: Oxford, 2004) 382.

363 *Farley v Skinner* [2002] 2 AC 732 (HL) [21] (Lord Steyn).

364 For example, Martial-Braz (n 356) [2].

365 Although in *MSC Mediterranean Shipping Company SA v Cottonex Anstalt* [2016] EWCA Civ 789 (CA) the Court of Appeal found that it was not open to the injured party to affirm the contract where the defaulting party was not able to perform.

366 For a statutory exception, see Consumer Credit Act 1974, s 90.

of agreed amounts are commonly made and prohibitory injunctions are generally available, specific performance and mandatory injunctions are exceptional—very much the poor relation of compensatory damages, which is the primary remedy. This is due to a combination of historical idiosyncrasies, a reluctance to resort to the severe sanction of contempt of court through which such orders are enforced, and perceived difficulties in supervising compliance. The result is that specific relief is not nearly as protective of performance as in France.

Damages awards are also narrower than in France. Non-pecuniary loss is not generally compensable, largely based on an assumption that the interests of the parties are principally commercial.[367] The scope for recovery is further restricted by the duty to mitigate, which requires the victim of a breach to act reasonably to minimize their loss. A failure to do so will result in any damages award being reduced commensurately.

Whilst the guiding principle in both jurisdictions is *pacta sunt servanda*, which means that one must perform that which one has promised, countervailing considerations are given more weight in England than in France. These include the inappropriateness of conferring a windfall on the injured party, the potentially negative implications of over-burdening the defaulting party, the desirability of encouraging self-reliance in the injured party, the avoidance of waste, whether an outcome makes economic sense and commercial pragmatism.

Other differences are identifiable in the context of termination. One is the absence in English contract law of any significant procedural requirements for unilateral termination. The injured party needs only to communicate to the defaulting party—orally or in writing—that the contract is at an end.[368] There is no requirement to give a reason, provided that a valid reason and an entitlement to terminate exist.[369] Termination takes effect immediately. The court does not have the power to allow the defaulting party additional time to perform.[370] This is due to a desire for commercial certainty and speedy resolution of disputes.[371] This is in contrast with the requirements in new article 1226 of the Civil Code that the injured party

[367] There has been growing recognition that the interest in contractual performance is not measurable exclusively by the pecuniary disadvantage that results from the breach. Exceptions to the rule have been created and recently extended: see Rowan, *Remedies for Breach of Contract* (n 173) 129–30.

[368] *Vitol SA v Norelf Ltd (the 'Santa Clara')* [1996] AC 800 (HL) (Lord Steyn).

[369] *James Spencer Co Ltd v Tame Valley Padding Co Ltd* 8 April 1998, unreported (CA); *SNCB Holding v UBS AG* [2012] EWHC 2044 (Comm); [2012] All ER (D) 259 [73] (Cooke J); on this point, see R Brownsword, 'Retrieving Reasons, Retrieving Rationality? A New Look at the Right to Withdraw for Breach of Contract' (1992) 5 Journal of Contract Law 83.

[370] Whittaker, 'A Period of Grace for Contractual Performance?' (n 33) 1083. For examples of statutory exceptions, see the Law Property Act 1925, s 146; the Consumer Credit Act 1974, ss 76, 87, and 98; see the exceptions mentioned to this general principle in S Rowan, 'Resisting Termination: Some Comparative Observations' in A Dyson, J Goudkamp, and F Wilmot-Smith (eds), *Defences in Contract* (Hart Publishing: Oxford, 2017), 163.

[371] Rowan, 'Resisting Termination: Some Comparative Observations' (n 370); see also R Hooley, 'Controlling Contractual Discretion' (2013) 72 CLJ 65, 84.

serves a notice on the defaulting promisor stating that the contract is at an end and the grounds of termination

There are also notable differences in the grounds on which the defaulting party can resist termination and the role of the court in protecting their interests. In English law, once the right to terminate has arisen, there is usually little the defaulting party can do to resist.[372] Unlike in France, the remedy for wrongful termination is not generally to compel performance but damages to compensate the resulting loss.

In reality, and as openly acknowledged by the drafters of the reforms, the main source of inspiration for the new provisions on remedies was not English law but a number of the international projects on contract law.[373] This is true of the way that the provisions are arranged and their substantive content. As to the former, both the PECL and UNIDROIT Principles contain sections that are entirely dedicated to, and group together, the various available remedies. This is now mirrored in the reformed Civil Code.

Similarly, the substantive content of the new French regime 'borrows'[374] extensively from these instruments. Both provide for performance to be withheld—including anticipatorily[375]—and price reduction.[376] Enforced performance—of which replacement is seen as a species—is their main remedy, at least as a starting point.[377] Its centrality is, however, subject to exceptions that are referable to the economic cost and disproportion of the remedy,[378] which the drafters also drew upon.[379] The comments to article 7.2.2(b) of the UNIDROIT Principles note that performance will be 'unreasonably burdensome or expensive' only in exceptional circumstances,[380] confirming that, as in France, the right to performance is very much the rule.

The French reforms also move the rules on termination in the direction of the PECL and UNIDROIT Principles. Where the breach is fundamental in nature,[381] in both the PECL and the UNIDROIT Principles as now in France, the injured party can terminate the contract by notice.[382] There is also scope under both

[372] Ibid.

[373] Ancel, Fauvarque-Casson, and Gest (n 289) [24.71] and [24–101].

[374] Ibid., [24.91]

[375] Article 9:201 of the PECL; article 7.3.4 of the UNIDROIT Principles goes further: 'a party who reasonably believes that there will be a fundamental non-performance by the other party may demand adequate assurance of due performance and may meanwhile withhold its own performance'.

[376] See article 9:401 of the PECL; article III 3:601 of the Draft Common Frame of Reference; article 50 of the Vienna Convention (CISG).

[377] H Schelhaas, 'Commentary on article 7.1 of the UNIDROIT principles' in S Vogenauer (ed), *Commentary on the UNIDROIT Principles of International Commercial Contracts (PICC)* (2nd edn, OUP: Oxford, 2015) [2]–[12] in commentary to article 7.2.2 of the UNIDROIT Principles. See articles 7.2.1 and 7.2.2 of the UNIDROIT Principles; articles 9:101 and 9:102 of the PECL.

[378] Article 7.2.2 (b) refers to an 'unreasonably burdensome or expensive' enforcement.

[379] Ancel, Fauvarque-Casson, and Gest (n 289) [24.91].

[380] Schelhaas (n 377) 893–4.

[381] Article 7.3.1 of the UNIDROIT Principles; article 9:301 of the PECL.

[382] Under article 7.3.2 of the UNIDROIT Principles and article 9:303 of the PECL.

instruments for the notice to allow additional time for the defaulting party to perform, effectively giving them a second chance.[383]

However, the drafters stopped short of adopting the remedial regimes in these instruments in full. There are a range of differences. One example already mentioned relates to the criteria for establishing when a serious breach entitles the injured party to terminate.[384] Another is that, unlike in France (but as in England), termination before the date for performance is available under both the PECL[385] and the UNIDROIT Principles.[386] The UNIDROIT Principles also do not permit the court to grant a grace period, out of concern not to delay the injured party in exercising the right to terminate.[387] The defaulting party does though have a right to cure defective performance where done promptly and the injured promisee has no legitimate reason to refuse, unless time is of the essence.[388]

383 Article 8:106 of the PECL.
384 See above for the requirement of a sufficiently serious breach [cross-refer xx].
385 Article 9:304 of the PECL.
386 Article 7.3.3 of the UNIDROIT Principles.
387 Schelhaas (n 377) 827–8.
388 See article 7.1.4 of the UNIDROIT Principles and article 8:104 of the PECL.

# 11
# Concluding Remarks

The reform of the contract law section of the Civil Code was intended to mark the dawn of a new era after the extraordinary longevity of the 1804 Code. There would at last be a contemporary framework for contractual relationships, at once more comprehensive and in tune with the challenges of the twenty-first century and a rapidly globalizing world. It would be more up-to-date, accessible, certain, predictable, attractive to business, and credible as an alternative to the major common law systems, whilst also fairer. Have these ambitious objectives been met?

Some clearly positive steps forward have been made but in other respects the drafters appear to have struggled to reconcile the classical tensions between freedom of contract, transactional certainty, and the protection of the weak. The result is that the main tenets of the new French law of contract are not always easy to discern. There is a particular and overarching concern that the powers of French courts to interfere with the substantive terms of the contract have been expanded. This is likely to be a source of ongoing uncertainty that is compounded by the absence of clear guiding principles by which the courts must abide. Although perhaps of comfort to some, this will hardly escape the notice of prospective international users of the Civil Code, who are unlikely to be enthused.

## A More Accessible and Predictable?

The first objective of the reforms was to make the Code more up-to-date, accessible, and predictable. There is a consensus that largely this has been achieved. The text and terminology are simpler and more modern. Structurally, the new articles are helpfully ordered in a sequence that corresponds to the life cycle of the contract. This begins with formation, followed by validity, interpretation, the effect between the parties, privity and, lastly, remedies for breach. In certain areas, the articles were reorganized in a more logical way. For example, the provisions on remedies, which were previously dispersed across the 1804 Code, are now grouped together in a single section and a coherent order (articles 1217 to 1231-7).

With the codification of many principles that had been developed in decided cases and the resolution of a number of long-running controversies and debates, the new Code is an altogether fuller and more accurate statement of French contract law. As a result, the need to delve into past cases to interpret the Code is now much reduced. One illustration is the introduction of a new subsection on contract

*The New French Law of Contract.* Solène Rowan, Oxford University Press. © Solène Rowan 2022.
DOI: 10.1093/oso/9780198810872.003.0011

formation. As Chapter 4 on the formation of contracts explained, this is an area on which the 1804 Code was completely silent, with the applicable rules developed and to be found exclusively in the cases. By contrast the new Code contains a total of fifteen articles on pre-contractual negotiations, offer and acceptance, and pre-contractual agreements (articles 1112 to 1127-6). Other examples analysed in the preceding chapters include the codification of fundamental principles such as freedom of contract, the binding force of the contract and good faith (articles 1102, 1103, and 1104), the formal recognition of the *dénaturation* power of review of the *Cour de cassation* in the context of contractual interpretation (article 1192), and the codification of the centrality of the remedy of specific enforcement (article 1221).

## B More Commercially Orientated, Competitive, and Fair?

Another objective was to make French contract law more commercially attractive and competitive whilst at the same time promoting substantive fairness (*justice contractuelle*). In some respects, the reformed Code is more business friendly. A number of the innovations that were introduced in the reforms are likely to appeal to commercial parties. An obvious example is the new provisions on remedies for breach of contract, which are now less rigid, more flexible, and strike a better balance between the competing interests of the parties. The new exception to specific enforcement where there is 'manifest disproportion' between the cost of performance and the interest of the injured party in enforcing performance enables the court to reach more proportionate results that avoid punishing the defaulting party (article 1221). Similarly, the options that are newly available to the injured party to suspend performance (article 1220), reduce the contract price (article 1223), and terminate unilaterally combine greater flexibility with reduced scope for interference by the court (article 1226). In the case of termination, for example, the injured party can escape from the failed contract and reallocate their resources to other opportunities more quickly, minimizing the losses on both sides of the contract. This can only serve the interests of commercial parties.

There are, however, other innovations which it seems will be unlikely to appeal to commercial parties or reformers in other countries.[1] Whilst the reforms have curtailed the reach of the court in some contexts, paradoxically, there are new powers for the court to rebalance the contract in others. These are intended to promote substantive fairness and protect the weaker party but come at the expense of transactional certainty.[2] The most striking examples are the greater prominence

[1] J Cartwright, 'Un regard anglais sur les forces et les faiblesses du droit français des contrats' RTD 2015.691.

[2] B Fauvarque-Cosson, 'The French Contract Law Reform and the Political Process' (2017) 13 European Review of Contract Law 337, 348; H Barbier, 'Les grands mouvements du droit commun des contrats après l'ordonnance du 10 février 2016' RTD civ 2016.247; M Fabre-Magnan, 'What is a

for the principle of good faith (article 1104), the expanded powers to strike down unfair terms (articles 1168 to 1171), and the new provisions on *imprévision* that allow the court to adjust the risk allocation agreed by the parties (article 1195).

A related concern is that the reforms provide no clear guidance as to how these new powers should be exercised, inevitably compounding the already significant uncertainties. For example, the new powers in respect of unfair terms and *imprévision* are worded very broadly with key terms not defined.[3] Similarly, the reformed Code gives new prominence to good faith both as an over-arching principle and in specific articles but the concept is not defined even though it is notoriously elusive and considered by many to be vague. The enlarged scope for court intervention and the attendant uncertainties seem more likely to deter international businesses than act as an enticement away from familiar common law rules.

## C Explaining the Lack of Coherency

The absence of a coherent approach to the competing values of freedom of contract, transactional certainty, and the promotion of fairness makes aspects of the new French contract law hard to fathom. There is a sense that the drafters tried too hard to accommodate the divergent views and interests of the many and various constituencies that were consulted during the process. The result is that no clear underlying philosophy emerges, or is even discernible, and some of the compromises can be difficult to reconcile.[4]

This has also been attributed to the reforms being in gestation for almost fifteen years, but with no real continuity amongst those working on the project[5] and instead a changing array of participants and influences. A further contributory factor may be that the process began with the Ministry of Justice 'cherry-picking' certain provisions from prior reform projects in 2005[6] and 2007,[7] but seemingly without any attempt to adopt the theoretical foundations and internal coherency of either. The Ministry of Justice also consulted widely, including amongst academics, judges, practitioners, businesses representatives, and consumer lobby groups, as

Modern Law of Contracts?' (2017) 13 European Review of Contract Law 376, 378–80; H Muir-Watt, 'The Reform of the French Civil Code at a Distance: An International and Comparative Perspective' (2017) 13 European Review of Contract Law 445, 449.

[3] See Chapter 7 on unfair terms; see Chapter 9 on *imprévision*.

[4] J-S Borghetti, 'Le nouveau droit français des contrats, entre continuité et Européanisation' in *Annuario del contratto* 2016, 2017.3, 9.

[5] Ibid.

[6] *Avant-Projet de Réforme du Droit des Obligations (Art 1101 à 1386 du Code civil) et du Droit de la Prescription (Art 2234 à 2281 du Code Civil) under the direction of P Catala, 22 Sept 2005* (Paris: Documentation française, 2006) translated in English by J Cartwright and S Whittaker: http://www.justice.gouv.fr/art_pix/rapportcatatla0905-anglais.pdf accessed 1 September 2021.

[7] F Terré, *Pour une réforme du droit des contrats* (Paris: Dalloz, 2008).

well as initiating in 2015 a public consultation on a draft of the decree, which received more than 3,000 pages of comments.[8] It sought to take account of as many views as possible and find some degree of middle ground.[9] The draft decree that emerged was then reviewed by the National Assembly and the Senate at the ratification stage, resulting in a significant number of substantive amendments and ultimately culminating in an end product that was a real patchwork of ideas.

With the benefit of hindsight, there is also a question as to the extent of the commitment of the drafters to making French contract law more attractive internationally and competitive with common law regimes. To achieve this objective would have required some degree of convergence with the features that make these regimes attractive to commercial parties. By common consensus, in England these include transactional certainty and predictability of outcome over absolute justice;[10] significant autonomy for parties to agree the terms that they wish; principles that give effect to those terms and enable enforcement with minimal judicial intervention; and the absence of any general jurisdiction to invalidate terms based on notions of reasonableness, fairness, unconscionability, or good faith, which are perceived to create uncertainty.[11] It was unrealistic to aspire to compete seriously with these regimes without material realignment with them.

The reality, however, is that the reforms were never going to be a significant break from the past. French contract law has always adopted what in common law jurisdictions would be regarded as a more moralistic approach[12] and that was highly unlikely to change. The interests of the injured party are not conceived of only in economic terms.[13] As a consensual bond, the contract has intrinsic value[14] and the relationship between the parties is of paramount importance. In the words of the eminent French contract lawyer, Mestre, 'the *raison d'être* [of the contract] is to unite individuals ... It is to be performed loyally ... and is ... above all a human affair ... The contract cannot be reduced, in an economic approach, to a transfer of values or a modification of estates.'[15]

[8] Borghetti (n 4) 7.

[9] T Revet, 'L'achèvement de la réforme du droit commun des contrats du régime général et de la preuve des obligations, regard général' RDC 2018 Hors-série, [34].

[10] R Goode, 'The Concept of "Good Faith" in English Law' in Saggi (ed), *Centro di studi e ricerche di diritto comparato e straniero* (Conferenze e seminari: Rome, 1992) 7; *Union Eagle Ltd v Golden Achievement Ltd* [1997] AC 514 (PC); Cartwright (n 1).

[11] Law Society report 'England and Wales: the Jurisdiction of Choice': https://www.eversheds-sutherland.com/documents/LawSocietyEnglandAndWalesJurisdictionOfChoice.pdf accessed 1 September 2021 and H Kötz 'The Jurisdiction of Choice: England, or Wales or Germany?' European Review of Private Law 1243, 1251–2; Cartwright (n 1); M Fabre-Magnan 'What Is a Modern Law of Contracts?' (2017) 13 ERCL 376 at 378; S Rowan, 'The New French Law of Contract' (2017) 66 ICLQ 805.

[12] S Whittaker, 'Contracts, Contract Law and Contractual Principle' in J Cartwright and S Whittaker (eds), *The Code Napoléon Rewritten: French Contract Law after the 2016 Reforms* (Hart Publishing: Oxford, 2017) 29.

[13] Cartwright (n 1) 289.

[14] Ibid.

[15] J Mestre, 'Préface' to B Fages, *Le comportement du contractant* (PUAM: Aix-en-Provence, 1997).

Whilst the drafters sought to make French contract law more commercially orientated, this was not intended to be at the expense of core values. The drafters in the 'Report to the President of the Republic' explained that 'enhancing the attractiveness of our law does not, however, require us to relinquish balanced legal solutions that are not only protective of the parties but also effective and responsive to changes in the market economy'.[16] Legal certainty and commercial attractiveness were balanced with the desire to promote substantive fairness, which in most instances was given precedence. In retrospect, it might have been preferable for the drafters to have been more cautious in managing expectations by setting more modest aspirations and accepting that French law is unlikely to compete seriously with common law regimes for the favour of international business.

It is also possible that the international businesses that the drafters had in mind are not those that typically choose to resolve their disputes under common law regimes such as English law. Commercial parties of international scale that litigate in the senior English courts are often organizations of substantial size and geographical footprint which are adept at looking after their own interests and judging the commerciality and fairness of opportunities and their agreements. English contract law has to some extent been developed by, and even for, these parties, to whom greater individualism and freedom of contract are suited.

These factors may have been thought to hold less sway in France, which does not have comparable status as an international centre of litigation. In commercial disputes, small- and medium-sized enterprises are more prominent.[17] Many will have limited access to legal advice and insufficient sophistication to scrutinize and challenge disadvantageous terms. Protective rules that blunt the perceived harshness of freedom of contract might have been thought to be more appropriate for this core group of users. It is in their interests that interventionism continues to prevail.

## D The New Face of French Law Is Still to Be Shaped

Since many of the new articles expand the powers of the court and contain only high-level propositions and notions that are not defined, it will be for the courts, through creative development, to shape how they are applied. Only when this happens will the new face of French law become clearer.[18] Whether the courts take a coherent approach and follow discernible guiding principles cannot be known

[16] 'Report to the President of the Republic relating to Ordonnance no 2016–131 of 10 February 2016 on the reform of contract law, the general regime and proof of obligations', JORF no 0035 of 11 February 2016, 2.

[17] S Rowan, 'The New French Law of Contract' (2017) ICLQ 66 (4) 805, 828.

[18] D Fenouillet, 'Les valeurs morales' RDC 2016.589; S Whittaker and J Cartwright 'Introduction' in J Cartwright and S Whittaker (eds), *The Code Napoléon Rewritten, French Contract Law after the 2016 Reforms* (Hart Publishing, Oxford: 2017) 10–11.

at this early stage. The absence in France of any doctrine of binding precedent, the innumerable appellate cases that do not always speak with a single voice, and the laconic style of judgments mean that uncertainty could persist for some time. Paradoxically this seems likely to slow progress towards, and could potentially even undermine, the original goal of a more accessible and predictable law of contract that does not rely for clarification upon a large body of decided cases. Perhaps the main consolation is that many of the new provisions introduced by the reforms are not mandatory and the parties can contract out of them.

From a comparative perspective, the main differences between English and French contract law prior to the reforms seem to remain and, if anything, have been exacerbated. In particular, the greater prominence of good faith in France is in notable contrast with continuing resistance to the principle in England;[19] the now formalized and general protection against unfair terms in France is at variance with the limited and piecemeal powers of English courts to invalidate terms on grounds of unfairness;[20] and the new French rule on *imprévision* has no equivalent in English law, where only the narrow doctrine of frustration can rescue a party that is unable to point to a force majeure or undue hardship clause, although in practice this rarely happens and in any case its effect is simply to discharge the contract rather than any more tailored solution. Whilst it is true that the formal recognition of self-help termination brings French law closer to the position in England, telling differences remain.[21]

The reforms do, however, achieve a striking *rapprochement* with international contract law instruments,[22] in which there are similarities with many of the innovations in the new Civil Code. International contract law projects such as the Principles of European Contract Law (PECL) and the UNIDROIT Principles inspired the drafters in a range of respects. To cite the most striking examples, new article 1195 on *imprévision* resembles article 6.2.2 and 6.2.3 of the UNIDROIT Principles and article 6:111 of the PECL. These provisions require or enable renegotiation and give the court the power to rebalance the contract in the light of changed circumstances. Similarly, new article 1171 on unfair terms resembles

[19] *Interfoto Picture Library Ltd v Stiletto Visual Programmes Ltd* [1989] QB 43 (CA) 439 (Bingham LJ). For a summary of English law on this point, see H Beale (ed), *Chitty on Contracts* (33rd edn, Sweet & Maxwell: London, 2020) [1:039]–[1:054A]. As Moore-Bick LJ recently said in *Mediterranean Shipping Co SA v Cottonex Anstalt* [2017] EWCA Civ 365 at [45]: 'There is . . . a real danger that if a general principle of good faith were established it would be invoked as often to undermine as to support the terms in which the parties have reached agreement.'

[20] Consumers are protected by the Consumer Rights Act 2015. For businesses, see the protection provided by the Unfair Contract Terms Act 1977 against unreasonable exclusion and limitation clauses. The extension of the remit of the court to other terms on grounds of unfairness and unconscionability was firmly rejected, even in exceptional circumstances, in *Union Eagle Ltd v Golden Achievement Ltd* [1997] AC 514 (PC) 518.

[21] S Rowan, 'Termination for Contractual Non-performance' in J Cartwright and S Whittaker (eds), *The Code Napoléon Rewritten: French Contract Law after the 2016 Reforms* (Hart Publishing: Oxford, 2017).

[22] Rowan, 'The New French Law of Contract' (n 17) 825.

article 4:110 of the PECL. The same is also true of many of the innovations relating to remedies for breach.[23]

This *rapprochement* has been interpreted by some commentators as a further indication that the drafters were seeking to achieve consensus. Many such international instruments are, after all, the embodiment of consensus and compromise. It also reveals a further paradox, which is that, whilst the drafters might have wished to restore and boost the influence of French law over or even counter European-level harmonization projects, they have also reduced its distinctiveness.[24]

[23] Ibid.
[24] Borghetti (n 4) 9.

# Bibliography

## Materials in English

### Books and Articles


Aikens R, '"The Obscure, the Implied and the Illegal": English and French Approaches to the Interpretation of Contract, Implication of Terms and Contracts Affected by Illegality' in C Mitchell and S Watterson (eds), *The World of Maritime and Commercial Law: Essays in Honours of Francis Rose* (Bloomsbury Publishing: London, 2020) 215

Aubert de Vincelles C, 'Validity of Contract: Dol, Erreur and Obligation d'Information' in J Cartwright and S Whittaker (eds), *The Code Napoléon Rewritten: French Contract Law after the 2016 Reforms* (Hart Publishing: Oxford, 2017) 79

Beale H (ed), *Chitty on Contracts* (33rd edn, Sweet & Maxwell: London, 2020)

Beale H (ed), *Chitty on Contracts* (34th edn, Sweet & Maxwell: London, 2021)

Beale H, Fauvarque-Cosson B, Rutgers G, and Vogenauer S, *Cases, Materials and Text on Contract Law, Ius Commune Casebooks for the Common Law of Europe* (3rd edn, Hart Publishing: Oxford, 2019)

Bell J, Boyron S, and Whittaker S, *Principles of French Law* (2nd edn, OUP: Oxford, 2008)

Bell J and Lichère F, *Contemporary French Administrative Law* (CUP: Cambridge, 2022)

Borghetti J-S, 'Punitive Damages in France' in H Koziol and V Wilcox (eds), *Punitive Damages: Common Law and Civil Law Perspectives* (Springer: New York, 2009) 55

Borghetti J-S, 'The Effects of Contracts and Third Parties' in J Cartwright and S Whittaker (eds), *The Code Napoléon Rewritten: French Contract Law after the 2016 Reforms* (Hart Publishing, 2017) 227

Borghetti J-S and Whittaker S (eds), *French Civil Liability in Comparative Perspective* (Hart Publishing: Oxford, 2019)

Bridge M, 'Does Anglo-Canadian Contract Law Need a Doctrine of Good Faith?' (1984) 9 Canadian Bus LJ 385

Bridge M, 'Doubting Good Faith' (2005) 11 NZBLQ 449

Bridge M, 'Good Faith, the Common Law and the CISG' (2017) 22 Unif L Rev 1, 18

Bridge M, 'Limits on Contractual Freedom' (2019) 7 The Chinese Journal of Comparative Law 387

Brownsword R, 'Retrieving Reasons, Retrieving Rationality? A New Look at the Right to Withdraw for Breach of Contract' (1992) 5 Journal of Contract Law 83

Cappelletti M, 'Comparative Reflections on Punishment in Tort Law' in J-S Borghetti and S Whittaker (eds), *French Civil Liability in Comparative Perspective* (Hart Publishing: Oxford, 2019) 329

Cartwright J, *Contract Law: An Introduction to the English Law of Contract for the Civil Lawyer* (3rd edn, Hart Publishing: Oxford, 2016)

Cartwright J and Whittaker S, 'Introduction' in J Cartwright and S Whittaker (eds), *The Code Napoléon Rewritten: French Contract Law after the 2016 Reforms* (Hart Publishing: Oxford, 2017)

Cartwright J and Hesselink M (eds), *Precontractual Liability in European Private Law* (CUP: Cambridge, 2008)

Catala P and Weir J-A, 'Delict and Torts: a Study in Parallel—Part II' (1963–1964) 38 Tul L Rev 221

Chen-Wishart M, *Contract Law* (6th edn, OUP: Oxford, 2018)

Collins H, 'Implied Terms: The Foundation in Good Faith and Fair Dealing' (2014) 67 CLP 297

Collins H, 'Is a Relational Contract a Legal Concept?' in S Degeling, J Edelman, and J Goudkamp (eds), *Contract in Commercial Law* (Thomson Reuters: London, 2016)

Cottier B, Rocha B, and J Voyame, 'Abuse of Rights in Comparative Law' in *Council of Europe, Abuse of Rights and Equivalent Concepts: The Principle and Its Present Day Application* (Council of Europe: Strasbourg, 1990) 23

Crabb J-H, 'The French Concept of Abuse of Rights' (1964) 6 Inter-Am L Rev 1

Davies P-S, 'Recent Developments in the Law of Implied Terms' [2010] LMCLQ 140

Davies P-S, *JC Smith's The Law of Contract* (OUP: Oxford, 2018)

Fabre-Magnan M, 'Termination of Contract: A Missed Opportunity for Reform' in J Cartwright, S Whittaker, and S Vogenauer (eds), *Reforming the French Law of Obligations, Comparative Reflections on the Avant-Projet de Réforme du Droit des Obligations et de la Prescription* (Hart Publishing: Oxford, 2009) 169

Fabre-Magnan M, 'What Is a Modern Law of Contracts?' (2017) 13 European Review of Contract Law 376

Fauvarque-Cosson B, 'Does Review on the Ground of *Imprévision* Breach the Principle of the Binding Force of Contracts?' in J Cartwright and S Whittaker (eds), *The Code Napoléon Rewritten: French Contract Law after the 2016 Reforms* (Hart Publishing: Oxford, 2017) 187

Fauvarque-Cosson B, 'The French Contract Law Reform and the Political Process' (2017) 13 European Review of Contract Law 337

Genicon T, 'The *Exception d'Inexécution*' in J Cartwright and S Whittaker (eds), *The Code Napoléon Rewritten: French Contract Law after the 2016 Reforms* (Hart Publishing: Oxford, 2017) 291

Goff R (Lord), '"Opening Address", Second Annual JCL Conference in London on 11 September 1991' (1992) 5 Journal of Contract Law 1, 4

Goode R, 'The Concept of "Good Faith"| in English Law' in Saggi (ed), *Centro di studi e ricerche di diritto comparato e straniero* (Conferenze e seminari: Rome, 1992) 4

Gordley J, 'The Abuse of Rights in the Civil Law Tradition' in R De La Feria and S Vogenauer (eds), *The Prohibition of Abuse of Law: An Emerging Principle of EU Law?* (Hart Publishing: Oxford, 2011) 33

Granger E, 'Sweating over an Implied Duty of Good Faith' [2013] LMCLQ 418

Gutteridge HC, 'Abuse of Rights' (1933) 5 CLJ 22

Harris D, 'Incentives to Perform, or Break Contracts' (1992) 45 CL 29

Hooley R, 'Controlling Contractual Discretion' (2013) 72 CLJ 65

Hooley R, 'Implied Terms After Belize' (2014) 73 CLJ 315

Jackson B, 'Injured Feelings Resulting from Breach of Contract' (1977) 26 ICLQ 502

Jansen N and Zimmerman R (eds), *Commentaries on European Contract Laws* (OUP: Oxford, 2018)

Keffenick C, '*Violence* in the Reformed Napoleonic Code: The Surprising Survival of Third Parties' in J Cartwright and S Whittaker (eds), *The Code Napoléon Rewritten: French Contract Law after the 2016 Reforms* (Hart Publishing: Oxford, 2017) 109

Kötz H, 'The Jurisdiction of Choice: England, or Wales or Germany?' (2010) 18(6) European Review of Private Law 1243

Kötz H, *European Contract Law* (2nd edn, OUP: Oxford, 2017)

Laithier Y-M, 'The French Law of Remedies for Breach of Contract' in N Cohen and E McKendrick (eds), *Comparative Remedies for Breach of Contract* (Hart Publishing: Oxford, 2005) 103

Laithier Y-M, 'Exécution Forcée en Nature' in J Cartwright and S Whittaker (eds), *The Code Napoléon Rewritten: French Contract Law after the 2016 Reforms* (Hart Publishing: Oxford, 2017) 257

Laithier Y-M, 'The Relationship between Contractual and Extra-Contractual Liability as between Parties to a Contract' in J-S Borghetti and S Whittaker (eds), *French Civil Liability in Comparative Perspective* (Hart Publishing: Oxford, 2019) 37

Lawson FH, 'Notes on the History of Tort in the Civil Law' (1940) 22 Journal of Comparative Legislation and International Law 136

Lawson FH, 'Fault and Contract—A Few Comparisons' (1975) 49 Tul LR 295

Leggatt L, 'Contractual Duties of Good Faith' Lecture to the Commercial Bar Association, 18 October 2016 <https://www.judiciary.uk/wp-content/ uploads/2016/10/mr-justice-leggatt-lecture-contractual-duties-of-faith.pdf>

Le Pautremat S, 'Mitigation of Damages: A French Perspective' (2006) 55 ICLQ 205

MacMahon P, 'The Englishness of English Contract Law' (paper on file with author, presentation at the LSE Law Department on 28 February 2020)

Markesinis B, '*Cause* and Consideration: A Study in Parallel' (1978) 37(1) CLJ 53

Mazeaud D, 'Contracts and Third Parties in the *Avant-projet de réforme*' in J Cartwright, S Vogenauer, and S Whittaker (eds), *Reforming the French Law of Obligations: Comparative Reflections on the Avant-projet de réforme du droit des obligations et de la prescription* (Hart Publishing: Oxford, 2009)

McCunn J, 'Contra Proferentem Rule: Contract Law's Great Survivor' (2019) 39 OJLS 483

McKendrick E, 'Good Faith in the Performance of a Contract in English Law' in L DiMatteo and M Hogg (eds), Comparative Contract Law: British and American Perspectives (Oxford: OUP, 2015)

McKendrick E, *Contract Law: Text, Cases and Materials* (9th edn, OUP: Oxford, 2020)

McKendrick E, *Contract Law* (13th edn, Macmillan: 2019)

McLauchlan D, 'Construction and Implication: In Defence of Belize Telecom' [2014] LMCLQ 203

Mekki M, 'The General Principles of Contract Law in the "Ordonnance" on the Reform of Contract Law' (2016) 76 Louisiana LR 1193

Michaud A, 'Mitigation of Damage in the Context of Remedies for Breach of Contract' (1984) 15 RGD 293

Muir-Watt H, 'The Reform of the French Civil Code at a Distance: An International and Comparative Perspective' (2017) 13 European Review of Contract Law 445

Nicholas B, 'Rules and Terms—Civil Law and Common Law' (1973-1974) 48 Tul L Rev 946

Nicholas B, *The French Law of Contract* (Clarendon Press: Oxford, 1992)

Pédamon C, 'The Paradoxes of the Theory of *Imprévision* in the New French Law of Contract: A Judicial Deterrent?' [2017] Amicus Curiae 12

Peel E, *Treitel on the Law of Contract* (12th edn, Sweet & Maxwell: London, 2007)

Pérès C, 'Mandatory and Non-Mandatory Rules in the New Law of Contract' in J Cartwright and S Whittaker (eds), *The Code Napoléon Rewritten: French Contract Law after the 2016 Reforms* (Hart Publishing: Oxford, 2017) 167

Rowan S, 'Comparative Observations on the Introduction of Punitive Damages in French Law' in J Cartwright, S Vogenauer, and S Whittaker (eds), *Reforming the French Law of*

*Obligations, Comparative Reflections on the Avant-projet de réforme du droit des obligations et de la prescription ('the Avant-projet Catala')* (Hart Publishing: Oxford, 2009) 325

Rowan S, 'Reflections on the Introduction of Punitive Damages for Breach of Contract' (2010) 30 OJLS 495

Rowan S, 'Fault and Breach of Contract in France and England: Some Comparisons' (2011) 22(4) European Business Law Review 467

Rowan S, *Remedies for Breach of Contract: A Comparative Analysis of the Protection of Performance* (OUP: Oxford, 2012)

Rowan S, 'Termination for Contractual Non-performance' in J Cartwright and S Whittaker (eds), *The Code Napoléon Rewritten: French Contract Law after the 2016 Reforms* (Hart Publishing: Oxford, 2017) 317

Rowan S, 'The New French Law of Contract' (2017) 66 ICLQ 805

Rowan S, 'Resisting Termination: Some Comparative Observations' in A Dyson, J Goudkamp, and F Wilmot-Smith (eds), *Defences in Contract* (Hart Publishing: Oxford, 2017) 163

Rowan S, 'Problems of Contractual Interpretation: English and French Law Compared' [2020] LMCLQ 273

Rowan S, 'The Reform of French Contract Law: The Struggle for Coherency' in TT Arvind and J Steele (eds), *Contract Law and the Legislature: Autonomy, Expectations, and the Making of Legal Doctrine* (Hart Publishing: Oxford, 2020) 219

Rowan S, 'Abuse of Rights in English Contract Law: Hidden in Plain Sight?' (2021) 84 (5) MLR 1066

Saintier S, 'The Elusive Notion of Good Faith in the Performance of a Contract, Why Still a "bête noire" for the Civil and the Common Law?' [2017] JBL 441

Schelhaas H, 'Commentary on article 7.1 of the UNIDROIT Principles' in S Vogenauer (ed), *Commentary on the UNIDROIT Principles of International Commercial Contracts (PICC)* (2nd edn, OUP: Oxford, 2015)

Sefton-Green R, 'Formation of Contract: Negotiation and the Process of Agreement' in J Cartwright and S Whittaker (eds), *The Code Napoléon Rewritten: French Contract Law after the 2016 Reforms* (Hart Publishing: Oxford, 2017) 59

Simpson B, 'Innovation in Nineteenth Century Contract Law' (1975) 91 LQR 247

Steiner E, *French Law: A Comparative Approach* (2nd edn, OUP: Oxford, 2018)

Steyn, J, 'The Role of Good Faith and Fair Dealing in Contract Law: A Hair-Shirt Philosophy?' [1991] Denning Law Journal 131

Stoffel-Munck P, 'The Revolution in Unfair Terms' in J Cartwright and S Whittaker (eds), *The Code Napoléon Rewritten: French Contract Law after the 2016 Reforms* (Hart Publishing: Oxford, 2017) 145

Stoffel-Munck P, 'Liability of Contracting Parties Towards Third Parties' in J-S Borghetti and S Whittaker (eds), *French Civil Liability in Comparative Perspective* (Hart Publishing: Oxford, 2019) 55

Sumption J (Lord), 'A Question of Taste: The Supreme Court and the Interpretation of Contracts' (2017) 17 OUCLJ 301

Tan ZX, 'Disruptive Doctrine? Revisiting the Doctrinal Impact of Relational Contract Theory' (2019) Legal Studies 39

Treitel G, *Remedies for Breach of Contract: A Comparative Account* (Clarendon Press: Oxford, 1988)

Treitel G, *An Outline of the Law of Contract* (6th edn, OUP: Oxford, 2004)

Valcke C, 'On Comparing French and English Contract Law: Insights from Social Contract Theory' (2009) 4 Journal of Comparative Law 69

Vogenauer S, 'Interpretation of Contracts: Concluding Observations' in A Burrows and E Peel (eds), *Contract Terms* (OUP: Oxford, 2007)

Vogenauer S, 'The *Avant-projet de Réforme*: An Overview' in J Cartwright, S Vogenauer, and S Whittaker (eds), *Reforming the French Law of Obligations, Comparative Reflections on the Avant-Projet de Réforme du Droit des Obligations et de la Prescription* (Hart Publishing: Oxford, 2009)

Vogenauer S, 'The Effects of Contracts on Third Parties: The *Avant-projet de réforme* in a Comparative Perspective' in J Cartwright, S Vogenauer, and S Whittaker (eds), *Reforming the French Law of Obligations, Comparative Reflections on the Avant-Projet de Réforme du Droit des Obligations et de la Prescription* (Hart Publishing: Oxford, 2009)

Vogenauer S, *Commentary on the UNIDROIT Principles of International Commercial Contracts (PICC)* (2nd edn, OUP: Oxford, 2015)

Webb C, 'Performance and Compensation: An Analysis of Contract Damages and Contractual Obligation' (2006) 26 OJLS 41

Whittaker S, 'Privity of Contract and the Law of Tort: the French Experience' (1995) 15 OJLS 327

Whittaker S, 'How Does French Law Deal with Anticipatory Breaches of Contract?' 45 (1996) ICLQ 662

Whittaker S, 'Performance of Another's Obligation: French and English Law Contrasted' in D Johnston and R Zimmerman (eds), *Unjustified Enrichment: Key Issues in Comparative Perspective* (CUP: Cambridge, 2002) 433

Whittaker S, *Liability for Products: English Law, French Law and European Harmonisation* (OUP: Oxford, 2005)

Whittaker S, 'A Period of Grace for Contractual Performance?' in M Andenas et al. (eds), *Liber Amicorum Guido Alpa, Private Law Beyond the National Systems* (British Institute of International and Comparative Law: London, 2007) 1100

Whittaker S, 'Termination Clauses' in A Burrows and E Peel (eds), *Contract Terms* (OUP: Oxford, 2007) 253

Whittaker S, 'Comments on "Abuse of Law" in European Private Law' in R De La Feria and S Vogenauer (eds), *The Prohibition of Abuse of Law: An Emerging Principle of EU Law?* (Hart Publishing: Oxford, 2011) 253

Whittaker S, 'Good Faith, Implied Terms and Commercial Contracts' (2013) 129 LQR 463

Whittaker S, 'Contracts, Contract Law and Contractual Principle' in J Cartwright and S Whittaker (eds), *The Code Napoléon Rewritten: French Contract Law after the 2016 Reforms* (Hart Publishing, 2017) 29

Whittaker S, 'Unfair Terms in Commercial Contracts and the Two Laws of Competition: French Law and English Law Contrasted' (2019) 39(2) OJLS 404

Whittaker S, 'A Common Framework for Civil Liability' in J-S Borghetti and S Whittaker (eds), *French Civil Liability in Comparative Perspective* (Hart Publishing: Oxford, 2019) 15

Whittaker S and Zimmermann R, *Good Faith in European Contract law* (CUP: Cambridge, 2000)

Zweigert K and Kötz H, *An Introduction to Comparative Law*, trans T Weir (3rd edn, Clarendon Press: Oxford, 1998)

Zweigert K and Drobnig U, *International Encyclopaedia of Comparative Law* (Brill, Nijhoff: Online Edition, 2018)

## Materials in French

### Books and Articles

Alfandari E, 'Le contrôle des clauses pénales par le juge' JCP 1971.I.2395

Amrani-Mekki S, 'La résolution unilatérale des contrats à durée déterminée' Defrénois 2003.369

Ancel B, 'L'encadrement de la liberté contractuelle en droit comparé, vers une reconfiguration de l'office du juge' Revue Lamy Droit civil, 2019, no 172

Ancel F, Fauvarque-Cosson B, and Gest J, *Aux sources de la réforme du droit des contrats* (Paris: Dalloz, 2017)

Ancel N, 'Le juge et les remèdes à l'inexécution du contrat' RDC 2016.408

Ancel P, 'Faut-il faire avec?' RDC 2007.538

Ancel P, Brun P, Forray V, Gout O, Pignarre G, and Pimont S, 'Points de vue convergents sur le projet de réforme du droit des contrats' JCP 2008.I.213

Ancel P, 'Le concours de la responsabilité délictuelle et de la responsabilité contractuelle' RCA 2012.2, dossier no 8

Ancel P, *Droit des obligations. Séquence 5—Contenu du contrat: par la volonté et au-delà de la volonté* (Dalloz: Paris, 2018)

Antonmattei P-H, *Contributions à l'étude de la force majeure* (LGDJ: Montpellier, 1993)

Atias C and Debeaurain J, 'L'abandon du chantier de construction' D 1990 Chron 291

Aubert J-L, *Notions et rôle de l'offre et de l'acceptation dans la formation du contrat* (LGDJ: Paris, 1970)

Aubert J-L, 'La victime peut-elle être obligée de minimiser son dommage?' RJDA 2004.355

Aynès A, 'Accroissement du pouvoir de la volonté individuelle' Droit & Patrimoine 2016

Aynès L, 'A propos de la force obligatoire du contrat' RDC 2003.323

Aynès L, 'Le contrat, loi des parties' Cahiers du Conseil Constitutionnel, Dossier: Loi et Contrat 2005.17

Aynès L, 'Le contrôle des nouveaux pouvoirs unilatéraux du contractant—Synthèse' RDC 2018.528

Barbier H, 'Les grands mouvements du droit commun des contrats après l'ordonnance du 10 février 2016' RTD civ 2016.247

Barbier H, 'L'exécution et la sortie du contrat' RDC 2018.40

Bazin E, 'La résolution unilatérale du contrat' RRJ 2000–4

Beale H, 'La réforme du droit français des contrats et le "droit européen des contrats": perspective de la Law Commission anglaise' RDC 2006.146

Behar-Touchais M, 'L'amende civile est-elle un substitut satisfaisant à l'absence de dommages et intérêts punitifs?' LPA 2002.36

Beignier B, *L'honneur et le droit* (LGDJ: Paris, 1995)

Bellivier F and Sefton-Green R, 'Force obligatoire et exécution en nature du contrat en droits français et anglais: bonnes et mauvaises surprises du comparatisme' in *Études offertes à Jacques Ghestin, Le contrat au début du XXIe siècle* (LGDJ: Paris, 2001) 89

Bénabent A, *Droit des obligations* (18th edn, LGDJ: Paris, 2019)

Bénabent A, 'Les nouveaux pouvoirs unilatéraux du contractant—Présentation' RDC 2018.503

Blanc N, 'Le juge et les standards juridiques' RDC 2016.394

Boccara B, 'La réforme de la clause pénale: conditions et limites de l'intervention judiciaire' JCP 1975.I.2742

Boffa R, 'Juste cause (et injuste clause)' D 2015.335

Boismain C, 'Étude sur l'évaluation des dommages-intérêts par les juges du fond' PA 2007 no 39.7

Borghetti J-S, 'Le nouveau droit français des contrats, entre continuité et Européanisation' in *Annuario del contratto* 2016, 2017.3
Borghetti J-S, 'L'avant-projet de réforme de la responsabilité civile (1)' D 2016.1442
Borghetti J-S, 'Faut-il distinguer les dommages et intérêts compensatoires des dommages et intérêts en lieu et place de la prestation?' RDC 2016.787
Borghetti J-S, 'La responsabilité des contractants à l'égard des tiers dans le projet de réforme de la responsabilité civile' D 2017.1846
Borghetti J-S, 'Un pas de plus vers la réforme de la responsabilité civile: présentation du projet de réforme rendu public le 13 mars 2017' D 2017.770
Boucard H, 'Responsabilité contractuelle de droit commun' in *Répertoire de droit civil* (Dalloz: Paris, 2014)
Bourassin M, 'L'emprise inéluctable des juges sur le nouveau droit des contrats' LPA 2017.9
Brière de L'Isle G, 'La faute dolosive, tentative de clarification' D 1980 Chron 133
Brochier E, 'Le point de vue de l'avocat sur le nouveau droit des obligations après ratification' RDC 2018.37
Brochier M, 'Les nouveaux rôles du juge dans l'inexécution du contrat' Droit & Patrimoine 2016
Brun P, 'Le droit de revenir sur son engagement' Droit & Patrimoine 1998.79
Brun P, 'Rapport de synthèse' RDC 2016.416
Buffelan-Lanore Y and Larribau-Terneyre V, *Droit civil Les obligations* (16th edn, Dalloz: Paris, 2018-2019)
Cabrillac R, 'Réforme du droit des contrats: révision-modification ou révision-compilation' RDC 2006.25
Cabrillac R, 'Le projet de réforme du droit des contrats: Premières impressions' JCP 2008.190
Carbonnier J, 'Le code civil' in P Nora (ed), *Les lieux de mémoire* (Gallimard: Paris, 1986)
Carbonnier J, *Droit civil, Les obligations* (22nd edn, PUF: Paris, 2000)
Cartwright J, 'Un regard anglais sur les forces et faiblesses du droit français des contrats' RDC 2015.691
Carval S, *La responsabilité civile dans sa fonction de peine privée* (LGDJ: Paris, 1995)
Carval S, 'Limitation de la responsabilité contractuelle au dommage prévu ou prévisible' RDC 2015.790
Carval S, 'L'amende civile—Avant-projet de loi portant réforme de la responsabilité civile, Observations et propositions de modifications' JCP 2016.42
Carval S, 'Le projet de réforme de la responsabilité civile' JCP 2017.401
Catala P, 'Il est temps de rendre au Code civil son rôle de droit commun des contrats' La Semaine Juridique Edition Générale 2005
Catala P, 'La genèse et le dessein du projet' RDC 2006.11
Catala P, 'Interprétation et qualification dans l'avant-projet de réforme des obligations' in *Études offertes à Geneviève Viney* (LGDJ: Paris, 2008) 243
Cassin R, 'Réflexions sur la résolution judiciaire des contrats pour inexécution' RTD civ 1945.12
Cermolacce A, 'L'article 1159 du Code civil' RLDC 2004.7 no 302
Chabas F, 'La réforme de la clause pénale (loi no 75-597 du 9 juillet 1975)' D 1976 Chron 229
Chabas F, *Fasc 224-2: Régime de la réparation—Action en réparation—Décision judiciaire—Astreintes* (LexisNexis Jurisclasseur, 2002)
Chagny M, 'La notion de dommages et intérêts punitifs et ses répercussions sur le droit de la concurrence—Lectures plurielles de l'article 1371 de l'avant-projet de réforme du droit des obligations' JCP 2006.I.149
Chantepie G and Latina M, *La réforme du droit des obligations, Commentaire théorique et pratique dans l'ordre du Code civil* (Dalloz: Paris, 2016)

Chantepie G and Latina M, *Le nouveau droit des obligations, Commentaire théorique et pratique dans l'ordre du Code civil* (2nd edn, Dalloz: Paris, 2018)
Chartier Y, *La réparation du préjudice* (Dalloz: Paris, 1983)
Chatain A, 'Le rôle du juge dans la réforme du droit des contrats' RDC 2016.12
Chatain A and Erb JP, 'Les conséquences de la réforme du droit des contrats sur l'intervention du juge' La Semaine Juridique Entreprise et Affaires 2017.1245
Chazal J-P, 'De la signification du mot loi dans l'article 1134, alinéa 1er du code civil' RTD civ 2001
Chénedé F, 'Les conditions d'exercice des prérogatives contractuelles' RDC 2010.709
Colin A and Capitant H, *Cours élémentaires de droit civil français* (8th edn, Dalloz: Paris, 1935)
Constantinesco L-J, *Inexécution et faute contractuelle en droit comparé (droits français, allemand, anglais)* (W Kohlhammer Verlag: Stuttgart, 1960)
Cornu G, 'Un Code civil n'est pas un instrument communautaire' D 2002 Chron 351
Couret A, Le Nabasque H, Coquelet M-L, Granier T, Poracchia D, Raynouard A, Reygrobellet A, and Robine D, *Droit financier* (3rd edn, Dalloz: Paris, 2019)
Courtieu G, *Arts 1382 à 1386—Fasc 131-20: Droit à la réparation—Abus de droits et abus de pouvoirs* (Lexis Nexis Jurisclasseur, 2005)
Couturier G, 'Vers un droit du reclassement?' Dr Soc 1999.497
Croze H, 'La loi no 91-650 du 9 juillet 1991 portant réforme des procédures civiles d'exécution: le nouveau droit commun de l'exécution forcée' JCP 1992.I.3555
D'Alès T and Terdjman L, 'L'introduction envisagée de mécanismes répressifs dans le droit de la responsabilité civile: le Rubicon sera-t-il franchi?' AJ Contrat 2017.69
De Cabarrus C, Jamin C, and Pimon S, *Nouveau droit des contrats—Le nouveau droit des contrats. Entre pouvoir du juge, efficacité économique et justice contractuelle* (Cahiers de droit de l'entreprise: LexisNexis Jurisclasseur, 2018)
De David Beauregard-Berthier O, *La notion de détournement de procédure en droit administratif* (Dr Admin: Lexis Nexis Jurisclasseur, 2006)
De la Marnierre E-S, 'De la construction édifiée en violation d'une servitude' D 1963 Chron 251
Delebecque P, *Fasc 22: Régime de la réparation—Modalités de la réparation—Règles particulières à la responsabilité contractuelle—Clause pénale* (LexisNexis Jurisclasseur, 2005)
Delebecque P, 'L'exécution forcée' RDC 2006.99
Demogue R, *Traité des obligations en général* (Rousseau: Paris, 1923-1933)
De Montholon C-F, *Récits de la captivité de l'Empereur Napoléon à Sainte-Hélène* (Paulin: Paris, 1847)
Deshayes O, 'L'introduction de l'obligation de modérer son dommage en matière contractuelle—Rapport français' RDC 2010.1139
Deshayes O, '"Existe-t-il un devoir de minimiser son dommage en matière contractuelle?"—Une question mal posée' RDC 2014.27
Deshayes O, 'Les directrices d'interprétation du Code civil: la cohérence des textes' RDC 2015.159
Deshayes O, 'La formation des contrats' RDC 2016/HS, 21
'Le nouveau droit des contrats après la loi de ratification du 20 avril 2018' RDC Hors-série June 2018
Deshayes O, Genicon T, and Laithier Y-M, *Réforme du droit des contrats, du régime général et de la preuve des obligations, Commentaire article par article* (2nd edn, LexisNexis: Paris, 2018)

Dissaux N and Jamin C, *Projet de réforme du droit des contrats, du régime général et de la preuve des obligations, rendu public le 25 février 2015, Commentaire article par article* (Dalloz: Paris, 2015)

Do V and Chang M, 'La résolution unilatérale du contrat en droit français: vers une harmonisation au sein de la Cour de cassation' LPA 2004.3

Domat J, *Les lois civiles dans leur ordre naturel* (Rollin et fils: Paris, 1745; reprint Hachette Livre: Paris, 2018)

Dreyer E, 'L'amende civile concurrente de l'amende pénale?' JCP 2017.1344

Dreyer E, 'La sanction de la faute lucrative par l'amende civile' D 2017.1136

Dupichot P, 'Regards (bienveillants) sur le projet de réforme du droit français des contrats' Droit & Patrimoine 2015

Durry G, 'Responsabilité délictuelle et responsabilité contractuelle: dualité ou unité?' Responsabilité Civile et Assurances 2001.20

Elland-Goldsmith M, 'La "mitigation of damages" en droit anglais' RDAI 1987.347

Engel L, 'Vers une nouvelle approche de la responsabilité. Le droit français face à la dérive américaine' Esprit 1993

Esmein P, 'Le fondement de la responsabilité contractuelle rapprochée de la responsabilité délictuelle' RTD civ 1933.627

Esmein P, 'L'obligation et la responsabilité contractuelle' in *Le droit privé français au milieu du XXème siècle, Études offertes à Georges Ripert* (Pichon et Durand-Auzias: Paris, 1950) 101

Etienney de Sainte Marie A, ' "L'interprétation créatrice": l'interprétation et la détermination du contenu du contrat' RDC 2015.166

Etienney de Sainte Marie A, 'Les principes, les directives et les clauses relatives à l'interprétation' RDC 2016.384

Fabre-Magnan M, 'Le mythe de l'obligation de donner' RTD civ 1996.85

Fabre-Magnan M, 'Réforme du droit des contrats: un très bon projet' JCP 2009.I.199

Fabre-Magnan M, *Droit des obligations, Contrat et engagement unilatéral* (2nd edn, PUF: Paris, 2010)

Fabre-Magnan M, *Droit des obligations, Contrat et engagement unilatéral* (4th edn, PUF: Paris, 2016)

Fabre-Magnan M, *Droit des obligations, Contrat et engagement unilatéral* (5th edn, PUF: Paris, 2019)

Fages B, *Le comportement du contractant* (PUAM: Aix-en-Provence, 1997)

Fages B, *Droit des obligations* (7th edn, LGDJ: France, 2017)

Fasquelle D, 'L'existence de fautes lucratives en droit français' in *Faut-il moraliser le droit français de la réparation du dommage? (à propos des dommages et intérêts punitifs et de l'obligation de minimiser son propre dommage)* (Colloque) PA 2002 no 232.27

Faure-Abbad M, 'Article 1222: la faculté de remplacement' RDC 2015.784

Fauvarque-Cosson B, 'L'obligation de restituer les profits tirés de la violation du contrat: l'arrêt Attorney General v Blake (2001) ou la consécration, par la Chambre des Lords, d'une nouvelle variété de dommages-intérêts, fondée non plus sur l'existence d'un préjudice, mais sur le profit tiré de la rupture du contrat' RDC 2005.479

Fauvarque-Cosson B, 'La réforme du droit français des contrats: perspective comparative' RDC 2006.147

Fauvarque-Cosson B, 'L'interprétation du contrat: observations comparatives' RDC 2007.481

Fauvarque-Cosson B, 'L'avant-projet français de réforme du droit des obligations et de la prescription: présentation générale' ERPL 2007.761

Fauvarque-Cosson B, 'Les nouvelles règles du Code civil relatives à l'interprétation des contrats: perspective comparative et internationale' RDC 2017.363

Fauvarque-Cosson B and Mazeaud D, 'L'avant-projet français de réforme du droit des obligations et du droit de la prescription et les principes du droit européen du contrat: variations sur les champs magnétiques dans l'univers contractuel' LPA 2006

Fauvarque-Cosson B and Patris-Godechot S, *Le code civil face à son destin* (La Documentation Française: Paris, 2006)

Fauvarque-Cosson B and Amrani-Mekki S, 'Droit des Contrats' in *Recueil Dalloz* (Dalloz: Paris, 2008)

Fédou J-F, Le juge et la révision du contrat RDC 2016.382

Fenet P-A, *Recueil complet de travaux préparatoires du Code civil* (Videcoq: Paris, 1836)

Fenouillet D, 'Les valeurs morales' RDC 2016.589

Fenouillet D, 'Le juge et les clauses abusives' RDC 2016.358

Flour J, Aubert J-L, and Savaux E, *Les obligations, Le rapport d'obligation* (8th edn, A Colin: Paris, 1999)

Flour J, Aubert J-L, and Savaux E, *Droit civil: Les obligations, l'acte juridique* (12th edn, Sirey: Paris, 2006)

Flour J, Aubert J-L, and Savaux E, *Les obligations, Le rapport d'obligation* (7th edn, A Colin: Paris, 2011)

Flour J, Aubert J-L, and Savaux E, *Droit civil: Les obligations, l'acte juridique* (14th edn, Sirey: Paris, 2014)

Fouillée A, *La science sociale contemporaine* (2nd edn, Librairie Hachette: Paris, 1885)

Foyer J, 'Exposé des motifs' (JOAN Annexes no 1365; JOAN 17 May 1975) 2861–2

Gautier P-Y, 'Contre Bentham: l'inutile et le droit' RTD civ 1995.820

Gautier P-Y, La hiérarchie inversée des modes de résolution du contrat' Droit & Patrimoine 2014.70

Gelot, B, *Finalité et méthodes objectives d'interprétation des actes juridiques* (LGDJ: Paris, 2003)

Genicon T, *La résolution du contrat pour inexécution* (LGDJ: Paris, 2007)

Genicon T, 'Observations' LPA 2009.81

Genicon T, 'Point d'étape sur la rupture unilatérale du contrat aux risques et périls du créancier' RDC 2010.44

Genicon T, 'Contre l'introduction du "coût manifestement déraisonnable" comme exception à l'inexécution forcée en nature' Droit & Patrimoine 2014.63

Genicon T, 'Défense et illustration de la cause en droit des contrats— à propos du projet de réforme du droit des contrats, du régime général et de la preuve des obligations' D 2015.1551

Genicon T, '"Résiliation" et "résolution" dans le projet d'ordonnance portant réforme du droit des contrats' JCP G 2015.1605

Ghestin J, *La formation du contrat* (3rd edn, LGDJ: Paris, 1993)

Ghestin J, 'La résolution pour inexécution (en droit français)' in *Il contratto inadempiuto* (G Giappichelli: Turin, 1999) 109

Ghestin J, 'Le futur: exemples étrangers. Le Code civil en France aujourd'hui' RDC 2004.1152

Ghestin J, JCP 2009.I.138

Ghozi A and Lequette L, 'La réforme du droit des contrats: brèves observations sur le projet de la chancellerie' RDC 2008.2609

Gibirila D, *Fasc 10: Louage d'ouvrage et d'industrie—Contrat d'entreprise* (LexisNexis Jurisclasseur, 2009)

Graziani F, 'La généralisation de l'amende civile: entre progrès et confusions' D 2018.428

Gridel J-P and Laithier Y-M, 'Les sanctions civiles de l'inexécution du contrat imputable au débiteur: état des lieux' JCP 2008.I.143
Grimaldi C, 'Toute faute contractuelle est une faute délictuelle, mais encore faut-il s'entendre sur le préjudice réparable!' RDC 2007.563
Grimaldi C, 'Paradoxes autour de l'interprétation des contrats' RDC 2008.207
Grimaldi C, 'La valeur normative des directives d'interprétation' RDC 2015.154
Grosser P, *Les remèdes à l'inexécution du contrat, Essai de classification* (Thèse: Paris I, 2000)
Grynbaum L, 'Réforme du droit des contrats' Revue Lamy Droit de l'immatériel, 2016, no 124
Guevel D, 'Le juge, auteur et acteur de la réforme du droit des contrats—Propos introductifs' RDC 2016.352
Guinchard S, *Droit et pratique de la procédure civile* (Dalloz: Paris, 2004)
Haftel B, 'La conclusion du contrat dans le projet d'ordonnance portant réforme du droit des obligations' Gaz Pal 2015.120
Haftel B, 'La responsabilité contractuelle' RDC 2017.143.
Hamelin JF, 'L'exercice des nouveaux pouvoirs du cocontractant RDC' 2018.514
Hanotiau B, 'Régime juridique et portée de l'obligation de modérer le dommage dans les ordres juridiques nationaux et le droit du commerce international' RDAI 1987.393
Heinich J, 'Le contrôle des nouveaux pouvoirs unilatéraux du contractant' RDC 2018.521
Helleringer C, 'Quand les parties font leur loi. Réflexion sur la contractualisation du pouvoir judiciaire d'interprétation' in M Xifaras and G Lewkowicz (eds), *Repenser le contrat* (Dalloz: Paris, 2009) 275
Heuzé V, *La vente internationale de marchandises, Droit uniforme* (LGDJ: Paris, 2000)
Houtcieff D, *Le principe de cohérence en matière contractuelle* (PUAM: Aix-en-Provence, 2001)
Houtcieff D, 'L'étendue des nouveaux pouvoirs unilatéraux du contractant' RDC 2018.505
Hugon C, 'Regard sur le droit des voies d'exécution' RDC 2005.183
Ivainer T, 'Le pouvoir souverain du juge dans l'appréciation des indemnités réparatrices' D 1972 Chron 7
Ivainer T, 'La lettre et l'esprit de la loi des parties' JCP G 1981.I.3023
Jabbour R, *La bonne foi dans l'exécution du contrat* (LGDJ: Paris, 2016)
Jacquemin Z, *Payer, réparer, punir. Étude des fonctions de la responsabilité contractuelle en droit français, allemand et anglais* (Thèse: Paris, 2015)
Jacquemin Z, 'Pour une reconnaissance de la spécificité contractuelle dans les effets de la responsabilité' RDC 2016.808
Jamin C, 'Les sanctions unilatérales de l'inexécution du contrat: trois idéologies en concurrence' in *L'unilatéralisme et le droit des obligations* (Economica: Paris, 1999) 71
Jamin C, 'Les conditions de la résolution du contrat: vers un modèle unique?—Rapport français' in M Fontaine and G Viney (eds), *Les sanctions de l'inexécution des obligations contractuelles, études de droit comparé* (Bruylant: Bruxelles and LGDJ: Paris, 2001) 451
Jauffret-Spinosi C, 'Les dommages-intérêts punitifs dans les systèmes de droit étrangers' in *Faut-il moraliser le droit français de la réparation du dommage? (à propos des dommages et intérêts punitifs et de l'obligation de minimiser son propre dommage)* (Colloque) PA 2002 no 232.8
Jauffret-Spinosi C, 'Les dommages-intérêts punitifs dans les systèmes de droit étrangers' LPA 2002.8
Jault A, *La notion de peine privée* (LGDJ: Paris, 2005)
Javaux B, 'L'amende civile, entre sanction pénale et punitive damages?' JCP 2019.152
Jeandidier W, 'L'exécution forcée des obligations contractuelles de faire' RTD civ 1976.700
Josserand L, *De l'abus des droits* (1st edn, Rousseau: Paris, 1905)

Jourdain P, 'La réparation des dommages immobiliers et l'enrichissement de la victime' Revue Droit Immobilier 1995.51

Jourdain P, 'Réflexion sur la notion de responsabilité contractuelle' in *Métamorphoses de la responsabilité* (PUF: Paris, 1998) 65

Jourdain P, 'Les dommages-intérêts alloués par le juge. Rapport français' in M Fontaine and G Viney (eds), *Les sanctions de l'inexécution des obligations contractuelles, Études de droit comparé* (Bruylant: Bruxelles and LGDJ: Paris, 2001) 263

Jourdain P, 'Rapport Introductif' in *Faut-il moraliser le droit français de la réparation du dommage? (à propos des dommages et intérêts punitifs et de l'obligation de minimiser son propre dommage)* (Colloque) PA 2002 no 232.1

Jourdain P, *Fasc 120: Droit à la Réparation, Responsabilité Fondée sur la Faute, Notion de Faute: Contenu Commun à Toutes les Fautes* (LexisNexis: Paris 2003)

Lachieze C, 'Critères justifiant une résolution unilatérale d'un contrat de fourniture d'électricité' JCP 2003.II.629

Laithier Y-M, *Étude comparative des sanctions de l'inexécution du contrat* (LGDJ: Paris, 2004)

Laithier Y-M, 'La prétendue primauté de l'exécution en nature' RDC 2005.161

Laithier Y-M, 'Clause pénale et dommages et intérêts incitatifs' in C Jamin (ed), *Droit et Économie des contrats* (LGDJ: Paris 2008) 141

Laithier Y-M, 'La *Cour de cassation* refuse d'imposer au créancier le devoir de minimiser le dommage' RDC 2010.52

Laithier Y-M, 'Le prononcé de dommages et intérêts punitifs en cas de faute lucrative' in N Ferrier and A Pélissier (eds), *L'entreprise face aux Évolutions de la responsabilité civile* (Economica: Paris, 2012) 117

Laithier Y-M, 'Les règles relatives à l'inexécution des obligations contractuelles' JCP 2015.47

Laithier Y-M, 'Les sanctions de l'inexécution du contrat' RDC 2016.40

Laithier Y-M, 'Les rapports entre responsabilités contractuelle et extracontractuelle entre les parties contractantes' RDC 2019.158

Lando O, 'L'avant-projet de réforme du droit des obligations et les Principes du droit européen du contrat: analyse de certaines différences' RDC 2006.167

Lapoyade Deschamps C, 'Le mythe de la responsabilité contractuelle en droit français' in F Rose (ed), *Failure of Contracts—Contractual, Restitutionary and Proprietary Consequences* (Hart Publishing: Oxford, 1997) 175

Lardeux G, 'Plaidoyer pour un droit contractuel efficace' D 2006.1406

Larroumet C, 'Pour la responsabilité contractuelle' in *Le droit privé français à la fin du XXe siècle, Études offertes à Pierre Catala* (Litec: Paris, 2001) 543

Larroumet C, *Droit civil, Les obligations, Le contrat* (5th edn, Economica: Paris, 2003) vol 3

Latina M, 'Contrats négociés et contrats d'adhésion' in *Répertoire de droit civil* (Dalloz: Paris, 2020)

Latina M, 'Généralités' in *Répertoire de droit civil* (Dalloz: Paris, 2020)

Latina M, 'Principes directeurs' in *Répertoire de droit civil* (Dalloz: Paris, 2020)

Latina M, 'Source du droit des contrats' in *Répertoire de droit civil* (Dalloz: Paris, 2020)

Laude A, 'L'obligation de minimiser son propre dommage existe-t-elle en droit privé français?' in *Faut-il moraliser le droit français de la réparation du dommage? (à propos des dommages et intérêts punitifs et de l'obligation de minimiser son propre dommage)* (Colloque) PA 2002 no 232.55

Laurent F, *Principes de droit civil français* (3rd edn, Bruylant-Christophe A Marescq: Bruxelles, Paris, 1878) vol 15

Le Bars B, 'La résiliation unilatérale du contrat pour cause d'intérêt légitime' D 2002.381

Le Tourneau P and Cadiet L, *Droit de la responsabilité et des contrats* (4th edn, Dalloz: Paris, 1996)

Le Tourneau P and Cadiet L, *Droit de la responsabilité et des contrats* (6th edn, Dalloz: Paris, 2006)

Le Tourneau P and Cadiet L, *Droit de la responsabilité et des contrats, Régimes d'indemnisation* (11th edn, Dalloz: Paris, 2017)

Le Tourneau P, Cadiet L, and de Poumarede M, *Répertoire de droit civil: bonne foi* (Dalloz: Paris, 2017)

Lecuyer H, 'L'inexécution du contrat', Contrats, Concurrence Consommation 2016.5

Lequette Y, 'Quelques remarques à propos d'un Code civil européen de Monsieur von Bar' D 2002 Chron 2202

Lequette Y, 'La résolution unilatérale du contrat aux risques et périls des créanciers' Revue de droit des affaires 2003.149

Lequette Y, 'Bilan des solidarismes contractuels' in *Mélanges Paul Didier* (Economica: Paris, 2008) 247

Leturmy L, 'La responsabilité délictuelle du contractant' RTD civ 1998.839

Leveneur L, 'Projet de la Chancellerie de réforme du droit des contrats: à améliorer' Contrats, Conc, Consomm 2008.10

Leveneur L, 'La résolution unilatérale' RDA 2010.88

Leveneur L, 'Une solution convaincante pour l'engagement de la responsabilité des contractants par les tiers. A propos de l'article 1234 du projet de réforme de la responsabilité civile' JCP G 2017.1182

Lichère F, Akoka F, Meynier-Pozzi A, and Lamy V, 'Crise sanitaire et contrats publics, une approche de sociologie juridique' AJDA 2021.1425

Liet-Veaux G, *Fasc 201–50: Construction—Responsabilité contractuelle de droit commun des entrepreneurs* (LexisNexis Jurisclasseur, 2008)

Loiseau G, 'Les vices du consentement' Contrats Concurrence Consommation 2016.5

Lonis-Apokourastos V, *La primauté contemporaine du droit à l'exécution en nature* (PUAM: Aix-en-Provence, 2003)

Malaurie P, 'Présentation de l'avant-projet de réforme du droit des obligations et de la prescription' RDC 2006.7

Malaurie P, Aynès L, and Gautier P-Y, *Les contrats spéciaux* (Defrénois: Paris, 2003)

Malaurie P, Aynès L, and Gautier P-Y, *Droit des contrats spéciaux* (10th edn, LGDJ: Paris, 2018)

Malaurie P, Aynès L, and Stoffel-Munck P, *Les obligations* (Defrénois: Paris, 2003–2004)

Malaurie P, Aynès L, and Stoffel-Munck P, *Droit des obligations* (10th edn, LGDJ: Paris, 2018)

Maleville M-H, *Pratique de l'interprétation des contrats: étude jurisprudentielle* (PU de Rouen, 1995)

Malinvaud P, 'Le "contenu certain" du contrat dans l'avant-projet "chancellerie" de code des obligations' D 2008.2551

Malinvaud P and Jestaz P, *Droit de la promotion immobilière* (7th edn, Dalloz: Paris, 2004)

Marais A, 'Le maintien forcé du contrat par le juge' LPA 2002.197

Marraud des Grottes G, 'Entretien avec Jean-Jacques Urvoas' Revue Lamy Droit Civil, 2016.6211

Martial-Braz N, 'L'objectivation des méthodes d'interprétation: la référence à la "personne raisonnable" et l'interprétation *in favorem*' RDC 2015.193

Marton G, 'Obligations de résultat et obligations de moyens' RTD civ 1935.33

Mathieu B, 'Le nouveau droit de l'inexécution du contrat en pratique—Quelques conjectures' La Semaine Juridique Entreprise et Affaires 2019.1126

Mazeaud D, *La notion de clause pénale* (LGDJ: Paris, 1992)
Mazeaud D, 'Loyauté, solidarité, fraternité: la nouvelle devise contractuelle?' in *Mélanges François Terré* (PUF Dalloz, Juris-Classeur: Paris, 1999) 604
Mazeaud D, 'Le nouvel ordre contractuel' RDC 2003.295
Mazeaud D, 'Exécution forcée de l'obligation contractuelle de faire' RDC 2006.323
Mazeaud D, 'Observations conclusives' RDC 2006.177
Mazeaud D, 'Les conventions portant sur la réparation' RDC 2007.149
Mazeaud D, 'L'introduction de la résolution unilatérale pour inexécution—Rapport français' RDC 2010.81
Mazeaud D, 'L'encadrement des pouvoirs du juge: l'efficacité des clauses relatives à l'interprétation' RDC 2015.187
Mazeaud D, 'La place du juge en droit des contrats' RDC 2016.353
Mazeaud H, Mazeaud L, and Chabas F, *Leçons de droit civil, Obligations, Théorie générale* (9th edn, Montchrestien: Paris, 1998)
Mazeaud H, Mazeaud L, and Tunc A, *Traité théorique et pratique de la responsabilité civile délictuelle et contractuelle* (6th edn, Montchrestien: Paris, 1965)
Méadel J, 'Faut-il introduire la faute lucrative en droit français?' LPA 2006.6
Mekki M, 'Les remèdes à l'inexécution dans le projet d'ordonnance portant réforme du droit des obligations' Gaz Pal 2015.1342
Mekki M, 'Le juge et les remèdes à l'inexécution du contrat' RDC 2016.400
Mekki M, 'La loi de ratification de l'ordonnance du 10 février 2016—une réforme de la réforme?' D 2018.900
Mesa R, 'L'opportune consécration d'un principe de restitution intégrale des profits illicites comme sanction des fautes lucrative' D 2012.2754
Mestre J, 'Réflexions sur l'abus de recouvrer sa créance' in *Mélanges Pierre Raynaud* (Dalloz-Sirey: Paris, 1985)
Mestre J, 'Observations sur l'attitude du juge face aux difficultés d'exécution du contrat' in *Le juge et l'exécution du contrat* (PUAM: Aix-en-Provence, 1993) 91
Mestre J, 'Préface' to B Fages, *Le comportement du contractant* (PUAM: Aix-en-Provence, 1997)
Mestre J, 'Rupture abusive et maintien du contrat' RDC 2005.99
Molfessis N, 'Force obligatoire et exécution: un droit à l'exécution en nature?' RDC 2005.37
Muir Watt H, 'La modération des dommages en droit anglo-américain' in *Faut-il moraliser le droit français de la réparation du dommage? (à propos des dommages et intérêts punitifs et de l'obligation de minimiser son propre dommage)* (Colloque) PA 2002 no 232.45
Nguyen Thanh-Bourgeais D, 'Contribution à l'étude de la faute contractuelle: la faute dolosive et sa place actuelle dans la gamme des fautes' RTD civ 1973.497
Oppetit B, 'L'engagement d'honneur' D 1979 Chron 107
Osman F, 'Le pouvoir modérateur du juge dans la mise en œuvre de la clause résolutoire de plein droit' Defrénois 1993.65
Paisant G, 'Dix ans d'application de la réforme des articles 1152 et 1231 du Code Civil relative à la clause pénale (Loi du 9 juillet 1975)' RTD civ 1985.647
Paisant G, 'La clause pénale' in *Répertoire civil Dalloz* (Dalloz: Paris, 2003)
Perru E, *L'impayé* (LGDJ: Paris, 2005)
Perus-Bichot S, 'La résolution unilatérale anticipée' Revue de Droit d'Assas 2010.85
Piedelièvre S, 'Les dommages et intérêts punitifs: une solution d'avenir' in *La responsabilité civile à l'aube du XXIe siècle—Bilan prospectif* (Colloque) Responsabilité Civile et Assurance 2001.68
Picod Y, 'La clause résolutoire et la règle morale' JCP 1990.I.3447

Picod Y, 'Obligations' in *Répertoire de droit civil* (Dalloz: Paris, 2017)
Pinna A, *La mesure du préjudice contractuel* (LGDJ: Paris, 2007)
Planiol M, *Traité élémentaire de droit civil* (9th edn, LGDJ: Paris, 1923)
Plantamp D, 'Le particularisme du remplacement dans la vente commerciale' D 2000 Chron 243
Pothier R, *Traité des obligations* (Debure, Rouzeau-Montaut: Paris, Orléans, 1764; reprint Dalloz: Paris, 2017)
Portalis JEM, 'Discours préliminaire du premier projet de Code civil' in PA Fenet, *Recueil complet de travaux préparatoires du Code civil* (Vidocq: Paris, 1836)
Prorok J, 'L'amende civile dans la réforme de la responsabilité civile. Regard critique sur la consécration d'une fonction punitive générale' RTD civ 2018.327
Radé C, 'L'impossible divorce de la faute et de la responsabilité civile' D 1998.301
Ranieri F, 'Bonne foi et exercice du droit dans la tradition du droit civil' RIDC 1998.1055
Rawach E, 'La portée des clauses tendant à exclure le rôle des documents précontractuels dans l'interprétation du contrat' D 2001.223
Reifegerste S, *Pour une obligation de minimiser le dommage* (PUAM: Aix-en-Provence, 2002)
Rémy P, 'Critique du système français de responsabilité civile' Droit et Cultures 1996.31
Rémy P, 'La "responsabilité contractuelle": histoire d'un faux concept' RTD civ 1997.323
Rémy-Corlay P, 'Exécution et réparation: deux concepts?' RDC 2005.13
Rémy-Corlay P and Fenouillet D (eds), *Les concepts contractuels français à l'heure des principes européens des contrats* (Dalloz: Paris, 2003)
Revet T, 'L'uniformisation de l'interprétation: contrats types et contrats d'adhésion' RDC 2015.199
Revet T, 'Le juge et la révision du contrat' RDC 2016.373
Revet T, 'L'achèvement de la réforme du droit commun des contrats du régime général et de la preuve des obligations, regard général' RDC 2018 Hors-série
Revet T, 'L'incohérent cantonnement, par l'Assemblée nationale, du domaine du contrat d'adhésion aux contrats de masse' D 2018 Chron 124
Ripert G, *La règle morale dans les obligations civiles* (4th edn, LGDJ: Paris, 1949)
Ripert G and Boulanger J, *Traité de droit civil d'après le traité de Planiol* (LGDJ: Paris, 1957)
Roche-Dahan J, 'L'exception d'inexécution, une forme de résolution unilatérale du contrat synallagmatique' D 1994.255
Rochfeld J, 'Résolution et exception d'inexécution' in P Rémy-Corlay and D Fenouillet (eds), *Les concepts contractuels français à l'heure des Principes du droit européen des contrats* (Dalloz: Paris, 2003) 216
Rochfeld J, 'Remarques sur les propositions relatives à l'exécution et à l'inexécution du contrat: la subjectivisation du droit à l'exécution' RDC 2006.113
Rodière R, 'Une notion menacée: la faute ordinaire dans les contrats' RTD civ 1954.201
Roujou de Boubée M-E, *Essai sur la notion de réparation* (LGDJ: Paris, 1974)
Rowan S, 'Le coût manifestement déraisonnable, nouvelle limite à l'exécution forcée en nature' Revue de Droit d'Assas 2010.81
Rudden B and Juilhard P, 'La théorie de la violation efficace' RIDC 1986.1015
Saint-Pau JC, *Fasc 171-10: Droit à la Réparation, Conditions de la Responsabilité Contractuelle, Fait Générateur, Obligations* (Lexis Nexis: Paris, 2003)
Sanz S, 'La consécration du pouvoir judiciaire par la loi du 9 juillet 1975 et ses incidences sur la théorie générale de la clause pénale' RTD civ 1977.268
Savaux E, 'La fin de la responsabilité contractuelle?' RTD civ 1999.1
Savaux E, 'La notion de théorie générale, son application en droit des contrats' LPA 2012.4
Savaux E, 'Article 1223: la réduction du prix' RDC 2015.3

Schulze R, 'Table ronde: Le regard des juristes européens' RDC 2009.380

Sefton-Green R, 'L'influence de l'analyse économique en droit anglais des contrats: le renversement des idées reçues' in *L'analyse économique du droit des contrats: outil de comparaison, facteur d'harmonisation* (Colloque) Gaz Pal 2005.25

Sériaux A, 'Réflexions sur les délais de grâce' RTD civ 1993.78

Simler P, 'L'article 1134 du code civil et la résiliation unilatérale anticipée des contrats à durée déterminée' JCP 1971.I.2413

Simler P, *Fasc 10: Contrats et obligations—Classification des obligations—Distinction des obligations de donner, de faire et de ne pas faire* (LexisNexis Jurisclasseur, 2011)

Simler P, 'Propos introductifs—A la recherche des frontières de l'interprétation' RDC 2015.146

Simler P, 'Art 1188 à 1192—Fasc 10—Contrat—Interprétation du contrat—L'instrument: notion, normes, champ d'application' (2017) JCL

Simler P, 'Art 1188 à 1192—Fasc 20—Contrat—Interprétation du contrat —La mise en œuvre: rôle respectif des juges du fond et de la Cour de cassation' (2017) JCL

Smorto S, 'La Justice Contractuelle' Revue Internationale de Droit Comparé 2008.60

Starck B, *Essai d'une théorie générale de la responsabilité civile, considérée en sa double-fonction de garantie et de peine privée* (Thèse: Paris, 1947)

Starck B, 'Domaine et fondement de la responsabilité sans faute' RTD civ 1958.475

Starck B, Roland H, and Boyer L, *Obligations—Contrats* (5th edn, Litec: Paris, 1995)

Stijns S, 'La résolution pour inexécution en droit belge: conditions et mise en oeuvre' in M Fontaine and G Viney (eds), *Les sanctions de l'inexécution des obligations contractuelles, études de droit comparé* (Bruylant: Bruxelles and LGDJ: Paris, 2001) 512

Stoffel-Munck P, *L'abus dans le contrat: Essai d'une théorie* (LGDJ: Paris, 2000)

Stoffel-Munck P, 'Le contrôle a *posteriori* de la résiliation unilatérale' Droit & Patrimoine 2004.106

Stoffel-Munck P, 'La relativité de la faute contractuelle' RDC 2007.587

Stoffel-Munck P, 'L'imprévision et la réforme des effets du contrat' RDC 2016.30

Stoffel-Munck P, 'Le nouveau droit des obligations: les questions en suspens' RDC 2018.52

Stoffel-Munck P, 'La préparation d'une réforme des contrats spéciaux' RDC 2020.1

Tallon D, 'Dommages et intérêts et exécution en nature. Quelques observations entre la common law et le droit français' JT 1985.601

Tallon D, 'Pourquoi parler de faute contractuelle?' in *Droit civil, procédure, linguistique juridique, Ecrits en hommage à Gérard Cornu* (PUF: Paris, 1994) 429

Tallon D, 'L'inexécution du contrat: pour une autre présentation' RTD civ 1994.223

Tallon D, 'L'article 1184 du Code civil. Un texte à rénover?' in *Université Panthéon-Assas, Clés pour le siècle* (Dalloz: Paris, 2000) 253

Terré F, *Pour une réforme du droit des contrats: Réflexions et propositions d'un groupe de travail sous la direction de François Terré* (Dalloz: Paris, 2009)

Terré F, Simler P, and Lequette Y, *Pour une réforme du droit des contrats* (Dalloz: Paris, 2008)

Terré F, Simler P, Lequette Y, and Chénedé F, *Droit civil, Les obligations* (12th edn, Dalloz: Paris 2018)

Texier G, 'L'abus de droit en matière de droit public' in J Mestre, *L'abus dans le droit des affaires*, Droit & Patrimoine 2000.83

Thibierge L, 'La mesure des dommages-intérêts: question de fait ou question de droit? Libres réflexions au travers du prisme de la minimisation du préjudice' RDC 2019.193

Tisseyre S, *Le rôle de la bonne foi en droit des contrats: essai d'analyse à la lumière du droit anglais et droit européen* (PUAM: Aix-en-Provence, 2012)

Tournafond O and Tricoire J-P, 'Les contrats de construction face aux nouvelles orientations du droit des contrats' RDI 2016.391

Tricot D, 'Le juge: le contrôle de dénaturation et la liberté d'interprétation des conventions' RDC 2015.149

Tunc A, 'Force majeure et absence de faute en matière contractuelle' RTD civ 1945.17

Vialard A, 'L'offre publique du contrat' RTD civ 1971.750

Viney G, 'La responsabilité contractuelle en question' in *Études offertes à Jacques Ghestin, Le contrat au début du XXIe siècle* (LGDJ: Paris, 2001) 921

Viney G, 'Exécution de l'obligation, faculté de remplacement et réparation en nature en droit français' in M Fontaine and G Viney (eds), *Les sanctions de l'inexécution des obligations contractuelles, Etudes de droit comparé* (Bruylant: Bruxelles and LGDJ: Paris, 2001) 107

Viney G, 'Rapport de synthèse' in *Faut-il moraliser le droit français de la réparation du dommage? (à propos des dommages et intérêts punitifs et de l'obligation de minimiser son propre dommage)* (Colloque) PA 2002 no 232.66

Viney G, 'Projet de réforme du droit des obligations: les éléments clés en matière de droit de la responsabilité' Revue Lamy droit civil, 2005, no 22.13

Viney G, 'Exposé des motifs: Sous-titre III. De la responsabilité civile (Article 1340 a 1386)' in *Avant-projet de réforme du droit des obligations et de la prescription: Rapport remis au garde des Sceaux* (La Documentation française: Paris, 2006)

Viney G, 'La victime n'est pas tenue de limiter son préjudice dans l'intérêt du responsable' RDC 2015.24

Viney G and P Jourdain, *Traité de droit civil, Les effets de la responsabilité* (3rd edn, LGDJ: Paris 2010)

Viney G and P Jourdain, *Traité de droit civil, Les conditions de la responsabilité* (4th edn, LGDJ: Paris 2013)

Wéry P, *L'exécution forcée en nature des obligations contractuelles non pécuniaires (essai). Une relecture des articles 1142 à 1144 du Code civil* (Kluwer: Liège, 1993)

Wéry P, 'L'exécution en nature de l'obligation contractuelle et la réparation en nature du dommage contractuel. Rapport belge' in M Fontaine and G Viney (eds), *Les sanctions de l'inexécution des obligations contractuelles, Études de droit comparé* (Bruylant: Bruxelles and LGDJ: Paris, 2001) 205

Wéry P, *Droit des obligations* (2nd edn, Larcier: Brussels, 2011)

Wester-Ouisse V, 'Le préjudice moral des personnes morales' JCP 2003.I.145

Whittaker S, 'Les sanctions de l'inexécution des contrats. Droit anglais' in M Fontaine and G Viney (eds), *Les sanctions de l'inexécution des obligations contractuelles, Études de droit comparé* (Bruylant: Bruxelles and LGDJ: Paris, 2001) 977

Whittaker S, 'Un droit à la prestation plutôt qu'un droit à l'exécution? Perspectives anglaises sur l'exécution en nature et la réparation' RDC 2005.49

Whittaker S, 'Un cadre commun pour la responsabilité civile' RDC 2019.145

Wicker G, 'La sanction délictuelle du manquement contractuel ou l'intégration de l'ordre contractuel à l'ordre juridique général' RDC 2007.593

Witz C, 'L'obligation de minimiser son propre dommage dans les conventions internationales: l'exemple de la Convention de Vienne sur la vente internationale' in *Faut-il moraliser le droit français de la réparation du dommage? (à propos des dommages et intérêts punitifs et de l'obligation de minimiser son propre dommage)* (Colloque) PA 2002 no 232.50

Zavaro M, *La responsabilité des constructeurs* (LexisNexis Litec: Paris, 2005)

# Index

*For the benefit of digital users, indexed terms that span two pages (e.g., 52–53) may, on occasion, appear on only one of those pages.*